THE
PRESIDENTS
AND THE
PEOPLE

THE
PRESIDENTS
AND THE
PEOPLE

Five Leaders Who Threatened Democracy
and the Citizens Who Fought to Defend It

COREY BRETTSCHNEIDER

W. W. NORTON & COMPANY
Independent Publishers Since 1923

For information about permission to reproduce selections from this book, write to
Permissions, W. W. Norton & Company, Inc., 500 Fifth Avenue, New York, NY 10110

For information about special discounts for bulk purchases, please contact
W. W. Norton Special Sales at specialsales@wwnorton.com or 800-233-4830

Manufacturing by Lake Book Manufacturing
Book design by Beth Steidle
Production manager: Lauren Abbate

ISBN 978-1-324-00627-5

W. W. Norton & Company, Inc., 500 Fifth Avenue, New York, N.Y. 10110
www.wwnorton.com

W. W. Norton & Company Ltd., 15 Carlisle Street, London W1D 3BS

1 2 3 4 5 6 7 8 9 0

This book is dedicated to the memory of my inspiring mother-in-law, Virginia G. Weisz, a champion of children's rights who believed in the power of committed citizens to realize the promises of democracy.

CONTENTS

SECTION III

EQUAL PROTECTION

THE LONG MARCH AGAINST SECOND-CLASS CITIZENSHIP

SECTION IV

THE RULE OF LAW

THE BATTLE FOR PRESIDENTIAL ACCOUNTABILITY

Introduction

THE PRESIDENT GLOWERED WITH UNSPEAKABLE RAGE. THE OBJECT OF HIS FURY, THE SOURCE of his unrelenting obsession, was the national press corps. Each day, as the next election loomed, the media poured partisan criticism on his agenda. They criticized his family and defiled his public image. A man of impulse, he read scores of headlines, lingering on every insult, until his loathing consumed him. The president's party had sprung to his defense, plotting to undermine the certification of the upcoming election result unless he was victorious. But the plot failed when it was exposed by the press. Now he would have his revenge. The president summoned the attorney general and schemed for a simple goal: to lock them up.

The president did not believe in equality under the law—especially when it came to race. He secretly lobbied the Supreme Court to deny civil rights protections, arguing they were not guaranteed by the Constitution. Publicly, he made clear he believed white people were a superior race. He invited racial extremists into the Oval Office and screened racial propaganda movies at the White House. All the while, he discriminated within the federal workforce—aggressively demoting African Americans and other racial minorities to keep them from serving their country in government positions. Predictably, his term saw the horrifying return of racial violence and white supremacist activity. By the end of this presidency, America would see massive violence in major cities—supporters drawn out by the president's rhetoric, spilling into the streets.

The president cultivated dreams of unchecked power—silently at first, then aloud. He began ordering his staff to surveil enemies and harass opponents. To bolster his fantasy, he peddled a legal theory that he claimed came from the Constitution; and emboldened by a Justice Department that pushed the legal powers of the presidency to near limitless heights, he announced that the president is literally above the law—licensed to reject congressional subpoenas or fire on a whim investigators who scrutinized him. Whatever the president chose to do in office was, according to him, never illegal.

The presidential acts described in the previous three paragraphs bear a striking similarity to events during Donald Trump's presidency. Yet these acts were not committed by one president but five. Well before Trump, these leaders posed great threats to democracy. John Adams waged war on the national press of the early republic, prosecuting as many as 126 people who dared criticize him, including a newspaper editor and a sitting congressman, and lambasting a story revealing his party's plot to steal the election of 1800 by refusing to certify electoral ballots. In the 1850s, James Buchanan colluded with the Supreme Court to deny constitutional personhood to African Americans. A decade later, Andrew Johnson urged violence against his political opponents as he sought to guarantee a white supremacist republic after the Civil War. And in the 1910s, Woodrow Wilson nationalized Jim Crow by segregating the federal government, fueling white supremacist sentiment and racial violence. Finally, in the 1970s, Richard Nixon committed criminal acts—ordering the Watergate break-in and other illegal efforts to undermine political opponents—that flowed from his corrupt ideas about presidential power: "When the president does it," Nixon said, "that means it is not illegal."

Each of these five presidents stoked the fire of a constitutional crisis. Each wielded the nation's most powerful office to undermine a core aspect of democracy. And each stands as a conspicuous example of the damage a single president can do.

The events of January 6, 2021, reminded us that the nation's system of elections, culminating in a peaceful transfer of power, is fundamental to our democracy. But American democracy is also about other fundamental guarantees beyond having one's vote counted. It requires the *freedom to dissent* from government policy, independently or through an opposition party. It means that legal and political rights cannot be denied to anyone on the basis of race or ethnicity, including rights to legal personhood and more broadly to equal protection of the laws—guarantees of *equal citizenship*. Finally, it requires adherence to the *rule of law* for all: the president cannot be a dictator, able to commit crimes with impunity. Each of these three pillars of democracy is as fragile as it is fundamental.

This book is about the threats five presidents posed to these fragile pillars of American democracy. But it is also about what happened next. Each of the crises we will explore was followed by a concerted effort at democratic recovery. These efforts did not come from self-correcting mechanisms inherent in the Constitution's structure. They were not the inevitable result of formal institutional checks by the Supreme Court or Congress. Instead, the efforts to reverse the damage done to United States democracy were often catalyzed directly by citizens with no official government position.

So where did the authority of these citizens to redress presidential wrongs come from? In calling presidents to account, they appealed to the Constitution—the fundamental law of the land. They believed the Constitution granted them legal authority to restore democracy against presidents who threatened it—and they were right. That stance, however, often placed these citizens at odds with presidents and other public officials, including Supreme Court justices. Because most of them lacked legal training, these citizens played David against a presidential Goliath. Presidents John Adams and Woodrow Wilson were among the most noted constitutional scholars of their time and were not shy in scorning laypeople's understanding of their field. James Buchanan, Andrew Johnson, and Richard Nixon were lawyers who used their training to justify their attacks on democracy; in the process, they often sought to prosecute the Davids who challenged them. But the citizens who sought to restore democracy fought back—and they knew the Constitution was on their side.

Because of this common strategy of turning to the Constitution to bolster their efforts at democratic restoration, I call these groups *democratic constitutional constituencies*. Defined by their use of the Constitution to oppose presidents who threaten the basic pillars of democracy, they sought to restore democracy by enlisting successor presidents in their cause. They thus relied primarily on politics, not litigation, to achieve their goals. These groups are appropriately considered democratic not only because of their defense of those democratic pillars—the *freedom to dissent, equal citizenship,* and the *rule of law*—but also because they symbolize democracy in its purest form. They are regular citizens, not public officials, and their authority comes from their reading of the Constitution and their ability to galvanize the support of other citizens.

Each of the democratic constitutional constituencies I examine in this book succeeded because they convinced subsequent presidents to adopt their vision of democratic restoration—not merely to undo the previous president's damage, but to build a new foundation of political values that strengthened the constitutional order going forward. These democratic constitutional constituencies, the citizen *readers* of the Constitution who played a crucial role in defending and furthering our democracy, therefore disrupt a standard story told by constitutional law scholars and political scientists—experts who declare that checks on the president come mainly from Congress or the Supreme Court, or locate the foundation of our democracy with the *writers* of the Constitution in 1787. Understanding the role of these constitutional constituencies reframes the story of the complicated relationship between democracy and the founding of the United States.

Some members of these democratic constitutional constituencies you may know; others are lesser known. They include relatively anonymous newspaper editors prosecuted by Adams who used their trials to galvanize readers to champion the *right to dissent*. Abolitionist orator Frederick Douglass birthed another constituency seeking to realize the promise he read in the preamble to the Constitution: a multiracial democracy that guaranteed not just legal personhood but *equal citizenship*. Another constituency, formed during the Wilson administration, worked to reclaim the meaning of equal protection—as enshrined in the Fourteenth Amendment ratified in 1868—from a Supreme Court and president who undermined it. This group was originally led by the journalists and activists William Monroe Trotter and Ida B. Wells, who later passed the baton to other figures pivotal in the Civil Rights Movement. The stories of these democratic constitutional constituencies illustrate the roles individuals outside of government have played in defending our democratic Constitution.

Although they organized in different eras and over different issues, these constituencies shared the common goal of pushing fellow Americans, and eventually presidents, to adopt a more democratic understanding of the Constitution. They then mobilized to ensure subsequent presidents protected the pillars of democracy. But even the most admirable citizen readers sometimes fail. As we will see, despite the valiant efforts of Daniel Ellsberg and a grand jury to demand accountability from an authoritarian president in the 1970s, a movement never fully developed in their defense, leaving our democracy at risk today. America's constitutional history often follows this recurring pattern: a president causes a period of acute democratic crisis, which is then met head-on by aggressive efforts led by democratic constitutional constituencies—not courts, legislatures, or political parties—to thwart this crisis and spread a new popular understanding of the Constitution that enhances the democratic values under attack. These citizens, the embodiment of the preamble's "We the People," resist "crisis presidents" by appeal to a democratic understanding of the Constitution. Ideally—but not always—they also erect new guardrails and work with "recovery presidents" to preserve hard-won democratic gains. Through this recurring battle, democratic constitutional constituencies help to shape the meaning and impact of the Constitution.

If history is any guide, today's crisis makes this a time ripe for constitutional recovery. In that sense, this book offers hope for current citizens seeking to restore democracy. The recoveries I detail in this book are not callbacks to some prior period of greatness; they are instead attempts to recapture an ideal of the Constitution that foregrounds the pillars of democracy, pillars trampled upon by crisis presidents. These stories of constitutional recovery also do not reveal laws of history, nor are they guarantees of how to stop a crisis president. They are instead a testament to the power of citizens to push past authoritarian moments toward democratic ones. To realize that potential for citizen success, we need to learn our history's pattern of crisis and recovery and the role constitutional constituencies played.

This book explores four periods in which a president threatened democracy and citizens fought to restore it.

The first was stoked by John Adams, who signed the Alien and Sedition Acts and used them to demand the prosecution of his political opponents. In response, some prosecuted newspaper editors fought against Adams and made the 1800 election a referendum on his constitutional desecration. These journalists formed a constitutional constituency among their readers and followers that prevailed upon Vice President Thomas Jefferson and framer James Madison to oppose Adams and ensure future presidents upheld a Constitution that championed the central pillar of democracy of *the right to dissent*. That recovery began during Jefferson's two terms and was enhanced during Madison's presidency.

The second crisis was precipitated by James Buchanan and furthered by Andrew Johnson. Buchanan was essentially a co-conspirator in the Supreme Court's catastrophic *Dred Scott* ruling, which expanded slavery and invited civil war. Johnson sought to further white supremacy, even after slavery's legal end. A call to realize the democratic promises of the Constitution's preamble came from orator and constitutional interpreter Frederick Douglass. Douglass escaped slavery only to later be literally hunted by Buchanan and denounced by Johnson. By arguing for his constitutional vision—one that rejected slavery and envisioned a multiracial democracy of equal citizenship—Douglass stood in contrast to abolitionists who rejected constitutional authority altogether. Backed by his democratic constitutional constituency, he found favor in the presidencies of Abraham Lincoln and Ulysses Grant and went on to stimulate what historian David Blight called a "reborn America."

Woodrow Wilson incited the third democratic crisis. Wilson segregated the federal government, nationalizing discrimination to combat what he called "friction" between white and Black Americans, while also reviving white supremacist ideology. Subsequent pushback came from a nascent Civil Rights Movement, galvanized into a democratic constitutional constituency by William Monroe Trotter and Ida B. Wells, and later by Sadie Alexander, the first African American woman to receive a PhD in economics in the United States. Alexander worked behind the scenes to convince Harry Truman, an unlikely civil rights hero, to set an agenda for recovering a Constitution that protected equality, an effort that would continue during the Eisenhower and Johnson presidencies, spurred by the constitutional understanding of Martin Luther King Jr.

While the first crisis spurred by Adams around the silencing of dissent could happen in any democracy, the second and third crises were distinctly American. These two crises were fomented by the glaring contradiction born out of our country's original sin of slavery: the constitutional promises of equality and popular sovereignty made when a significant proportion of the population lacked even the most basic sovereignty over their own bodies and destinies. Two different generations of constitutional constituencies would confront that glaring contradiction, demanding its resolution by appeal to the document's ideals, and using those ideals to hold presidents to account. If the right to dissent is essential to any democracy, the calls for legal personhood and equal protection respond to the distinctly American contradiction between the nation's founding ideals and its practice of slavery.

The fourth and final democratic crisis was instigated by Richard Nixon. The crisis Nixon stoked included the Watergate conspiracy, the attempt to bug the Democratic National Committee, which touched everyone from Nixon's "Plumbers" unit to Attorney General John Mitchell. Less famously, Nixon threatened democracy through his criminal effort to silence Vietnam protestor Daniel Ellsberg. Nixon's authoritarian understanding of the Constitution was effectively challenged by a group of grand jurors, everyday residents of Washington, DC. But despite their valiant efforts to hold the president accountable to law, this crisis did not end with restoration. While Ellsberg and the jurors defended the democratic pillar that no leader is above the law, no constituency formed around it—allowing the crisis of the Nixon presidency to linger to this day.

This study of crisis and recovery, an account of the dangers of the presidency and citizen responses to those dangers, should bring hope, not despair. While we haven't reached constitutional recovery from Nixon yet, history shows recovery is possible through the efforts of citizen readers of the Constitution and the constituencies they lead.

★ ★ ★

UNDERNEATH THESE EPISODES of despair and triumph lies a deeper question: Why does American constitutional history experience a continual tug-of-war between crisis and recovery?

I am not the first scholar to describe cyclical American political currents. Yale political scientist Stephen Skowronek initiated the study of presidents in relation to their predecessors and successors. Some presidencies are defined by continuing the vision of past presidents, he argues. Others are marked by their rupture with that vision, changing the path of history. Skowronek thus highlighted the presidency's vast ability to alter or maintain the nation's policy agenda. Like him, I focus on crisis and recovery among clusters of presidents. But I focus less on the give-and-take of normal policy making and instead consider the relationship of the presidents toward democracy itself. The presidents I study all threatened to push America off the path of democracy altogether, a danger averted by recovery presidents and constitutional constituencies.[2]

These cycles do not happen by accident. They reflect a tension within America's constitutional design. The Constitution creates a powerful, central, singular chief executive. But the first three words of its preamble, "We the People," signal this power is granted through popular sovereignty, the will of the people.

When the Constitution was ratified in 1788, the presidency it created was nothing like the weak "president" that had existed under the Articles of Confederation during the failed post–Revolutionary War government. Instead, the framers of the new Constitution designed an office of far more significant power, making the president the commander in chief of the military, the chief executor of the laws, and the head of state.³ The president would lead the executive branch and would serve alone, not on a committee. The office's power would be vested in a single person, a "unitary executive" as it is sometimes labeled.

The framers robustly debated this design and its particularities. Alexander Hamilton said the executive needed "energy" to both protect the nation from threats and to secure "liberty against the enterprises and assaults of ambition, of faction, and of anarchy."⁴ He believed a committee of executives—or a disempowered unitary executive—would become dysfunctional and ill-equipped to tackle the pressing issues a head of state must address. Influential voices such as James Madison worked to limit the president's authority, but the convention ultimately agreed that the Articles of Confederation were too weak, and to make this new republican experiment succeed, the states would need a much stronger executive.

Not everyone was convinced. Anti-Federalists who opposed ratification of the Constitution warned of the presidency's dangers. Revolutionary War heroes such as Patrick Henry predicted that the office was so powerful that a president with authoritarian ambitions could simply lay claim to the "American throne," and asked the Constitution's supporters, "what have you to oppose this force?"⁵

Though Hamilton and the anti-Federalists disagreed, both views help us understand the presidency's potential and perils. The anti-Federalists illustrate the danger the office poses to people's rights; Hamilton illuminates its potential to restore democracy in the aftermath of threats. The presidency is therefore both a poisonous recipe for tyrannical overreach, lurking in each president's shadows, and its antidote, found in the power of the office when its occupant responds to a democratic constituency.

Henry was right to worry about the presidency. Scholars often point to the difference between the American presidential system and more stable democracies that follow a parliamentary structure. Of the twenty-two oldest democracies, twenty have rejected the American model.⁶ One strength of parliamentary systems is they are less rigid; prime ministers may be replaced at any time by parliament if they lose its confidence—a check against tyranny.⁷ In contrast, the presidency can collapse into dictatorship, a phenomenon that has happened often in Latin American countries mirroring the American model.

Despite the direness of Henry's warning, the American constitutional system has a check on the presidency embedded into its design—one distinct from the familiar idea of the three branches' checks and balances. This second extraordinary feature of our constitutional design is an innovation brought into the modern world in 1787: popular sovereignty. Popular sovereignty means that the legitimacy of government flows from the people, and from the people alone. As the Declaration of Independence proclaims, governments derive "their just powers from the consent of the governed." Kings claim a divine right to rule, but in American democracy, the president or Congress cannot alone change a constitution—only supermajorities of the people can. While such notions strike us as obvious today—our Constitution begins with "We the People"—in the eighteenth century, popular sovereignty was a radical idea. As historian Gordon Wood writes, the early United States became "the first society in the modern world to bring ordinary people into the affairs of government—not just as voters but as actual rulers."[8]

Popular sovereignty as initially practiced in America was deeply exclusionary. "We the People" was mostly limited to propertied white men, with others forcefully excluded from exerting the power to govern. This reality mars the execution of popular sovereignty at the founding, where an all-white group of mostly wealthy men wrote the Constitution in Philadelphia. Still, popular sovereignty began to have meaning in the populace's first major act in 1788: ratifying the Constitution, a proposition that was put to a vote in what legal scholar Akhil Amar has called "the most participatory, majoritarian . . . event the Earth had ever seen" until then.[9] We cannot today consider that vote fully democratic; few women or non-white people were involved, ensuring that a select minority of Americans had a say in constitutional ratification. But out of the depths of monarchy, for those who were allowed to participate in the state-by-state process of ratifying the Constitution, it was a profound act—one that put "We the People" in the driver's seat of democratic government.

As the nation's history began unfolding, from the earliest days of the republic, the American people—spanning from farmers to bankers to laborers, later expanding to include women, African Americans, and others written out of the country's early history—demanded a central role in reading, interpreting, and arguing over their Constitution. Not for nothing is the founding document, a mere 4,543 words—a half-hour's read, small enough to fit in a farmer's pocket. Because people could read it, they could claim it as their own, such that all Americans—even the most powerful—were subject to its provisions. Even today, the Constitution ratified in 1788 remains the third shortest Constitution in the world.

These two ingredients—popular sovereignty and a powerful executive—are an odd pair for the same constitutional system. One calls on the people, a huge and diverse mass, to be the ultimate source of legitimate government. The other grants extraordinary opportunity to the executive, a single person, to act. To mix these two compounds in the same beaker is to invite the constant dangers of crisis, conflict, and recovery. Presidents have the power to push the government off the rails, crashing through constitutional constraint. Typically, these conflicts are rooted in crisis presidents who confuse their personal ambitions with the office's requirements, or in those who are overcome with personal paranoia or excessive fear of threats to American security. Often enough, in the stories we will examine, their dangerous overreaching was couched in authoritarian interpretations of the Constitution that were actually fairly common among contemporary jurists and legal scholars.[10] In fact, some of the foremost constitutional abusers were leading constitutional scholars of their day. They were not explicitly anti-constitutional demagogues simply bent on seizing power at any cost; instead, they appealed to widely shared antidemocratic interpretations of the document to advance their goals.

Democratic constitutional constituencies invoke *the people's* authority to distinguish legitimate constitutional behavior from illegitimate. They call out abuse, demand respect for democratic rights, and do so by marshalling the Constitution's democratic ideals. This exercise of popular sovereignty often takes place in published articles that are critical

of presidents, or they occur in Oval Office confrontations that are publicized to galvanize the public. Democratic constitutional constituencies, knowing their work must be transformative, not transitory, enlist
subsequent presidents to erect better guardrails to ensure the train can't
leave the rails again, or at least not in the same way. The work of popular
sovereignty comes not just in the *method* constitutional constituencies
employ, rallying Americans around recovery, it also is realized in the
content of the constitutional reforms sought. Democratic constitutional
constituencies therefore reject the populist formulation of "the people"
to which authoritarian presidents sometimes appeal. Populist presidents sometimes claim their authority is virtually unlimited because
they were elected, meaning they embody the people's wishes. But these
constituencies reject that formulation, their resistance proving that
the sovereignty and rights of the people cannot be handed away to an
authoritarian ruler.

As the investor Warren Buffett has observed, it takes twenty years
to build a reputation, and only five minutes to ruin it. Applying this
maxim to the presidency provides interesting insights. The presidency is
so powerful that one reckless occupant of the White House can throw
the country into crisis in a single term. Rebuilding from this crisis to
recover a new and stronger version of the Constitution, on the other
hand, requires time—a process that involves mobilizing a constituency,
persuading citizens, and winning elections. Even then, the work continues, because to preserve those gains constitutional constituencies must
pressure new presidents to uphold their vision.

The push and pull between citizens' democratic understandings of
the Constitution and crisis presidents' authoritarian ambitions reflects
the structural danger embedded within the Constitution. That structure is partly defined by the fact that only one government official
embodies the powers of an entire branch: the president controls the
levers of executive power. That means that the beliefs, theories, and
quirks of a president have an outsize effect on policy compared to any
other government official. It also means those beliefs or quirks can lead
presidents, and therefore the executive branch, to oppose fundamental

democratic rights. Constitutional design therefore contains a danger and a solution. The danger lies in the power of an office that can misread the Constitution to threaten democracy. The solution lies in democratic constitutional constituencies and their power to challenge the authority of these presidents and reclaim the Constitution.

★ ★ ★

THE PRESIDENTIAL INAUGURATION OF 1793 would be unrecognizable by today's standards. It had almost nothing in common with today's inaugurations, where millions shiver outdoors in Washington, DC, for a nationally televised event. Instead, George Washington's second inaugural was a small affair. That March, a few dozen people, mostly elected officials, crammed into the Senate chamber of Congress Hall in Philadelphia, a small room on the second floor.

The size and setting conveyed Washington's modesty and his vision for the office; there was no bragging about how large the audience was. Without speaking a word, Washington made clear that the presidency was not about him, but his duty to the people and their representatives. Early in the ceremony, William Cushing, a justice of the Supreme Court, prompted him to recite the oath of office.

What happened next was telling. Washington turned to the assembly and delivered an inaugural address that at 135 words remains the shortest ever. It was as brief as it was important—the essential exposition on how citizens should judge a president and evaluate the presidency itself.

To close the address, Washington said:

> This oath I am now about to take, and in your presence: That if it shall be found during my administration of the Government I have in any instance violated willingly or knowingly the injunctions thereof, I may (besides incurring constitutional punishment) be subject to the upbraidings of all who are now witnesses of the present solemn ceremony.[11]

In that one sentence, Washington invited Americans to understand several key things about the presidency. The first was that the presidential office was distinct from the person occupying it. The second was the need for criticism. The third was the accountability of this officeholder to the people and their representatives.

The framers had literally designed the role of president for Washington. However, it was Washington who used his tenure to clarify for the public and for future presidents the distinction between the person and the office. Rejecting the moniker of "Your Highness," Washington accepted the more reserved title of "President." That title—lost upon leaving office—made clear the person occupying the presidency does so temporarily and that the values of the office defined by the Constitution—not those of any individual president—are the country's guide.

Washington took his title's symbolism to heart. As a man, he adored money—with his land holdings and ownership of enslaved people, he was one of the richest people in America. His personal tastes ran toward the exuberant, including a luxurious room at Mount Vernon devoted to hosting his many guests. Yet Washington the president insisted that he not profit from the office, following the Constitution's emoluments clauses. Monarchs can enrich themselves because the king is the state; but the American presidency was merely held in trust by its occupant, not to be used for personal gain.

Moreover, Washington resisted the temptation to enrich himself in terms of vast political power. A discontented colonel once suggested Washington should become a king. Washington was appalled, telling the colonel, "You could not have found a person to whom your schemes are more disagreeable."[12]

In his second inaugural, Washington advised Americans that presidents were not above criticism; in fact, presidents who violate their oath were to be criticized and subjected to "upbraidings" and "constitutional punishment." Indeed, only when those from whom the president's power derives—"We the People"—demand their chief executive protect and defend the Constitution's high ideals, can the country's experiment in self-government succeed.

★ ★ ★

RELATED TO WASHINGTON'S INVITATION for necessary criticism was the demand that citizens and other branches of government hold him (and all future presidents) to constitutional standards. The oath of office for the president of the United States establishes the Constitution as the standard by which citizens must judge presidents. At a minimum, it requires presidents not to oppose the document or its values. There's more, however. Presidents must "preserve, protect and defend" the document for the future. The oath thus requires presidents not to merely refrain from crashing through guardrails of the Constitution; it demands presidents guard the Constitution, affirming and recovering the rights of citizens.

Crucially, Washington's second inaugural makes clear the Constitution isn't the exclusive province of lawyers or judges. When Washington welcomed "the upbraidings of all who are now *witnesses of the present solemn ceremony*," some of the literal witnesses in the Senate room in Philadelphia were not legal experts or judges. While those witnesses were mostly white, male officeholders and so were not representative of the American people, the principle has broad application. As citizen readers of the Constitution throughout history have made clear, all Americans can be considered "witnesses" tasked with holding the president accountable to the Constitution.

Washington's ideas about presidential accountability—that presidents' interests are secondary to constitutional requirements; that they should welcome criticism; and that they should be judged by how well they protect the Constitution's core values—provide a bulwark for citizens to call the highest officeholder to account.

★ ★ ★

WE OFTEN SEE THE SUPREME COURT as our chief constitutional interpreter, the fundamental check on the president. Through its rulings, the court forces the officeholder to honor the constitutional rights enjoyed by all Americans. But, in fact, history is replete with examples of the court abusing its supposed role as a defender of constitutional rights. Just as the Supreme Court has the power to prevent a constitutional crisis, it also has the power to hasten one. (It may even conspire with a sitting president to do so.) When presidents push America through the guardrails of the Constitution, the court often goes along with it.

Democratic constitutional constituencies make clear that the Supreme Court doesn't have the final say over constitutional meaning. The democratic values represented by the preamble—"We the People"—gives the lie to the notion that our rights are best defended by nine life-appointed people in robes.[13] Recognizing the fallibility of the branches of government, constitutional constituencies insist on advancing their democratic readings of the Constitution.

These citizens are often motivated to demand constitutional restoration because they know firsthand the harms that could be inflicted by crisis presidents; they have skin in the game.[14] Their accounts of rights deprivations illustrate how presidents have failed to preserve, protect, and defend the Constitution. While courts and presidents often cite constitutional text and case law while excusing abuses of power, constitutional constituents fight back differently; they rescue the Constitution from crisis presidents by reading it in line with democracy and popular sovereignty. When constitutional constituencies speak, recovery presidents—in stark contrast to crisis presidents—translate those ideas into action, reinforcing the role each of us plays in our democracy and the unique role presidents can play in realizing its central values.

★ ★ ★

DEMOCRATIC CONSTITUTIONAL CONSTITUENCIES do not battle just with crisis presidents. Their ideas are often opposed by groups seeking other goals. Some of these groups openly reject democracy. Others promote democracy through an approach that would scrap the Constitution. For instance, William Lloyd Garrison, Frederick Douglass's mentor turned foe, called the Constitution a "covenant with death" and an "agreement with hell," believing it an inherently proslavery document.[15] In contemporary debates, it is popular to urge abandoning the Constitution to secure democracy.[16] But historically, recovery from democratic crises has come from reclaiming the Constitution rather than opposing it wholesale. Central to that process has been an insistence by constitutional constituencies to read the document as securing the democratic rights of "We the People."[17] Douglass's approach to defending democracy through constitutional reclamation is this book's animating framework.

Douglass provides a model of how the people can hold presidents to account. And while not a perfect president, not least because he unforgivably enslaved his fellow Americans, Washington clarified that presidents need to welcome constituents who hold them accountable. Together, Douglass and Washington explain how the people and the presidents ought to stand in relation: the people should demand presidents abide by the Constitution and protect the highest values of the office, which stands above any one occupant. This principle calls for all of us, the witnesses to the president's oath, to demand accountability from our chief executives—like constitutional constituencies have done.

It wouldn't be long after Washington's second swearing in before citizens were called to hold a sitting president to account, perhaps far sooner than Washington anticipated. That's because America's first crisis came from someone Washington trusted—a person conspicuously absent from the Senate chamber that day—who had a very different idea of the presidency.

SECTION I

THE RIGHT TO DISSENT

The Journalists Who Demanded It

CHAPTER 1

John Adams versus Cooper, Bache, and Duane

A President's Attempt to Shut Down the Opposition

A RECENT STUDY CASTS A PALL ON THE FUTURE OF PRESIDENTIAL SYSTEMS IN A DEMOCRACY. Adam Przeworski's research finds that, among all forms of democracy, presidential systems have proven the most brittle; they fail at the highest rate, and they are almost twice as likely to collapse as parliamentary democracies.[1]

Some might draw solace from the study, claiming American democracy is a shining example of a presidential system perfectly designed to never fail. With this view, our glorious past attests to our stability and strength. A closer look at the early republic reveals a different sobering truth: we are and have always been one wrong turn away from a starkly different future.

The Constitution's two-century-long endurance, a course that saw the United States become the world's dominant superpower, has created a myth that our system of government is everlasting. This is a notion with purchase on both the political left and right. Yet our fragile early republic—and the road to autocracy onto which it briefly veered—reveals just how close we came to snuffing out the world's first modern democracy.

The danger of self-government collapsing is particularly acute for systems in their infancy, a fate that could easily have befallen the fledgling United States. In its early years, nothing was guaranteed. Today, we ask whether institutions will "hold," as if describing mighty oaks in a hurricane. In 1796, America's institutions were saplings, if they existed at all, and their novelty—lacking norms to violate, or experienced officials to protest—made them extraordinarily vulnerable to abuse. During this period, the entire federal staff consisted of just 126 people.[2] In Philadelphia, the now-mighty State Department worked from a three-story house—or rather, part of one, shared with the office of the postmaster general, like cheap roommates—splitting the rent to pay the landlord, a local man named James Simmons.[3] To say American democracy was an "experiment" then wasn't cliché, as it is today. It was true—even understated.

What nearly upended the young republic was a crisis. The severity of this crisis has been largely glossed over in history books, from high school courses to postgraduate programs. Like the several crises that would convulse the country in the ensuing two hundred years, its spark was a war. At issue was the right to criticize the government and its leaders—including the president—a right without which American democracy could never have been possible. Today, a regime that limits citizens' freedom to oppose government officials is rightly called autocratic. But less than a decade after the First Amendment was ratified, thus banning Congress from abridging free speech, a president and his party sought to stamp out political opposition and cloak his attack on democracy in the veneer of the Constitution.

★ ★ ★

IN 1796, PHILADELPHIA POLITICS was dominated by one event: the French Revolution. That cataclysmic rebellion from monarchy was inspired, in part, by America's revolt against the British king. To some Americans, however, it was not a celebration of their revolutionary ideas, but a sign of the possible degeneration of republican government. Looking across the ocean, some Americans were concerned that popular rule could descend into mob rule.

The French Revolution drew France into a long and bloody conflict with Britain. Given their revolutionary ideals and earlier assistance in the American Revolution, the French expected American aid. To their understandable shock (and outrage), George Washington refused to involve his young country in a foreign war; he signed the Proclamation of Neutrality in 1793, America's first major foreign policy decision.

Washington's decision—right or wrong—had an unintended consequence: the French and British conflict became America's first polarized culture war. The battle between Britain and France was, for many Americans, like watching two parents fight to the death. The United States had both countries in its DNA. From the British, Americans derived the legal structure that formed the basis for their Constitution. Vast swaths of the document, from impeachment to pardon power, came from Britain.

From the French, however, America received something equally vital: revolutionary spirit. The French aided the American colonies in the Revolutionary War. The Marquis de Lafayette helped lead ragged American troops through the winter at Valley Forge in one of the war's darkest hours. French philosophers like Rousseau, who had written an ode to equality and popular sovereignty in his treatise *The Social Contract*, influenced revolutionary pamphleteers such as Thomas Paine and inspired the Declaration of Independence.[4] And the money, infantry, and naval support of King Louis XVI helped the Americans win their independence. The British legal tradition gave America her head; the French revolutionary spirit gave America her heart.

This debt to America's two parent nations took a new form in the country's political parties: the Federalists, who largely held British sympathies, and the Democratic-Republicans, whose sympathies leaned toward France. This party divide is essential to understanding the extreme behavior of the leaders of each party, who would soon lead the United States into chaos with their partisan behavior.[5] Then, as now,

elites polarized by negative partisanship—the belief that political opposition poses an existential threat—become capable of reckless action.

Both American political parties had heavy hitters. The most notable French sympathizer was the leader of the Democratic-Republicans,
Thomas Jefferson, a Francophile who had spent years in Paris and championed the French Revolution whenever he got the chance. Among
the Federalists, meanwhile, there was perhaps no greater advocate for
the British—and despiser of all things French—than Vice President
John Adams.

Long before becoming America's first vice president under Washington, Adams was shaped by his experience with the British. Before the
revolution, Adams had been a lawyer for British soldiers after the Boston Massacre. After the war, but before Washington became president,
Adams became America's first minister to Great Britain. Adams loved
London and its tradition of legal thought. He was particularly immersed
in the British system of judge-made law, or "common law."[6] As foreign
minister after the war, Adams worked—with limited success—to repair
the relationship between the former colonies and the British empire.[7]

However, Adams was not so fond of the French. When Adams
first visited King George III as minister to Great Britain, the monarch laughed and said he had heard Adams described as "not the most
attached of all your countrymen to the manners of France." Adams
replied smoothly that the opinion was "not mistaken"; he was only
loyal to his "own country."[8] Adams's distaste for France may have begun
during the Revolution, when he accompanied Benjamin Franklin to
the court of Louis XVI. When Adams ventured again to France, King
Louis refused to publish the news in the *Gazette*, the official organ of
the French monarchy. Adams took the insult personally. When a senior
advisor to the king dismissed Adams for not knowing French, it also left
him feeling aggrieved.[9]

Adams's affinity for the British ran far deeper than personal taste: he
had adopted British ideas about self-government. Unlike anti-royalists
like Jefferson, Adams took a more nuanced, sympathetic view of monarchy. Adams had been a central architect of a revolution that created
a "government of laws, not of men." However, Adams mostly thought

that the British monarchy *was* such a government. Drawing from the philosopher Montesquieu, Adams believed a republic could take many forms—including a constitutional monarchy with a king. "England is a republic," Adams wrote in 1789. "A monarchical republic it is true, but a republic still."[10]

If you are puzzled by these claims, you are not alone. Adams insisted there was much worth emulating in a king, and it informed his view of the presidency. His main assertion (shared by several founders) was that America needed a strong chief magistrate to lead the executive branch, with powers like a veto. More quizzically, however, Adams advocated for government officials to have royal-sounding titles; allied senators proposed that the president be called "His Highness the President of the United States of America and Protector of the Rights of the Same." All these ideas found antecedents in the "royal prerogative" of the British king—leading James Madison to suspect Adams was secretly a monarchist. Recently, new scholarship has emerged around Adams. Harvard historian Eric Nelson argues Adams was among a group of founders who believed the Revolution wasn't fought against a king, but waged against his abusive Parliament. Indeed, Adams may have believed King George was not abusing his powers, but rather was not powerful *enough.*[11]

Adams did not just have affection for constitutional monarchy. He opposed a fundamental concept embedded in "We the People": the notion of popular sovereignty. The Constitution's central innovation was that its authority emanated from "We the People," the first three words of the preamble. Remarkably, Adams disagreed that the preamble or any constitutional text made the people the final authority in our democracy. Indeed, Adams rejected the idea that the republic was at core democratic, instead championing a "mixed constitution," in which sovereignty lay in the Congress and presidency together. Here Adams drew on the British idea that both Parliament and king were sovereign.

The mixed constitution Adams admired denied the popular sovereignty central to democracy. In Great Britain, the king was insulated from legal accountability. For instance, under British sedition laws, anyone who dared slander the king in writing could be imprisoned or fined.[12] Adams's approval of this aspect of the mixed constitution led naturally to endorsing similar sedition laws at home. Indeed, as Montesquieu argued, much to Adams's appreciation, a people's direct confrontation with a king (or a president) invited instability, or worse, total collapse. The goal of a mixed constitution, Adams thought, was to *prevent* such confrontation by channeling popular desires into the legislature, where they would be checked by the aristocratic House of Lords, or its American analogue, the Senate. In Adams's ideal society, this balance between the people and aristocracy preserved the power of the king or president.

Adams believed revolutionary France proved his ideas about monarchy with bloody clarity. Angry mobs beheading the Parisian political elite were, to Adams, a logical progression of what can happen when popular tempers spin out of control. *Here*, thought Adams, was "popular sovereignty." Unchecked by a monarch, the French descended into violence. In a letter to his son written January 1793, Adams doubted France could prosper without monarchy: "My Opinion has always been that in France a free Government can never be introduced and endure without both an hereditary Executive and Senate."[13] In other words, he recommended a mixed constitution. But just weeks after this letter, new leadership in France showed their intentions. King Louis—who had aided the American revolutionaries decades earlier—was marched to the guillotine. In public view, the blade fell, and so did the king's head.

About a month later, in early March 1793, Washington took his second oath of office. Tending his ill wife, Adams was notably absent as the dignitaries assembled, including from the most democratic branch, the House of Representatives, to hear Washington ask them to "upbraid" him should he overstep his authority. Had he been there, Adams would have cringed. A president—like a king—did not *invite* criticism from the people or their representatives. To do so would set the match to tinder. Washington's call to criticize a president who has become unmoored from the office champions a right to dissent we now see as crucial to democracy. But as he amassed power, Adams had other ideas.

★ ★ ★

THREE YEARS LATER, Adams got his chance to correct Washington's error. He narrowly won the 1796 election, becoming the nation's second president. However, because the Constitution awarded the vice presidency to the presidential runner-up, Thomas Jefferson—the opposition leader and Adams's personal nemesis—was elected vice president.

During Adams's first year as president, relations with France continued to spiral. The French were angry at America for declaring neutrality and continuing to trade with Britain. By the end of Washington's administration, the French had resorted to seizing American merchant ships and had refused to receive an American foreign minister. Both sides were incensed; the tinder was ready for a spark.

That spark arrived in a fiasco known as the XYZ Affair. In 1797, Adams sent three diplomats to Paris to seek an audience with the French foreign minister and resolve the countries' tensions. They were stopped by three French officials—who became known as X, Y, and Z—who demanded the Americans pay bribes to get a fair hearing. Outraged, the diplomats refused. While the Americans eventually got their audience, the relationship damage was done.

That's not all the French officials imparted, however. They made it known to the Americans that, to France, there *already* was a loyal party in American government: the Democratic-Republicans. They could always deal with them, they mused, instead of the "British party"— the demeaning term the French used to describe Adams and the Federalists.

It took several months for the news to reach the United States. When it did, in spring 1798, the blowback was ferocious. Some Federalists called for war, including Adams's secretary of state, Timothy Pickering.[14] Incredibly, the French escalated again, resuming attacks on merchant ships, this time in American waters. The panic for a military response seized the federal government. Adams appointed his first secretary of the navy, a new office. Finally, in July 1798, Congress nullified its treaty with France and authorized attacks on French warships.

America's first undeclared war began. Sometimes called the Quasi-War, the naval conflict lasted two years.

As the war cry rose among Federalists, so did their panic and paranoia. X, Y, and Z were not entirely wrong about Democratic-Republicans. They *were* enamored with France and largely opposed Federalist calls for war. In Philadelphia salons and the partisan press, Federalists began to suspect that Democratic-Republicans might choose France over the United States. In a private letter to fellow Federalist Alexander Hamilton, Secretary Pickering said France's actions were "so monstrous as to shock every reasonable man." Soon the Federalists, including Adams, made the next paranoid leap in logic: if the French could not be trusted, then neither could their American allies.[15]

Adams could have cooled off this rhetoric. Instead, his paranoia fed the flames. He wondered what having Jefferson as his vice president meant, considering the French claims about "their" party in the government. It didn't help that Adams was ensconced in Philadelphia, the capital city, where French influence pervaded. French was widely spoken, as it was the second language of the political elite, and some store signs were written in French.[16] Partisan Democratic-Republicans there physically fought Federalists in Congress and the streets.

The combination of Jefferson and French influence in Philadelphia led Adams to imagine the worst: he feared a rebellion by Philadelphians, stoked by pro-French radicalism—the kind of mob action that beheaded King Louis. Privately, he began to nourish another nightmare: What was to stop a French invasion?[17] This fear was not totally unfounded. Weak by comparison, the United States was ripe for attack. If anything might entice the French to invade, Adams thought, it was the presence of allies in the government, as X, Y, and Z had claimed. Adams had long allowed himself to imagine the invaders being welcomed by the Democratic-Republicans in his government. As early as December 1796, he wondered to his wife, Abigail, whether "in their Trances and Deliriums of Victory [the French] think to terrify America."[18]

These fears were widespread enough that the Federalists decided to act. In June and July of 1798, President Adams signed a suite of unprecedented emergency measures that Congress passed—reflecting a sense of impending war with France and her American allies—which became known as the Alien and Sedition Acts. These infamous laws were four specific bills. The first three concerned noncitizens, granting Adams power to imprison or deport any resident "aliens" and retract civil liberties for virtually all noncitizens. The fourth was the Sedition Act. The bill made it a federal crime to publish "false, scandalous, and malicious writing" that criticized the president, the government generally, or congressmen. Anyone convicted faced up to two years in prison and a $2,000 fine, about $48,000 today.[19]

Despite being written in neutral terms, these laws were understood as blatantly political. Because it targeted citizens directly, the Sedition Act was the most controversial. The act prohibited criticism of Congress and the president, which meant criminalizing any criticism of *Federalists*, who controlled both branches. However, in one of the law's most extraordinary feats of partisan contempt, the Sedition Act allowed criticism of the *vice* president—Thomas Jefferson, a Democratic-Republican. As if the partisan bullseye in the law wasn't obvious enough, the law's politics were clear: its expiration date was set for March 3, 1801, the day before the next presidential inauguration. This was a Federalist move to ensure the law couldn't be used against *them*. The Sedition Act was a power grab and election manipulation scheme masquerading as a security measure.

The combined acts addressed both sides of Adams's paranoia: the Sedition Act to head off destabilizing dissenters and the Alien Acts to suppress French influence. Together, the acts divided the citizenry between the loyal citizens respectful of the president and the disloyal opposition, namely the Democratic-Republicans and their noncitizen allies.

This purpose was lost on no one, not least the Democratic-Republicans, who lambasted the law. Their rage and emotional appeals for the rights of citizens makes clear that Federalists knew what they were doing. Albert Gallatin, a Swiss-born, French-speaking Democratic-Republican congressman from Pennsylvania, put the terms starkly:

Laws like the Sedition Act emulated the "worst Emperors of Rome." He invoked the idea that a republic was supposed to debate ideas, not punish them: the way "to combat error is truth, and . . . to resort to coercion and punishments in order to suppress writings attacking their measures, is to confess that these could not be defended by any other means."[20]

★ ★ ★

ADAMS SIGNED TWO OF THE ALIEN ACTS IN JUNE, and the third on July 6, 1798. The Sedition Act came on July 14, one week after Congress authorized attacks on French ships. Adams implied he was a reluctant signer, acting only on wartime necessity, later saying: "I knew there was need of them both, and therefore I consented to them." Adams's implied reluctance may have given cover to his admirers, since the Sedition Act appeared to be at odds with his professed belief in a "government of laws, not of men."[21]

However, the Sedition Act cohered with the constitutional vision of both Adams and the Federalists. Like Adams, many Federalists were influenced by Montesquieu, who wrote extensively of the dangers public mockery and criticism posed to the dignity of public office. The Sedition Act aligned with two ideas that forged Adams's worldview: the mixed constitution and British common law. At common law, sedition against the king was punishable, at times by death. True, public executions for a newspaper editorial would have been beyond the pale for most Federalists. But the capital offense in British sedition law made a prison sentence in America appear more acceptable. Adams's devotion to these ideas combined with some desire to protect his ego likely made him a ready signer of the acts.

However, the Sedition Act contradicted a central constitutional ideal. During the Philadelphia Constitutional Convention of 1787, delegates who feared a weak central government created a powerful presidency. Many, though, still leery of an overreaching government, took steps to limit government power. The First Amendment, adopted by Congress in 1789 and ratified in 1791, prohibited Congress from "abridging the freedom of speech." More directly, the Constitution's structure aimed to halt such overreach: Congress had vast powers, such as taxing and spending, but lacked general "police powers" to regulate people's morality. Among the many framers of the Constitution still alive, James Madison, who initially drafted the First Amendment, was particularly incensed about the Sedition Act, a law he thought unconstitutionally violated freedom of speech. He said the law meant Democratic-Republicans were "not equal" and "may be exposed to the contempt and hatred of the people without a violation of the act." He added, "What will be the situation of the people? Not free."[22] For Madison, the right to "free speech" meant the right to dissent. This was a broader view than that of Adams, who thought free speech included the right of newspapers to exist and opine on many topics—but not to criticize him or his party.

By far, the greatest outrage about the Sedition Act came from the law's intended targets: Democratic-Republicans in the partisan press. In eighteenth-century America, journalistic notions of objectivity had yet to be invented: newspapers were partisan organs, proudly owned and operated by Democratic-Republicans or Federalists deeply enmeshed in their nascent parties. In 1790, the US had an estimated 96 newspapers. By 1800, that had grown to 234 papers—available nearly everywhere, with widespread reach: more than 1.9 million newspapers were mailed nationwide in 1800.[23]

Make no mistake: these news outlets were harsh. The year before Adams became president, the revolutionary pamphleteer Thomas Paine, writing a letter to George Washington published in the *Philadelphia Aurora*, critiqued Adams for his monarchical views. Deliberately provoking him by using his first name, Paine wrote, "John has said . . . the Presidency should be made hereditary," a view which was "of a degree beyond common treason" and "a sin against nature."[24]

The publisher of that newspaper was Benjamin Bache, an Adams opponent and twenty-seven-year-old grandson of Benjamin Franklin, whom Adams had thought too solicitous of the French during a diplomatic mission they had taken together. In 1796, Bache opposed Adams's campaign, supporting Jefferson. Since candidates then did not openly campaign, Bache was Jefferson's surrogate, arguing the choice between the men was between "a steadfast friend to the Rights of the People, or an advocate for hereditary power and distinctions."[25] After Adams won by three electoral votes, Bache's *Aurora*, among the preeminent Democratic-Republican publications, briefly tried a conciliatory tone. One writer wrote, "May success, happiness and tranquility yet await [Adams's] measures." Soon, however, this optimism faded. By May 1797, the *Aurora* accused Adams of giving a "war speech" and needlessly inciting conflict with France.[26] Infamously, Bache published a letter speaking of "querulous and cankered murmurs of blind, bald, crippled, toothless Adams."[27]

Some of the day's insults went too far, as when Democratic-Republican newspaper editor James Callender called Adams a "hideous hermaphroditical character, which has neither the force of a man, nor the gentleness and sensibility of a woman." However, the Federalist press exaggerated how much the Democratic-Republicans propounded personal attacks rather than policy debate. Even Callender's ill-conceived remark, while clearly an attack on Adams's character, was in the context of a broader attack on his policies and spending power; the remark was not intended to reveal some personal secret about Adams's private life.[28] The bulk of the comments ultimately causing Federalist ire (and prosecution) were core political speech, the kind of reasoned-if-colorful dialogue that today would be fully protected by the courts and would be viewed as central to the robust debate that is needed in any functioning democracy.

Adams, a man who thought he deserved a royal title, had a deep, festering egotism and a thin skin. The insults and criticisms of his policies hit him hard. This insecurity manifested as contempt for Democratic-Republicans and even intraparty rivals—he once called Hamilton a "bastard brat of a Scotch Pedler."[29] His condescension also included, incredibly, George Washington. In a letter decades later, Adams described Washington as "too illiterate, unlearned, [and] unread, for his Station and reputation."[30] (Ironically, if read uncharitably, this commentary about Washington would have been illegal had the Sedition Act operated in 1812. Add self-awareness to the virtues Adams lacked.)

Adams's emotional sensitivities and political philosophy help explain his support for the Alien and Sedition Acts. Rather than calm him, his spouse and confidante, Abigail, encouraged him to retaliate against criticism. One man in particular drew her focus: Benjamin Bache. After reading the editorials in the *Aurora*, the First Lady dreamed of imprisoning Bache. "Dairingly [sic] do the vile incendaries keep up in Baches paper the most wicked and base, voilent & caluminiating abuse," she wrote her sister. Then, she ominously hinted at the fate of Democratic-Republicans at the *Aurora*: "The wrath of the public," she wrote, "ought to fall upon their devoted Heads." Bache had no idea he had made an enemy. But once he had, the *Aurora*'s fate was sealed when the Sedition Act was introduced. The president's wife had been clamoring for a bill to stop Bache, as "nothing will have an Effect untill congress pass a Sedition Bill."[31] Vice President Jefferson, appalled by the sedition bill, remarked that Bache was thought to be its "main object."[32] Adams proved him right, as his administration soon arrested Bache. Washington had also drawn Bache's ire during his presidency, but he had never prosecuted this severe critic. Adams was a different kind of president.

★ ★ ★

ON JUNE 26, 1798, Bache was charged with sedition. The cause must have been for political revenge, because the facts that spurred his prosecution are so benign. Bache was targeted because he had published a letter from French foreign minister Charles-Maurice de Talleyrand before it reached Congress. Though publishing the letter was not obviously illegal, the Federalists attempted to smear Bache as a French agent while discrediting the letter's substance, which suggested France was not looking for war. Bache was charged with the vague accusation of seditious libel against Adams and "the Executive Government." In an odd twist, this prosecution came before the Sedition Act had been formally signed (it was introduced the same day). Thus, Bache was charged under the "common law" of criminal libel. Bache planned to fight back, using his newspaper to defend the free press while he fought the courts' jurisdiction to try him. Tragically, before this plan could go into effect, he died in a yellow fever epidemic.

Despite the demise of Bache, the Adams administration wasn't done with the *Aurora*. They meanwhile rushed to wield the new laws widely against their other enemies. Until recently, common wisdom was that prosecutions under the Sedition Act were few, minor blemishes on an otherwise proud founding history. Now, thanks to historians such as Wendell Bird, we know that there were as many as 126 defendants prosecuted under the Sedition Act.[33] Their offenses were as minor as contributing to the publication of a letter bemoaning that Adams had not been sent to a "mad house" for his policies.[34] One person prosecuted, Matthew Lyon, a congressman from Vermont, was sentenced to four months in prison and issued a $1,000 fine for noting the president's "unbounded thirst for ridiculous pomp, foolish adulation, or selfish av[a]rice."[35] (Lyon then ran for reelection—and won—from jail.)

Lyon fought the charges, arguing the First Amendment protected his right to criticize the president. If Lyon or Bache were charged today, their conviction would be struck down immediately, because presidential criticism is protected political speech. In 1798, however, that tradition did not exist, and the judiciary was dominated by Federalist-appointed judges sympathetic to the Sedition Act, including arguably its most influential proponent: Samuel Chase, a justice on the Supreme Court.

Chase was a distinguished jurist, penning the 1798 opinion in *Calder v. Bull*, which is still taught in constitutional law classes today. In *Calder*, Chase offered a seminal explanation of the Constitution's ban on ex post facto laws, which are laws that make an action illegal retroactively. (That is, new laws cannot be used to prosecute people for offences that were not illegal before the law went into effect.) Chase also discussed the Constitution's ban on bills of attainder—criminal laws that target particular individuals for punishment.

Yet without irony, Chase supported the Alien and Sedition Acts, laws designed primarily to target specific Democratic-Republican newspaper editors. Political partisanship for him was no source of embarrassment: while on the court, he openly campaigned for Adams.[36] In fairness, standards of judicial independence were different at the time, preceding the not-yet-formed American Bar Association, which insisted on a rigid divide between politics and law.[37] Nonetheless, Chase's behavior was inappropriate even then. He went beyond mere partisanship and sought to diminish political opponents' ability to criticize his party's leaders or have a fair trial.

This is exemplified by the action taken against the *Aurora* by the Adams administration and the Federalists. After Bache's death, it was unclear how they could proceed. The *Aurora* meanwhile faced short-term tumult, though it soon returned with a new leader: Bache's apprentice, William Duane. Duane was practically a novice in Philadelphia politics, and the Adams administration and its allies, eager to see the sedition laws wielded against Democratic-Republicans, assumed they could make an easy example of Duane. They were wrong.

Duane was raised in New York, by Irish parents, in the 1760s. As a teen, Duane lived in Ireland, and eventually India, in the British colony in Calcutta. There, writes historian Jeffrey Pasley, Duane received his "first taste of arbitrary power."[38] Duane initially enlisted in the service of the East India Company's army, then joined a local English newspaper. Things went smoothly at first. But Duane became a passionate supporter of the French Revolution and published criticisms of French royalists in India, receiving a seditious libel charge that lost him his editorship. When he soon founded another publication featuring prorevolutionary sentiment and complaints against the East India Company, he was deported to Britain as a criminal.[39]

Duane had tasted the oppression of British libel laws, and having seen their threat to liberty, sailed to the United States—seeking the land of the First Amendment. Just months after Duane arrived in Philadelphia, Washington delivered his Farewell Address. Duane trashed it, writing under a pseudonym that Washington was a hypocrite the country was better off without. The brazen piece caught the attention of Bache, who hired Duane two years later. With Bache's sudden death, the renegade, largely unknown Duane stumbled into leadership of the capital's most prestigious political paper, just in time for the Sedition Act.[40]

At the *Aurora*, Duane made clear that he was no happier with the second president and his politics, claiming that Adams was controlled by Great Britain. Just as the Federalists stoked paranoia about French control, Duane responded by doubting whether high officials were always autonomous American actors. He wrote in July 1799: "The high character for private and public virtue . . . has been tarnished by British intrigue," claiming to have evidence that even Adams admitted (though did not like) Britain's power in American government.[41] As an Irishman, Duane was doubly incensed by Adams, both for the Sedition Act and Alien Acts; lacking documentation of his New York birth, Duane was vulnerable to deportation. Adams knew that, too. Furious over Duane's writings, Adams wrote to Secretary Pickering: "The matchless effrontery of this Duane merits the execution of the alien law. I am very willing to try its strength upon him."[42] Duane's activism amplified the Federalist desire to see him prosecuted. In Philadelphia, Duane helped organize a petition to repeal the Alien Acts. In response, he was charged by Federalists with "seditious riot"—but was acquitted by a sympathetic Philadelphia jury.

As he accumulated status, Duane was emboldened. In winter 1799, the *Aurora* attacked a bill introduced in the Senate that blatantly attempted to tilt the election toward Federalists—a little-known scheme, eerily familiar today, that Duane's reporting revealed. It would have created a committee stacked by Federalists to effectively discard and refuse to certify electoral votes on a case-by-case basis, a proposal similar to those floated by Senator Ted Cruz and others regarding certifying the 2020 electoral vote, but more brazen in its attempt to legally codify the scheme.[43] Duane's editorial pulled no punches: the Federalists had become a party against democracy, he wrote—"hostile to the popular interests" and eager "to engross every power which the people enjoy" and instead place the "constitution in the hands of a few."[44] Democratic-Republicans had feared that the Sedition Act was a thinly veiled attempt to destroy their political chances and popular sovereignty, striking at the people's right to criticize (and replace) their leaders. Now, they saw the Federalists taking bolder steps to undermine democracy, plotting to usurp the electoral college to ensure Federalist victory.

Duane's exposé of the Federalist plot was so embarrassing that Senate Federalists demanded he be brought to heel; some wanted Duane tried in the Senate instead of by jury, claiming extraconstitutional power, so they could convict him themselves. Duane appeared at first in the Senate to protest, requesting lawyers to defend his case. Yet when two lawyers refused, citing the farce of the Senate's request, Duane rejected the Senate's subpoena and declined to show up for the phony trial. The Senate held him in contempt and ordered him found, forcing Duane into hiding while Federalists attempted to catch their longtime nemesis. The Senate resolved that the administration should try Duane under the Sedition Act, and President Adams eagerly complied, instructing his attorney general to prosecute.[45]

Throughout his travails, Duane kept fighting, publishing a defense of his original exposé when the House failed to pass the Federalist election scheme. Poignantly, Duane connected his story about the bill to the sedition law's threat to democracy.[46] If Duane had not defied the sedition law, the power grab might have succeeded, thus undermining democracy. Ultimately, Duane and his attorney managed to delay his trial long enough for Jefferson to take office and the law to expire, and so avoided prosecution.

Not everyone was that lucky. Thomas Cooper, a lawyer and former editor, faced an all-out prosecution under the sedition law. Exhibiting savvy that was the envy of any contemporary publicist, Cooper's defense against the law showcased why the Sedition Act was an all-out assault on democracy by a would-be authoritarian president.

Duane had originally asked Cooper to represent him at his pending Senate trial. Privately, Cooper had taken up his cause, secretly writing to Vice President Jefferson, who served as Senate president, with suggestions for how to subvert or delay the Senate's conviction attempts.[47] But Cooper publicly refused to represent Duane in the Senate, claiming, "I will not degrade myself by submitting to appear before the senate with *their gag in my mouth.*"[48]

Like Duane, Cooper was an immigrant—traveling from England during the French Revolution—and was familiar with British libel law. Like Duane, he had a healthy disrespect for authority, and he channeled his rage at the Federalists as a newspaper editor at the *Sunbury and Northumberland Gazette.* A year after the infamous laws passed, Cooper penned a satire about what a president who sought authoritarian power would do, writing in the voice of the president that he would create a standing army that he could control "not for defense against invaders from without, but for use against the friends and principles of liberty from within." Seeing himself in the thinly disguised character, Adams wrote to his attorney general: "I despise it," adding, "I have no doubt it is a libel against the government, and as such ought to be prosecuted."[49]

In Cooper's words, his writing aimed to inspire resistance to despotism, "opposed in the only justifiable way of opposition under a free government, by discussion in the first instance, and a change of persons by constitutional election, if no other method will succeed." Cooper accused Adams of hiding behind the Sedition Act and interfering with the judicial process, "a Stretch of authority which the Monarch of Great Britain would have shrunk from."[50]

This time, Cooper had crossed a line, appalling Abigail Adams by his "Mad democratic Stile." The Federalists had been seeking a way to prosecute Cooper since his refusal to defend Duane. Now, they made a move, arresting Cooper for seditious libel, nominally due to a handbill he had published months earlier, but really the culmination of months of criticism. Just as Bache had passed the torch of free speech defense to Duane, now Duane passed the public battle to Cooper.

Cooper welcomed the attention and worked to publicize the cases widely. His plan was to flip the script and, as one historian phrased it, put the sedition law itself "on trial." Indeed, as Cooper developed his defense, he aimed squarely at Adams and the entire Federalist Party.[51]

The other reason the trial seized the attention of the country was because of who presided: the Sedition Act's most vocal judicial supporter, Justice Chase. Federalists might have hoped the presence of this sitting justice would quiet rogue Democratic-Republican editors nationwide. But Democratic-Republicans saw Chase's involvement as an opportunity to publicize his clash with one of the law's chief architects and defenders.

At trial, bolstered by his own writing and both sides of the partisan press, Cooper became the face of the Democratic-Republicans' national campaign to defeat the Sedition Act. Duane had modeled defiance of prosecution and how to use the accusations leveled against him to demonstrate the importance of the constitutional right to dissent as given by the First Amendment. This strategy would be perfected by Cooper, an editor and skilled lawyer with a flair for political drama. Cooper addressed the judges and the jury throughout the trial, though with a bigger audience in mind. The American people soon would cast ballots in the election of 1800. Cooper aimed to convince them that the Sedition Act was a threat to constitutional self-government and their status as democratic citizens. He wanted voters, not Chase, to condemn the acts by voting the Federalists out of power. To this end, Cooper published the details of his argument in what he claimed was a word-for-word transcript of the trial, hoping to paint Chase and the president as authoritarian enemies of democracy.[52]

The trial opened in April 1800 at the federal circuit court in Philadelphia. Cooper could not have gotten better publicity in the persons of his adversaries: watching from the gallery was the secretary of war and Congressman Robert Goodloe Harper, who helped author the act, while Secretary Pickering sat on the bench with the judges, as William Rawle, the Federalist district attorney, served as prosecutor. This was a partisan law and a partisan prosecution.[53]

In opening statements, Rawle made his case. He argued Cooper was guilty of a crime that "all civilized nations ha[ve] thought it right . . . to punish with severity," committing an "abuse [of] the men with whom the public has entrusted the management of their national concerns." He added that Cooper's charge that the president was authoritarian was a dangerous "error" that "leads to discontent, discontent to a fancied idea of oppression, and that to insurrection."[54] The prosecutor then read to the jury the Sedition Act followed by Cooper's writing, intending to show that Cooper clearly violated it.

On his turn, Cooper took two primary tacks. The first was to claim that what he wrote was true insofar as it was opinion, using in his defense the definition of truth as described by the Sedition Act itself. Even if the jury disagreed with his claims about Adams, the jury should recognize that opinions could not be true or false, a point at the heart of modern First Amendment doctrine.[55]

More important, Cooper argued that his right—the right of any citizen—to criticize Adams was fundamental to democracy. He doubled down that the standing army Adams sought exemplified his authoritarian ambitions. As Cooper said, people could not "exercise on rational grounds their elective franchise, if perfect freedom of discussion of public characters be not allowed." He continued by reminding jurors of the upcoming presidential election, where "[e]lectors are bound in conscience to reflect and decide who best deserves their suffrages; but how can they do it, if these prosecutions . . . close all the avenues of information, and throw a veil over the grossest misconduct of our periodical rulers."[36] In other words, American citizens—and the electors who would choose their president—had a right not just to discuss politics but to hear all political opinions; and as such a law that criminalized viewpoints had no place in constitutional government.

This was a masterclass in the democratic principles underlying constitutional law. Cooper appealed to the logic of the Constitution, linking its basis in popular sovereignty with the rights of the freedoms of speech and press. He also used his charm, dramatic flair, and wit on the jury, cracking that being from Britain, he knew the king of England was infallible. "But I did not know till now that the President of the United States had the same attribute."[37]

Cooper's sense of drama illustrated his constitutional point. He attempted to serve a subpoena on President Adams as an illustration that no citizen should be above the law or courts, and further that it was right to compel Adams to appear because Adams was the subject of Cooper's supposed libel, the subject of the trial. Predictably, Justice Chase denied the subpoena, saying it was improper and indecent. Cooper's request and Chase's rejection symbolize a larger conflict. From the perspective of popular sovereignty, a subpoena of the president by a citizen is perfectly natural, but from the perspective of a mixed constitution, it seems absurd.

Disallowed from subpoenaing the president, Cooper brilliantly sought to bring a former president to his side. In the midst of the trial, Cooper argued he was adopting Washington's policies against foreign entanglements. He quoted Washington's Farewell Address, illustrating its overlap with his own criticisms. He then concluded, "Gentlemen of the jury, do I stand before you, indicted for being an advocate for the doctrines, solemnly and deliberately recommended to his fellow citizens, by George Washington."[38] The implication was clear: Cooper stood with Washington against the authoritarian president.

Cooper's antics aggravated Chase, who thus far had resisted the clash Cooper and the Democratic-Republicans were gunning for. He allowed most of Cooper's testimony but grew frustrated at the subpoena attempt. Chase reprimanded Cooper in front of the jury: "You are mistaken in supposing the prosecutor of this indictment is the president of the United States." As the judge, Chase was supposed to instruct the jury about its role deciding Cooper's guilt or innocence. Instead, amid a lengthy exposition on libel and sedition, he repeatedly implied that Cooper should be convicted, at one point saying that "[Cooper's] publication is evidently intended to mislead the ignorant, and inflame their minds against the President, and to influence their votes on the next election."

With Justice Chase set against him, the jury convicted Cooper. He was fined $400 and sentenced to six months in prison. Despite losing, Cooper succeeded in his wider ambitions, resisting the authoritarianism of Adams and the Federalists and publicizing why the sedition laws were incompatible with democracy. Years later, Jefferson acknowledged Cooper's brilliance on display in the trial: "Cooper is acknowledged by every enlightened man who knows him to be the greatest man in America, in the powers of mind . . . that without a single exception."[39]

The courtroom confrontations between Chase and Cooper were a proxy battle in the deeper war over the First Amendment's guarantee of free speech. For Chase and the Federalists, the First Amendment only reiterated what British common law acknowledged: newspapers might have a right to publish, but anyone who criticized a king or a president was not insulated from criminal punishment. Cooper had a very different understanding. He read the First Amendment as a rejection of the monarchical conception that the people are subservient to their leaders, unable to challenge or criticize them in any way. But Cooper's contribution to democracy was as much in his method of dissemination as in the ideas themselves. The audience he sought to persuade was not just in the courtroom, but the people writ large, the electorate, following along in his paper. Though Cooper lost the case, he sought victory for his democratic understanding of the Constitution in the court of public opinion.

★ ★ ★

IN 1789, WELL BEFORE ADAMS TOOK OFFICE, James Madison said that judges would play a key role in protecting constitutional rights and liberties, calling them an "impenetrable bulwark."[60] But Madison likely lost his optimism when he saw that courts only enabled Adams further as he stifled dissent. Cooper's trial served as a dramatic illustration of how judges have often undermined democratic rights, not protected them. Justice Chase, the man who earlier lobbied for the Sedition Act, was not going to strike down that law. To protect the Constitution when all three branches had abandoned it to pursue partisan aims, the First Amendment would have to find its champions among the sovereign people, Cooper among them.

Of course, Adams and the Federalists saw the moment and the wider ideas they battled over in starkly different terms. Adams opposed direct criticism of a president by the people—not merely out of vanity, but from a sincere belief that it would lead to the political instability of the type that gripped France. But Cooper's performance in the courtroom showed that speech—even biting and critical of a president— could be carried out within the procedures of law. Even as editorials lauded Cooper and Americans were fixated on the trial's outcome, there was no violence, nor guillotine. Rather, the real risk to the republic came from Adams himself. By intentionally targeting a political party, Adams risked creating a one-party state that mimicked monarchy.

The criticisms Adams saw as a threat to the republic—from Bache, Cooper, Duane, and their readers—were the budding of America's first constitutional constituency, fighting for a robust democratic expression of the First Amendment against Adams's monarchical one. In their view, the people's sovereignty was the source of the president's power. That meant the people's rights could not be brushed aside based on the supposed dignity of the office of the president or an appeal to independent presidential sovereignty. They needed to be allowed to criticize and even mock the chief executive. Furthermore, they had a written guarantee of their "freedom of speech" enshrined in the text of the First Amendment. Written for all Americans, the First Amendment allowed editors to publish their observations so that readers could see for themselves that the Sedition Act passed by Congress directly contradicted the Constitution. Eventually, the editors' beliefs would come to dominate our common understanding of the First Amendment and of American democracy itself. In contemporary American politics, at least until very recently, it has been rare, indeed almost unheard of, to find an opponent of the right to dissent.

Cooper and his fellow editors were not simply defending themselves against individual charges but giving voice to an idea bigger than themselves and bigger even than the president: that criticizing the president was no act of betrayal of the so-called mixed constitution but an instantiation of the sovereign rights of the people enshrined in this document. These nominal criminals, not the president, would see to it that the democratic understanding of the Constitution drove the nation forward. The constitutional constituency they led would become closely aligned first with the Democratic-Republican party and later the Federalists. And this movement's first order of business was replacing Adams with a more sympathetic president.

Ultimately, Adams was a threat to democracy not just because of his ideas, but because of his personality and the danger he himself posed to the office he held. Washington, in his second inaugural, had stressed the difference between the presidential office and its temporary occupant when he asked those who evaluate chief executives to judge their actions against the constitutional ideal of the office. But for Adams, partly because of his ego and thin skin, he and the office were synonymous; an attack on him was an attack on the office. If Adams's vision had succeeded, the presidency and the nation would have taken a different political path, where authoritarian prosecutions could have become the norm. That close call during the Adams period illuminates an alarming but enduring truth about the presidency: because presidents can help establish and preserve our understandings of rights, they also have the power to undermine them. This danger is made all the more prominent by the fact that just one individual, quirks and all, inhabits the office. If Adams rather than the editors had prevailed, the right to dissent and to criticize a chief executive might never have been fully realized.

Still, despite the dangers of the presidency, the vast power of the office allows its occupant to play a lead role in recovering from attacks on democracy. Presidents, rather than prosecuting democratic constitutional constituents, sometimes ally with them to vindicate democracy. That is a possibility of a redemptive presidency, which is especially important in the aftermath of an attack on the fundamental rights of the people. While the Federalists demonstrated key ingredients for constitutional overreach in the form of an oversensitive president, a partisan Congress, a willing attorney general (complicit in the president's schemes), and an enabling judicial system, they also initiated something else that would become an American tradition: a cycle of constitutional reckoning and recovery. The Sedition Act, a political means to stifle Democratic-Republican dissent, would become a key tool in the case for a constitutional democracy based on popular sovereignty. Under Adams, Bache, Cooper, Duane, and Lyon were painted as irresponsible citizens, indicted as criminals who violated the dignity of the presidential office. But two future presidents would redeem their ideas and make those ideas central to their own administration's ambitions to reframe the way we understand the relationship of a president to the people.

The battle lines between the constitutional understanding of the editors and that of Adams soon played out during the election of 1800, an election that put the right to dissent on center stage. With the Federalists in control of all three branches of government, the future of the meaning of the Constitution—authoritarian or democratic— hung in the balance.

CHAPTER 2

Thomas Jefferson and the Editors' Campaign

The Recovery Begins

IN APRIL 1798, THOMAS JEFFERSON WROTE A MYSTERIOUS LETTER. TO ONE OF HIS CLOSEST confidantes, none other than Secretary of State James Madison, Jefferson revealed something he dared tell no one else: he suspected he was under surveillance.

Jefferson feared his mail was being intercepted, read, and then carefully reinserted into the postal system.[1] He worried the Adams administration was watching him. It is unclear whether Jefferson's worry was well founded. But given the proclivity Adams showed for prosecuting his political opponents, it was possible. Jefferson's private correspondence was a Federalist operative's dream—a treasure trove of intelligence with real-time insight into the opposition leader's thoughts—and after the passage of the Sedition Act a possible means for prosecution.

Jefferson's suspicions had history. He and Madison had for years used ciphers in their correspondences to avoid detection.[2] Eventually, Jefferson resorted to closing his letters with a wax seal so that Madison could know whether they had been improperly opened.[3] Given his suspicions of government tampering, Jefferson asked Madison to make sure the seals were left untouched.[4] In November 1799, not six months after the passage of the Sedition Act, Jefferson's fear of prosecution grew, as did his distrust in the mail. He wrote to Madison, "I shall trust the post offices with nothing confidential, persuaded that during the ensuing twelvemonth they will lend their inquisitorial aid to furnish matter for new slanders." He would send no more sensitive letters.[5]

By the time of the Alien and Sedition Acts crisis, Jefferson was almost halfway through a term as vice president. He had become a figure of immense public scrutiny and a top Federalist target. The situation was further complicated, as he was simultaneously part of the Adams administration and the obvious candidate to challenge Adams for the presidency. This arrangement was more than awkward. It turned the fierce disagreements between Adams and Jefferson into delicate matters that, for Jefferson, required extraordinary caution.

The Alien and Sedition Acts had put Jefferson in a difficult position. For Jefferson, his opposition was not just personal. He was outraged by the acts, which enabled attacks on his political allies. But beyond that, principles of a democratic constitution were at stake. He had helped to pass the Bill of Rights, which contains the first ten amendments to the Constitution, and he believed these new laws violated the First Amendment because they ran "so palpably in the teeth of the Constitution as to shew they mean to pay no respect to it." This violation extended to the Alien Acts, which Jefferson decried as stripping noncitizens of rights and so making them subject to "absolute government," not a government of "We the People."[6]

Jefferson knew that speaking out against Adams would bring extraordinary risk. For one thing, the sedition law all but targeted Jefferson by name, since the protections it gave to the president did not apply to the vice president. If Jefferson spoke out angrily against Adams, he could face legal reprisals, even prison. One of the first people imprisoned for violating the Sedition Act, after all, was Congressman Matthew Lyon, proving that holding office was no safeguard against prosecution. For Jefferson, such legal prosecutions were but half of the matter: the spectacle of an arrest, trial, and imprisonment would hurt his presidential prospects.

As it turned out, his suspicions of Adams were at least partly warranted. That year, Abigail—Adams's chief domestic minister without portfolio, as historian Joseph Ellis has called her[7]—declared the vice president and the opposition to be potential threats. Abigail even worried for Adams's safety after he received a letter saying the president was in danger and should be wary of "that infernal Scoundrel Jefferson," the "grandest of all grand Villains" and a "traitor to his country."[8] The First Lady played a key role in prosecuting Bache. Why should Jefferson be different?

Jefferson feared that if Adams knew the extent of his opposition, the president wouldn't hesitate to prosecute him. Adams, in fact, would have been right to fear Jefferson: the vice president had bigger concerns—and bigger plans, with Madison—that called for absolute discretion.

Allied with a leading constitutional thinker in Madison and deeply fearful about the threats that the Alien and Sedition Acts posed to the Constitution, Jefferson plotted. Silenced from speaking out as vice president, and before he could protect the right to dissent as President Jefferson, he had to resist the gross violations of the First Amendment and be an anonymous ally and supporter of a resistance movement turned democratic constitutional constituency led by the newspaper editors Adams targeted.

★ ★ ★

JEFFERSON SPENT MUCH OF LATE 1798 pondering his response to the Alien and Sedition Acts. The prosecutions in the summer and fall against Bache and Lyon likely confirmed to Jefferson that he was right to become an active participant in the fight against the despotism of these laws. Jefferson was a friend of Bache's, and he advised the young editor on how to grow his newspaper and increase his influence.[9] By the end of the decade, the *Aurora* had become the leading newspaper of Jefferson's party. Jefferson was outraged by the fact that his ally was targeted, and Bache's prosecution must have only inflamed his anger.

As enraging as the attacks on Bache and other allies were, they may have been inspiring, insofar as they revealed that when the judiciary failed to protect constitutional rights, citizens could step in. Jefferson later articulated a deep skepticism about the role of the judiciary in protecting constitutional rights. His distrust was possibly stoked when he witnessed Justice Samuel Chase openly lobby for the Sedition Act and Justice William Paterson's role in applying it in the Lyon trial, despite the law's clear conflict with the First Amendment.

Jefferson later argued that if courts alone were trusted as the sole interpreters of constitutional rights, they could mold those rights like "wax" into whatever they wished.[10] Over time, the guarantees of the document would be left meaningless, mangled and remangled by generations of unelected judges. Even though both Lyon and Cooper lost their criminal cases, their defiance of Supreme Court justices spoke to Jefferson's core idea of the Constitution. In Jefferson's view, judges didn't have a monopoly on the meaning of the Constitution—but they often warped it. The document existed in words and spirit apart from what any judge said. Through their trials, these citizens showed that the Constitution was theirs to interpret.

Jefferson's actions paralleled the resistance exhibited by Duane. Whereas those on trial resisted in courtrooms and newspapers, Jefferson tried to enlist state legislatures, working his contacts—anonymously—to stop Adams's tyrannical laws. On the eve of the Sedition Act being signed in July 1798, Jefferson left Philadelphia and traveled to his home, Monticello, in Virginia.[11] On the way, approximately 230 miles into the journey, he stopped at Madison's home, Montpelier, also in Virginia. Given what happened soon after, it is likely that there they began deliberating about how to fight the tyranny of the impending acts, a fight that took months. Because they faced the danger of being prosecuted, their business was conducted unofficially, and anonymously, and behind Adams's back.

To resist the laws, Madison and Jefferson collaborated on a strategy that allowed them to galvanize the power of state governments. If the federal government passed a terrible law—and a corrupt Supreme Court did not stand in the way—could states weigh in on the constitutionality of the law? Jefferson and Madison thought yes. Since the federal government and the judiciary had failed to declare the Alien and Sedition Acts unconstitutional, the states would have to take up that duty.

Though they agreed on that general goal, the two men disagreed on the extent to which states could use their legal powers for this resistance. During their deliberations, Jefferson proposed an especially radical interpretation: states could not only declare federal laws unconstitutional, but they could "nullify" them if they wished—rendering them entirely void in their state. Madison thought this went too far. To him, in order for there to *be* a Constitution worth preserving, there had to be a supreme federal law that operated the same in every state. Nullifying federal law would confuse justified resistance with illegal action.

Madison's argument rested on the insight that there was nothing to stop states from refusing to *enforce* a bad federal law. That meant that if the federal government sought to arrest citizens for libeling the president, states need not cooperate. That mattered tremendously, given how law enforcement worked then: although a small number of federal marshals offered protection for federal courts and occasionally made arrests, they were nothing like today's FBI. The federal government was mostly reliant on sheriffs and constables to enforce federal laws. If those state officials refused to comply, there was little the federal government could do to arrest someone.

Yielding to Madison's measured strategy, Jefferson joined him in drafting resolutions that condemned the acts as unconstitutional and committed states not to enforce them. Intended as guiding documents that could be introduced into state legislatures, the resolutions spelled out the lawful means of noncompliance that states could use to resist federal action.[12] In essence, Jefferson and Madison were making a statement: if the Federalists wanted to enforce their acts, they would have to do it themselves. Rather than despair or complain privately, these two future presidents wrote one of the country's first resistance manuals.

Madison and Jefferson stoked a campaign to adopt the resolutions in state legislatures countrywide. For months, multiple states debated the acts' unconstitutionality, kicking up publicity from politicians, newspaper editors, and citizens.[13] While most states ultimately did not adopt the resolutions, they sparked debate among citizens, inspiring their own resistance to the acts and Adams.

In the end, the resolutions were formally adopted by two states, Kentucky and Virginia.[14] These states declared the Alien and Sedition Acts unconstitutional and committed to refusing assistance to the federal government in prosecuting anyone indicted under them. Even the states that did not adopt the resolutions fiercely debated them, with some residents agreeing that states had the power to opine on the constitutionality of a national law.[15] Tennessee and Georgia even argued that the laws were "in several parts opposed to the constitution, and are impolitic, oppressive, and unnecessary."[16]

Furthermore, Madison's report on the Virginia resolution made clear why Adams's authoritarian conception of the Constitution was wrong and the newspaper editors' democratic understanding was correct. Alluding to the monarchial underpinnings of the sedition laws, Madison claimed that the idea that a "king, [could] ... do no wrong" had no place in the American Constitution. He emphasized that the Sedition Act undermined the Constitution's commitment to democracy because it regarded the citizens as "not equal" and rendered a people "not free; because they will be compelled to make their election between competitors, whose pretensions they are not permitted by the act, equally to examine, to discuss, and to ascertain."[17] In other words, the prosecution of the editors undid the possibility of a free and fair election because without their freedom to publish, the American people would lack the information needed to choose among competing candidates. Like Cooper, Jefferson and Madison did more than just highlight the specific injustices of the Sedition Act. Their goal was to defend their young country's democracy by galvanizing the public against a president with an authoritarian understanding of the American Constitution.

★ ★ ★

AS JEFFERSON SOUGHT TO UNSEAT ADAMS IN 1800, it was crucial that his anonymous resistance be bolstered by a more public campaign. Because of the looming threat of prosecution, not to mention the norms for nineteenth-century presidential campaigns, Jefferson needed citizens to campaign for him. Jefferson had initially tried to stump for himself, intending to give a campaign speech in Richmond. But Governor Monroe argued that a direct campaign by Jefferson could backfire by triggering opponents' campaigns, leading to a public relations war. Given that Jefferson was a weak public speaker, Jefferson did not stump.[18] Not having to campaign also insulated Jefferson from the risk of arrest for libeling Adams under the act, which was a distinct possibility if he took to the campaign trail himself.

The groundwork for a citizen-led campaign on behalf of Jefferson had been laid by the newspapers that published editorials opposing the Alien and Sedition Acts. While Adams and the Federalists wielded the Sedition Act in an attempt to destroy opposition newspapers and their editors, that attack served only to feed the growth of these opponents. Indeed, Democratic-Republican newspapers were ascendent as the election grew nearer.[19] Moreover, the papers were not just winning more readers. They were galvanizing citizen action. Thousands came to the small town of Lexington, Kentucky, responding to a call by the Democratic-Republican *Kentucky Gazette* to protest the acts. The gathering passed resolutions declaring that "all laws made to impair or destroy [free speech] are void."[20] The New Jersey *Sentinel of Freedom* lauded the Virginia and Kentucky resolutions and called on "real republicans" to "conv[e]ne together in either township or county meetings . . . by way of remonstrance to repeal the alien and sedition laws, which have been enacted in open violation of the constitution."[21] In Essex County, New Jersey, citizens passed resolutions condemning the acts as unconstitutional. Each newspaper beckoned citizens to action then reported on their work, spreading resistance further. Citizens also decried the acts' unconstitutionality in hundreds of petitions written to Congress.[22]

Cooper's trial also personalized resistance, paving the way for the editors' campaign for Jefferson in the public mind. The reports of the trial appeared not only in Cooper's paper but in the growing number of Democratic-Republican papers around the country, a proto-Twitter complete with retweets against Adams's assault on democracy. But in April 1800, when Cooper was convicted, the editors' campaign needed a new captain at the helm. James Callender took on that role. Callender was an immigrant who arrived from Scotland early in Washington's second term, fleeing persecution for his biting writings. Following in Cooper's footsteps, he openly defied Adams, then used his prosecution to demonstrate Adams's tyranny.[23] Callender started his American career in Philadelphia as a collaborator of Bache and Duane, writing for the *Aurora*. After Bache's arrest, Callender feared he was next, so he fled to Richmond, Virginia, which was friendlier territory for an Adams critic.[24]

Callender published his anti-Federalist pamphlet, *The Prospect Before Us*, in 1800. There he openly defied the Sedition Act's prohibition on criticizing Adams. Callender called Adams corrupt, the "father of the alien and sedition acts," and declared that his party hated "American independence."[25] The network of Democratic-Republican newspapers leaped into action, reprinting Callender's writing and building the opposition to Adams, activating the proto-Twitter network.

Jefferson lent support financially to the editors. "Every man must lay his purse and pen under contribution,"[26] Jefferson wrote to Madison, emphasizing the need to fund these papers because they were the lifeblood of their nascent political party. He further wrote that "we should really exert ourselves to procure [funds], for if these papers fall, republicanism will be entirely brow-beaten."[27] They directly funded some editors, including Callender, and they indirectly supported other editors by purchasing copies of their publications in bulk.[28] When Jefferson read a draft of Callender's pamphlet, he expressed satisfaction, writing that Callender's piece "cannot fail to produce the best effect."[29] Jefferson approved of making Adams's attack on the Constitution central to the campaign. As he wrote to one supporter, his surrogates should "rally round the Constitution" in order to "rescue it from the destruction with which it has been threatened."[30]

Not everyone was pleased with the editors. Secretary of State Pickering ordered the federal district attorney to look for illegal material in Callender's writings. That inquiry was followed by Callender's arrest in 1800 for so-called "seditious" attacks on the president.[31] Once again, Justice Chase presided over the trial.[32] Chase, perhaps thinking he hadn't been harsh enough with Cooper, doubled down. When Callender's attorneys tried to argue that the Sedition Act violated the Constitution, Chase refused to allow the argument.[33] Callender's lawyers also urged that their client was entitled to express opinions critical of the president. But Justice Chase rejected this line of argument, telling the jury to regard Callender's statements—such as his reference to Adams as a "detestable and criminal man"—as falsehoods, not opinions.[34] Chase would not even allow a senator with firsthand knowledge to testify that Adams held aristocratic views and that Callender had not libeled him in saying so.[35] Chase so impeded Callender's lawyers' ability to provide a defense that they resigned in protest.[36]

Convicted and incarcerated in the Richmond jail, Callender upped his defiance, publishing a follow-up criticism of how the Adams administration stifled dissent. He called one of his new chapters "More Sedition,"[37] and sent copies to Jefferson and Madison.[38] Chase's repression backfired and played right into Cooper's playbook. The more Chase sought to prosecute Callender, the more the editors wrote about it, pinning the Federalist attack on democracy on both the justice and the president. To the editors, Justice Chase epitomized the tyranny of the laws—a supposedly neutral figure who instead endeavored to neutralize his political opponents.

Not everyone was convinced that the editors' campaign was the best way to unseat Adams. Governor Monroe warned that the Callender prosecution might bolster Federalist chances. He warned if Democratic-Republican dissent turned into violent resistance, the party could be seen as lawless. But Jefferson thought the editors were pursuing the right course. He wrote to ally Elbridge Gerry, a delegate during the XYZ Affair, that "The Alien and Sedition Acts have already operated in the south as powerful sedatives of the XYZ inflammation."[39] In other words, the editors' focus on the acts had shifted public attention away from France's insult of the Adams administration, which was a black eye on the French-aligned Democratic-Republicans. Yet Jefferson also thought the campaign might go too far if the public perceived Democratic-Republicans were bringing an "attack of force" against the government. That perception could cause the electorate to "rally them round the government," where what was needed was "firmness, but a passive firmness."[40]

Newspapers transformed their criticisms of Adams into campaign messages for Jefferson, and were careful to avoid violent rhetoric. The campaign pitched the election as a choice between two visions of the Constitution: the Federalist authoritarian one and the Democratic-Republican one that championed dissent. The *Aurora*, for instance, published a piece that compared "Things As They Have Been" under Adams—a "reign of terror created by false alarms, to promote domestic feud and foreign war"—and "Things As They Will Be" under Jefferson— "The Principles of the *Revolution* restored . . . *Republicanism* allaying the fever of domestic feuds, and subduing the opposition by the force of reason and rectitude . . . The Liberty of the Press . . . truth and Jefferson."[41]

Several Democratic-Republican citizen groups, prompted by the themes from the newspapers, found creative ways to campaign for Jefferson and highlight that he would defend the right to dissent. They planted "liberty poles," one of which in Newburgh, New York, read: "1776. LIBERTY. JUSTICE. THE CONSTITUTION INVIO-LATE. NO BRITISH ALLIANCE. NO SEDITION BILL." In Vassalborough, Maine, Democratic-Republicans burned a copy of the Alien and Sedition Acts.[42] Some Democratic-Republicans pursued a satirical path to urge the end of the sedition law and the election of Jefferson. One citizen joked of starting a "THINKING CLUB" to avoid prosecution under the act, because it outlawed speech, not thoughts.[43]

The Federalists fought back, pivoting away from arguments about the right to dissent to portrayals of Jefferson as an atheist. They used Jefferson's support for the Virginia Statute for Religious Freedom— which banned the creation of an official state religion—against him, distorting his commitment to limit the role of religion in politics. They claimed Jefferson was an atheist seeking to rid America of any religion. Jefferson's media surrogates turned that accusation to their advantage. If Adams and his supporters rejected Jefferson's defense of the freedom of religion, they argued, perhaps they sought to impose an official religion on American citizens.[44]

The campaign was fraught, the stakes high, and the rhetoric harsh. Once the ballots were cast, it was clear Adams had been soundly defeated. Yet due to a quirk in the electoral system, Jefferson and his running mate, Aaron Burr, received the same number of votes, throwing the election to the House of Representatives, where each state's delegation got one vote. After many rounds of balloting, Matthew Lyon, one of the first people prosecuted under the Sedition Act, proudly cast one of the decisive votes for Jefferson.

The constitutional constituency of Democratic-Republican newspaper editors and their readers who condemned Adams's attacks on democracy played a central role in the 1800 election.[45] Despite his behind-the-scenes efforts, Jefferson had said little publicly about the acts or the right to dissent. Now in power, would Jefferson honor this right?

★ ★ ★

JEFFERSON TOOK THE OATH OF OFFICE ON MARCH 4, 1801. It was the first inauguration held in Washington, DC. The election had tested the stability of the Constitution. Because Washington had not been associated with a political party, when Adams stepped down, it was the nation's first voluntary exchange of power between political parties. This peaceful transition—possible partly because of Duane's efforts to uncover and foil the Federalist plot to disrupt it—would continue a chain of peaceful transitions between administrations that would last for more than two hundred years, until January 2021.

The country wondered what Jefferson would do now with his presidential power—power he could wield over his political enemies as Adams had. Jefferson used his inaugural address to answer that question. In a move that was doubly symbolic, he provided an advance copy of his address to a local newspaper—the first president to do so—hoping that Americans everywhere would read the message he would deliver.

Today, Jefferson's first inaugural is rightfully considered one of the finest in American history, a masterpiece of political reconciliation. Jefferson devoted his entire speech to constitutional restoration of democratic principles. That included the document's sacred ideals:

"freedom of religion; freedom of the press," and freedom from arbitrary imprisonment "under the protection of the habeas corpus," principles that form a "bright constellation." These, he added, "should be the creed of our political faith, the text of civic instruction."[46] Jefferson invoked political rights that Federalists had just attacked. Federalists and Democratic-Republicans alike, he argued, while bitterly divided, should rise above partisanship to see commonality among all citizens in recognition of the fundamentality of the Constitution, a higher loyalty he articulated in the speech's famous, stirring call. "We have called by different names brethren of the same principle," Jefferson announced. "We are all Republicans; we are all Federalists." The historian John Ferling notes a subtle detail about this sentence. In the original speech, the words *republicans* and *federalists* were not capitalized. Some newspapers mistakenly capitalized them, suggesting that Jefferson was referring to political parties.[47] Ferling, however, sees this initial use of lowercase letters as evidence that Jefferson was not talking about party at all, but universal values. More likely, Jefferson was playing on ambiguity, appealing to the populace to transcend their own parties and invoking ideals that could serve as common ground.

A commitment to those values and to transcending party meant rectifying the harm caused by Jefferson's predecessor. The new president allowed the Sedition Act to expire. Then he issued a general pardon to everyone convicted under the act, including Callender. In issuing the pardons, Jefferson did several things at once. First, he reiterated his view that the act was unconstitutional. Second, since he was essentially overturning the convictions presided over by Chase (among other judges), Jefferson channeled his belief that presidents, not just courts, must interpret the Constitution; he also made clear that presidents weren't just obligated to refrain from constitutional abuses but to counteract them.

Jefferson's use of these levers of presidential power was both radical and new. It captured his departure from Hamilton's understanding of the Constitution as a document best interpreted by courts. Jefferson would refine his theory, which scholars later called departmentalism. Under this view, Jefferson believed that the president had equal power

as the Supreme Court to decide what was constitutional.[48] Like his flir-
tation with nullification, Jefferson's notion of departmentalism would
occasionally veer into extreme waters. He briefly considered expanding
the theory to even allow presidents to disobey court orders (which he
later did in a case about the Embargo Act.)[49]

But as much as the pardons vindicated the role of presidential interpretation, they also highlighted the legitimacy of *citizen* interpretation of
the Constitution. Jefferson's pardons are usually seen as an early instance
of departmentalism. Less noticed is their affirmation of the citizen editors' democratic interpretation of the Constitution over the authoritarian understanding of Adams. By issuing pardons for the Sedition Act,
Jefferson sided with Cooper and the editors, reading the Constitution
to require the right to dissent. The pardons were an act of constitutional
reclamation of the democratic right to dissent both on the substance of
the matter and in the method the editors had employed to demand it: the
editors had a right to dissent and a right to interpret the Constitution to
support that right. Jefferson's pardons affirmed their stance.

Jefferson's ideas were too radical for many of his supporters, much
less his Federalist adversaries. On Adams's quasi-monarchical view of
the presidency, they held that an incoming president should respect
the decisions of his predecessors as well as the courts—no matter how
controversial—or risk anarchy. Perhaps most incensed by Jefferson's pardons was Abigail Adams, who three years later wrote an angry letter to
the new president: "In your ardent zeal, and desire to rectify the mistakes, and abuses as you may consider them," Jefferson was being "led
into measures still more fatal to the constitution, and more derogatory
to your honor."[50] For his part, Jefferson had presented Abigail Adams
with his carefully stated view of departmentalism. "You seem to think it
devolved on the judges to decide on the validity of the sedition law," he
wrote, "but nothing in the constitution has given them a right to decide
for the executive, more than to the Executive to decide for them."[51] The
president's interpretation wasn't supreme to the courts' interpretation;
they were equal.

Jefferson's debate with Abigail Adams is crucial to understanding his role in deciding the fate of Samuel Chase. While Jefferson had

begun his presidency with a spirit of reconciliation, he viewed Chase's conduct as grave enough to warrant an exception. The immediate harm of the Alien and Sedition Acts had been felt by those prosecuted. The harm to the country was even broader. In championing the acts, Justice Chase had already overstepped the bounds of his role as a justice. His biased use of the acts to crush political opponents in the courtroom was beyond the pale. Any veneer of a neutral judiciary was tarnished with Chase on the Supreme Court. (His increasing public drunkenness also didn't inspire confidence.) Chase had helped to enable the Federalist assault on the right to dissent, and in Jefferson's view, constitutional recovery now required his removal.

Chase's behavior under Adams now received close scrutiny. In addition to lobbying for and seeking prosecutions under the Sedition Act, his opponents highlighted another disturbing case evincing his lack of fitness to serve on the court: he blatantly disregarded the power of ordinary citizens to interpret the Constitution by abusing the grand jurors tasked with protecting the rights of the accused. Grand jurors are ordinary citizens who decide whether to approve criminal indictments. They are a fundamental bulwark for the constitutional rights of the accused against would-be tyrannical public officials. But the trial of a Pennsylvania man named John Fries showcased Chase's hatred of the citizens' right to dissent and citizens' role in protecting it. In 1799, John Fries, an auctioneer from Pennsylvania, led a group to rescue from jail citizens arrested under two new controversial property tax laws. Although armed, the mob disbanded when ordered; no one was injured. Nevertheless, Fries was charged with treason. His trial was largely a sham, with the judges determined in advance to work against him. He was convicted, but before he could be sentenced to hang, the case was ruled a mistrial over a juror's comment.

Undeterred, the government brought the case against Fries again, with Justice Chase now presiding over the trial—if it could be called that. Chase had opened the April 1800 session by reiterating that the grand jury had no right to rule on the "validity of the Law." Shockingly, Chase wrote a written opinion *before* the second Fries trial, declaring that opposition to any federal law constituted treason. When Fries's lawyers heard this, they walked out of the courtroom, leaving Fries to defend himself. (Chase had also earlier shown his lack of independence, calling Adams "our illustrious and patriotic beloved President.") On this second unfair trial, Fries was convicted, and Chase sentenced him to death by hanging. (Fries averted this fate when Adams had the good sense to pardon him.)[52]

Chase had largely lain low after the inauguration of 1800. But in 1803, after watching the Democratic-Republicans govern, he couldn't contain himself. Presiding over a grand jury in Baltimore, he gave a partisan rant, arguing that with Democratic-Republicans in power, the nation would "sink into a mobocracy, the worst of all possible governments."[53] Jefferson had never forgiven Chase for seeking to crush his party. With the Sedition Act expired, and Jefferson's opposition to it, imprisoning Chase was not an option. Still, did Chase have a right to his job if he kept rejecting his duty to play a neutral judicial role? Jefferson had enough. He wrote to an ally in Congress, "You must have heard of the extraordinary charge of Chace [sic] to the grand jury at Baltimore. Ought this seditious & official attack on the principles of our constitution, and on the proceedings of a state, to go unpunished?"[54] Ten months after this letter, articles of impeachment were drawn up against Chase, the only Supreme Court Justice ever to be impeached.

In 1804, the House of Representatives voted up eight articles of impeachment. Most focused on Chase's role in the Sedition Act trials. In particular, congressmen argued that Chase's conduct in the Fries and Callender trials was so egregious that he could not remain on the court. The charges also highlighted other instances of Chase's behavior, like his nakedly partisan tirade to the Baltimore grand jury.[55]

But Chase argued back that his impeachment was evidence that his accusers were abusing power. He had committed no crime and therefore no "high crime," the textual standard for impeachment. Democratic-Republicans leading the impeachment rebutted that "high crimes and misdemeanors" transcended criminal illegality.[56] Chase ultimately prevailed in the Senate. A majority voted to remove him on several charges, including the charge regarding his role in the Baltimore grand jury, yet the final vote did not reach the supermajority required for conviction.

Despite the failure to convict Chase, Jefferson scored a broader victory. As constitutional scholar Keith Whittington argues, Chase's impeachment "helped recalibrate expectations about how life-tenured judges should behave in a democratic but partisan political environment."[37] Chase had been formally rebuked on behalf of the grand jurors and newspaper editors he had bullied and terrorized. But the impeachment was more than pushback against Chase's partisanship, it was a vindication of the right to dissent defended by the editors prosecuted under the Sedition Act. It was also a bold defense of the power of ordinary citizens to protect the constitutional rights of the accused, like those on the Fries grand jury that Chase so badly disrespected. Absent a Supreme Court that would strike down the Sedition Act, the impeachment was a statement by Congress on behalf of the sovereign people to criticize their government. In short, it was an impeachment in defense of democracy. Finally, the impeachment solidified Jefferson and the editors' belief that the Supreme Court and Chase did not have the final say about the legitimacy of the Sedition Act—or any law. Chase served out his lifetime appointment quietly, but he never campaigned for a politician again, nor was he given an opportunity to prosecute citizens for dissent. Part of the battle for democracy came with Adams's defeat in 1800. A second came with the pardons. A third victory for government of "We the People" came with Chase's impeachment, which served as a partial vindication of the citizens he had long abused and the democratic rights he disregarded.

★ ★ ★

EARLY IN HIS TERM, Jefferson had done much to engineer the first major constitutional recovery from a presidential assault on democracy. He had been elected with the aid of the editors who fought against the Alien and Sedition Acts. His mandate was the restoration of the right of dissent. Publicly, Jefferson played the role of a recovery president, reacting to the demands of the constitutional constituency that brought him to power. But Jefferson would allow personal vanity to undermine presidential achievement and any claim of pure protection of dissent. As much as he revealed the promise of the presidency, using its vast power to vindicate the rights Adams had trampled on, he also revealed the perils of the office. Jefferson allowed his ego to tarnish his restoration of the right to dissent.

A glaring example of the gap between Jefferson's ideals and personal failings was his treatment of one-time ally Callender. After his journalistic work helping to defeat Adams, Callender sought a federal appointment. Jefferson declined. In retaliation, Callender in September 1802 began bitterly publishing a series of exposés about Jefferson. He revealed that during the 1800 election, Jefferson had funded him; Jefferson responded (falsely) that Callender was lying. That was probably a mistake. Callender responded by printing an accusation we now know to be true: Jefferson was having sex with one of the people he enslaved, Sally Hemmings, and had fathered several children by her.

Jefferson was furious. He could not call for prosecution of Callender under federal law, as the Sedition Act had expired, and renewing the act would invite charges of hypocrisy, betraying the reason his constituents supported his candidacy. Jefferson was, however, a man not above ego. While he didn't want to be seen limiting the right to criticize the president, he later wrote a confidential letter to the governor of Pennsylvania suggesting that under *state* law, criminal libel might be used to prosecute offending editors.[58]

It wasn't just Callender who prompted Jefferson to betray his commitment to protecting dissent. Harry Croswell, the editor of the New York Federalist newspapers the *Wasp* and the *Balance*, attacked Jefferson as unfit for office and accused him of paying Callender to write critical articles against Adams and Washington years earlier. The New York attorney general, a Jefferson ally, responded by indicting Croswell under state law. Despite the obvious parallel with the Adams prosecutions, Jefferson remained quiet.

Ironically, this time it was Jefferson's rival—Alexander Hamilton— who stood up for Croswell and defended freedom of speech. Hamilton took the case on appeal after Croswell was convicted at trial. He argued that New York state law was wrong to exclude truth as a defense to criminal libel. Hamilton lost before a divided court, and Croswell's conviction stood.[59] Despite Jefferson's failure to speak out against this prosecution, the condemnation that the Croswell trial received was part of the broader constitutional recovery Jefferson's election had helped to engineer. When Jefferson's Federalist enemies sought to cast the New York indictment as a violation of freedom of speech, they were invoking the norm against political prosecutions that Jefferson's Democratic-Republicans had previously fought so hard to protect.

Jefferson's actions indeed merited the charge of hypocrisy. But there is an important difference between the actions of Jefferson and those of Adams. As president, Adams had called publicly for the prosecutions of his political enemies. Jefferson had never done the same; his entreaties were always private. To his credit, while Jefferson nursed his wounded ego, he never turned to Adams's vicious brand of open partisan warfare. That might have been a tribute to the power of Jefferson's constitutional constituency, the editors and citizens who elected him as protest against the Alien and Sedition Acts. Jefferson's allies had prominently used their own trials to fight against Adams and the acts and push for Jefferson's election. Now, these citizen resisters had elected a president who knew he was accountable to the ideals that had brought him to power. Despite Jefferson's private inclinations, the public norms his supporters had helped instantiate in the nation's conscience made it unthinkable that he could renew the Alien and Sedition Acts that had defined Adams' presidency.

★ ★ ★

IN HIS FIRST TERM AS PRESIDENT, Jefferson began a constitutional restoration of free speech and a reclaiming of the idea of presidential accountability core to Washington's second inaugural. In contrast to Adams's monarchial vision of the Constitution, Jefferson—urged on by the editors' democratic constitutional constituency—championed a democratic understanding that protected a right to dissent. But Jefferson's private efforts to stifle speech critical of himself marred that early recovery.

This partial restoration of free speech rights needed to be followed by a more robust recovery from Adams by a president who would defend the right to dissent for both allies and opponents.

CHAPTER 3

James Madison and Hanson

Protecting Speech during War

DURING THE WAR OF 1812, ON THE EVENING OF AUGUST 24, 1814, BRITISH FORCES APPROACHED the capital city of Washington, DC. First Lady Dolley Madison rushed to save a portrait of George Washington before the president's mansion, "the president's house," was set ablaze. Later, Francis Scott Key wrote a poem to the tune of a drinking ballad, "The Star-Spangled Banner," commemorating American efforts in the war, a tune that would take an improbable journey to becoming the national anthem.

However, the details of the War of 1812 are murky for most Americans. The war was the result of a long-simmering conflict, spurred by the British kidnapping of American sailors to draw the United States into the continental fight against Napoleon. Strangely, it is a war that produced no clear victor despite resulting in approximately twenty thousand casualties. Even America's most widely remembered victory in the war, the Battle of New Orleans, was somewhat absurd—fought in 1815, entirely *after* a peace treaty had been signed in Europe, but before the news had reached US shores.

But on that August 1814 evening, America's second war with Great Britain was anything but murky. British ships controlled the Chesapeake Bay just outside DC. Beginning that evening, 4,500 British infantries marched into Washington, pushing past resistance from American troops at Bladensburg, Maryland.[1] With orders to burn government buildings, they set fire to the Treasury Department, the War Department, and the Capitol, where the British used the Library of Congress's three thousand volumes as tinder.[2] The flames grew so high that glass skylights melted from the heat.[3]

From the Capitol, two lines of British soldiers, one hundred total, marched silently toward the president's house.[4] Major General Robert Ross gave an order that the invasion was not to destroy private property, but the president's house would not be spared. As soldiers headed to the mansion, in addition to Washington's portrait, Dolley Madison preserved some silver and a copy of the Declaration of Independence for safekeeping, but the house remained filled with objects of American history—along with food on the table for a now-abandoned dinner. Some British soldiers helped themselves. Then they set the home ablaze.

With its exterior standing but interior destroyed, Madison's presidential home would never house him again. He called the act "a deliberate disregard of the principles of humanity" that had marked the war's "extended devastation and barbarism."[5] The soldiers were on the ground in Washington for only twenty-six hours in total, as a storm forced them to flee.[6]

Madison and his family fled Washington for a Quaker refuge in Maryland.[7] Tensions with the British had been mounting since 1807 when the USS *Chesapeake* was attacked by the British. In the interim, the British blocked American trade with France, the United States blamed the British for skirmishes with Indian tribes at the Canadian border,[8] and Democratic-Republicans called for war. In 1812, honoring Congress's constitutional role, Madison sought and received a declaration of war.

Two years after that declaration, as Madison sat in the Quaker house, things were not going well. The DC invasion was a sign of larger losses, including the surrender at Fort Detroit by General William

Hull, a Revolutionary War veteran, who thought his 2,500 troops would have no chance against the British preparing an attack—a call Madison had second-guessed.

Madison was also managing a bitterly divided population. Federalists (still pro-Britain) opposed the war, calling it "Mr. Madison's War."[9] Federalist Rufus King called for an opposition presidential campaign with a platform to end the war. The *Salem Gazette*, responding to the government's effort to conscript the Massachusetts militia into service, reprinted Federalist No. 46, which discussed how the states would be able to resist such overreach, to throw Madison's own words at him.[10] Large and angry rallies sprung up against the war, especially in New England. In response, Democratic-Republicans called it the Second War of Independence—and labeled Federalist opponents as traitors. The vitriol eclipsed the French panic during 1798—with Democratic-Republicans labeling Federalists as Tories to emphasize they were beholden to that British party.[11] Regularly, Democratic-Republicans wrote to Madison to emphasize that Federalist criticisms were "treason" in the service of aiding Britain. Domestic civil unrest loomed.[12]

The war continued on, and the situation in 1814 was the photographic negative of 1798—the conflict this time with Britain, not France; with Democratic-Republicans supporting war, and Federalists balking at their rhetoric; and with Democratic-Republicans harassing their opponents for disloyalty and treason, as Federalists claimed the mantle of free speech.

Yet the main difference between these two eras was as clear as the flames that licked the Washington sky. Unlike Adams's paranoid fears about a quasi-war, there was nothing quasi about the war Madison faced. It was, and remains, the only time in American history that the armed forces of an enemy nation occupied the capital. It also created a crisis on orders of magnitude more serious than any Adams faced: What to do about political opponents who opposed the war—and his own supporters who harassed them and called for their imprisonment on the grounds of alleged disloyalty—while the nation's capital was sieged?

Now that he was facing war and vociferous partisan criticism, the simplest approach would be to mimic Adams and lock up those opponents. But Madison's already lofty political stock had risen by resisting Adams's abuses of constitutional rights and defending the free speech rights of newspapers editors and his own political party, a battle he rode to the presidency a decade later. As British forces gathered, how Madison dealt with this conflict and criticism would test the sincerity of his commitment to democracy and to a Constitution founded on popular sovereignty. Would his principles hold?

* * *

THE EXPIRATION OF THE SEDITION ACT at the start of Jefferson's presidency had ended the federal imprisonment of political dissidents and clarified that freedom of conscience applied to all partisans. But despite Jefferson's call for unity, partisan conflict had intensified dramatically during his terms. Like his fellow Democratic-Republicans, Jefferson had compared Federalists to Revolution-era loyalists, calling them Tories to emphasize their British sympathies. At the time, words like these, thick with implications of treason, could trigger duels and other violence.

And now, as the nation inched closer to war, partisan insults exploded into violence. In August 1812, with Federalist opposition in New England growing, an anti-war Federalist mob in Plymouth, Massachusetts, grabbed a Democratic-Republican judge, Charles Turner, and "kicked [him] through the town."[13]

On the pro-war Democratic-Republican side, more violence erupted. In 1808, prominent Baltimore lawyer and Federalist Alexander Contee Hanson had launched a newspaper, the *Federal Republican*, which quickly became a fierce anti-Madison outlet. The paper even accused Dolley Madison of being a polygamist.[14] Hanson's eviscerating editorials were eyebrow-raising for another reason: Baltimore was one of the most Democratic-Republican cities in America.[15] In 1812, as hawks in Madison's cabinet called for war, Hanson opposed the conflict and the *Federal Republican* joined a chorus of Federalist newspapers nationwide lambasting the plan "to create civil contest through the pretext of a foreign war." As Hanson saw it, Democratic-Republicans were using the conflict with Britain to fight Federalists at home. He predicted they would seek to limit Federalist's civil liberties in the name of the national good—forcing Federalists to "cling to the rights of freemen."[16]

Baltimore's Democratic-Republicans were outraged.[17] On June 22, two days after the editorial appeared, a mob descended on the *Federal Republican*'s building. Rioters destroyed the printing press, seeking to silence Hanson. Mayhem ensued. A window was ripped from the second story; the rioter removing it fell to his death. The building was destroyed. Hanson was lucky to have been away.

Defiantly, a month later, Hanson and his defenders restarted the paper, clinging to his right to publish. Resuming work risked more violence, as Democratic-Republicans kept implying Federalists were untrustworthy enemies. In July, a mob returned to Hanson's new office.[18] As American forces lined the Canadian border to fight the British, Democratic-Republicans assembled outside Hanson's headquarters threatening violence. Inside, Hanson prepared to fight back. He gathered allies and friends, including Revolutionary War officer James Lingan, who had once been held as a British prisoner of war,[19] and former Virginia governor Henry Lee, a Revolutionary War hero and father of five-year-old Robert E. Lee. Lingan and Lee—no friends of the British— were ardent defenders of the press.

Angry partisans circled the premises, screaming "We'll drink their blood!" and "We'll eat their hearts!"[20] This time, Hanson and his veteran allies were ready. When the first rocks crashed through the windows, the defenders fired warning shots. The furious crowd burst through the door only to find Hanson's men waiting for them. Armed, they opened fire and killed a mob leader, whose limp body was pulled away. Enraged, the mob stalked the building the entire night, exchanging fire while the wounded grew on both sides. A drum beat outside, calling more Democratic-Republicans to fight.[21]

Partisan civil war was imminent when the mayor, Edward Johnson, a fierce Democratic-Republican, came to the Federalists' aid. Johnson, flanked by the commander of the local militia, promised Hanson's crew, holed up in the printing house, safe passage to the only secure location: the city jail.

That evening, a crowd of hundreds assembled outside the jail. A bloodbath ensued. The crowd charged the jail, breaking past the guards and taking over the complex. Inside, a brawl began. Some of Hanson's men escaped. The remaining men, including Hanson, were less fortunate. They were dragged into the street and beaten and tortured for hours with knives and searing oil. The crowd beat Lingan to death. They held down Lee and attempted to cut off his nose. Hanson and the remaining eight men survived, as well as Lee, whose motionless but still-breathing body was discovered nearby, "his head cut to pieces" and "covered with blood."[22] A shell of a man afterward, he succumbed to his injuries within years.[23]

These so-called Baltimore Riots, a crescendo of diffuse and increasingly random destruction, lasted over a month. First sparked by Congress's war declaration, the wildfire of violence exhausted its patriotic rationale and sustained itself on partisan, racial, and religious antagonisms. Just as a paranoid fantasy had seized the Federalists in 1798, Democratic-Republicans now indulged conspiracies of a British-led slave revolt, which sparked mob actions that targeted Baltimore's substantial free Black population, including a mob that reduced the home of James Briscoe, a free Black man, to rubble. Catholics and Protestants also sparred; animosities sparked almost wholly apart from the politics that had commenced the violence. The Baltimore Riots remain some of America's most significant urban violence.[24]

Both the ongoing violence and the attack on Baltimore's jail—torturing one Revolutionary War hero and murdering another—left the country shaken and embittered. Both parties judged the other with contempt. Ominous reaction came in the partisan press, where Democratic-Republicans excused the violence as an appropriate response to Federalist treason. Secretary of State James Monroe, then one of Madison's closest advisors, expressed his dread as he scrambled to respond: "I fear that if some distinguished effort is not made, in favor of the authority of the law, there is danger of a civil war."[25]

It is a remarkable irony, then, that the War of 1812—to the extent it is recalled at all—invokes a vague spirit of national unity to this day through song, providing a momentary swell of patriotic fellow-feeling to open baseball games. In fact, the war sparked partisan vitriol that some historians suggest rivaled Vietnam-era protests in their intensity.[26] As noted previously, this violence spurred several constitutional challenges Madison faced as president. Not only did he have to wage a war against the British while preventing a civil war among Americans, he had to curb the constant calls from his own party to shut down civil liberties so as to ensure domestic tranquility. Indeed, the right to dissent was now threatened by the Democratic-Republicans, who had championed it to defeat a Federalist in 1800. Now it was the Federalists, led by an injured but persistent Hanson, calling for the president to respect democracy and dissent. Hanson had assumed the mantle of what had been a Democratic-Republican constitutional constituency. How would Madison respond?

★ ★ ★

MADISON OFFERS AN IDEAL CASE of how a president devoted to a democratic understanding of the Constitution can pursue urgent goals without shutting down civil liberties. Madison's presidency is also a case study in how a president should respond to a constitutional constituency at odds with his party. Once aspiring to the ministry, Madison was swept into the Revolution and soon became a passionate advocate for freedom of conscience. As a delegate in the state legislature of Virginia, he opposed a proposal to fund religious instruction through tax dollars, anonymously writing a piece that propelled that state to adopt a historic guarantee of religious freedom. In 1787, Madison played an indispensable role at the Constitutional Convention, helping to craft the Virginia Plan, a model of government that championed a limited presidency whose structure, he thought, would protect rights of conscience like religious freedom and free speech. While the extent of his intellectual dominance has been debated, Madison is often called the Father of the Constitution.[27]

At the Constitutional Convention and immediately afterward, Madison opposed the inclusion of a Bill of Rights that included explicit protection for the freedoms of speech and religion. He did this not because he opposed these protections; rather, his stance was akin to how a chef balks at being told her specialty dish needs more salt. As Madison later emphasized in the Report of 1800 to the Virginia General Assembly, he thought the Constitution already protected the rights that proponents of the Bill of Rights were seeking. Eventually, however, he was convinced of the value of explicitly reaffirming these core rights, and he promised to support a Bill of Rights in the first Congress. Representing Virginia, Madison helped draft and defend the first ten amendments to the Constitution, known as the Bill of Rights, including the First Amendment protections of freedom of speech, press, and religion.[28] Madison's theory of freedom of conscience could not have been more different than that of Adams's. Madison believed popular sovereignty lay at the heart of the Constitution: the people's authority was the basis for the legitimacy of all government actions, so no president could shut down dissent.

Another feature to Madison's view of politics also became indispensable to his presidency. Although Madison believed the Constitution could embody popular sovereignty, he foresaw the threats to democracy baked into the document. In fall 1787, joined by Alexander Hamilton and John Jay, Madison had concocted a national public relations strategy to support ratification of the Constitution, using the popular press as the primary vehicle. Writing what would become known as *The Federalist* (commonly referred to as the Federalist Papers), the three men published eighty-five essays that promoted and defended the Constitution. Madison wrote one-third of them. The essays appeared first in newspapers in New York and later across the country. Among them, the most famous essay, still taught in introductory government courses, is Federalist No. 10, Madison's prescient warning about the dangers of "factions."[29]

Now that he was president, the factionalism he feared had seized political life. As the country's most powerful Democratic-Republican, Madison found himself at the head of one such faction. To add to the irony, the Democratic-Republicans were now calling to shut down free speech, a liberty Madison worried that factionalism might destroy.

Madison was elected president in 1808, campaigning on the early ideals of democratic republicanism. His first inaugural address mirrored Jefferson's in promising to protect the freedom of conscience, pledging to "avoid the slightest interference with the right of conscience or the functions of religion, so wisely exempted from civil jurisdiction; to preserve in their full energy the other salutary provisions in behalf of private and personal rights, and of the freedom of the press."[30] He was the opposite of a warmonger, and he desperately tried to avert conflict with the British during his first term. As relentless pressure mounted, both from within his party and the public, Madison caved, seeing no choice but to challenge Britain militarily. A devotee of the Constitution, however, Madison insisted that a formal declaration of war be ratified by Congress—something Jefferson had not done, for example, in his campaign against the Barbary pirates. Madison could have followed Jefferson in claiming that the conflict was defensive, and thus required no war declaration. Instead, he sought the authorization anyway in an effort to preserve the rule of law even in an emergency.

The war tested Madison's long-held commitment to the Constitution, particularly to the Bill of Rights he had helped birth. As the war with Britain intensified, people from Maine[31] to Mississippi lobbied him. Democratic-Republican clubs both emphatically supported the war and called for a second front against the Federalists. The letters sounded a common theme: Federalists threatened the union and must be stopped. A group of Democratic-Republicans in Natchez, Mississippi, said, not-so-subtly referencing Federalist opposition: "We hold it not only an absolute duty, but it shall be our pride to resist and hush to silence in time of war, ther [sic] utterance of sentiments and doctrines tending to sow the seed of discontent & sedition among our citizens, or the encouragement of our enemies by persons who live in the bosom of our land."[32] The Democratic-Republicans of Middlesex, Massachusetts, published a memorial announcing their intention to "repel and defeat the seditious attempts of the opposers of constitutional authorities, to unite in their support, and in the defense of our country against the invasion of a relentless, perfidious enemy."[33] Democratic-Republican citizens like these formed the backbone of Madison's party, and as such forced him to choose between his constituency and his constitutional obligations.

Incredibly, many editors who had fought with Madison against the Sedition Act now reversed their stances about free speech. Thomas

Cooper argued that any criticism of the government with "unworthy motive" should be severely punished. He argued, "the only way to preserve the liberty of the Press, is to punish its prostitution."[34] Cooper noted he was in the wrong against Adams because while free speech was important for elites who could respond to criticism appropriately, the lower classes could not be trusted to contain their passions. Cooper suggested about his own prosecution that "I had no right to complain" to the extent he had stirred up the passions of less discriminating readers.[35] The norm of respecting free speech was still fragile, even after Jefferson's efforts to vindicate it.

Intense pressure to pursue legislation akin to a new sedition act came from within Madison's administration. Vice President Elbridge Gerry had been friends with Adams and was one of the emissaries involved in the XYZ Affair. He now was a Democratic-Republican, having fallen out with the Federalists. He warned that a Federalist faction aimed to institute monarchy, and he argued impending violence justified anti-sedition measures. Describing the partisan conflict, Gerry quoted the Bible, saying "If we do not kill them, they will kill us."[36] Among the most vocal supporters of a new sedition act[37] was the noted Supreme Court Justice Joseph Story, nominated by Madison. Story echoed Chase's earlier calls for a sedition law.[38] In the aftermath of the Baltimore Riots, Democratic-Republican members of Congress went beyond talk, introducing legislation to give military courts authority over civilian "traitors." Senior military officer Henry Dearborn explained that repression of civil liberties was necessary given that the Federalists were pursuing "serious & sistematic measures taken for producing a revolution in the Northern States." Dearborn added, "I most ardently hope that Congress will take early & strong measures for putting down those Treasonable proceedings."[39]

Madison had helped build the Democratic-Republican Party in part to rescue the right of free speech from a president threatening it. Now that party, his own party, was urging him to restrict it. Editors like Thomas Cooper had opposed Adams and championed free speech. And they did so partly by joining forces within the Democratic-Republican party urging Jefferson's election. But now Cooper's call for a new sedition act showed that partisan loyalty had overwhelmed the free-speech mission. In its original incarnation, the democratic constitutional constituency sparked by Duane, Bache, and Cooper, was dead. Its legacy, however, was very much alive. From a most unlikely corner, a new set of citizen readers emerged to test Madison's commitment to the Constitution and the right to dissent.

The Federalist Hanson, like the Democratic-Republicans Bache, Cooper, and Duane, had been the victim of a partisan attack. And like them, rather than succumb to his victimhood, he used it to double down on his dissent from the orthodoxies of the opposition party. Specifically, Hanson used the Baltimore Riots to rally citizens around the right of free speech and pressured the president to respect it, highlighting the irony of Democratic-Republicans' reversal to pressure Madison. He said that Democratic-Republicans were attempting "to destroy the freedom of speech and of the press . . . through a system of French revolutionary terror."[40]

But Hanson needed to do more than criticize the Democratic-Republicans for abandoning free speech. He needed to show that his party was devoted to constitutional preservation. George Washington's step-grandson, George Washington Parke Custis, gave him that opportunity with a funeral oration after the riots that evoked the second inaugural in its focus on the Constitution. Hanson's defiantly re-reopened paper printed Curtis's words about how "the right of opinion, the liberty of speech, and the liberty of the press, are prostrated at the feet of lawless power," a reference to the willingness of Democratic-Republicans to let violence limit liberty.[41] Hanson had followed the newspaper editors of the Adams era in championing the right to dissent while engaging in it. And echoing their invocation of Washington in support of this cause, by printing Parke Custis's words, Hanson implicitly appealed to the president who stood for constitutional fidelity rather than party loyalty.

To form a constituency behind these ideals, Hanson had to rally Americans to the cause just as the editors of the early era had. Although the people joining him were different, the idea was the same. The mantle of America's first democratic constitutional constituency would cross parties, taken up by new adherents.

Just writing about the threat to liberty was insufficient. Hanson needed to galvanize this nascent constituency to pressure the president to respect free speech. The Baltimore Riots provided the impetus for citizen meetings around the country in which assemblies called on Madison to buck his party's demands and protect free speech for all, regardless of partisan affiliation, even those opposing war. A meeting in Montgomery County, Maryland, showed Hanson's impact, as they resolved "That the thanks of this assembly are due to ALEXANDER C. HANSON and his Heroic Companions, who with unexamined bravery and magnanimity risked their lives . . . against the subversion of our constitution." The citizens of Loudoun County, Virginia, resolved that "every press has a right, at all times, whether of war or peace, to canvass freely the wisdom, justice, or policy of public measures, and the character, conduct, and motives of public men, subject to no other restraint than that of constitutional laws." At least nine such resolutions were passed throughout the country.[42] Hanson had framed the attack on his paper as an assault on the right to free speech and galvanized citizens to defend it. Now it was the Federalists who lobbied the president to respect fundamental democratic rights.

To whom would Madison listen? The voices within his party calling for a new sedition act? Or the voices of his conscience, amplified by Hanson's Federalist constitutional constituency? This dilemma is common to wartime leaders since time immemorial: whether to use the cover of real violence to crack down on political opposition. That Madison was simultaneously running for reelection in 1812 might have made the temptation greater.

After the Baltimore Riots, Madison turned to Monroe, a confidante since their days plotting against Adams. Monroe's advice was straightforward. Monroe argued that while the Federalists were hardly blameless, the Democratic-Republican "mobs . . . must be prevented." He recommended Madison support the protection and distribution of Hanson's paper.[43] When Hanson reopened his office following the riots, there was no violence. Moreover, the federally controlled Maryland militia secured the post office to protect the paper's distribution; circulation increased.[44]

Madison's commitment to free speech was tested further when Hanson won a seat in Congress, promising to defend press freedoms. Within Madison's cabinet came calls to keep Hanson at arm's length, given his criticisms of the war. Secretary of War John Armstrong particularly loathed Hanson, seeing his criticism as dangerous to national security. Armstrong also joined the calls for a new sedition act. Ironically, Armstrong had won a Senate seat on a free speech platform himself in 1800. But with war brewing, he now saw dissenters like Hanson as public enemies.[45] [46]

Madison, however, bucked Armstrong and his allies over now-Congressman Hanson. Madison refused to re-up a sedition act and symbolically defended the right of the opposition party to speak out against the war by inviting Hanson to the president's mansion. He then did something even more dramatic. After Hanson demanded that Madison fire Armstrong, Armstrong was soon forced to resign. Armstrong's ire seared as he confronted the president in person on August 29, 1814, telling Madison he knew Hanson received an audience, and accusing Madison of abandoning the Democratic-Republicans.[47]

Madison made no dramatic public speeches announcing opposition to a new sedition act. And he never publicly condemned those in his party who proposed military tribunals for opponents of the war. However, he effectively resisted his party's calls to shut down free speech. Without presidential support, the movement to shut down the opposition fizzled. In his second inaugural address, Madison implicitly criticized these calls for censorship, focusing on why liberty must be maintained even during war, as "we can reflect with a proud satisfaction that in carrying [the war] on no principle of justice or honor, no usage of civilized nations, no precept of courtesy or humanity, have been infringed."[48] Madison here called attention to why respecting foreign soldiers' rights during war was a national strength. We should also understand his words, however, as recognizing that respect for liberty domestically, even people seen as enemies, was essential in a democracy. That commitment to democracy and the right to dissent made Madison willing to oppose his own party and respect Federalists' dissent. But Madison's commitment to democracy was soon tested again by a general with a different view of war and free speech.

★ ★ ★

AFTER MADISON WON REELECTION IN 1812, he devoted much of his term to war, facing perhaps the most direct constitutional challenge of his presidency. Like the Baltimore Riots, this constitutional threat involved political dissent during wartime and a choice between civil liberties and political popularity. This time, however, the problem wasn't about how to resist fellow partisans. It was a battle with Andrew Jackson.

Before 1815, few Americans had heard of Andrew Jackson. The war changed that. Unlike Madison, who fought with his pen, Jackson was a soldier, first witnessing war as a thirteen-year-old helping Revolutionary War troops at the Battle of Hanging Rock. Born to a poor family, Jackson became a wealthy plantation owner, exploiting the labor of enslaved people to build a fortune. After a brief stint in Congress, representing Tennessee, Jackson served as a state judge and later in the state militia. He also developed an approach to the Constitution far different from Madison's.

As the War of 1812 proceeded, a long simmering conflict within the Creek Indian tribe came to a head, with one faction battling the United States government to defend long-held land and another seeking peace. Jackson's fame grew as he brutally massacred Creek civilians he viewed as sympathetic to the warring faction. Militia member David Crocket reported, "We shot them like dogs," referring to the brutality of Jackson's massacres.[49]

Madison, disturbed by Jackson's brutality, reprimanded Secretary Armstrong for hiring him; in fact, this decision may have contributed to Armstrong's forced resignation. But even with Armstrong gone, Madison was stuck with Jackson. Jackson's greatest triumph was also the war's grandest absurdity. By late 1814, both nations were weary of the fighting, and peace negotiations began in what is now Belgium. At home, however, the fighting continued. In January 1815, British troops marched on New Orleans. General Jackson stood his ground, and his ragtag band of militia and pirates thwarted the advance. It was a resounding victory for the brash military leader and the nation. There was just one problem. The Treaty of Ghent that ended the war had been signed fifteen days earlier. Nonetheless, the Battle of New Orleans catapulted Jackson into national celebrity.[50]

Jackson's fame is where his clash with Madison began. Before the battle, fearing disloyal residents would join the British, Jackson declared martial law in New Orleans on December 16, 1814. At one point, fearing critics in the state legislature, he threatened that the legislature should be "blown up."[51] After word of the treaty arrived, Jackson continued to rule like a dictator. Trouble began when state senator Louis Louaillier wrote an article in the *Louisiana Courier* denouncing Jackson's contin-uation of martial law. As Louaillier saw it, with the war over, no emer-gency justified this extreme action, and "it is time the citizens accused of any crime should be rendered to their natural judges and cease to be brought before special or military tribunals."[52]

Louaillier in New Orleans, using the press to decry limits on civil liberties, became the analog of Hanson in Baltimore. Jackson wasted lit-tle time responding, and his approach was starkly different from Mad-ison's: he threw Louaillier into prison. But with the help of attorney Pierre Morel, Louaillier petitioned the federal district court for a writ of habeas corpus—using the constitutional principle that no person can be held without charges and without basis for detention. Habeas corpus can be suspended by Congress in some circumstances, but Congress had not done so, and Madison had insisted on not seeking such emergency measures. That didn't stop Jackson from unilaterally and without legal authority suspending habeas corpus himself.

Federal district court judge Dominic Hall, a Madison appointee, ordered Jackson to immediately release Louaillier. What did Jackson do? He arrested Judge Hall! The federal district attorney for Louisiana, John Dick, jumped into action. Since Congress had not suspended habeas corpus and Jackson was acting beyond any constitutional authority, he demanded that Jackson free Hall. What did Jackson do? He arrested Dick! Dick wrote directly to James Madison, giving a full accounting of what Jackson had done.[53] Madison was livid. He wrote to Monroe, enclosing Dick's prison letter, and demanded the cabinet be convened immediately to respond to Jackson's no less than "astonishing" conduct. Madison acknowledged the difficulty in sanctioning a well-liked general who won the Battle of New Orleans, "But the duty of the Executive, and the prerogatives of the Judiciary & the Press, can never be sacrificed to any individual considerations, or even to any popular enthusiasm."[54]

Consequences followed. Judge Hall, released from jail after martial law had expired, ordered a trial of Jackson to adjudicate his flagrant violation of the rule of law. Defiant, Jackson submitted a written defense of his actions, but refused to answer questions. Judge Hall found him guilty of contempt of court and ordered him to pay a $1,000 fine.[55] Jackson, livid about having been convicted, reprinted his defense in newspapers, and also sent it to the president. But Madison had his new acting secretary of war, Alexander Dallas, send Jackson a message about his conduct. Madison knew the wording was paramount, and he exchanged drafts with Dallas to get it right.[56] In the end, the letter bluntly rebuked Jackson, stating there was no legal justification for his actions. Jackson had argued that the country was still in an emergency circumstance that supported his decisions. But Madison responded that Jackson's drastic actions could not be justified—even under the banner of war—and were inconsistent with law.[57]

Despite this private rebuff, no public rebuke came. Madison, knowing Jackson might run for governor of Tennessee, pragmatically avoided conflict with his general.[58] The Louaillier fiasco was not an anomaly for Jackson. His behavior in New Orleans foreshadowed his authoritarian impulses as president where, seventeen years later, he refused to respect the Supreme Court's ruling that Georgia stop infringing on Cherokee sovereignty. By not giving the court's decision the full backing of the federal government, Jackson neglected his duty to faithfully execute the law.[59] In contrast, after the Battle of New Orleans, President Madison had rejected a shutdown of Louaillier's criticism of Jackson, even in the aftermath of war, even when his popular general rebuffed him. Madison held true to the ideal he had spoken of in his second inaugural: liberty always applies to allies and opponents alike.

James Madison was in many ways the anti-Jackson. Jackson was quick to anger and famous for a rash temper that sparked violent duels, including one where he killed his opponent for insulting Jackson's wife and publicly maligning him.[60] Madison was mild-mannered and never dueled. He even talked Monroe out of dueling Hamilton, despite a direct challenge.[61] Madison was cerebral, a generational thinker. Jackson was a man of action, not disposed to contemplation.

Madison's unaggressive public image hurt his popularity among contemporaries and historians, who usually give him middling reviews. Jackson, however, was celebrated for his aggressiveness. He was called Old Hickory, in reference to a particularly tough hardwood. During his 1828 presidential campaign, Jackson's victory during the Battle of New Orleans would be lauded in the first campaign song in history, "Hunters of Kentucky."[62]

> *But Jackson he was wide awake,*
> *And was not scar'd at trifles,*
> *For well he knew what aim we take*
> *With our Kentucky rifles.*

Madison never cut the same dashing, heroic figure as Jackson. US currency provides an interesting lens for viewing their respective popular fame: Madison appeared on the now out-of-print $5,000 bill, whereas Jackson still graces the $20 bill. Yet through the lens of preserving the right to dissent, Madison's supposed weakness is really a strength. Jackson justified his imprisonment of opponents after the war as a wartime necessity, a seemingly popular decision, given his future political success. Madison, by contrast, did the less popular but critical work of securing the right to dissent and showing restraint, a bravery exhibited on behalf of democracy.

★ ★ ★

THE OATH OF OFFICE REQUIRES THE PRESIDENT to "preserve, protect and defend" the Constitution. But we have seen in this section that how a president understands the Constitution leads to very different interpretations of that duty. In 1798, John Adams relied on his quasi-monarchical constitutional philosophy to justify the Sedition Act and his prosecutions of dissenters. Those prosecutions were met with resistance by a citizen interest group, newspaper editors, who turned constitutional *defense* into a duty of "We the People" in the face of a president who disregarded it. This democratic constitutional constituency defended their own right to dissent by charging that Adams, not them, trampled on the Constitution. But if the newspaper editors were to spur a lasting constitutional preservation of that right, they needed a political strategy not only to defeat Adams but to ensure future generations could criticize their leaders without reprisal.

The editors used the election of 1800 as a way for Americans to condemn Adams's tyranny and cement the right to dissent, not through the courts but through the venue of public opinion. They campaigned for Jefferson, giving him a mandate to oppose Adams's monarchical views and policies and to promote popular sovereignty. This Jefferson did, but only partially, as he was marred by his half-hearted defense of dissent.

Madison, who found that the right to dissent was insecure, had to strengthen and preserve it. The War of 1812 could have given Madison cover for a new sedition act, as his party demanded. Instead, Madison chose restraint. Rebuffing his party was a heroic defense of the fundamental democratic idea that citizens have a right to criticize public officials, including a president. By the end of Madison's presidency, incipient concepts like the freedoms of speech and press were cemented in the minds of most Americans.

While Madison's commitment to free speech was crucial, it was not pursued in a vacuum. A new democratic constitutional constituency that had taken the mantle of free speech from the anti-Adams editors held Madison to his principles. Hanson and his supporters claimed that mantle by highlighting the glaring irony of Democratic-Republicans who insisted on censorship when opposition to the sedition laws had brought them to power in the first place. Madison could have responded with prosecution. Instead he listened to his opponents, heeding their call to respect the right to dissent. Madison's rebuff of Jackson further showed a president who put constitutional preservation over popularity.

It was far from given that the right to dissent would be preserved after the War of 1812. Imagine if Adams had been in power while a foreign force burned the president's mansion. How many of his political opponents would have been jailed? The difference between that outcome and reality rested largely on both the insistence of Hanson's constituency to respect democratic rights and for Madison to willingly listen. The result was a president who embraced the idea of popular sovereignty; even during war, the people remained the source of the government's power. But which people? Madison's presidency showed that even a principled democratic constitutional constituency can have leaders like Thomas Cooper, who abandon their beliefs when politically expedient. It is up to a president who wishes to respect their oath to distinguish those who claim to represent the people's rights from those who actually do. That Madison embraced Hanson's vision despite his party affiliation may have demonstrated disloyalty to the individuals in his party—as Armstrong charged after Madison fired him—but Madison's loyalty was to constitutional principles of democracy.

While principled, Madison's constitutional forbearance was also politically clever; had he thrown Federalists in prison, he might have enhanced their political standing, fomenting the sort of backlash that had swept Jefferson and himself into office. Instead, he withheld this political fuel, watching the Federalists fade into obscurity by the end of his presidency. In practicing the constitutional restraint that Adams lacked, Madison may have helped end his rival's party.

While Jefferson's and Madison's presidencies helped establish the democratic right to dissent as central to the American Constitution, their actions and lack thereof on slavery helped postpone the birth of true democracy. Both presidents had a complex relationship to the "peculiar institution," an American evil that destroyed Black lives and was a horrific stain on the country's soul. To various degrees, they each claimed to believe slavery morally wrong. Jefferson, despite owning over six hundred enslaved people throughout his life and repeatedly separating enslaved children from their families, expressed an abstract hope that abolition might come in the future,[63] and Madison knew his own actions in enslaving more than one hundred people placed him on the wrong side of history.[64] By the end of Madison's presidency, America continued to protect the institution of slavery, and so was far from the truly democratic republic his writings invoked.

Yet the work of both Jefferson (despite his hypocrisy) and Madison throughout their lives to protect a robust conception of the freedom of speech provided the architecture for a fuller democracy, one that would prove crucial for part of the nascent abolitionist movement's eventual transformation into a democratic constitutional constituency. The freedom of speech that Jefferson and Madison held as the basis for their administrations became a critical tool in abolitionists' antislavery arguments. The right to free speech would therefore act as a scaffold from which to build a truer democracy out of a slave society.

In understanding how to honor the convoluted legacy of these two presidents, we should look to an early voice in the abolition movement. David Walker was born free in North Carolina around 1796, at the end of Washington's presidency. The son of an enslaved father and a free mother, Walker devoted his life to fighting slavery, publishing numerous abolitionist essays. Walker's work would often be distributed and read free from censorship partly due to Jefferson's and Madison's efforts to recover the right of free speech. Southern states called for a national ban on Walker's writing. Some made possession of Walker's work a capital offense. But much of the North resisted calls to suppress Walker's work.[65] When Boston mayor Harrison Gray Otis received a letter from the mayor of Savannah, Georgia, asking him to arrest David Walker, Otis responded that no law nationally or locally prohibited the publishing of Walker's work, even if he disagreed with it. Massachusetts governor Edward Everett shared Otis's view, saying, "The genius of our institutions and the character of our people are entirely repugnant to laws impairing the liberty of speech, and of the press, even for the sake of repressing its abuses."[66] Had the Sedition Act still been in place, the mayor of Savannah may have had a case, but the recovery of free speech meant that those who might seek to censor Walker's work had no federal laws to aid them. And as it happened, the dissemination of Walker's ideas provided the groundwork for an orator who would soon emerge from his own enslavement to use the contradictions at the heart of the American founding as a cudgel against slavery and in defense of democracy.

SECTION II

LEGAL PERSONHOOD

Frederick Douglass and the Promise of "We the People"

CHAPTER 4

James Buchanan versus Frederick Douglass

A Fake Neutrality

IN 1798, PRESIDENT JOHN ADAMS SOUGHT TO SHUT DOWN POLITICAL OPPOSITION. CITIZENS responded, seeking to save a lost ideal of constitutional democracy. By 1840, a new citizen movement was building. This time, however, the citizens did not seek to recover the Constitution. They sought its destruction. The movement was led by William Lloyd Garrison, America's most vocal antislavery activist and a leading abolitionist. Garrison's primary weapon was the *Liberator*, the abolitionist newspaper he founded and edited in Boston. The *Liberator* had only about three thousand paid subscribers, most of them free Black people.[1] These numbers belied the renegade's political influence.

A mesmerizing orator and immensely talented organizer, Garrison seeded a groundswell of antislavery events countrywide. The events were covered in the *Liberator* and often organized by its readers. This group of activists later blossomed into a larger network who arranged local gatherings and speeches. The organization that grew out of those meetings, the American Anti-Slavery Society, eventually became the largest abolition organization in the United States, with over 150,000 members.[2] At Society events, organizers could arrange few more compelling speakers than Garrison, whose comments stoked controversy practically everywhere he went. Garrison's words in lectures and the *Liberator* illustrated his mission of radically reimagining America; no compromise within the existing constitutional system was adequate. "I will be as harsh as Truth, and as uncompromising as Justice," Garrison wrote in the *Liberator's* first issue, in January 1831, announcing his mission. "I will not excuse—I will not retreat a single inch—and I will be heard."[3]

Garrison's mission was ambitious, and building a successful movement was slow going. By 1833, two years after founding the *Liberator*, the end of slavery was not in sight. However, American abolitionist ideas found a home in Great Britain where, in that same year, another antislavery movement legally abolished slavery in British colonies.[4] But at home, despite fierce abolitionist writing by Garrison and other figures such as David Walker, the abolition movement made little legal progress nationally against proslavery politicians and their backers, who were getting stronger. In 1836, responding to the activism of antislavery societies, Congress passed a rule—known later as the gag rule—silencing its own members from even considering bills that mentioned slavery.[5]

In 1787, just shy of 700,000 Black people were enslaved; by 1840, the number was nearly 2.5 million.[6] Madison's hopes that the Constitution might leave the door open for the abolition of slavery proved catastrophically wrong in the near term. One reason was the addition of new territories, with accords such as the Missouri Compromise that enabled the expansion of slavery. A more fundamental reason, however, was the often-misunderstood Three-Fifths Clause—a constitutional provision regarding the census, whose sin wasn't undercounting enslaved Black people but overcounting them in a way that enhanced proslavery power. By dishonestly counting slaves as if they were "constituents" in the South—despite being denied basic rights, including the vote—the Three-Fifths Clause inflated the South's congressional representation, disproportionately increasing Southern influence in government. As the political power of the Southern states grew, so did the power of slavery's supporters.

To Garrison, a primary reason slavery had grown unchecked wasn't merely the power of slaveholders. It was some politicians' naive hope that the Constitution could guide a settlement to end slavery. The surest way to eliminate slavery, Garrison believed, was to eliminate the Constitution itself. By 1840, this anti-Constitution message made Garrison one of America's most controversial citizens. His columns and speaking events occasionally sparked riots. A Boston mob had once dragged him through the streets at the end of a rope; he was narrowly rescued by the mayor.[7] With progressively more radical ideas, Garrison's notoriety grew. The Constitution of the United States of America is "the source and parent of all the other atrocities—'a covenant with death, and an agreement with Hell,'" he said on July 4, 1854, before the Massachusetts affiliate of his antislavery society.[8] So opposed was Garrison to the Constitution that he proselytized against any form of participation in American democracy, which he argued entailed complicity with slavery. He urged his supporters to avoid voting, and even refrain from endorsing candidates, no matter how antislavery they appeared.[9] Garrison called for a boycott of the Constitution. As he put it, while dramatically burning a copy of the document, "So perish all compromises with tyranny!"[10]

Garrison's anti-constitutionalism might well have driven American abolitionism. But seeds of a new direction for the movement were planted one morning in 1841. During three days in mid-August, Garrison convened an antislavery convention on Nantucket Island. The second night, Garrison delivered the keynote address to the nearly thousand abolitionists who had gathered. The following morning, a little-known speaker took the podium at the Nantucket Athenaeum—a formerly enslaved person who had escaped to the North and was now earning a living as a dockworker in nearby New Bedford.[11]

The young man, Frederick Douglass, stumbled at first, gripped by nerves. Then he began a riveting account of his life. Born in bondage on a plantation in Maryland, he later made an improbable escape to freedom on the Underground Railroad, finding refuge in New Bedford.

By the time Douglass finished his remarks, the crowd was entranced. So was Garrison. He later described what he heard as "more eloquent" than any speech by Patrick Henry himself.[12] The convention's unknown speaker would go on to become one of America's greatest orators. Even without formal training or education, Douglass was a masterful speaker, learned and engaging—startling his white audiences weaned on Southern lies of Black inferiority.

Garrison pushed his way to the front of the room. "Have we been listening to a thing, a piece of property, or to a man?" Garrison asked the crowd. "A man!" they shouted repeatedly in unison. Garrison replied, "Shall such a man ever be sent back to bondage from the free soil of old Massachusetts?" and the crowd roared No!, drowning out Garrison's voice.[13] Douglass was a sensation. Launched to fame in Nantucket, he would change the fortunes of the abolitionist movement forever. Within weeks, Douglass was traveling by train to attend speaking events for the American Anti-Slavery Society.[14]

Thus began one of the most famous friendships in American politics. Garrison became Douglass's mentor, making Douglass a regular writer for the *Liberator*, helping him build a national audience and earn a living as a full-time abolitionist. For the next seven years, with Garrison's help and publicity, Douglass became the most sought-after abolitionist speaker in the country. In due course, protégé eclipsed mentor—presaging a descent from a famous friendship to an equally famous falling-out. Douglass was uneasy serving as a lieutenant—or worse, a prop—in Garrison's army. By 1848, their relationship had deteriorated beyond repair, stemming from a disagreement focused on a single issue: the Constitution.

At first, Douglass had embraced Garrison's interpretation of politics, agreeing that the Constitution was not salvageable. Only a new founding document and political system devoted to abolitionist goals, a new set of fundamental laws, could renew America. Over time, however, Douglass began to question his position. He doubted the wisdom and efficacy of his mentor's anti-Constitution views, and he wanted his own Black-led platform to develop his own ideas.[15]

What started as Douglass's skepticism toward Garrison's approach developed into a new theory of how to understand the Constitution's relationship to slavery, reached through extensive study of the document. Douglass found himself increasingly convinced by the ideas of abolitionist writers like Lysander Spooner, who believed the Constitution as ratified did not legally permit slavery. Garrison, along with other commentators, stressed the *intent* of the framers, but Spooner noted the framers had diverging intents about slavery; Madison believed abolition was on the horizon, while South Carolina delegates thought the document protected slavery. Since the framers had no monolithic intent, Spooner argued, constitutional interpreters needed instead to look at the text itself, a view now widely shared by constitutional scholars. More important, he stressed that the only intent with legal force was that of the people who voted to ratify it, as expressed in the plain text of the document, not the secret beliefs of those who wrote it down. Spooner was encouraging readers to find the Constitution's core meaning in its text, not court cases or government practice. Douglass took up that charge.[16]

In 1847, Douglass moved to Rochester, New York,[17] where he came to firmly believe that Garrison was wrong in thinking the Constitution a proslavery document. Instead, Douglass agreed with Spooner that the document, in its text and values, should be read to ban slavery at both the federal and state levels.[18] Inspired to spread the message, and to make his break with Garrison official, in December 1847, Douglass created a new newspaper, the *North Star.*

Driven by Douglass's star power and a network of sympathetic contributing writers, the *North Star* grew to four thousand subscribers.[19] Douglass's fame grew with it. The subscriptions were won through Douglass's speeches and the efforts of coeditor Martin Delany, who traveled throughout the North and Midwest persuading free Black people to subscribe.[20] Douglass largely financed the paper through funds raised on a speaking tour through Britain and Ireland. Those efforts painstakingly built a constitutional constituency devoted to ending slavery and promoting the idea of a country devoted to equal protection of the law.

A few years after founding his paper, by which time Douglass had solidified his views during his slow break with Garrison, Douglass endorsed the following creed: "That the Constitution . . . might be made consistent in its details with the noble purposes avowed in its preamble; and that hereafter we should . . . demand that it be wielded in behalf of emancipation." Douglass began to share his insights from his reading of the Constitution. Behind "the letter" of the Constitution was an understanding of liberty broadly conceived that allowed the citizen reader to see that slavery "never was lawful, and never can be made so." Douglass said that not one word in the Constitution endorses, much less mentions, slavery. And the document, properly read, required something of readers: "The first duty of every American citizen ... [was] to use his *political* as well as his *moral* power for [slavery's] overthrow."[21]

Douglass used the paper to highlight the voices of Black Americans within this new constitutional constituency. In 1849, Douglass published the essay of Ohio barber and activist Alfred Anderson. Anderson, echoing Douglass, argued against "partial legislation," exemplified by a supposedly antidiscrimination law in his state, that nevertheless maintained segregation in schools, failed to address the constitutional right of Black people to serve on juries, and made Black people ineligible for government poverty benefits. Partial legislation denied "the doctrine of the equality of all men" and failed to outlaw "invidious distinctions on account either of caste or color, sect or condition."[22]

Douglass also took aim at Garrison's constitutional understanding. Garrison was wrong to conflate participation in American democracy with complicity in slavery. To the contrary, Black people should demand the right to participate because, rightly understood, the Constitution regarded them as political equals. Douglass also jumped into the political arena, attending the convention of the Liberty Party, a minor party that had splintered from the American Anti-Slavery Society because of a different interpretation of the Constitution. Garrison fought back, arguing that Douglass read the Constitution wrong and had sold out to the Liberty Party.[23] This criticism was unfair. Douglass stood apart from Liberty Party leaders like future Supreme Court Chief Justice Salmon Chase in his radicalism. For Chase and many of his followers, the Constitution allowed Congress to abolish slavery in federal territory but did not require it.[24] However, while Chase urged abolition in the states where it already existed, he thought this was a local matter, not something Congress had the constitutional power to outlaw. Douglass's more radical understanding—shared with some other members of the Liberty Party—sought to build a movement around the idea that the document, when read correctly, required more—the immediate abolition of slavery throughout the country and the conferral of equal citizenship.

Although Douglass aligned himself with the Liberty Party, he was not shy about voicing his interpretation of the Constitution; he was more than a mere Liberty Party appendage. As that party fizzled by 1853, ceding to other antislavery parties,[25] Douglass's democratic constitutional constituency was just beginning. With other activists, Douglass created a network of Black leaders devoted to his understanding of the Constitution. He helped to organize a Black-led convention in Rochester in 1853, inviting abolitionists from around the country.[26] There, he contended with an alternative strand of Black thought—the emigrationists, led by former *North Star* coeditor Martin Delany. Delany, pessimistic that whites could accept Black people as equals, urged mass migration out of the United States because Black people would never become equal citizens under a fundamentally proslavery founding document. At the convention, Douglass marginalized Delany's followers, doubling down on his pro-Constitution abolitionism. Boldly, he argued that those assembled were full citizens of the United States. He said, "We address you not as aliens nor as exiles . . . but we address you as American citizens asserting their rights on their own native soil."[27] Douglass's allies thundered at these words, rebuking those who believed Black people needed to leave the country to gain their full rights.

Douglass used the Rochester event to jumpstart a "national council" with state affiliates who would fan out and begin their own Black-led pro-Constitution antislavery organizations.[28] At a follow-up Black-led conference in Chicago on October 6, Douglass argued that an Illinois law that made it illegal for free or enslaved Black people to enter the state was unconstitutional. According to John Jones, one of the convention's organizers, Douglass gave zest to the in-state antislavery activity. One editor, Zebina Eastman, praised Douglass's address in Illinois, chiding the antislavery press for not giving his efforts the attention they were due.[29] This nascent movement pushed the country to adopt a democratic understanding of the Constitution that required equal citizenship for

Black people at a time when most supposed-expert interpreters were suggesting nothing of the sort.

Like the editors Bache, Cooper, and Duane, Douglass aligned himself with a constitutional tradition of citizen readers who sought to build a political movement around a Constitution based in popular sovereignty. However, Douglass went further than the Adams-era editors had, insisting that popular sovereignty required an end to slavery and a new guarantee of equal protection for Black people. That understanding of the Constitution soon met its opposite, championed by a president and a Supreme Court who threatened democracy in Douglass's time, much as Adams did in his battle against the editors. That president and Supreme Court would challenge the very right of Black Americans to legal personhood.

Douglass's democratic constitutional constituency didn't just differ from the early editors' in its primary goal; it also used different methods and had a different timeline. After galvanizing public support through their publications, Bache, Cooper, and Duane quickly joined forces with a political party to enact change by urging their supporters to elect a new president. Douglass's supporters, however, couldn't simply enact change by voting in a new president; because they were not considered legal persons, most of this constitutional constituency, Douglass included, had no voting rights. Douglass and his fellow constituents must have known that they were playing a long game. Perhaps this realization led them to build a more robust organizational structure that could achieve the kind of sustained action needed for a change as radical as the one they were demanding. That structure—a network of advocacy organizations that hosted conventions and published pamphlets and editorials—spread the fight for equal citizenship to a growing chorus of Black Americans and allies who would in turn prevail upon others. This infrastructure of advocacy expanded exponentially on the impact of Douglass's legendary oratorical and writing skills. The long game of this constituency would last several presidencies, but eventually both white and Black supporters of Douglass's vision—male supporters, that is—would be able to vote in a president, not simply speak out against one.

★ ★ ★

DOUGLASS'S RIVAL, a president every bit the threat to democracy Adams had been, was elected as a moderate for his time. While Adams openly held quasi-monarchial views, this president claimed he championed popular sovereignty. James Buchanan ran in 1856 advocating that states and ter-ritories should have power to decide the slavery question within their jurisdictions—a position often associated with the term popular sover-eignty. Buchanan claimed that the presidency was a limited office, obli-gated to respect constitutional limits on national power. The presidency, as he publicly claimed he saw it, should neither try to end slavery nor promote its spread. Although he asserted that he personally abhorred slavery, he argued that the presidential office was a constitutional one, distinct from his own moral beliefs. That idea was emphasized in his inaugural address, in which Buchanan made respect for the Constitu-tion central. (In the speech, he mentioned the document fifteen times.) He "[owed his] election to the inherent love for the Constitution," and emphasized that danger came when readers tried to "strain the language of the Constitution."[30] Buchanan said he believed the Constitution, as it was already written, resolved the nation's most pressing problems. Nowhere was this truer than Buchanan's beliefs about slavery.

Buchanan was born in Pennsylvania to a financially successful merchant and farming family that did not own enslaved people. He attended Dickinson College (which still has a residence hall named after him) and later became a lawyer. Buchanan was at first a Federalist and opposed the War of 1812 like most of his party. But he still signed up as a volunteer for that war out of a sense of patriotism to stop the British invasion of Baltimore.[31] He despised that era's chaos and division, and he became a harsh critic of President Madison. He later won a seat as a Federalist in the Pennsylvania legislature, and was subsequently elected to the US House and the Senate.

On slavery, Buchanan had long claimed to draw a distinction between his personal views and legal ones. In 1826, he had written that slavery was a "Great Political and a great moral evil." But, he added, it was "one of those moral evils, from which it is impossible for us to escape, without the introduction of evils infinitely greater." That evil, to the conflict-averse Buchanan, was the dissolution of the United States. Trying to outlaw slavery would only "manifest to the people of the South that they cannot live with us," Buchanan wrote. "Touch the question of slavery seriously," he warned, "and the Union is from that moment dissolved."[32] In public speeches and statements, Buchanan painted himself as moderate, emphasizing the need to put the Constitution above personal morality when it came to slavery. In an 1836 speech, he vowed to "never violate the Constitutional compact which we have made with our sister States. Their rights will be held sacred by us. Under the Constitution, [slavery] is their own question."[33] Key to Buchanan's claims of moderation was his insistence that he would neither support abolition nor work to protect slavery nationally.

Douglass still did not trust Buchanan. By the time of Buchanan's 1856 campaign, Douglass had broken with an increasingly irrelevant Liberty Party and was exploring other vehicles to support his goal of abolition. After Buchanan gained the Democratic Party's nomination, Douglass condemned his candidacy. That was no surprise, as that party, which had been largely defined by the proslavery president Andrew Jackson, was associated with the position that slavery should grow, not be abolished. Douglass initially supported a third-party candidate, though he ultimately endorsed the Republican candidate, former California senator John Frémont.[34] In an editorial, Douglass issued an ominous warning: Buchanan did not tell the truth and was not to be trusted in any of his promises, including those on slavery. Most consequentially, Douglass predicted that Buchanan's moderation masked a virulent proslavery agenda: "So we can expect at the hands of Mr. Buchanan, if elected, nought but whips, and chains, bludgeons, bloodhounds, the powers of the Federal Government wielded for the support of Slavery, the Constitution trampled in the dust."[35]

Douglass was right. Despite his superficially modest rhetoric, Buchanan arguably did more to nationalize the institution of slavery than any other president. Once elected, he eschewed his idea of a restrained presidency by lobbying to expand the rights of slaveholders nationally. This unprecedented power grab spun the country into crisis and, eventually, civil war. Buchanan achieved it secretly, partly through lobbying the Supreme Court in a notorious case known as *Dred Scott.*

Dred Scott was a man born into slavery in Virginia in the late 1790s. In the 1830s, Scott was purchased by an army surgeon named John Emerson. In 1834, Emerson relocated for military duty, forcing Scott to travel with him to Illinois. In 1836, Emerson took Scott to Fort Snelling in what was then the free territory of Wisconsin (now part of Minnesota), where Scott married his wife, Harriet. In both places, slavery was illegal—but Scott stayed enslaved. Emerson died in 1843, and the ownership of Dred Scott and Harriet passed on to Emerson's widow, Irene. In 1846, Dred Scott and Harriet tried to purchase their freedom from Emerson's widow but were refused. Undeterred, they went to the courts. Although they were initially turned away on a technicality, the St. Louis Circuit Court granted them their freedom in 1850. Irene Emerson appealed the decision, bringing the case before the Missouri Supreme Court, where it attracted the attention of abolitionist allies and the anxieties of slaveholders. Scott had argued that under the principle of "once free always free" established by prior courts, when Emerson had taken him to live in free territories, Scott had been made free forever.[36] The Missouri Supreme Court denied his claim with a twisted logic. Yes, Scott had strong legal claims to his freedom, but the nation faced a crisis—not from slavery, but from abolitionist instability—that suspended old understandings of the law. To stem the upheaval, the court believed it must deny Scott's rights.[37]

Scott refiled his case in federal court, bringing claims under the Constitution. Scott's lawyers appealed to the Full Faith and Credit Clause, arguing that if Scott's freedom was recognized in Illinois and Wisconsin, then Missouri had to recognize those same rights. Scott also invoked Congress's power to regulate slavery in the territories, like Wisconsin, where he had lived as a free person. That power was thought to be clearly established because Congress had limited the growth of slavery with legislation such as the 1820 Missouri Compromise, which guaranteed that areas north of an imaginary line with precise coordinates would be free territories. This guarantee was based on

Congress's power under Article IV, Section 3 of the Constitution to make "rules and regulations" for the territories including the power to limit slavery. Slaveholders understood that to forcibly bring slaves into free territories meant they could be set free under the "once free, always free" principle.

To just-elected President Buchanan, Scott's case presented an extraordinary political opportunity. The United States Supreme Court heard Scott's case on appeal in 1856, while Buchanan was preparing for the presidency. Around that time, Buchanan, who had not intended to directly confront slavery until after beginning his term, realized that he could influence the case. In February 1857, Buchanan wrote to his old friend, Justice John Catron, a slave owner, to check *Dred Scott*'s status. Catron eagerly informed Buchanan of their progress. In two letters he conveyed that the court was moving more slowly than anticipated, and that it would not determine the Missouri Compromise's constitutionality and would instead rule more narrowly.

Then suddenly, Catron said the court *would* rule on the Missouri Compromise, and that Buchanan would be wise to use his inaugural to validate the court as the appropriate body to decide. For that ruling to take shape, though, the court needed an extra vote, so Catron urged Buchanan to "drop [Justice] Grier a line . . . saying how necessary it is . . . to settle the agitation by an affirmative decision of the Supreme Court."[38] Buchanan obliged, writing to Grier soon after.[39]

This was an extraordinary suggestion. Although for decades Congress was the unquestioned arbiter of slavery regulations in federal territory, a power Buchanan publicly claimed to respect, privately he believed that congressional compromise had made slavery more controversial. There are clues to his private belief. Years before, in 1847, Buchanan, as secretary of state, had written a letter to the editor of an Albany newspaper, saying that continuing to debate the legality of slavery would "produce no effect but to alienate the people of different portions of the Union from each other."[40] Buchanan saw the *debate* over slavery—not slavery itself—as the source of sectional rage. With Dred Scott's case, Buchanan likely thought he had stumbled on a solution that would finally legally settle the slavery question and quell the raucous debate. Instead of tamping down on a crisis, however, he ignited one.

Justice Grier responded to Buchanan how he had hoped. Grier had shared the letter with Chief Justice Roger Taney and Justice James Wayne, who both agreed with the aggressive approach in defense of slavery. Aware of the vast implications of the decision, Grier, who like Buchanan was from Pennsylvania, joined the majority in part to ensure the votes of the court did not divide North versus South, and meanwhile promised Buchanan he would not divulge "the cause of [Grier, Taney, and Wayne's] anxiety to produce this result."[41]

To describe this behavior—by the justices and the president—as unethical would be a vast understatement. While Buchanan was fashioning himself as a constitutionally restrained president who was not pushing the slavery views of either side,[42] he used the court as a key part of his charade. At his inaugural address—delivered just two days before the *Dred Scott* opinion—Buchanan, feigning his ignorance about the decision, announced that his personal position on slavery was "happily a matter of but little practical importance," as it was about to be resolved "speedily and finally" by the Supreme Court.[43] Buchanan's coordination with Catron and Grier to subvert a crucial aspect of democracy, the idea that Black people had rights under the Constitution, resembled the coordination Adams had with Chase to undermine the right to dissent. Yet it differed in an important way. While Chase did little to hide his partisanship, earning himself an impeachment, Catron and Grier coordinated with Buchanan secretly. And President Buchanan, unlike Adams, hid his true views about slavery behind a veneer of supposed deference to the court.

When the court issued its opinion on *Dred Scott*, the 7–2 ruling was so proslavery that it stunned practically the entire country, including the South. Writing for the majority, Chief Justice Taney drew on precedents that he believed laid the groundwork for a national protection of slavery. Striking down the Missouri Compromise, the court declared "that the act of Congress which prohibited a citizen from holding and owning property of this kind in the territory of the United

States north of the line therein mentioned, is not warranted by the Constitution, and is therefore void; and that neither Dred Scott himself, nor any of his family, were made free by being carried into this territory."[44] It was only the third time the court had struck down an act of Congress.[45]

The court ruled that enslaved African Americans weren't people, but property. In Taney's words, "We think [people of African ancestry] are not, and that they are not included, and were not intended to be included, under the word 'citizens' in the Constitution, and can therefore claim none of the rights and privileges which that instrument provides for and secures to citizens of the United States."[46]

Any legislation that denied slaveholders the right to own slaves, it followed, unconstitutionally denied their right to property. Because the Missouri Compromise prohibited white people in certain territories from owning slaves, it too was unconstitutional—leading abolitionists to worry that *Dred Scott* created a new national right to own slaves that might entitle enslavers to bring enslaved people into any state, no matter how strong its antislavery protections. As for Dred Scott, the court ruled that he did not have standing to bring a lawsuit at all. He was, in their view, property—not a person.

A Supreme Court that had done virtually nothing to interfere in Congress's lawmaking powers throughout American history had suddenly eviscerated one of its most significant laws. And it did so by intervening in the country's most consequential moral and political issue. President Buchanan helped make this radical breach possible, signaling to the justices that their unprecedented national decision protecting slavery would be well-received by the incoming president.

What prompted the famously "slavery-neutral" and nonslaveholding Buchanan to lobby the court to protect the evil institution? In one sense, Buchanan was presciently fearful of an impending conflict and believed that continuing compromise short of full resolution would be futile. Averting a near-inevitable clash demanded stability, and stability required that the legal system choose a side. In the end, Buchanan saw abolitionists, not the slaveholders, as the greater threat to that stability. Buchanan likely told himself that the Constitution was born in compromise, and that in *Dred Scott*, the court had made the same calculation the framers had. But at bottom, Buchanan's decision derived from the way he read the Constitution. It was a binding legal document, he thought, not a container of moral promises about the nature of life and purpose of liberty. Whatever Buchanan thought, his actions would be imbued with a tragic irony that is difficult to overstate. The conflict-averse president thought his approach would settle the slavery question. But in cutting off any hope of ending slavery through normal politics, he all but ensured the nation's most dire violent crisis, one that brought the United States to the brink.

★ ★ ★

THE DRED SCOTT CASE, as tragic as it was, created a moment *designed* for Frederick Douglass. It lay bare the difference between the Supreme Court's reading of the Constitution—in which enslaved Black people were regarded as property, not persons, and even free Black people were not citizens—and his vision of the document as guaranteeing equal liberty for Black Americans. No longer could politicians claim to seek eventual abolition through a gradual process of legislation and compromise. Under the decision, slavery was protected throughout the country, imperiling the right of even the most antislavery Northern states to outlaw the practice. As Douglass noted in a speech decrying the decision, its drastic implication seemed to be that "Congress has no right to prohibit slavery anywhere; that slavery may go in safety anywhere under the star-spangled banner."[47]

The court's decision cut off crucial political means to constitutionally end slavery. In fighting back, abolitionists faced a crucial choice—would they pursue Douglass's strategy or Garrison's?

The *Dred Scott* ruling led the Garrisonians to deepen their calls for disunion, as the Supreme Court had now literally upheld their idea (albeit for different reasons) that the Constitution was proslavery.[48] Douglass called out the similarity between Taney's and Garrison's understandings of the Constitution: "It may be said that it is quite true that the Constitution was designed to secure the blessings of liberty and justice to the people who made it, and to the posterity of the people who made it, but was never designed to do any such thing for the colored people of African descent. This is Judge Taney's argument, and it is Mr. Garrison's argument, but it is not the argument of the Constitution."[49] Once a flight of theoretical fancy, Garrison's call for scrapping the Constitution now seemed to many abolitionists like the only plausible response to a Supreme Court that had declared slavery constitutionally protected. Douglass had to show there was still another way.

In May 1857, Douglass appeared at an American Anti-Slavery Society meeting in Rochester, New York.[50] Brimming with indignation and resolve, he presented his rebuttal to *Dred Scott*. Both Justice Benjamin Curtis and Justice John McLean had written dissents—Curtis's actually called out the fact that Black people could be citizens at the time of the Founding—but neither dissent conveyed the depth of the decision's depravity. Delivering a speech circulated widely in the abolition movement, Douglass gave *Dred Scott* the dissent it deserved. With fire and passion, he decried a "lying decision" that had misled Americans about the meaning of their Constitution.

Douglass began by describing the purpose of the Constitution. Taney's core failure, he observed, was that, like Buchanan, he viewed the document as a cold legal instrument. Taney and his allies "delight in supposed intentions—intentions nowhere expressed in the Constitution, and everywhere contradicted in the Constitution." In contrast to Taney's flawed appeal to the framers' original intent, Douglass argued that implicit in the Constitution's text were fundamental values like liberty and justice. He further argued that for the court to overturn a law of Congress, including the Missouri Compromise, the "rules of interpretation" should be "in harmony with the true idea and object of law and liberty." A proper reading of the Constitution "must be construed strictly in favor of liberty and justice."[51]

As Douglass saw it, Taney's mistakes in constitutional method allowed him to posit his biggest lie: that the Constitution was proslavery. Taney had claimed the Constitution's proslavery intent was revealed in the text itself, saying that there are "two clauses in the Constitution which point directly and specifically to the negro race as a separate class of persons, and show clearly that they were not regarded as a portion of the people or citizens of the Government then formed."[32] Douglass, in multiple speeches after the decision, responded that there *was* no textual basis for slavery in those provisions or anywhere else. The so-called Fugitive Slave Clause Taney referenced, for example, stated that people involved in "Service or Labour in one state" cannot be "discharged from such Service or Labour" simply by going to another state.[33] Douglass argued that the reference to "service or labor" rather than "enslavement" was telling. Even this ostensibly proslavery clause failed to mention slavery, and applied also to indentured servants. In Douglass's view, this wording indicated the pains the framers took to avoid using the term and thus endorse or protect slavery.[34] Indeed, the other constitutional provision cited by Taney, dating from 1808, was the grant to Congress of a power to eliminate the "migration or importation of persons." The term "persons" not "slaves" is telling.

To Douglass, the text revealed principles that were *incompatible* with slavery. The Constitution's prohibition on bills of attainder—a rejection of the British Parliament's practice of punishing an entire family bloodline, a practice known as the corruption of blood—should be understood as an antislavery principle, as Douglass stated: "The law of slavery is a law of attainder. The child is property because its parent was property and suffers as a slave because its parent suffered as a slave. Thus the *very* essence of the whole slave code is in open violation of a fundamental provision of the Constitution and is in open and flagrant violation of all the objects set forth in the Constitution."[35]

Then there was the matter of what the Constitution omitted. At the Constitutional Convention, South Carolina delegate and future governor and ambassador Charles Cotesworth Pinckney wanted the Constitution to explicitly protect property in the form of enslaved people.[36] Madison had previously refused. Despite being a slaveholder, he wanted the document to never explicitly acknowledge slavery. In short, Pinckney lost, and Madison won. In outlining the Three-Fifths Clause, the text described "all other Persons" (that is, those who were not "free") for the purpose of representation and taxation. The original Constitution never explicitly recognized the legal personhood of African Americans, but neither did it label them property. On this basis, Douglass argued that when read in the context of its overall values, the document should be understood to confer and protect equal rights. He sought to show that Taney and the court were "disregarding the plain and common sense reading of the instrument itself."[57]

In Douglass's view, the Constitution had been "pressed into the service of slavery" by Taney, who appealed to a "secret and unwritten understanding of its framers."[58] For Douglass, Taney superimposed the beliefs of some framers and founding-era Americans about slavery onto the Constitution's text, falsely rewriting the document. The framers' intent was more nuanced to Douglass, even regarding framers who owned slaves. He pointed out that George Washington expressed his wish to see the end of slavery.[59] He could have also cited James Madison, who had argued that slavery was a moral evil and believed the institution should be abolished over time. Far from mere moral posturing, these antislavery arguments, Douglass said, were earnestly inserted into the founding documents.

The battle between Taney and Douglass over constitutional terminology was more fundamentally about the document's guarantee of democracy. For Taney, "The words 'people of the United States' and 'citizens' are synonymous terms . . . They are what we familiarly call the 'sovereign people,' and every citizen is one of this people, and a constituent member of this sovereignty."[60] That sounds like an endorsement of democracy. But Taney next said, "The question before us is, whether [the enslaved] . . . compose a portion of this people, and are constituent members of this sovereignty? We think they are not, and that they are not included, and were not intended to be included, under the word 'citizens' in the Constitution, and can therefore claim none of the rights and privileges which that instrument provides for and secures to citizens of the United States."[61] Douglass's rebuttal again turned to the text of the founding documents to identify democratic protections for equal rights. The Declaration of Independence declared that all men were created equal—not just white men. The Constitution's preamble begins with the immortal credo "We the People," an inclusive phrase that does not distinguish based on race. Just as it mentions slavery zero times, it never references the race of any person or group.[62] As Douglass emphasized, it does not say "We the White People."

What good, however, was Douglass's interpretation of the Constitution as an inclusive democratic document, no matter how well-argued,
if the Supreme Court had officially rendered it proslavery? Wasn't the
court the authoritative reader of the document, while he was a mere
escaped enslaved person? Douglass viewed the suggestion that only public officials could interpret the document as lunacy—the court didn't
have the right interpretation of the Constitution's view of slavery just
because they wore judicial robes; nor did the president simply because
he'd been elected: "To fling away [rights against slavery] because James
Buchanan is President, or Judge Taney gives a lying decision in favor of
slavery, does not enter into my notion of common sense."[63] In the previous century, newspaper editors resisted President Adams's interpretation of the Constitution, and now Douglass fought against Buchanan
and Taney's understanding, demanding his own rights as a citizen
reader. Under *Dred Scott*, according to the court, Douglass lacked the
status of citizenship and was excluded from the sovereign body of "We
the People." But as Douglass saw it, the document itself provided him
the authority to speak and to be treated as an equal citizen, a member of
a promised but never realized racially inclusive democracy. As a citizen,
he could claim the rights the Supreme Court had failed to recognize.

Douglass's simultaneous defense of the Constitution and attack on
Dred Scott was echoed by free Black people in the North. In conventions in Ohio, Boston, and New Bedford, free Black people attempted
to reclaim constitutional promises against *Dred Scott*. These citizens
asserted their constitutional rights like Douglass had, assailing *Dred
Scott* as illegitimate. A convention, chaired by John Mercer Langston, a
later longtime Douglass ally and collaborator, met in Ohio and passed a
resolution that was a clear rebuke to *Dred Scott*, declaring that the convention was formed in accordance with "the right to assemble and petition
for a redress of grievances," calling attention to their First Amendment
rights. It set the fee for attendees at fifty cents and declared that if *Dred
Scott* was the "law of the land," then "colored men are absolved from all
allegiance to a government which withdraws all protection."[64]

Attendees at a Boston convention came from all over New England
and as far as Pennsylvania, Illinois, and Canada. After singing a rous-

ing hymn about making the "fettered bondman free," attendees created a committee on "permanent organization." "Throngs" came
through the door. The president of the convention, George Downing,
a crucial abolitionist ally of Douglass, presided from a stand "graced
with elegant bouquets." The convention resolved that *Dred Scott* was
"marked by a brutality of spirit, a daring disregard of all historical
veracity, a defiant contempt of State sovereignty, a wanton perversion
of the Constitution of the United States in regard to the rights of
American citizens."[65] These conventions showed that Douglass's voice
was not alone—and Douglass amplified his allies by publishing an
extensive record of the Boston proceedings and other Black conventions. As Douglass's message about the Constitution reverberated
in these conventions, a constitutional constituency that sought to
reclaim the promises they read in the Declaration of Independence
and the preamble of an inclusive democracy was being born. This
constituency was threading a needle. They were seeking to reclaim
a document that had long been thought to countenance slavery in
defense of a yet unseen multiracial democracy. In their efforts to
reclaim the Constitution, Douglass and his allies looked backward,
insisting the text of the eighteenth-century document protected their
rights, despite *Dred Scott*; they also looked forward, attempting to
craft a different future in which Black people were both legal persons
and equal citizens under law.

★ ★ ★

THE GARRISONIANS THOUGHT DOUGLASS'S RESPONSE to *Dred Scott* showed complicity with slavery. By defending the Constitution, and arguing within its
framework, they charged, Douglass lacked the radicalism appropriate to
the moment. While the Garrisonians despised slavery, they thought the
Constitution endorsed it, so the decision by the Supreme Court, they
reasoned, was correct. Whether Douglass liked it or not, the Constitution was, for the time being, officially proslavery.

Douglass rejected the assertion that the Constitution could not be
saved. He also demonstrated by example that the Garrisonians were

wrong about his lack of radicalism. While the current situation was untenable, he believed tearing up the Constitution would make matters worse. "Mr. Garrison and his friends have been telling us that, while in the Union, we are responsible for slavery; and in so telling us, he and they have told us the truth. But in telling us that we shall cease to be responsible for slavery by dissolving the Union, he and they have not told us the truth," he argued.[66] Instead of abandoning the document, the right step was action to make the Constitution consistent with its deep principles.

Far from a compromising moderate, Douglass was a radical, emboldened by his vision of what rights Black people already were entitled to under the law. He attempted to marry his pro-Constitution vision with an agenda of radical action—an agenda symbolized by his friendship with John Brown.

An itinerant businessman bursting with moral fervor, Brown was a prominent antislavery crusader, inspired to action by his Christian faith. His approach to violence is summed up with the last note he wrote before his execution: "I, John Brown, am now quite certain that the crimes of this guilty land will never be purged away, but with blood."[67] Blood is what helped Brown cement his reputation as one of America's most radical abolitionists.

In 1854, Congress passed the Kansas-Nebraska Act—another attempted compromise—that allowed the eponymous territories to decide for themselves whether they would be a free or slave state. Aware of the crucial stakes for the future of slavery, Brown and his family moved to Kansas to help the antislavery forces. The political conflict turned into years of bloodshed that came to be known as Bleeding Kansas. By 1857, proslavery forces organized and, thanks to a boycott of the vote by free-state Kansans, passed a proslavery state charter known as the Lecompton Constitution. Its most prominent supporter was President Buchanan, backing the measure over the objections of Democrats such as Stephen Douglas from Illinois, who thought the measure violated popular sovereignty, which was part of Buchanan's supposedly moderate approach to slavery.[68] Buchanan's secret support of the *Dred Scott* ruling was his first contribution to constitutional crisis; his endorsement of the Lecompton Constitution was his second. Here again, the president showed his supposed moderation was a lie. In claiming to respect "popular sovereignty," and a state's right to decide for itself whether or not to allow slavery, the president was usurping the role of Congress in regulating the national spread of slavery. But he went further in acting to protect the institution, intervening for Kansas's proslavery referendum despite its lack of popular support.[69] Unlike his role in *Dred Scott*, here there was no hiding his true colors; Douglass had been right all along to call Buchanan a proslavery president. While Buchanan promoted the Lecompton Constitution as evidence of "popular sovereignty," for Douglass, the federal Constitution offered a deeper, more meaningful idea of democracy, one guaranteeing equal citizenship for Black people.

Was Douglass's commitment to an inclusive racial democracy as weak as the Garrisonians had claimed, given his attachment to the Constitution? The answer would come in the form of John Brown.

After losing his son to the violence of Bloody Kansas, John Brown left Kansas. His subsequent arrival in Rochester put Douglass's radicalism to the test. Brown found aid and comfort from Douglass and his family, boarding at his house. There, as both men reckoned with the fallout from *Dred Scott* and Bloody Kansas, Brown plotted his most ambitious act of resistance yet.[70]

For years, Brown had fought against proslavery forces in Kansas. Most famously, in response to an attack on the free-state settlement of Lawrence by proslavery troops, Brown and his men killed five proslavery men outside of their homes. Douglass said it was "a terrible remedy for a terrible malady," suggesting some sympathy with Brown.[71] After Kansas, Brown began to design a plot that would liberate Virginia from slavery—a massive undertaking, likely involving huge numbers of men, munitions, and logistical coordination.

Douglass took an active, albeit secondary, role in helping Brown. He served as a de facto banker, receiving donations for the insurrection plot that he channeled to Brown.[72] Meanwhile, much of Brown's planning took place around Douglass's meal table, where the men deliberated about strategy, looking over maps and plans. Brown had even written a constitution to govern former slave states once they had been liberated. Douglass's support for Brown echoed one of his earlier pro-Constitution arguments: the Constitution guaranteed that each state shall have a republican form of government, with which slavery was fundamentally incompatible.[73]

Douglass had misgivings, however. For one, Brown settled on Harpers Ferry, Virginia, a federal arsenal, as his main attack point. Transporting slaves out of Virginia was one thing; attacking the federal government was another. Thinking Brown's raid a suicide mission, Douglass advised against it on strategic grounds, refusing to participate.[74] Brown pressed ahead, and the raid failed dramatically. When President Buchanan received word that Brown seized the federal armory and military personnel in Harpers Ferry, he ordered Robert E. Lee, who lived nearby, into service. Lee's marines and local militia killed ten of Brown's men and captured Brown, who was tried for treason and hanged.[75]

Brown's attempted insurrection left Buchanan enraged; it confirmed his belief that Northern agitators, not Southern slaveholders, were the true threat to constitutional democracy. Perhaps Buchanan couldn't see—or simply didn't want to see—that his interventions in *Dred Scott* and Kansas pushed men like Brown and Douglass toward radical action. Whatever the reason, like all paranoid and powerful men, Buchanan endorsed a crackdown. When Virginia governor Henry Wise issued a warrant for Douglass's arrest, charging Douglass as Brown's co-conspirator, Buchanan evidently backed the effort. Federal marshals soon appeared in Rochester to arrest Douglass.[76]

Just days following Brown's raid, after receiving word that the New York lieutenant governor was prepared to assist Governor Wise in capturing him, Douglass fled Rochester with the aid of his friends, Amy and Isaac Post. Douglass and the Posts traveled to Lake Ontario, where he boarded a ferry to Canada. When the marshals arrived in Rochester, they discovered they were too late. America's greatest constitutional interpreter had fled the country.

Douglass went to Canada West, in what is present-day Ontario, while his family remained in Rochester, which added to the anguish

of his exile. Douglass was no longer a fugitive slave, since British abolitionists purchased his freedom after he had escaped enslavement.[77] Now,
however, he was a fugitive of another sort, running again from the law,
accused of conspiring with Brown.[78]

Douglass's exile would prove symbolic. The nation now not only
disregarded and betrayed the values of the Constitution but also disregarded him. In a farewell message to the United States, published in the
Rochester Democrat and American, Douglass vowed never to be "caught
by the hounds of Mr. Buchanan."[79] He planned to return, he declared,
when he and Buchanan were on "equal terms."

Douglass felt unsafe in Canada West, fearing he might be kid-
napped. In November 1859, he boarded a steamboat bound for England,
where he would be "beyond the reach of Buchanan's power and Virginia's prisons."[80] He stayed until the spring of 1860, using his time in exile
to study and to disseminate his antislavery understanding of the Constitution.[81] In lectures, Douglass argued it was not enough to push for
emancipation or "equal protection" of the law. Black people must claim
their right to vote under the federal Constitution, a right that offered
the best hope of equal citizenship, and which he believed the Constitution already legally promised.[82] For Douglass, a democracy with only
white voters failed to realize the meaning of "We the People."

Douglass quietly returned to Rochester in spring 1860 to mourn the
death of his daughter. Although he felt safe enough to come back to the
United States and return to public speaking, he remained pessimistic
that American democracy would ever recover from the Buchanan presidency. While the federal constitutional right to vote remained prominent in his speeches, pragmatic strategy recommended he first focus
on local reform in Northern states like New York. As such, he focused
on passing a ballot initiative ridding New York of an onerous property
requirement for voting that applied to Black residents but not white
ones. The New York ballot initiative failed, disheartening him.[83] Moreover, Douglass was not willing to follow his fellow abolitionists who
had thrown their support to another non-abolitionist candidate, Abraham Lincoln. While Lincoln had earned fame for speaking out against

Dred Scott, his approach differed in what seemed an order of magnitude from Douglass's. True, Lincoln's antislavery credentials ran deeper than Buchanan's, but Lincoln's position was too tepid; he still did not advocate for Congress to end slavery nationally and saw no constitutional obligation for it to do so. He even doubted that Congress had the power to abolish slavery in the states where it existed. Although he'd narrowly avoided imprisonment by the previous president, Douglass knew his voice was powerful. While he pledged to support Republicans in the election, thinking them the most practical way forward for his antislavery agenda, he also wrote "I cannot support Lincoln" and voted for a radical minor party abolition candidate.[84]

Still, in a four-way race that saw candidates divided over slavery, Abraham Lincoln—a largely untested politician, a former Illinois congressman and now the face of the nascent Republican Party—won the electoral college. The gulf between the two men's views on slavery led Douglass to a healthy skepticism of the new president. But the next four years sparked an evolution of Lincoln's constitutional thinking toward the thinking of Douglass's, a change that forever altered our understanding of the American Constitution and the structure of our democracy.

★ ★ ★

BUCHANAN PRESENTED HIMSELF AS following in the mold of George Washington—upholding the Constitution, by which he meant implementing decisions of the court. As Buchanan saw it, the Constitution required a president to lead by minimizing disagreement and sectional tension over slavery. Even on his own terms, however, Buchanan was a failure. He did not simply seek to influence the law. He secretly sought to nationalize slavery.

Buchanan's flaw runs deeper than his duplicity. His major mistake is his understanding of the meaning of the Constitution. By reading the document as a plain legal instrument, Buchanan let the court try to rob it of legitimacy. As Douglass had shown, the first three words of the preamble, "We the People," were meant to provide the source of its power and its purpose: democracy. While a Constitution that was read so narrowly that it would rob Black people of citizenship and personhood might have the veneer of democracy given that it empowered many white voters, it rendered the almost four million enslaved Black people of the United States, and a further five hundred thousand free Black people, subordinates to the white population. Such a system of racial oligarchy failed to provide the government Douglass thought the preamble promised.

Douglass's reading of the document as imbued with a moral promise offered not just a destination, but an outline for a way to recover from the crisis Buchanan and the court created. During Adams's presidency, the Democratic-Republican newspaper editors responded to the president's aggression by pushing the country toward democracy. Douglass was following a similar playbook. He used his status as a fugitive to galvanize a democratic constitutional constituency through his speeches and writings. And like the editors before him, he soon used that leverage to seek support from the next president, prodding him to accept equal citizenship for Black people. The multiracial democracy Douglass sought was well beyond the more basic right to dissent. Still, Douglass drew upon that first democratic pillar as he spoke and wrote against Buchanan, seeking to create from it a wider foundation for democracy. Taken together, these different democratic constitutional constituencies were reclaiming the promises of "We the People," fighting back against two presidents' anti-democratic understandings of the founding document.

Douglass was a patriot, though not a dewy-eyed one. From abroad, he spoke bitterly of the contradiction between ideals of freedom and the practice of slavery in his country.[85] That irony juxtaposed the promise of an inclusive "We the People" with its opposite: the institution that enslaved millions of Black Americans. Buchanan's presidency brought that contrast into inescapable light. A Constitution that promised equality, supposedly guided by reason, was being used by the court and the president to justify the depravity of slavery. War, it was increasingly clear, would be necessary to resolve those contradictions. Writing of the repeated small insurrections that enslaved people waged against their masters, Douglass had already presaged the fight to come:[86]

> *The fire thus kindled, may be revived again;*
> *The flames are extinguished, but the embers remain;*
> *One terrible blast may produce an ignition,*
> *Which shall wrap the whole South in wild conflagration.*
> *The pathway of tyrants lies over volcanoes*
> *The very air they breathe is heavy with sorrows;*
> *Agonizing heart-throbs convulse them while sleeping,*
> *And the wind whispers Death as over them sweeping.*

CHAPTER 5

Abraham Lincoln and Frederick Douglass

The Transformation of a President

AMID A SEA OF WHITE, TWO BLACK FACES STOOD OUT, SEEKING ENTRY. EARLIER IN THE DAY ON March 4, 1865, a jubilant, multiracial crowd in Washington, DC, had witnessed President Lincoln's second inaugural address. That evening, onlookers gathered at the president's mansion for the official presidential reception, where members of the public were welcomed. Strangers filed into the president's house to give their congratulations. But police stopped two individuals, Frederick Douglass and his companion, the Philadelphia abolitionist Louise Dorsey, at the door.[1] They were informed that people of color were not allowed at this reception, and with faux politeness shown the way to a temporary exit passage. Douglass did not budge, protesting that he had a right to be there—even that his presence was desired. During the dispute, a passerby recognized Douglass, who, wielding his fame, asked the passerby to tell the president that Frederick Douglass was being detained at the door. Soon after, Douglass found himself inside the mansion, in the East Room. As Douglass later wrote in his autobiography, he found President Lincoln standing tall like a "mountain pine" above the others in the room. Lincoln recognized Douglass on sight and exclaimed loudly so no visitor would miss it, "Here comes my friend Douglass."[2] Taking him by the hand, Lincoln said, "There is no man in the country whose opinion I value more than yours."

Lincoln's gesture of welcome is well known—not because of Lincoln's generosity, but because it was utterly unthinkable just a few years earlier. It had been some five long years since Douglass had fled to Canada and England, living abroad as an exile and hunted by President Buchanan. When the opening shots of the Civil War were fired in the spring of 1861, Douglass, back in Rochester, again took the helm of his newspaper, now called *Douglass' Monthly*. He had a new target, the supposedly moderate President Lincoln. In one fall 1862 editorial, he called Lincoln and his administration "characteristically foggy" and "remarkably illogical."[3]

Throughout the war, the two often clashed—about "voluntary expatriation," the Fugitive Slave Act, and the role of the president in ending slavery. When Lincoln announced he would run for president in 1860, Douglass vacillated between cautious support and skepticism, simultaneously explaining that he could not vote for Lincoln[4] and promising to campaign for the Republican ticket (on which Lincoln was at the top). Douglass thought Lincoln's party's commitment to ending slavery was "tolerable."[5] After Lincoln's election, that skepticism grew to outright criticism as Douglass publicly lambasted the president for refusing to clearly oppose slavery or to recognize that the war should aim to end it. That criticism later turned to persuasion as Lincoln's term unfolded, and Douglass transformed from outside critic to internal confidant, counseling the president privately in the president's mansion. Lincoln, not yet the Great Emancipator, changed his mind in dramatic ways, due in large part to Douglass.

Lincoln's presidency marks an evolution toward Douglass's understanding of the Constitution and a recovery from the Buchanan presidency, albeit an incomplete one. Douglass influenced Lincoln's change of heart, meeting with him and offering criticisms that Lincoln tracked and sought to answer. Through it all, Douglass claimed that Lincoln paid him such heed because Douglass served as a de facto representative of Black America. Douglass, of course, couldn't be a formal representative of Black America because no enslaved Black people and few free Black people could vote. But Douglass strategically used his leadership position to promote the uncompromising idea that "We the People" meant full membership in the American polity, equal citizenship, and a constitutional right to vote. His readers and listeners became a democratic constitutional constituency on whose behalf he lobbied a president who was originally skeptical of him and his constitutional mission. In the process, Douglass forever changed not just Lincoln's constitutional understanding but the course of American democracy. But first the nation would delve deeper into the crisis ignited by Buchanan.

★ ★ ★

AT THE OUTSET OF THE CIVIL WAR, Lincoln would never have called Frederick Douglass "my friend." Long before Lincoln became America's most lauded president, widely credited with ending slavery, he held a range of views, at times muddled, about the constitutionality of the institution. Like Buchanan, Lincoln said he believed slavery was wrong. But, also like Buchanan, he divorced this moral sensibility from his understanding of the law.

Lincoln in 1864 described himself as "naturally anti-slavery," and said that he could not "remember when I did not so think, and feel."[6] In 1841, as a state representative in Illinois, Lincoln, when reflecting on witnessing the sale of twelve enslaved people, noted the cruelty of slavery.[7] After being elected as a Whig congressman in 1846, Lincoln drafted a bill to emancipate enslaved people in the District of Columbia, while compensating their former owners.[8]

Although Lincoln distinguished the law and morality of slavery, he broke with Buchanan in response to *Dred Scott*. Lincoln fiercely denounced *Dred Scott*, claiming it wrongly decided and fearing that it would legalize slavery nationwide. He said it desecrated the Declaration of Independence.[9] During his famous debates against Stephen Douglas, as the two campaigned for the US Senate in 1858, Lincoln claimed to represent those "who contemplate slavery as a moral, social and political evil."[10] And in 1860, as he prepared to run for president, Lincoln declared that the founders believed slavery to be wrong and intended for it to ultimately be eliminated—even partially echoing Frederick Douglass's argument that the Constitution omitted the mention of slaves on purpose to exclude "the idea that there could be property in man."[11]

Unlike Douglass, however, Lincoln never said outright that slavery was unconstitutional, even as the Civil War was underway. In his first inaugural address, Lincoln insisted that he had "no lawful right" to interfere with slavery.[12] Writing in 1862 to Horace Greeley, the antislavery editor of the *New-York Tribune*, Lincoln distinguished between his "oft-expressed *personal* wish that all men everywhere could be free" and his "*official* duty" to follow whichever course best preserved the United States, whether ending slavery or preserving it.[13] Accordingly, when one of his Union generals emancipated the slaves of Missouri rebels without first seeking his permission, Lincoln publicly overruled him, softening the edict so that it would only apply to slaves who were forced to fight for the Confederacy.[14] Even as late as 1864—when Lincoln declared that "if slavery is not wrong, nothing is wrong"—he wrote in the very same letter that he "never understood that the Presidency conferred upon me an unrestricted right to act officially" on his antislavery views.[15]

What, then, unified Lincoln's philosophy around slavery? In the 1862 letter to Greeley, Lincoln clarified his priority: "My paramount object in this struggle *is* to save the Union and is *not* either to save or to destroy slavery," he wrote. "What I do about slavery ... I do because I believe it helps to save the Union."[16] As Lincoln saw it, Article II of the Constitution obligated the president to execute the law, not make it.[17] Before *Dred Scott*, Lincoln believed that Congress could limit slavery in the federal territories and Washington, DC, even if it could not interfere within states that protected it. After the decision, even though he believed it was "erroneous" and encouraged a future court to "overrule" it, he felt that as president he needed to abide by the Court's holding, albeit in the narrowest possible sense. Lincoln did agree that he was bound to enforce the Fugitive Slave Act, as Buchanan eagerly did. In the war's first two years, Lincoln's official policy reflected his belief that slavery was wrong, but that the Constitution protected it in some respects.

The origins of this view—feeling conflicted about slavery, but resolute about the need to keep the United States together and enforce even its immoral laws—can be glimpsed twenty years prior, in a speech Lincoln gave to the Young Men's Lyceum of Springfield, Illinois. Delivered in January 1838 when he was a state legislator, Lincoln warned in precise detail how the United States might one day collapse. The address is one of the most famous in American history. Few Americans, however, know the address was prompted by two brutal lynchings.[18]

In St. Louis, on April 28, 1836, Francis McIntosh, a free Black American man, was abruptly accosted by two policemen. When a scuffle ensued, one of the policeman died. McIntosh was taken to the jail, where a white mob forced him out, chained him up, and lit him aflame. No one was prosecuted.[19] A newspaper editor, Elijah Lovejoy, later wrote about the lynching, condemning the racist violence. The following year, on November 7, 1837, Lovejoy, too, was murdered.[20]

Perhaps because he was a celebrity and perhaps because he was a white man, Lovejoy's murder shocked the nation. Former president John Quincy Adams called it "an earthquake."[21] When a young John Brown learned the news of the murder, he declared: "Here, before God, in the presence of these witnesses, from this time I consecrate my life to the destruction of slavery."[22]

About three months after the Lovejoy murder, and just eighty-five miles from the murder site, Lincoln addressed the Lyceum crowd in Springfield. He fiercely condemned the McIntosh lynching and several others like it, not in the manner of John Brown's pronouncement that slavery was an offense to God, but because such acts destroyed the rule of law. So long as mobs were free to "shoot editors, and hang and burn obnoxious persons at pleasure, and with impunity," Lincoln warned, "this Government cannot last."

Unlike Buchanan, who viewed *abolitionists* as the sowers of discontent, Lincoln saw slavery as the root of a growing national lawlessness. This lawlessness, Lincoln warned, could one day prompt a tyrant—a new "Napoleon," an American "Caesar"—to seize total power and over-throw the republic, much as what happened in ancient Rome. To con-clude, Lincoln proposed this collapse could be avoided by cultivating a "political religion" that called for "reverence for the constitution and laws." Such "reverence" for the rule of law would not be occasioned by impassioned ecstasy (read: John Brown), but by "reason—cold, calculat-ing, unimpassioned reason."[23]

The Lyceum address is famous because it is a window into Lincoln's mind when he ran for president, more than two decades later. Lincoln's reverence for reason led him to denounce *Dred Scott* as a calamity—but also to abide by the decision as the current law of the land, as he would "offer no resistance" to the specific holding.[24] Similarly, Lincoln's devotion to the law, even when wrong, illuminates why he enforced the Fugitive Slave Act. He did not want to risk becoming a Caesar, a tyrant. Accepting the presidential nomination for the Republican Party in 1860, Lincoln explained his nuanced view that slavery was wrong but legal and that he did not have unilateral executive authority to abolish it.

Not surprisingly, Lincoln's view worried many abolitionists. For all Lincoln's attempts to carve out a moderate position on the consti-tutionality of slavery, what little was left of the Liberty Party mounted a campaign among a crowded field to run against him. Frederick Dou-glass, while ultimately endorsing the Republican ticket, cast essentially a protest vote for the Liberty Party candidate, Gerrit Smith, over Lin-coln, reflecting his caution about Lincoln's position.[25] That might have been because Lincoln's moderation somewhat resembled Buchanan's (despite their major differences) in distinguishing between what the law required and what morality required. That was a far cry from Doug-lass's understanding of a Constitution that was morally and practically opposed to slavery and devoted to inclusive democracy. While "tolera-ble," the position was nothing like what Douglass sought in a president: respect for Black people as equal citizens, who were entitled to the fran-chise and legal equality.

Lincoln's various accommodations to slavery were enough to keep Douglass from voting for him, but his accommodations were not enough to appease proslavery forces. When Lincoln won the four-way contest in 1860, he became the first formally antislavery candidate ever elected president—instantly prompting cries from Southern state governments to secede from the United States. They soon did, and before Lincoln's hand touched the inaugural Bible on March 4, 1861—and with James Buchanan still president—seven states broke their compact with the United States and left the union.[26]

The crisis of secession tested the limits of Lincoln's "political religion." Could he win the looming war and still stay true to the law—including the specific legal guarantees written in the Constitution? Secession had fulfilled Lincoln's first prediction—that slavery's defenders would force a crisis of lawlessness. The war and chaos that resulted would together test whether Lincoln could prevent his second prediction: the rise of an American Caesar. Would he need to become the dictator he feared so as to save the document he revered and the nation it bound? As Lincoln grappled with that question, he would also face an equally important question about the meaning of the Constitution: Was this thing he struggled to save merely a rational legal document? Or did it, as Douglass had long contended, have a deeper moral commitment to the equality of persons and to multiracial democracy?

On April 12, 1861, the South fired the first shots of the Civil War, when Confederate forces attacked the Union-held Fort Sumter in South Carolina. Lincoln had been president merely a month. Suddenly, with little military experience, he had to lead the Union Army. While his generals scrambled to amass men and matériel, Lincoln also had to settle on a *philosophy* of the war. What, precisely, was the nature of the conflict?

Was the war about slavery? To the Confederacy, it was—despite a veneer of "state's rights" rhetoric to the contrary, slavery was front and center in many declarations of secession, including the so-called Cornerstone Speech by Alexander Stephens, the Confederacy's vice president.[27] For Lincoln, ending slavery could not be the main purpose of the Union cause, because some slave states had not seceded, and he saw a strategic need to keep them in the Union. Instead, he settled on viewing the war as a domestic insurgency. Defining it this way,

Lincoln took pains to demonstrate that the war was about quashing insurrection—and not, as Confederates believed, a Northern attempt to end slavery.

An early test of Lincoln's war philosophy came during the conflict's first year, caused by the Union general John Frémont. A fierce abolitionist with a history of disobeying orders, Frémont, in 1856, had preceded Lincoln as the Republican Party's first nominee for president. Frederick Douglass endorsed Frémont then because he believed he would act to curb slavery. In 1861, Lincoln dispatched Frémont to Missouri—an indispensable Union state where slavery remained legal—to take command of the Department of the West. There, while fighting Confederate rebels, and without warning, Frémont declared martial law and issued a military decree that all slaves in Missouri owned by Confederates were henceforth emancipated. Frémont's order caused panic in Washington. Terrified the decree would induce Missouri and Kentucky to secede, Lincoln ordered Frémont to rescind the edict. Frémont refused. Lincoln then publicly modified the emancipation decree himself, and soon fired Frémont, who Lincoln lamented "should not have dragged the Negro into [the war]."[28]

The Frémont affair left Douglass disillusioned. Pragmatic, principled, and no stranger to military strategy—qualities that helped him foresee the tactical folly of Harpers Ferry—Douglass understood Lincoln's strategic imperative to retain Missouri. But in firing Frémont, Lincoln had signaled a disagreement not over his general's judgment, but over the war's purpose. While Frémont may have acted recklessly, Douglass thought Frémont understood something that Lincoln did not: the issue of slavery was the essence of the war itself. The tide would turn, Douglass wrote, only when the Union made the conflict a "moral" war, a transformation that only the president's war powers could bring about.[29] By using his military prerogative to proclaim emancipation, Frémont had done what Douglass hoped one day Lincoln might do. But Lincoln would sooner fire his generals, Douglass now saw, than acknowledge the war's most important cause.

The Frémont affair pushed Douglass to criticize Lincoln loudly and publicly. Writing in *Douglass' Monthly*, he lamented that Lincoln "seems to possess an ever increasing impassion for making himself appear silly and ridiculous."[30] From that moment on, Douglass became a fierce Lincoln critic. To Douglass, in stopping Fremont's emancipation proclamation, Lincoln showed he would "take advantage of any legal technicalities for arresting the cause of Emancipation, and the vigorous prosecution of the war against slaveholding rebels."[31] Between 1861 and 1862, Douglass's speeches and publications were rife with invective against the president. He even compared Lincoln to Confederate president Jefferson Davis. In a speech titled "The Reason for Our Troubles," Douglass wrote that Davis "seems ashamed to tell the world just what he is fighting for," while "Abraham Lincoln seems equally so, and is ashamed to tell the world what he is fighting against."[32] For Douglass, "our troubles" were due to both Lincoln and the Confederacy.

Douglass's criticism surely stung, or at least frustrated, Lincoln. Douglass was one of the most influential voices among the expanding antislavery electorate, and he was criticizing the president's handling of a war that Lincoln essentially needed to win to be reelected. And Lincoln disagreed with Douglass over how to read the Constitution. In Lincoln's view, *Dred Scott* was wrongly decided, but its direct holding still had the force of law. Moreover, Congress was empowered to end slavery through legislation or if need be, pass a constitutional amendment (contingent on state ratification), while the president could not simply flick his pen and declare slavery abolished through executive order. In Lincoln's philosophy of the war, the United States was still intact, and slavery was still the law of the land. To end slavery through executive order would be to become what Lincoln feared, an American Caesar— and give the Confederacy more justification to secede than slavery ever could, as such action would be genuinely unconstitutional.

Such talk infuriated Douglass, who viewed this "political religion" as hifalutin legalistic posturing meant to obfuscate Lincoln's cowardice on slavery. Worse, it was a misreading of the Constitution, which was not a raw legal document, but a document infused with moral values with the inclusive idea of a democratic people as its core principle. Douglass's anger was more than just personal disappointment: he had good reason to doubt Lincoln's sincerity about his constitutional justifications. In other areas of the war, Lincoln showed a concerted willingness—if not exactly enthusiasm—to behave like Frémont and take controversial measures to win. Lincoln was willing to read some provisions of the Constitution as dispensable when a higher purpose was served by doing so. To Douglass, that made Lincoln's claims that he couldn't abolish slavery suspect.

Exhibit A was Lincoln's treatment of John Merryman. Just days after the attack on Fort Sumter, Lincoln called for troop reinforcements, panicked that Washington might be invaded. Traveling by rail, infantry regiments had to pass through southern Maryland, an area teeming with Confederate sympathizers who began a frenzy of sabotage in an effort to delay the Union reinforcements. Lincoln's advisors urged him to use the military to arrest anyone disrupting troop movements. Such an order, however, would require the president to unilaterally suspend habeas corpus—the constitutional guarantee that a person not be arrested without lawful grounds for detention approved by a court. The Constitution states: "The Privilege of the Writ of Habeas Corpus shall not be suspended, unless when in Cases of Rebellion or Invasion the public Safety may require it." This provision is found in Article I, the section of the document that establishes the powers of the legislative branch—which suggests that Congress must authorize the suspension. But Congress was out of session. Faced with an impossible choice, Lincoln himself suspended habeas corpus in the area, and ordered his generals to arrest anyone suspected of sabotage. A wave of arrests followed.

One of those arrested was Merryman, a plantation owner and secessionist alleged to have cut telegraph wires and set fire to multiple railroad bridges. Merryman was detained at nearby Fort McHenry. Immediately, he filed a petition for a writ of habeas corpus, arguing that Lincoln's suspension was invalid. Just days after Merryman's capture, his case was heard by Chief Justice Taney of *Dred Scott* infamy. Taney granted Merryman's request, ordering the commanding general to produce Merryman for a hearing in court. The general refused, guided by Lincoln's view that the suspension of habeas corpus was valid and strategically critical, given that releasing saboteurs like Merryman could endanger the Union war effort. Enraged, Taney ruled that Lincoln had no authority to suspend habeas corpus without Congress and ordered the arrests to stop immediately. Again, Lincoln refused, and the arrests continued under his orders. His orders remained in effect until Congress sanctioned the measures two years later.

Exhibit B was how Lincoln handled political dissent. During the war, Lincoln's administration took action to suppress more than three hundred newspapers, seizing printing presses and arresting staff.[33] In 1862, federal agents arrested more than twelve prominent editors.[34] Another group of editors was rounded up and sent to military prison at Fort Lafayette, which earned the nickname the "American Bastille."[35] These editors almost never faced formal charges, meaning Lincoln again was defying the guarantee of habeas corpus.[36] Union troops and supporters also regularly threatened and burned opposition newspapers without reproach. These aggressive orders often came from cabinet members like William Seward and Edwin Stanton, with Lincoln's quiet approval; occasionally Lincoln even acted directly. In one memorable case, the *New York World* and the *New York Journal of Commerce* published false documents claiming Lincoln was soon calling for a new military draft. Lincoln thought these forgeries endangered the war effort, and he personally ordered the shuttering of the papers and the arrest of their editors.[37]

Exhibit C was the Lincoln administration's tactics against political opponents. More than 12,500 people were imprisoned during the war. In one case, one of Lincoln's generals imprisoned Clement Vallandigham, a former Democratic congressman from Ohio and a harsh critic of the administration. Vallandigham inveighed against "King Lincoln" and suggested that Lincoln should be impeached if the arbitrary arrests continued. General Ambrose Burnside brought soldiers to arrest Vallandigham in the middle of the night at his home, alleging Vallandigham had violated General Order No. 38: showing sympathy to the Confederate enemy. The judge, upholding Lincoln's order, denied Vallandigham's petition for habeas corpus.[38] He was quickly convicted by a military tribunal and imprisoned. Three days later, Lincoln exiled him to the Confederacy.[39]

Lincoln claimed to have made none of these decisions casually. Always, his rationale was tailored to a single argument, saving the United

States. In a speech before Congress, Lincoln defended his habeas decision by appealing to a bigger cause: What good would obeying habeas corpus do, he asked, if by doing so the Constitution that guaranteed it was destroyed by letting the union fall apart? "Are all the laws *but one* to go unexecuted, and the Government itself go to pieces lest that one be violated?" Lincoln was suspending rights now, he explained, to save "free government upon the earth" forever.[40] Later, he made the metaphor even more compelling: he faced a choice to cut off a "limb," a constitutional right, to save a "life"—the Constitution.[41]

From Douglass's point of view, however, these justifications reeked of hypocrisy. Lincoln was willing to disobey federal judges, shutter newspapers, and arrest political opponents. But when it came to dismantling slavery, suddenly, disobeying the law went too far. Lincoln claimed to suspend rights to save "free government." But there could *be* no free government in a United States with slavery, Douglass argued. Lincoln claimed to believe that there could be no "property in man" because the Constitution never once mentioned slavery. But the Constitution did mention habeas corpus—right in Article I—and Lincoln seemed willing to run roughshod over that. Lincoln was squeamish, on the other hand, about overruling a right to own slaves even though such a right was not expressly stated in the Constitution. The result was a blatant hypocrisy that Douglass called out in a speech in January 1862. On the one hand, Douglass said, "The great writ of habeas corpus is suspended from necessity, liberty of speech and of the press have ceased to exist. An order from . . . Lincoln sends any citizen to prison, as in England, three centuries ago." But on the other hand, while "the president was in favor of martial law," he "was not in favor of freeing [the rebels'] slaves." According to Douglass, this was the "secret of all our misfortune in connection with rebellion," as the president took radical extralegal action except on the issue where it mattered most.[42] For Douglass, Lincoln rightly thought presidential power expanded when the future of the United States was at stake, though wrongly refused to extend that power to guarantee a foundational democratic principle at the heart of the preamble, the rights of Black people to be equal citizens.

The last straw for Douglass came in 1862. Privately, Lincoln had begun to accept that the war was indeed about slavery—that he could either preserve the United States or preserve slavery, but not both. Yet still he resisted Douglass's call of "moral crusade." Sensing an opportunity to rid himself of the problem entirely, Lincoln advocated for a policy he had long considered: voluntary expatriation of African Americans to a new country, such as the Chiriquí region in what is now Panama. Far from embracing Douglass's idea that Black people were an equal part of "We the People," Lincoln called for people of color to leave the country. In August 1862, Lincoln invited a group of Black residents of Washington, DC, to the president's mansion to build support for the policy. As one historian put it, it was more of a "lecture" than a discussion.[43] He told the Black guests assembled: "The aspiration of men is to enjoy equality with the best when free, but on this broad continent, not a single man of your race is made the equal of a single man of ours."[44] The first Black delegation ever invited to the executive mansion was thus convened to discuss their own deportation. Douglass was enraged when he heard the news.[45] That Lincoln would even consider expatriation for Black people—the people who had built the very house he lived in—proved to Douglass that Lincoln didn't even view Black people as Americans, much less equal citizens. Railing against Lincoln, Douglass wrote, "In this address Mr. Lincoln assumes the language and arguments of an itinerant Colonization lecturer, showing all his inconsistencies, his pride of race and blood, his contempt for Negroes and his canting hypocrisy." Lincoln, Douglass concluded, was stoking white supremacist prejudice.[46]

Publicly, the relationship between Douglass and Lincoln could not have been further apart. However, soon after calling for voluntary expatriation, Lincoln must have seen the error of his ways. As Douglass biographer David Blight notes, Lincoln's rhetoric began to shift around this time, his speeches evolving to reflect Douglass's views.[47] The Lincoln of the Lyceum Address, that emphasized the legal limits on the presidency, became a president increasingly devoted to a new goal, emancipation unfettered by the narrow legalism that presidents like Buchanan had leaned on to reject bolder action.

Readers today can speculate about the causes of the change, which were likely multiple, as Lincoln bore the weight of leading the country's most gruesome conflict. Perhaps Lincoln was swayed by Douglass's argument that his willingness to suspend actual constitutional rights like habeas corpus while clinging to fake ones, like the rights of slaveholders, was hypocritical. The criticism of Lincoln's expatriation strategy from Douglass and others also might have led him to see that this plan was a fool's errand, not logistically possible, and certainly not embraced by many Black Americans. The fact that Douglass's criticisms of Lincoln were being published abroad in the UK, where that nation was still considering aiding the South in the war, might also have added pressure on a president concerned about international perceptions.[48]

For whatever reasons, by 1863, Lincoln had started transforming himself from an opponent of Douglass to a committed ally, with the president increasingly adopting Douglass's understanding that the Constitution was infused with a democratic commitment to the rights of Black Americans. On January 1, 1863, more than six hundred bloody days into the war, Lincoln issued the Emancipation Proclamation, declaring, in part, "All persons held as slaves within said designated States, and parts of States, are, and henceforward shall be free." The Proclamation was operative only in enemy territories of the Confederacy (though not in the border states). Lincoln embraced emancipation as a "fit and necessary war measure" to destroy the Confederacy, authorized and "warranted by the Constitution."[49] It also allowed Black Americans to enlist in the Union Army for the first time.

Against the measure's critics, who called it evidence the president was acting as a dictator, Lincoln defended the Proclamation using the same formulation he had with Greeley the year before, emphasizing the preservation of the United States. Only toward the end did he assert the moral imperative of ending slavery as the Proclamation's purpose. But under the surface of such rhetoric, Lincoln's intent was clear. While the Proclamation may read as a legal brief, by signing it, Lincoln upended for the first time the consensus that slavery could not have national resolution. After the Emancipation Proclamation, the national end of slavery began to seem inevitable. In this way, the Emancipation Proclamation achieved in large measure what Douglass had long advocated: infusing the war with its true moral purpose.

Douglass was stunned, then overjoyed, by Lincoln's decision. The normally loquacious orator did not give a speech, and instead joined those around him in singing a celebration song upon hearing the Proclamation would soon be official.[50] Even if Lincoln did not speak explicitly in Douglass's terms, the orator saw his call to infuse morality into the war reflected in the president's policy. Lincoln, no longer sounding like Buchanan, dispensed with the rhetoric that justified the Fugitive Slave Act. Douglass showed his approval of the new aim of the war by approving his two sons' decision to enlist in the Union Army.

His sons' enlistment, it turned out, sparked the events that began Douglass's in-person dialogues with Lincoln. Initially thrilled about the Proclamation, Douglass was despondent upon seeing the unequal treatment of Black soldiers within the Union Army. Shortly after their induction into the 54th Massachusetts Infantry Regiment, his sons Charles and Lewis learned their pay was less than that of white soldiers, an injustice that held true across the Union Army. Until this moment, Douglass would have done what he always did: sit at his mahogany desk, write an attack against Lincoln, and circulate it to his thousands of newspaper subscribers. But now a supporter of the war, Douglass changed his approach, seeking to appeal to Lincoln as an ally.

When he arrived at the president's mansion one morning in August 1863, Douglass was escorted directly into Lincoln's office. Accustomed to the formalities of the occasion, Douglass began to introduce himself, before Lincoln stopped him. "I know who you are, Mr. Douglass," said Lincoln with a smile. "I am glad to see you."[51]

On that familiar note, the two men began their first discussion about race in America. Douglass first pressed Lincoln on the issue of pay equity for Union soldiers. He was alarmed, too, at the treatment of Black soldiers who were taken prisoner. If Black prisoners of war were executed by the Confederates, he urged Lincoln to retaliate in kind, executing Confederate prisoners if the Confederate generals did not stop. This was a revealing request. Only a few years earlier, Douglass had distanced himself from John Brown's more violent modes of rebellion. The thought of his sons beyond enemy lines, however, had charged Douglass with new emotion—one that Lincoln, still agonizing over the premature death of his two sons, no doubt understood.

Lincoln acknowledged the pay disparity problem. He said that while Black soldiers should temporarily be okay with lower pay, they would receive equal compensation eventually. On Douglass's demand for executions, however, Lincoln pushed back. According to Douglass, Lincoln told him that killing Confederate soldiers likely would not deter them and might even escalate violence. More important, Lincoln said, he could not condone executing a man who had not himself directly committed the heinous act of execution, just to pay for the actions of his callous superiors. The rule of law, even in such a bloody conflict, must prevail.[52] Douglass disagreed then, though later reconsidered, seeing how Lincoln's reply reflected his deep humanity.

The dialogue and its conclusion illustrated why the meeting was monumental. For the first time in American history, a representative of Black America stood with the president as an equal, bargaining, making demands, and conceding points. Albeit unelected, Douglass was received by the president as a representative of the interests of Black soldiers and Black Americans generally. He stood before him as a leader of a democratic constitutional constituency, aspiring to represent the interests of the entire Black population, free and enslaved. And Douglass, having been admitted to the president's mansion and earning Lincoln's respect, leveraged the president's respect to advance democratic equality. Playing out in the president's mansion was the fundamental force of the push and pull of a president and a citizen, their argument emblematic of American democracy itself. The dialogue was evidence of an evolving recovery from the Buchanan presidency. While the previous president hunted Douglass for his criticisms, Lincoln received him as an interlocutor whose opinions he considered carefully. The relationship quickly bore fruit. Later that day, Douglass conferred with Secretary of War Edwin Stanton, a sign that the administration was taking Douglass seriously. As he departed the president's mansion, Douglass felt as optimistic as he ever had. Reflecting in a later autobiography, he believed "that the true course to the black man's freedom and citizenship was over the battle-field, and that my business was to get every black man I could into the Union armies. Both the President and Secretary of War assured me that justice would ultimately be done my race, and I gave full faith and credit to their promise."[33]

★ ★ ★

IN DOUGLASS'S MIND, the "justice" promised by Lincoln needed to go beyond abolishing slavery. While Lincoln had come partway to infusing the war with moral purpose, they still differed on that purpose. For Lincoln, it was increasingly about ending slavery. Douglass wanted more—an America where Black people had full constitutional equality. Necessary for that status was a guaranteed right to vote. Despite having been welcomed into the president's mansion and his initial enthusiasm for the Emancipation Proclamation, Douglass returned to his role as critic within months of their meeting. Douglass lectured on the "mission of the war" throughout the country. At a major stop in New York, Douglass told his audiences that Lincoln might agree to an armistice without a guarantee of equal citizenship, selling out the cause of abolition. To applause from the New York crowd, Douglass said Lincoln should only agree to a peace which "declares free the whole-colored race and which gives the freedmen of the South every civil and political right with their white brethren including the right to vote."[34] Douglass acknowledged that Lincoln had made "progress," but warned that abolition absent a full endorsement of Black suffrage would be "hollow" and "deceitful," far from the full equality emblazoned in the Declaration of Independence.[55]

In a letter to a British correspondent reprinted in the *Liberator* and British newspapers, Douglass was even harsher in his criticism of the president. He said Lincoln was involved in a "swindle by which our Government claims the respect of mankind for abolishing slavery." And a year after his initial meeting with Lincoln, the president had failed to provide Black soldiers equal compensation or to include them in prisoner exchanges. "The treatment of our poor black soldiers," he wrote, had "worn my patience quite threadbare." He believed Lincoln was essentially proposing to "hand the negro back to the political power of his master" at the end of the war.[56]

Lincoln was aware of and troubled by Douglass's criticism. In the summer of 1864, he met with his advisor, military chaplain[57] John Eaton—who later played a major role in Reconstruction during the Grant administration—to better understand Douglass's views. Eaton had seen Douglass give the "mission of the war" lecture in Toledo, and the two men spoke in depth about where Douglass thought Lincoln had gone wrong. Eaton impressed on the president Douglass's demand for the franchise and his ongoing concerns about the treatment of Black soldiers. Lincoln responded by showing Eaton a letter he had written to the governor of what was at the time Union-controlled Louisiana in which he suggested suffrage for some Black soldiers. He wondered if Douglass had seen it, perhaps hoping that if he had not, Eaton should tell him about it. Lincoln then told Eaton that he regarded Douglass as "one of the most meritorious men in America," and asked Eaton to set up another meeting between Douglass and himself.[58]

In August 1864, the president invited Douglass to the president's mansion for a follow-up conversation, hoping to find common purposes.[59] Lincoln sought to quell domestic abolitionist dissent, and may have been aware that Douglass's stinging rebukes were appearing in British papers,[60] potentially pushing that country into supporting the South, risking Lincoln's belief that the emancipation "would help us in Europe." But if Douglass continued to insist the president wasn't sincere in seeking to abolish slavery, then Britain might agree, and, not having to choose sides in the moral conflict, might as well support their economic allies in the South, a major producer of cotton used in English textile mills. Regardless of which dangers he focused on, in deciding to make the case in person that their views were aligned, Lincoln clearly knew he needed to win over the famous Frederick Douglass.

In their second meeting, the president assured Douglass that he would not seek a premature peace conference that would stop short of ending slavery, and he complained about critics who were trying to move him in that direction. The meeting lasted longer than the scheduled time, and his secretary twice interrupted the president to remind him that Governor Buckingham of Connecticut was waiting for a meeting. Twice the president said he needed more time and asked his secretary to "tell Governor Buckingham to wait, for I want to have a long talk with my friend Frederick Douglass." This time, Douglass was both impressed and surprised by Lincoln's apparent commitment. Douglass noted a "deeper moral conviction against slavery" than Lincoln had expressed before. In Douglass's eyes, Lincoln's initial infusion of the slavery issue into the war as a pragmatic maneuver had evolved into a matter of principle. Lincoln even proposed that Douglass organize a group of African Americans to travel behind enemy lines into the South, alerting enslaved people of the Emancipation Proclamation and guiding them back North. Incredibly, given that the previous president had sought to prosecute Douglass for his association with John Brown, the current president indicated that he wanted Douglass to base this proposed mission on the Harpers Ferry raid.[61]

Was Lincoln sincere or trying to quell a critic? The test came when he asked Douglass about an open letter he had recently written to the South. In the letter, famously addressed "To Whom it may concern," Lincoln had conditioned the end of the war on the end of slavery.[62] Moderates were now pushing him to draft a new letter that would express a more general openness to a negotiated peace without demanding the end of slavery. Douglass objected that such a move would signal Lincoln was not sincere in the newly infused moral purpose of the war. Lincoln relented, scrapping the proposed letter, and choosing Douglass and his constituency over the moderates. The president's shift was as monumental as their historical first meeting. Not only did Douglass stand before Lincoln as the head of a democratic constitutional constituency, he had won an ally in the president, moving him toward his conception of equality. Here lay a mechanism once again of constitutional change. In the founding era, the editors had begun as outsiders, prosecuted by the Adams administration only to become insiders, embraced by Jefferson. Similarly, Douglass had also been sought for prosecution by the previous president; now, the current president was embracing him and adhering to his recommendations.

Douglass began a plan to enact the John Brown–style raid as requested. But he abandoned the plan when he saw the war was progressing rapidly, thinking it unnecessary. He had opposed the original John Brown raid, and perhaps suspected a similar strategy would not work this time either.[63] Still, the meeting and the president's trust in him altered his approach to Lincoln, and convinced him that for now his criticism of the president needed to end.[64] Douglass endorsed Lincoln for reelection, praising his sincerity in transforming the war into a fight against slavery.[65] He still had not promoted the full franchise for Black Americans, as Douglass noted, but there was progress. Douglass was fond of the metaphor that "peace will flow like a river, and our foundations will be the everlasting rocks." Lincoln was providing a foundation for a later, more ambitious realization of the Constitution's promise of equality that Douglass had long argued was at the document's core.

Lincoln's two most famous speeches, the Gettysburg Address and his second inaugural address, show a clear evolution from his initial view of the Constitution, as seen in his Lyceum Address. The influence of Douglass in this evolution is evident.

In Douglass's writings, the explicit equality-based principles of the Declaration of Independence should be read alongside implicit references to equality in the Constitution, and this parallel reading shows that slavery is banned by the Constitution. For instance, Douglass argued that the Constitution's ban on a "bill of attainder" banned a central idea of slavery that status was inherited through the mother and thus "the child is property because its parent was property." For Douglass, the morality of the Declaration of Independence was thus infused into the Constitution.[66] Lincoln never explicitly embraced Douglass's approach or fully endorsed merging the values of the Declaration of Independence and the Constitution in precisely the way Douglass advocated. But that link shines through in Lincoln's most famous speech, in which he brilliantly echoes Douglass in linking the preamble of the Constitution, which begins with "We the People," to the commitment to equality expressed in the Declaration of Independence.

On the site of the war's bloodiest battle, Lincoln arrived at Gettysburg, Pennsylvania, in November 1863 for a dedication ceremony of a battlefield memorial.[67] In his famously brief address, Lincoln began by implicitly changing the birth date of the country: not with the birth of the Constitution in 1787, but "fourscore and seven years ago"—the signing of the Declaration of Independence in 1776. In this way, the nation wasn't conceived in a charter of compromise, and certainly not conceived in Taney's proslavery history, but rather was "conceived in liberty, and dedicated to the proposition that all men are created equal." As Lincoln explained, the "great task remaining before" the country was no longer just to win the war. It was to make sure the country would realize its values—to ensure a "government of the people, by the people, for the people."[68] The Gettysburg Address was perhaps the most important statement ever made by a leader about the rule of law in a democracy. Lincoln never explicitly mentioned slavery in the Gettysburg Address. He didn't have to. Government "by" the people could now include Black people in the decision-making process. Government "for" the people would protect the fundamental rights of personhood and equality. And government "of" the people finally included in its definition of sovereign rulers a population that slavery had excluded. Thus, for the first time, a president adopted the Declaration's democratic principle of equality not simply as high rhetoric, but as the country's founding promise. The moment was all the more remarkable given that only a few years before, Lincoln had embraced the legalistic understanding that slavery was largely permitted by the Constitution. This moment marked a milestone in the complex relationship between Douglass and Lincoln; Lincoln had turned the tide toward Douglass's democratic reading of the Constitution, with equal citizenship at its core.

Lincoln's transformation deepened during his second inaugural address on March 4, 1865. Speaking from the steps of the Capitol before a massive crowd, Lincoln conveyed that slavery had always been the moral force underpinning the war. Many were uncertain what reunification with a defeated South would look like. Lincoln made clear that the war's conclusion would bring about the end of slavery, even if it hurt his party politically. On this position, Lincoln would not back down.[69] The prior peace could no longer be possible in a republic that allowed slavery. Looking on from nearby was Frederick Douglass. Once a slave, then a radical—and always an outsider—Douglass watched as his own understanding of the Constitution was endorsed before the nation on the presidential stage. Later that evening, Douglass would attempt entry to the inaugural gala—when Lincoln would override his guards to welcome "my friend Douglass." By now, he was.

In Lincoln's last public speech, on April 11, 1865, he addressed the need for a "reconstruction," which historian Eric Foner notes was a word known to connote a devotion to equality, as opposed to the more retrograde "restoration." Lincoln focused on why Louisiana must be readmitted to the United States. Although Louisiana seceded on January 26, 1861, Lincoln argued that the state had made progress in renouncing the values of the Confederacy, as was necessary to reenter the United States. He tried to hold Louisiana up as a model for other states that had seceded, praising it for enacting immediate abolition, giving the right to attend school "equally" to Blacks and whites, and supporting the proposed Thirteenth Amendment, which would formally end slavery after ratification by three-quarters of the states. Watching from the crowd, John Wilkes Booth reportedly remarked, "that means "n***** citizenship," and he promised to "put him through."[70] On the evening of April 14, 1865, Booth shot Lincoln in the head. The president died the next morning.

Lincoln had tied himself to the Thirteenth Amendment by signing it after Congress passed it before it was adopted by the states, even though the Constitution doesn't require a president to sign amendments. Historian Michael Vorenberg argues this showed Lincoln's conscious desire to forever tie the end of slavery to his legacy. Lincoln also famously worked with his aides to garner the necessary votes in the Senate to secure the passage of the amendment.[71] Lincoln, however, did not live to see its adoption, as the amendment was still being debated in state governments across the country when he was assassinated. In December 1865, the last of the required three-quarters of states ratified the amendment. Slavery was officially abolished in the United States.[72]

The amendment was structured in two parts. Section I ended "slavery" and "involuntary servitude" (with one exception, "as a punishment for crime").[73] Section II gave Congress "power to enforce this article by appropriate legislation." For all the attention appropriately given to Section I's rhetorical abolishment of slavery, it was Section II that would prove more important. It changed the balance of power under the Constitution. For nearly eighty years, the federal government had been limited in its ability to guarantee civil rights. *Dred Scott* had weakened that power further by eviscerating Congress's ability to limit slavery's growth, much less end it. Now, Congress was explicitly charged with the power and obligation to end all remnants of slavery and white supremacy—the "badges and incidents" of slavery—throughout the country.[74]

The promise of the Declaration of Independence, reiterated anew at Gettysburg, had now explicitly, albeit incompletely, been incorporated into the text of the amended Constitution. But amid the celebrations of the new amendment, Frederick Douglass found himself embroiled in a debate with his former mentor William Lloyd Garrison at the annual meeting of the American Anti-Slavery Society. Garrison argued that the Society should be disbanded in recognition of the ratification of the Thirteenth Amendment. To Douglass, the amendment and Lincoln's presidency had only been a middle point. White supremacy still reigned at the state level, and the federal government still fell short in its obligation to correct it. If local governments could still deny the franchise to Black people, slavery persisted, as "slavery is not abolished until the black man has the ballot."[75] The amendment had the promise of abolition, though had not yet achieved it. Elsewhere, Douglass used a metaphor that cements this point: "Protestants are excellent people, but it would not be wise for Catholics to depend entirely upon them to look after their rights and interests."[76] As Douglass saw it, legal rights conferred to Black people were not enough. Douglass insisted that the promise of the preamble was of full democratic citizenship, including an equal right to vote. Even with the new amendment, that promise was still far from realized.

* * *

THE RELATIONSHIP BETWEEN DOUGLASS AND LINCOLN exemplifies how a citizen can successfully prod a president to transform his constitutional understanding. Under pressure from Douglass and his democratic constitutional constituency, Lincoln's interpretation of the Constitution evolved from a focus on the rule of law to one that put a more inclusive understanding of a democratic people at its center. Lincoln, of course, was no mere passive receptacle of Douglass's ideas. Rather, it was the synthesis of these two great thinkers, deliberating together, that buried *Dred Scott* and its denial of legal personhood to Black people and birthed a Constitution that clearly prohibited slavery. According to Douglass, Lincoln's ability to deliberate with others made him "not only a great President, but a *Great Man*—too great to be small in anything."[77] That meant, unlike any president before him, he had a willingness to dialogue with a Black man, to respond to his concerns about what the Constitution required, and most of all to rethink his deeply held beliefs.

As Douglass saw it, this dynamic was possible because of Lincoln's personal respect for him. Yet, Douglass knew he was afforded an audience with the president not because he was a great constitutional and political thinker, but because he had gained the allegiance of many Black Americans. As Douglass put it, "I am quite sure that the main thing which gave me consideration with him was my well known relation to the colored people of the Republic, and especially the help which that relation enabled me to give to the work of suppressing the rebellion and of placing the union on a firmer basis than it ever had or could have sustained in the days of slavery."[78] Douglass used his fame, the support of his readers, and those who attended his lectures to convince Lincoln of the power of his constitutional ideas. The passage of the Thirteenth Amendment was a tangible result of this effort. Still, Douglass was not done yet. He set his sights on the franchise, the key to transforming a symbolic constituency into an actual constituency possessed with the power of the vote.

What should be said about Lincoln's willingness during the war to suspend habeas corpus and shut down free speech? Had he, in seeking to save the United States, created another constitutional crisis, destroying the hard-won freedoms that had defined the Madison recovery from Adams? The willingness to suspend democratic rights to save democracy is no doubt a dangerous precedent. Nixon would later cite Lincoln's suspension of civil liberties as evidence of expanded presidential power during times of crisis. Members of the Bush administration did the same after 9/11 to justify torture. But those comparisons were unfair. Douglass rightly saw that Lincoln faced a crisis incomparable to any other in American history. He also thought Lincoln's suspension of the rule of law didn't go far enough. He rightly sought to use Lincoln's willingness to shut down civil liberties as a lever for a more fundamental change: the end of slavery.

Despite Lincoln's eventual support for abolition, Frederick Douglass viewed Lincoln's legacy as imperfect. Douglass said Lincoln was a "white man's President," one who loved "the Union" more than he did its Black citizens and prioritized the interests of whites, leaving African Americans at best as his "step-children." But, Douglass continued, Lincoln's untimely death left to citizens the task of realizing a fuller democracy: "In doing honor to the memory of our friend and liberator, we have been doing highest honors to ourselves."

CHAPTER 6

Andrew Johnson versus Frederick Douglass

A New Threat in the Midst of Recovery

LINCOLN'S SECOND INAUGURAL ADDRESS, AN ELOQUENT STATEMENT OF EQUALITY UNDER LAW, offered a glimpse of what postwar America could be. But from the perspective of Frederick Douglass, the day of that speech also foreshadowed a dark turn. Before Lincoln spoke, a man had stumbled drunk onto the stage for his own swearing in: Vice President Andrew Johnson. When Johnson spoke, he ranted aimlessly and was so inebriated that he forgot the secretary of the navy's name and, at one point, kissed the Bible. Later, President Lincoln showed Johnson where Douglass was standing in the crowd. Douglass looked up to see Johnson leering at him, with an expression of "bitter contempt and aversion." Douglass was so perturbed that he concluded on the spot, "Whatever Andrew Johnson may be," he murmured to his friend, Louise Dorsey, "he certainly is no friend of our race."[1]

Lincoln chose Johnson as vice president for a simple, pragmatic reason: Johnson's Southern ties could be crucial to unify the union against the Confederacy, while as vice president, serving in a role that was largely powerless, his potential to cause damage would be slim. That calculus changed when Booth shot Lincoln at Ford's Theater—the night Douglass's fears came true. Johnson, sworn in as president on the morning of April 15, 1865, quickly revealed himself to be an unabashed white supremacist. In one of history's strangest ironies, the hard-won recovery from slavery that Lincoln had begun, and Douglass had worked to spark, was thrown into grave doubt by Lincoln's handpicked successor. Amid the recovery from the Civil War, Johnson's presidency emerged as a new threat to democracy. After the strides toward equal citizenship that Douglass and Republicans had made, they suddenly stood to lose everything. For Douglass to continue leading the fight toward equal citizenship for Black Americans meant overcoming a president devoted to reviving white supremacy. Johnson would test in real time whether a citizen-based recovery could succeed with a hostile president in power. And, since Douglass insisted that anything short of guaranteed political equality for Black people would continue slavery under a new name, Douglass and his constitutional constituency needed to battle not just the president but their supposed Republican allies in Congress. While Douglass had long sought to represent the interests of the enslaved, now things were different: the formerly enslaved could now speak for themselves, and this they did by joining Douglass in a series of Black conventions and strategizing how to make the promise of the preamble a reality.

★ ★ ★

JOHNSON'S IMPROBABLE RISE TO POWER BEGAN WHEN, as a young man working in a Tennessee tailor's shop, he discovered his talent for public speaking through stints in local government.[2] With no formal education, Johnson rose through the Democratic Party ranks by modeling Andrew Jackson, running vitriolic campaigns that harnessed contempt for the Southern aristocracy. But Johnson's idea of the common man was a racist one: he owned some eight slaves. Johnson believed Thomas Jefferson had meant only to include "the white race, and not the African race" in the Declaration's promise of equality. And like Taney, Johnson thought (before the Civil War) that the Constitution protected slavery.[3] When the Civil

War came, however, Johnson sided with the Union. He believed the Confederacy was a puppet of the aristocracy and would destroy democracy for poor white men, with whom he still identified despite his later wealth.[4] Johnson once said that if he ever became president, he would "see that [Confederates convicted of treason] suffer the penalty of law at the hands of the executioner."[5]

With the levers of presidential power at his disposal, Johnson began to enact the white supremacist "democracy" he had long envisioned. President Johnson could not overtly revoke the Thirteenth Amendment, which he supported when it was proposed and ratified. However, he could seek to ensure that the end of slavery did not entail equality for Black people, vetoing congressional efforts to legislate for civil rights. Johnson began his presidency with a bizarre attempt to court Black support, though soon looked the other way as Southern states passed laws aimed at undermining the rights of freedmen. And as his term developed, he more explicitly advocated white supremacy, seeking, as one friend put it, a "white man's government."[6]

When the Congress convened in December 1865, Republicans enjoyed a more than three-to-one majority, and they fought the Democratic president. Among them was Senator Charles Sumner of Massachusetts, who believed the Thirteenth Amendment opposed white supremacy beyond just slavery to eradicate all the badges and incidents of slavery that marked Black men as less than equal. In their view, even though Johnson was not trying to bring back antebellum slavery, the white supremacist policies of the president still violated the new constitutional provision. It also meant that Johnson failed his oath to preserve, protect, and defend the Constitution. To make good on their obligation to enforce the amendment, senators introduced a civil rights bill that would give ballast to the Thirteenth Amendment. This bill, which acted as the precursor to the Fourteenth Amendment, provided a definition of citizenship that included those newly emancipated, and affirmed the right to the "full and equal benefit of all laws."[7]

The proposed bill was a start, though Frederick Douglass lamented that it did not guarantee the franchise for Black people. Civil rights without the vote, as Douglass saw it, meant whites would continue to determine Black people's destiny. Douglass leaped into action, planning to lobby the president and Congress to guarantee the franchise. Douglass had convinced Lincoln to change constitutional course. Could he do the same with Johnson? Douglass had some cause to think Johnson wished to emulate Lincoln, insofar that Johnson had given a speech to Black people that indicated he would continue Lincoln's work and compared himself (in a bizarrely overblown way) to Moses in his desire to lead Black people out of bondage.

Whereas Douglass emerged as a singular symbolic leader of Black Americans in his meetings with Lincoln, he sought to represent this group more formally with Johnson. Absent the guarantee of the ballot, Douglass was unlikely to hold elected office, so he galvanized a movement that would press for full and equal citizenship. The groundwork had been laid in 1864, where in Syracuse, New York, Douglass had led a meeting of more than 140 delegates of a new organization that would advocate for suffrage for Black people. The newly dubbed National Equal Rights League[8] ratified a Declaration of Our Rights, which demanded that "all men are born free and equal; that no man or government has a right to annul, repeal, abrogate, contravene, or render inoperative, this fundamental principle."[9] At a September 1865 meeting in Cleveland, the League demanded that voting rights be granted to men of color in the Southern states, and resolved to support a new constitutional amendment to ban legislation that discriminated on the basis of race.

Douglass's effort to lobby for equal rights was bolstered by another parallel Black convention. In Boston in December 1865, Douglass spoke at the Convention of Colored People of New England, attended by his ally George Downing, who moved to admit Douglass as an honorary member. Downing's father had made his name running a New York restaurant frequented by the city's elite white families and politicians. Downing started his own restaurant, cultivating those customers and lobbying them for political favor. He then opened a catering and restaurant operation in Rhode Island, where Downing lobbied for integrated public schools in that state. The convention decided that Downing should lead a delegation to DC to lobby for "due respect for the entire colored people."[10]

Downing used his vast network, including his friendship with Senator Sumner, to secure a meeting on February 7, 1866, with Johnson in the president's mansion. He was joined by Douglass; his son Lewis Henry; John Jones, a former underground railroad leader;[11] and a handful of other African American leaders.[12] Douglass took the lead, turning to the topic of equal suffrage and setting a tone with the president to indicate that this was no mere meet-and-greet but a confrontation on behalf of a vast Black constituency who was demanding its constitutional right to vote. Douglass told Johnson that Black Americans needed the "ballot with which to save ourselves," and that without the vote, a Black person "is divested of all political power. He is absolutely in the hands of [his master]."[13] Slavery had legally ended, but Douglass's repeated use of the term *master* to refer to white Americans emphasized his long-held belief that without the franchise Black people would remain enslaved. The meeting could have not gone worse. Johnson, defiant and aggressive, gave a forty-five-minute lecture that left Douglass and the delegates little time to respond. He completely rejected giving Black people the franchise to vote, suggesting that it would lead to a "war of races."[14] Johnson even mused about the possibility of reviving repatriation[15] and also strangely sought credit for owning slaves but never selling one. He also reprised his self-comparison to Moses, making the supposed evidence of his allyship seem deeply ironic.

Douglass concluded by pledging to take his case "to the people." The meeting confirmed his worst fears: Johnson was hellbent on keeping Black people a subordinated class. Indeed, to Johnson, the real victims of the Confederacy were poor white people, who would be the real victims of emancipation in a world where Black people could vote. After the meeting, Johnson was said to have muttered to an aide: "Douglass; he's just like any other n*****, and he would sooner cut a white man's throat than not."[16]

The discussion with Johnson was recorded by the president's secretary, and Douglass made sure it was reproduced in newspapers nationwide, thereby expanding the constitutional constituency devoted to free and equal citizenship. Savvily, Douglass and Downing used the encounter to publicize the president's limited understanding of emancipation, hoping to open America's eyes to a stronger view of equal citizenship. As he had with Buchanan, Douglass again rallied support for a different understanding of the Constitution than the president's, using his public standing to challenge the officeholder. Then and now, Douglass didn't just publicize his arguments, he modeled that in a democracy, any American—even a formerly enslaved one—could go toe-to-toe with the chief executive debating the Constitution's meaning. Douglass and his democratic constitutional constituency had come a long way since his confrontation with President Buchanan before the war, but they still had a long way to go. Douglass made it clear to President Johnson that he and his supporters would settle for nothing less than full citizenship, including a guaranteed right to vote.

★ ★ ★

JOHNSON MADE KNOWN HE OPPOSED the interpretation of the Thirteenth Amendment sought by Douglass. Even the most expertly drafted constitutional amendment is vulnerable to a president who works to undermine it. The Thirteenth Amendment was particularly vulnerable, since it was written with a loophole—a "prisoner exception"—that legalized involuntary servitude as "punishment for crime." When the amendment was debated, the exception was included as a holdover from earlier legal abolitions of slavery in the territories controlled by Congress. Charles Sumner had proposed alternative language, sensing the dangerous role the prisoner exception might play in allowing slavery to be revived. But the strategic worry that the amendment might lose votes without the exception pushed him to let it go.[17] Southern states—which had to ratify the Thirteen Amendment to be readmitted into the union—saw the loophole and pounced. Passing laws called Black Codes, Southern states functionally re-enslaved African Americans, creating crimes of "vagrancy" under which former slaves could be arrested for lacking employment (which they couldn't get) or housing (which they couldn't find).[18]

The president, who had supported ratification of the amendment, knew that Southern states were using the prisoner loophole to reinstitute slavery by a different name. Johnson did nothing. Johnson's actions and statements revealed that he read the amendment narrowly, ending slavery but not white supremacy. Johnson endorsed readmitting the Southern states to the union rapidly, and—despite his earlier condemnation of Confederate traitors—he granted pardons and amnesty to many ex-Confederates in 1865. It was clear that Johnson's support for the union was never an endorsement of a multiracial democracy. When an extension on the original Freedmen's Bureau was sent to Johnson in February of 1866, he vetoed the bill as unnecessary, complaining that the government has never helped the "millions of the white race who are honestly toiling from day to day for their subsistence," implying a distinction between worthy whites and the unworthy freedmen the law would have helped. Congress failed to override Johnson's veto. Only after a more moderate version of the bill passed both chambers in July 1866—which again Johnson vetoed—did the House and Senate marshal the two-thirds majority required to override him.[19]

Johnson's clashes with Congress continued throughout 1866. A major conflict came with the proposed Civil Rights Act. In the spring, Congressional Republicans passed the act in what was then the country's most comprehensive effort on behalf of racial equality. The bill effectively overturned the Black Codes, explicitly established citizenship for freed Black people, protected property rights, and guaranteed "equal protection" of the laws. Johnson vetoed it. He doubted the newly freed slaves were qualified for the "privileges and immunities of citizenship" and worried that "the negro" would be privileged over more "intelligent" foreigners.[20] Nevertheless, Congress overrode Johnson's veto. For the first time ever, the United States had passed comprehensive civil rights legislation.

Congressional pushback against Johnson raised a new question in the push-and-pull of crisis and recovery: Could the recovery of the democratic ideals expressed in the Constitution continue against a president bent on using the same document to undermine them? The answer depended on Congress. The Radical Republicans faction in the body professed belief in equal citizenship, and although they opposed Johnson and would challenge him in an epic battle for the nation's future, they fell short of pushing for equal voting rights. They instead emphasized legal equality—the entitlement of Black people to pursue their rights in court—not enfranchisement at the ballot box. Douglass and his supporters in the Black conventions realized they had to fight for democracy on two fronts, challenging not just Johnson but also impelling Radical Republicans to expand their limited understanding of equal citizenship. The moment could either set the country back into the fire of slavery or forward toward Douglass's idea of equal citizenship as defined by the equal right to vote. Moderation on constitutional rights was not an option.

The Radical Republican members of Congress, despite their strong support of civil rights, counseled pragmatism. They reasoned that passing a civil rights bill would be for naught if a future white supremacist president with a sympathetic Congress repealed it. To ensure that did not happen, they needed to make explicit the Constitution's opposition to white supremacy. This was a step short of the equal voting amendment Douglass demanded. They drafted a fourteenth constitutional amendment that read: "All persons born or naturalized in the United States, and subject to the jurisdiction thereof, are citizens of the United States" and "No state shall . . . deny to any person within its jurisdiction the equal protection of the laws"—a commitment to legal equality with no exception. Moreover, the proposed Fourteenth Amendment went partway toward Douglass's vision, insofar that it protected voting rights indirectly by requiring that if any state disenfranchised its citizens, it would have its representation in Congress reduced.[21]

Despite its relative moderation, Johnson was livid about the proposed Fourteenth Amendment. In a letter to Missouri's governor, he proclaimed his horror: "This is a country for white men, and by God, as long as I am President, it shall be a government for white men."[22] Johnson was not the only one complaining about the amendment. To the chagrin of Republican proponents, Douglass opposed the amendment, even though it enshrined the language of "equal protection" he had championed for decades. In Douglass's view, the amendment promised equal citizenship but failed to provide the best path to protecting it: with a guaranteed right to vote regardless of race. Equality, he recognized, came through political power, and power required the franchise for Black people, which the amendment did not explicitly secure, and instead left that protection in the hands of whites and the legal system.[23] Douglass spent much of his energies throughout 1866 arguing with the Radical Republicans as much as he criticized Johnson, speaking at conventions, publishing articles, and urging Americans to demand a broader amendment.

The fight between Douglass and the amendment's supporters played out on a train ride between Rochester and Philadelphia in September 1866. Johnson had organized a rally to support his policies, including his opposition to the Fourteenth Amendment, so Republicans planned to counter Johnson's rally with their own convention in Philadelphia to support passage of the amendment. Douglass, who was elected as a delegate to the counterconvention, brought his own plans that fit neither the president's nor the Republicans' ambitions. As the train traveled, several white Republican counterconvention delegates noticed Douglass on the train and urged him to not attend. They argued the image of a Black man speaking at the convention posed a danger to the Republican Party. If Douglass spoke, they argued, that would bolster the claims of Johnson and Democrats that Republicans were favoring "social and political equality" beyond legal equality. Once he arrived in Philadelphia, pressure on Douglass to leave mounted. Organizers asked that he not march in the convention's parade—a procession that featured pairs of delegates and so would involve him walking side by side with a white person. When he insisted on marching, none of his supposed Republican allies would take his hand, until a fellow journalist, the white Theodore Tilton, joined hands and marched.

On September 6, Douglass's opponents, having failed to get him to leave the convention, motioned to adjourn before the issue of Black voting rights could be put to a vote. Defiant, Douglass took the stage to loud cries from supporters shouting his name. Meanwhile, according to a reporter covering the event, delegates from border states "looked grim" after the failed attempt to adjourn the meeting. Douglass, his voice hoarse from the convention, said, "If you mean anything by equal protection, by equal liberty, you mean that Frederick Douglass shall have equal right with every other citizen to protect his liberty." The audience cheered. He asked the audience, "Do you mean it?" The crowd roared back, "We do." He continued, "I have talked with reverend and distinguished men from the South and they have said to me, 'Douglass, don't put it on too heavy; have patience; let us get out of the well, and then we will take care of you.'" The language of "equal protection" left it to the courts to protect Black rights. But that was not enough. Instead, Douglass said plainly, "I am for the immediate, unconditional, and universal enfranchisement of the black man, in every State in the Union."[24] As much as his words, Douglass's presence at the convention spoke of the need for political, not just legal, empowerment for Black Americans.

Douglass continued his criticism as the states considered ratification of the Fourteenth Amendment. In an article called "Reconstruction" for the *Atlantic Monthly*, he detailed his criticisms. An amendment that clarified Black people's right to vote, which Douglass claimed was already present in the original Constitution, would be welcome, but this amendment did not include such a guarantee and would be a regressive move, failing to codify the Constitution's original promise. The mistake made by Congress, as Douglass saw it, was that the amendment granted an "emasculated citizenship" in contrast to the kind of equal citizenship originally "contemplated in the Constitution of the United States."[25]

Douglass's opposition was backed by the constitutional constituency he had cultivated, particularly the network of Black conventions, which lined up behind him. A meeting in DC, in January 1867,[26] echoed Douglass in opposition to the proposed amendment. Attendees issued a resolution declaring that because the amendment is "not founded in equal justice and impartial suffrage," and "it permits our disfranchisement, it is undemocratic, illegitimate, and unjust."[27] Despite his battle with his fellow Republicans in Congress, Senator Sumner agreed to read the resolution on the Senate floor. A delegate to the DC convention watched from the gallery, reporting that the resolutions were presented in a "very handsome manner" by "our friend and champion, Hon. Charles Sumner."[28]

★ ★ ★

WHILE DOUGLASS AND HIS ALLIES criticized congressional Republicans for supporting an overly weak amendment, Johnson challenged it for doing too much. The threat to America, as Johnson saw it, was that the Black vote meant white disenfranchisement. Incredibly, he argued falsely that Republican efforts were already causing violence and denying white people the right to vote. During the infamous Swing Around the Circle speaking tour in the late summer of 1866, Johnson ranted against Republicans and Blacks.[29] One talking point was about who to blame for a massacre in New Orleans in late July 1866. The massacre came about during a convention where Republicans, including the Louisiana Supreme Court justice Rufus King Howell and about twenty-five delegates, met in New Orleans to discuss granting the franchise to Black people in the Louisiana constitution, among other reforms. They were cheered on by approximately two hundred freedmen who rallied outside the convention building. The mayor of New Orleans ordered the meeting broken up. The sheriff deputized whites, who then attacked the freedmen, murdering thirty-four of them. Even the official report issued by Johnson's administration described it as an "absolute massacre by the police."[30] Douglass had referred to the massacre in his argument for the urgency of the franchise, writing "with us disenfranchisement means New-Orleans."[31]

Despite the findings of his own administration, on September 8, 1866, in a public speech, Johnson blamed Black people for their own massacre. The riot was caused, he said, by an attempt to "enfranchise one portion of the population, called the colored population, and who had been emancipated, and at the same time disfranchise white men." He added that Black people in New Orleans wanted "to arm themselves and prepare for the shedding of blood." Black people's desire to cause violence, Johnson claimed, had "its origin in the Radical Congress."[32] For these and other imagined threats, Johnson suggested Thaddeus Stevens, a Republican in Congress, should be hanged, earning a roar of approval from the crowd.

The threat Johnson posed to democracy was unmistakable. The country had emerged from the Civil War only to find its president explicitly proposing the murder of a political opponent and seeking a retrenchment on the question of equal citizenship for Black people. While the threat Johnson posed to the future of American democracy was clear, the question of how to stop him divided Douglass and the Republican Party.

Congress's tensions with the president over the future of civil rights increasingly focused on the controversial secretary of war, Edwin Stanton. Stanton was one of a few holdovers from Lincoln's administration still serving under Johnson. By the war's end, Stanton had become a strong supporter of Douglass and his postwar vision, conferring with Douglass after his first meeting with Lincoln, committing to enlisting Black troops and instilling in Douglass a new optimism. Stanton had also advocated for the Emancipation Proclamation and championed the Thirteenth Amendment.[33] After the war, he became one of the chief architects of Reconstruction, creating a plan that placed Southern governments under temporary military rule and enforcing the Military Reconstruction Acts, which ensured that the former Confederate states abided by the new Constitution and protected the rights of freed Black people.

Stanton pushed forward with this plan, against Johnson's wishes. Under his control, in January 1865, the Union Army issued Special Field Order No. 15. It delivered what Black leaders such as Douglass, and an emerging Black Southern intelligentsia, had thought necessary to build Black wealth, which undergirded equal citizenship.[34] The order granted portions of a large swath of land originally owned by white planters, whereby plots of "not more than (40) acres of tillable ground" would be awarded to families of freed slaves.[35] This was the famous promise described as forty acres and a mule. Such acts of radical empowerment for Black Americans were not what Andrew Johnson had in mind. He revoked Special Field Order No. 15 and actively undermined efforts of formerly enslaved people to own land, demanding his generals "endeavor to effect an arrangement mutually satisfactory to the freedmen and the [former] landowners."[36]

Through it all, this president, who had repeatedly claimed to be a Moses for Black people, was indifferent to appeals by formerly enslaved people. On Edisto Island, located off the coast of Charleston, South Carolina, thousands of freed people responded to Special Field Order No. 15 by taking up the lands they had formerly worked as slaves. But within months, at Johnson's direction, residents were asked to surrender the land back to their former owners. Panicked, formerly enslaved people on the island appealed to the president in a letter: "This is our home, we have made These lands what they are. We were the only true and Loyal people that were found in possession of these Lands," their letter read. "We therefore look to you In this trying hour as A true friend of the poor and Neglected race. for protection and Equal Rights."[37] Not surprisingly, the president who had dispensed any pretense that Black people were part of his constituency or entitled to equal rights never responded. Like Douglass argued, Black people needed the franchise because unaccountable whites could never be trusted to represent them.

By mid-1868, Johnson was prevailing over Stanton, ensuring that nearly all properties that had been redistributed to formerly enslaved people were returned to former Confederates.[38] Stanton, still, though, was a thorn in his side. In August 1868, Johnson had had enough; he asked Stanton to resign. Stanton refused, sparking a showdown; Johnson was legally prohibited by the Tenure of Office Act from firing his hugely popular war secretary without Senate approval, and Stanton was too proud to step down. Johnson's next move was to order Stanton "suspended." Taking his place as "interim" war secretary would be the commanding general of the US Army: Ulysses S. Grant.[39]

Understanding that Stanton's firing was a threat to Reconstruction, the Senate responded with an extraordinary move: in January 1868, they voted 35–6 to immediately remove Grant and to have Stanton reinstated.[40] In response, Johnson ordered Grant to ignore the vote and Stanton's authority. This placed Grant in an extreme dilemma: follow the instructions of the Senate or listen to the commander in chief. In the end, Grant rebuked Johnson's order, refusing to disobey an act of Congress, and allowed Stanton to return to his office. It was a breathtaking victory for the rule of law and a striking blow to Johnson. Enraged, Johnson temporarily retreated. But in February 1868, frustrated at being undermined by his own cabinet official, Johnson neglected the Tenure of Office Act and officially fired Stanton. Johnson hoped that his word would be final, but the controversy was just getting started. Stanton refused to step down, arguing the law protected him.

Years of obstructionist tactics to derail Reconstruction had left Republicans infuriated, and the Stanton imbroglio had finally lit the proverbial match. As Congressman John Bingham put it, "The President of the United States has deliberately, defiantly, and criminally violated the Constitution, his oath of office, and the laws of the country."[41] Bingham would lead the first-ever effort to impeach a president. The decision reflected Republicans' view of the extraordinary stakes. To many Republicans, allowing Johnson—who had promoted white supremacy, vetoed civil rights bills, opposed a constitutional guarantee of equal protection, derided Black voting, and reversed the provision of land—to remain in office risked collapsing the struggle for equality that had come to define the war.

Yet even while Johnson's threat to multiracial democracy was well understood, how to stop it remained a problem: Johnson could be impeached only for "high crimes and misdemeanors." What precisely were they? House leaders deliberated about what charges, specifically, their articles of impeachment should include. One faction of Congress wanted to focus narrowly on Johnson's dismissal of Stanton, since the firing appeared to violate the Tenure of Office Act. Another group, led by Thaddeus Stevens, thought a narrowly construed charge would obscure the broader moral and political crimes Johnson had committed in opposing Reconstruction. Stevens emphasized that the Republicans should impeach Johnson for his calls for violence against members of Congress and his attempts to deny protections for former slaves in the South, of which firing Stanton was just a part.

The legalists won the battle of how to impeach Johnson. Of the eleven counts of impeachment introduced, eight focused narrowly on Johnson's firing of Stanton and disregard for the Tenure in Office Act. One article quoted Johnson's blame of Black people for the New Orleans massacre. But the racism at the root of his speech was never called out directly.

★ ★ ★

THE IMPEACHMENT OF PRESIDENT JOHNSON by the full House of Representatives and the subsequent trial in the Senate took place from February to May 1868. The proceedings offered a chance for the American people to address his threat to democracy. Impeachment could have offered a direct way to challenge Johnson's opposition to the promise of multiracial democracy enshrined in the Thirteenth Amendment and the coming Fourteenth Amendment, which had passed Congress but awaited state ratification. But by using a narrow legalistic approach, congressional Republicans muddled the issue. Still, amid that clouded effort, Frederick Douglass's lucid voice clarified the real danger Johnson posed to democracy and the danger that lay in the weakness of the Republicans' response. The danger, Douglass argued, came not from firing Stanton, disregarding the Tenure of Office Act, or even calling for violence against congressmen. Rather, the danger lay in Johnson's commitment to white supremacy and his attempt to re-create the conditions of slavery under a different name. As Douglass wrote, impeaching Johnson should send a message "that the fair South shall no longer be governed by Regulators and the Ku-Klux Klan, but by fair and impartial law." Douglass lambasted Republicans for "quibbling about technicalities" instead of focusing on the real threat Johnson posed. The failure to call out Johnson's white supremacy would stand "in the way of the reform which his removal would produce."[42]

Douglass's hope of making the impeachment an indictment of Johnson's white supremacy faded as the impeachment proceeded and Republicans centered the "technicalities" he had urged them to avoid. The Republicans' focus on the Tenure of Office Act bored the public. Perhaps influenced by the lack of public interest in the impeachment and failure of the impeachers to explain what exactly was so threatening about the Johnson presidency, after months of intense debate, Johnson was acquitted in the Senate by one vote. Douglass remarked that the acquittal functioned as an exoneration of Johnson's racism. In Johnson's final months in office, Douglass grew increasingly skeptical that the nation was continuing its constitutional recovery from the depths of the *Dred Scott* decision. It seemed to him that Johnson had won. Some could rejoice that despite Johnson's obstruction of Black equality, the states were moving forward in ratifying the Fourteenth Amendment, which came on July 9, 1986. For Douglass, given the amendment's shortcomings, its ratification provided little evidence of real progress.

★ ★ ★

THE ROUTE TO DEMOCRATIC RECOVERY from the current crisis had no set path. The response to the Adams crisis had been somewhat linear, expressed first in a partial recovery driven by the newspaper editors and Jefferson and next in a more comprehensive one by Hanson and Madison. The quest to realize the promise of a democratic and multiracial Constitution after Buchanan's attack on it was more jagged: a partial move by Lincoln toward full democracy at the behest of Douglass, followed by a new threat to it from Johnson. At that moment, "We the White People" not "We the People" looked like the nation's future. Still, even at such a precarious point, the promise of equality was on the horizon, and a partnership between Douglass and a member of the Johnson administration would help realize that promise.

CHAPTER 7

Ulysses Grant and the Douglass Constituency

Securing the Right to Vote amid Violence

FREDERICK DOUGLASS'S DESPAIR OVER THE SENATE NOT REMOVING JOHNSON GAVE WAY TO HOPE as the 1868 election approached. Johnson had survived the impeachment proceedings, but Democrats thought he had hurt their electoral chances and refused to renominate him. However, they stuck with his white supremacy, as the Democratic nominee, Horatio Seymour, campaigned on the slogan, "This is a white man's country."[1] Douglass asked, "Does anybody want a revised and corrected edition of Andrew Johnson in the presidential chair for the next four years?"[2]

The best way, Douglass concluded, to make sure the Democrats lost the presidency and the fight for voting rights continued, was for him to endorse the Republican nominee for president, Ulysses S. Grant. Grant's commitment to the issue earned him some trust from Douglass. Still, there would have been reasons for concern. Grant had not publicly supported a voting rights amendment. And he had originally joined Johnson on his notorious speaking tour, albeit abandoning it midway as Johnson's violent rhetoric left him "disgusted." Douglass decided that, on balance, in 1868, Grant was the best chance "to extinguish every ray of hope to the rebel cause."[3]

Douglass campaigned for Grant, seeking to persuade Black voters to vote for the Republican; he argued that if this constituency could assure him victory, Grant would owe them a debt and see a voting rights amendment as benefitting *his* voters. Douglass also argued that a Grant administration would be devoted to "equal rights." This was a key point, because despite the ratification of the Fourteenth Amendment that granted African Americans the rights of citizenship, anything less meant "our work is not done." Douglass used the threat Andrew Johnson had posed to multiracial democracy to frame the stakes of the election. Highlighting the continuities between Seymour and the Confederate rebellion, Douglass intoned, "The foe is the same. Though we are to meet him on a different field and under different leaders."[4]

Supporting Grant required organizing voters behind Douglass's message. The Black convention tradition was mobilized for that purpose. In August 1868, in Baltimore, about sixty Black citizens met at the Douglass Institute.[5] Douglass had inaugurated the hall three years earlier with a speech calling for equality and describing future Black intellectual and political power. Now a speaker called on those assembled to "let the embodiment of your political salvation, Gen. U. S. Grant and Colfax, be perched upon every banner." Others called on those assembled to "be true to your race, your country, and your God by voting for Gen. U. S. Grant and Hon. Schuyler Colfax, in whose keeping your liberties, the liberties of the American people are safe." In a hall named for Douglass, attendees employed his arguments, tying support of Grant to the demand for a voting rights amendment promised by a "reading of the Constitution as originally framed."[6]

The support for Grant came with risks. Black people in the South heeded these calls to support the Republican nominee in massive numbers, risking their lives amid scorching violence. Concerned about the potential for Black people to gain the franchise—which was not yet explicitly guaranteed in the Constitution—white supremacists mobilized. In Louisiana, Black people had begun to elect a wave of state and local officials. Stoking the resentment of poor whites, they unleashed one of the most horrific reigns of terror in American politics. When Black Americans tried to vote, they were met by a vast and violent resistance. As the 1868 election neared, white Democrats in St. Landry Parish, Louisiana, assaulted a local Republican newspaper editor, which prompted Black families to arm themselves for protection. A massacre erupted. For two weeks, squads of armed white men took control of the area, brutally murdering around two hundred Black people. The scare tactics and murders were highly effective: in St. Landry Parish, not one single vote was counted for Grant. As a local official described, given that ballots were not then secret, "No man on that day could have voted any other than the democratic ticket and not been killed inside of twenty-four hours thereafter."[7]

Such campaigns of terror were widespread. Six other Louisiana parishes recorded zero votes for Grant, indicating the success of violent voter suppression.[8] It is estimated that around the election, approximately one thousand Black people were killed in Louisiana and an estimated two thousand were murdered in Arkansas.[9] In Georgia, white bands on horseback threatened death to a group of Black people attempting to attend a political rally—and carried through on the threat with at least seven innocent people, who were brutally murdered in what became known as the Camilla Massacre.[10] Democratic candidates and officials often condoned this violence.

Nevertheless, this campaign of terror failed to thwart large-scale Black turnout for Grant in 1868—the first presidential election in which Black people were allowed to vote in significant numbers. Although Grant handily won the electoral college 214–80, he eked out only three hundred thousand more popular votes than Seymour—a margin historians attribute to his Black supporters.[11] With these votes forming a core of his support, which Black people risked their lives to cast—Grant won the presidency.

Would Grant pay the debt he owed his Black constituency? As Election Day loomed, Grant remained silent on whether he supported a constitutional amendment to guarantee the franchise in no uncertain terms. This silence left Douglass unclear whether he had miscalculated in supporting Grant. In 1800, a constitutional constituency led by newspaper editors had backed Jefferson, hoping to reverse the authoritarian policies of Adams. Now in 1868, the first national Black constitutional constituency to influence a presidential election galvanized behind Grant to clearly secure the right to vote for Black people, hoping to reverse the policies of Buchanan and Johnson. Their aim was multiracial democracy. Would they succeed?

* * *

GRANT'S SILENCE MASKED AN EVOLVING STANCE on voting rights. Originally, in the Lincoln administration, Grant saw Reconstruction as a gradual and sequential process. For Grant, education for newly freed enslaved people was essential before the franchise should be granted. Grant called this a "time of probation," in which the emancipated population could "prepare themselves for the privileges of citizenship."¹² When Lincoln issued the Emancipation Proclamation, Grant worried that Black people might receive the ballot without being literate.¹³ Thus, while Grant enthusiastically helped establish Southern schools in the early years of Reconstruction, he was not an immediate supporter of the franchise.

But Grant's opposition to immediate voting rights to Black people changed when as commanding general of the Union Army during the Johnson administration he had seen the violence white supremacists were employing to prevent Black equality. When Grant had received the first official report of the 1866 massacre in New Orleans, he sought to convince President Johnson to crack down on "authenticated cases of murder." He ordered a report on the epidemic of anti-Black violence and turned it over to Johnson, who ignored the findings.¹⁴ Grant's aide, Cyrus Comstock, noted that the violence in Memphis and New Orleans led to "General [Grant] getting more and more radical."¹⁵ An account from Grant's brother-in-law indicates that when "the Kuklux endeavored to suppress the political rights of the freedmen of the South by the use of unscrupulous means," Grant "became convinced . . . that the ballot was the only real means the freedmen had for defending their lives, property, and rights."¹⁶

With the election of 1868, Republicans took the president's mansion and, on Grant's coattails, Congress, by an overwhelming majority. With the election over and Grant waiting in the wings to take the presidential oath of office, Republicans in Congress passed a proposed Fifteenth Amendment that would ban racial discrimination in voting and give the federal government a role protecting that right. Grant could now make public what, after his evolution, he had come to believe privately. At a massive parade in Washington, Grant showed his support for Black voting rights, calling them "the realization of the Declaration of Independence." The president-elect was now reflecting Douglass's view, the same one endorsed at the Baltimore convention.[17]

★   ★   ★

EVEN WITH PRESIDENTIAL BACKING, the fight for the amendment was just beginning. The constitutional constituency pushing for the amendment's ratification, including Douglass and allies, had successfully convinced the president to support it and Congress to pass it, but as they sought to urge ratification by the states, they faced powerful opposition by women's suffrage advocates such as Elizabeth Cady Stanton, who joined with Democrats against the amendment. Stanton and Douglass had originally pushed for female and Black suffrage together. But in 1866, Douglass decided that quick passage of an amendment to protect Black people from violence required severing Black voting from female suffrage. Stanton disagreed. Since the proposed amendment did not include women, she opposed it and Grant, given his support of it. Tensions between Stanton and Douglass spilled out at a meeting of the newly formed American Equal Rights Association on May 12, 1869. Douglass said, "I must say that I do not see how anyone can pretend that there is the same urgency in giving the ballot to women as to the negro. With us, the matter is a question of life and death."[18] Some prominent women's suffrage advocates joined Douglass in stressing the urgency of the amendment even though it abandoned female suffrage. Julia Ward Howe, the white writer of the "Battle Hymn of the Republic," remarked, "I am willing that the negro shall get the ballot before me."[19] Black writer Francis Harper also chided Stanton, stressing the need for the Black vote to protect against violence, saying she was willing to "let the lesser question of sex go."[20] She backed Douglass's distinction between the "desirable" vote for Black women and the "vital" vote for Black men.[21]

Douglass never wavered in his support for female suffrage, even as he refused to sacrifice ratification of the Fifteenth Amendment to include women. That uneasy tension was also reflected in the proceedings of the Black conventions as they met to organize for ratification. In 1869, at the start of the National Convention of the Colored Men of America in Washington, DC, some attendees moved to deny admission to a female delegate. Eventually, she was admitted. But the attempt to bar women made the priority of the convention clear: ratifying the amendment came before women's suffrage.[22] A convention of Black laborers chaired by longtime Douglass ally George Downing took a different approach. That convention passed a resolution formally inviting women to organize and participate in labor organizations.[23] Despite the objections of Democrats and some female suffragists, on February 3, 1870, the Fifteenth Amendment was ratified. But tensions had frayed the once strong alliance between Black suffrage supporters and women's suffrage advocates.

In the 1870 midterm elections, empowered by the new amendment, a massive number of Black people again risked their lives and voted. Propelled by Black votes, for the first time the halls of Congress became home to several Black congressmen serving full terms—as Douglass had envisioned. Five Black representatives were elected from three states during the midterm elections, following the three others who had been elected to the previous Congress in special elections in 1870.[24] Of those earlier elected was Joseph Rainey, a former state senator from South Carolina, who became the first Black member of the House of Representatives. Another, Hiram Revels, the first Black US senator, was a religious leader and state senator from Mississippi. The shift was so swift that white Democrats seemed blindsided. They attempted to prevent Revels from being seated in the Senate, seeking a vote by that chamber to exclude him. After a contentious and heated debate, the Republican-controlled Senate overwhelmingly voted to seat Revels. Still, the vote signaled that the coming change for Grant and Republicans would not be easy.

Watching from the public balcony as Revels took his seat was Douglass's son, Charles. He later wrote to his father that he overheard spectators whisper that Douglass himself should be a senator.[25] But while he was not on the Senate or House floor, a widely distributed print commemorating the event symbolized his major role, showing him at the center of a portrait flanked by Revels and Blanche Bruce, a political leader from Mississippi, who would go on to become the second Black US senator. The portrait telegraphed what everyone knew. Without Douglass, it was unlikely that the constitutional constituency that elected those men ever would have existed.

With Congress seated, Grant worked with the newly elected Black delegation and their allies to act on his constituents' demand for an aggressive federal response to white supremacist violence—often perpetrated by the Ku Klux Klan—against Black voters. Despite the Fifteenth Amendment, rampant violence against Black voters in 1870 severely blunted its effectiveness. Grant recognized that legislation to enforce it was necessary. In a speech to Congress in December 1870, Grant demanded a "pure, untrammeled ballot, where every man entitled to cast a vote may do so, just once at each election, without fear of molestation or proscription on account of his political faith, nativity, or color."[26] Thus began the Grant administration's efforts to crush the Ku Klux Klan.

Unlike previous Congresses, Black representatives could themselves answer the call from Grant and their own constituents, who spoke for themselves about the terror they had encountered and the need for legislation to tamp down Klan violence that was devoted to destroying Black political equality. No longer was an all-white Congress ostensibly representing the lived experience of Black people. Congressman Rainey described his perpetual fear of the Klan in his home district: "When myself and my colleagues shall leave these Halls," he remarked in a stirring speech on the House floor, "we know not that the assassin may await our coming." Rainey was followed by Representative Robert Elliott, another Black congressman. As an official in South Carolina, Elliott had led state militia efforts to thwart the Klan. He recounted how a local Black family had been awakened by whites in the middle of the night around the election and brutally beaten. Elliot then read

aloud a public notice from the Ku Klux Klan that threatened local officials with violence if they didn't step down from their positions.[27]

Rainey pushed for the first of a series of laws known as Enforcement
Acts, which aimed to effectuate the Fourteenth and Fifteenth Amendments by redefining the role of the federal government, obligating it to
protect Black people from political violence. Until this point American democracy largely evolved locally without federal protection at the
polls. But these acts, designed to protect against violence and provide a
critical step toward a democracy that included Black people, relied on
new powers given to the federal government under the newly ratified
amendments. The first Enforcement Act, signed in May 1870, empowered the president to deploy federal troops to thwart the Klan. It also
made it a federal crime for the Klan or other groups to go "in disguise
upon the public highways, or upon the premises of another" to prevent
the exercise of constitutional rights.[28] The second Enforcement Act,
signed by Grant in February 1871, gave the president supervisory power
to send federal judges and US marshals to guarantee ballot access.[29]

Douglass and his constitutional constituency had made the right bet
in supporting Grant, and they continued to do so while Democrats and
white supremacists denounced him. The Black conventions provided a
forum to support Grant's agenda, as in February 1871, when a Nashville convention endorsed the president's call for legislation to protect
Black voters: "The colored citizens of Tennessee, tender their grateful
acknowledgements to Congress for the passage promptly of laws enforcing the Fifteenth Amendment to the Constitution of the United States,
and to President. U.S. Grant, and his Cabinet for faithfully executing
and enforcing the principles of liberty and equal rights to all." The convention also provided the raw empirical data of "outrages" where the
Klan attacked Black voters.[30] They reported on a particularly pernicious
Klan practice, forced voting, in which Klansmen demanded Black people vote for Democrats or be murdered. The report noted, "We have to
cast our votes contrary to our wishes, and for the party which has kept
us in slavery, for fear of being thrown out of employment or suffering the
indignities and afflictions perpetrated by the Kuklux."[31] This forced voting was possible because of the still-common practice of public balloting.

A committee documenting these "outrages" reported as well on the Klan terrorizing schools. "Kuklux outlaws," the report noted, violently attacked almost every rural Black school in the state.[32] Meeting in April, a Black committee in Kentucky sent a report to Congress that noted, "We have been law-abiding citizens, pay our taxes, and in many parts of the State people have been driven from the polls, refused the right to vote; many have been slaughtered while attempting to vote." The report implored members of Congress to act quickly: "We ask, how long is this state of things to last? We appeal to you as law-abiding citizens to enact some laws that will protect us, and that will enable us to exercise the rights of citizens."[33]

In April 1871, Congress responded to these calls from Black conventions and newly elected Black representatives for additional legislation to enforce the Fifteenth Amendment. Grant soon signed the third and most significant Enforcement Act, known as the Ku Klux Klan Act. The act made it a crime to violate the civil rights of any Americans and empowered the federal government to prosecute these cases if state or local governments failed to—even if this required prosecuting local officials. The law also empowered citizens the right to sue officials in *federal* court for the violation of their civil rights.[34] Gone were the days when Black citizens had to beg for their rights, like Edisto Islanders had to do in their letter to Johnson. The law was also a warning shot to Southern states, as it gave Grant the power to suspend habeas corpus, declare martial law, and send in federal troops to protect equal rights if necessary.[35]

Grant formed the Department of Justice in 1870, many historians claim, with the purpose of carrying out the Enforcement Acts.[36] A large caseload quickly developed consisting of prosecutions under those acts.[37] In 1870, Grant appointed Amos Akerman the first attorney general to head the new department, giving him a clear mission to prosecute the Klan. Between 1870 and 1872, the Department of Justice convicted more than a thousand people under the acts. The convictions were won despite a small budget that limited the department's staff. New prosecutors, mindful that Southern whites might nullify successful prosecutions, tried these cases before majority Black juries. The victories over the Klan came, too, because of the bravery of Black victims who testified, risking their lives.[38] In a particularly urgent moment, Grant used military force to stamp out the Klan in South Carolina, while wielding his new power to suspend habeas corpus.[39]

After the passage of the Enforcement Acts, Black conventions continued to convene to support President Grant. In October 1871, the Southern States Convention of Colored Men met in Columbia, South Carolina, and there resolved to "commend the action of President Grant in suspending the writ of habeas corpus in the State of South Carolina, as wise and beneficial to our race." It also warned of continuing dangers and expressed the "hope that by the prompt action of the United States authorities, the members of the Klan will be brought to speedy justice."[40]

The plan of Douglass and his allies had worked. In supporting Grant in 1868, Black people had found a president beholden to them because they had placed him in power. They were finally citizens who had formed a constituency to which the chief executive was accountable.

As Black people faced Klan violence and the Grant administration fought back with prosecutions and legislation, Douglass used his latest paper, *New National Era*, which he edited with his son Lewis, to document the federal government's efforts of fighting anti-Black violence. Douglass's paper told the account of a Black household attacked by masked local men. When local officials refused to make any arrests because their sheriff was complicit in the crime, federal authorities arrested the sheriff and another perpetrator.[41] The tragedy of the story was undeniable. But unlike in previous decades where federal officials would have played no role, these new laws set an expectation that officials who condoned white supremacy would be stopped.

Douglass was now a prominent defender of the president—even honored by him. Grant appointed Douglass to an official commission investigating statehood for Santo Domingo (modern-day Dominican Republic). Once an outcast, Douglass now had a presidential ally who was implementing his constitutional vision, and a federal government devoted to protecting the civil and political rights of Black people against local forces of white supremacy.

★ ★ ★

IN 1872, HORACE GREELEY, a Republican like the president, opposed Grant's run for a second turn. He sought the presidency under the banner of an off-shoot party known as the "Liberal Republicans." Democrats, sensing that Greeley was their best opportunity to beat Grant, nominated him as their candidate for the presidency, too. Greeley's candidacy was defined by opposition to Grant, including the perception that federal enforcement of Black voting rights in the south had grown too aggressive.[42] A Grant victory would be seen as an endorsement of his aggressive enforcement of civil rights, whereas Greeley's election would surely set back that agenda.

With Grant's civil rights agenda threatened, Douglass campaigned fiercely for him. Grant in turn put Douglass front and center, in recognition of his success at galvanizing a core constituency for the president. Douglass used his influence to highlight and defend Grant's war against the Klan, arguing that "at this . . . dark hour of Ku-Kluxism, of war to the knife against the black man . . . a defeat of the Republican party . . . would be the greatest calamity that could befall our people throughout the States."[43] Douglass wrote to laud the president, claiming "to Grant more than any other man the Negro owes his enfranchisement."[44] Grant, Douglass believed, was devoted to "stamping out this murderous ku-klux as he stamped out the rebellion [of the Confederacy]."[45]

Douglass also highlighted lesser-known achievements of Grant's presidency. Grant, Douglass pointed out, had integrated large swaths of the federal government[46]—doing more to diversify federal employment than any other president yet. This diversification included record numbers of Blacks—as well as Jews and Native Americans—in major and minor positions in government, such as Ebenezer Bassett, the first African American diplomat. Seeing the state actively aid the fortunes of people it had formerly enslaved was, to Douglass, a tangible mark of progress. In the president, Douglass judged that the closest thing to his vision of equal citizenship had been enacted to that point, arguing that "no man in high position has manifested . . . a more entire freedom from vulgar prejudice of race and color, than Ulysses S. Grant."[47]

With overwhelming Black support, Grant defeated Greeley. The victory was bittersweet, however. On April 13, 1873, little more than a month after Grant's second inaugural, in Colfax, Louisiana, a mass murder that historian Eric Foner calls "the bloodiest single instance of racial carnage in the Reconstruction era," ended with at least seventy, and possibly more than one hundred, Black people dead.[48] Grant, under the authority of the Enforcement Acts, sent in federal troops. The South's "disregard for law, civil rights and personal protection," he later declared, "ought not to be tolerated in any civilized government."[49] The threat of violence was ever present, ready to strike at any moment. Douglass had long argued the right to vote offered the best insurance that the government would protect Black people against violence, and in 1873 he was proven right once again. Accountable to a constitutional constituency that had voted him into office once again, Grant brought prosecutions against the perpetrators.

★ ★ ★

GRANT MADE TOWERING STRIDES TO crush the Klan and protect the vote. But things were getting worse regarding Black people's basic right to occupy public spaces without legal prohibition. Across the country, not just in the South, a nascent system of public segregation was taking root. Grant didn't seem concerned about stopping this trend. Speaking at his second inaugural, he promised continued enforcement of political rights against the Klan, though he said "social equality is not a subject to be legislated upon." In Grant's view, his obligation was only to give each Black man "a fair chance to develop what there is good in him" by protecting him from violence and ensuring access to the ballot and schooling. Grant wanted the Black man to feel "assured that his conduct will regulate the treatment and fare he will receive" while he moves around the country, but he did not yet support what he regarded as the distinct "social equality" of integration in public accommodations.[50]

Douglass and the Black constituency he worked to shape pushed Grant to evolve. Almost from the time of Grant's second inauguration, the newly elected Black congressmen pushed for legislation that would end the nascent segregation cropping up in entertainment spaces, schools, and juries.[51] They proposed a new Civil Rights Act that would give additional teeth to the Equal Protection Clause of the Fourteenth Amendment. The proposed act could end segregation's systemic racism before it took root—which the bill's backers understood.[52] As the Massachusetts senator Charles Sumner lay on his deathbed in 1874, he summoned Douglass, Downing, and other allies, whispering a dying request: "You must take care of the civil rights bill—my bill, the civil rights bill—don't let it fail!"[53] Sumner had introduced the bill in 1870. Now, it would be Black congressmen and leaders such as Downing who would shepherd the controversial proposal into law. Black congressmen had integrated the House and Senate chambers. Now they would try to integrate the nation.

In 1874, Congress took up debate of the bill. The newly elected Black congressmen again offered what their white counterparts could not: firsthand accounts of the emerging racial apartheid's effect on their dignity and why this "social" degradation could not be divorced from political subordination. They showed that segregation would perpetuate second-class citizenship for Black people and undermine democracy. In the spaces where people lived their lives, they needed to stand as equals, not physically separated subjects.

Speaking in opposition to the bill was Alexander Stephens, the former Confederate vice president, and now congressman from Georgia. In faux-genteel rhetoric, Stephens argued that the Civil Rights Act violated the Constitution. He tried to narrow the meaning of the Fourteenth Amendment, arguing that its reference to "liberty" meant the right of each state to legislate as it wished, and that the federal government could not intrude on private actions such as what types of clients a shopkeeper welcomed into their business. The demand for "social equality" for African Americans in the bill, he argued, was foreign to this idea of liberty in the amendment and not central to the American creed.[54]

In one of the most extraordinary moments in Congressional history, Black members rose to rebut Stephens. The first was Alonzo Ransier, a brilliant lawyer elected to Congress from South Carolina in 1872. While "American slavery no longer curses our land," he began, "a relic of it remains in the conduct of a portion of our people toward another portion in nearly every part of our country." Personal stories of Black congress-

men forced to lead double lives hammered home the urgency of the bill;
James Rapier of Alabama, for example, described being forced to ride a
segregated train to Washington. Even the Black representatives to Congress, he said, still had "chains of civil slavery [hung] about him."[35] Then
Robert Elliott of South Carolina rose to reject Stephens's constitutional
claims. To Elliott, "the constitution of a free government ought always
to be construed in favor of human rights." Indeed, of Stephens's narrow
reading of the constitutional provision, Elliott argued, "the thirteenth,
fourteenth, and fifteenth amendments, in positive words, invest Congress
with the power to protect the citizen in his civil and political rights." He
concluded with a rousing call to realize the nation's founding principles:
the Civil Rights Act "proposes to enforce the constitutional guarantee
against inequality and discrimination by appropriate legislation," he
stated. "The Constitution warrants it; the Supreme Court sanctions it;
justice demands it."[36]

Playing out in this debate was a deeper disagreement about how
much the Constitution demanded multiracial democracy. While the earlier debate between Douglass and his opponents over whether the Constitution allowed slavery had ended with the Thirteenth Amendment,
a new debate emerged about how broadly to read that amendment and
the two that followed it. America's new Black representatives sought in
Congress to read themselves and other Black Americans into the preamble, rejecting any notion that American democracy was only for whites.

While the newly elected Black congressman took center stage in
demanding democratic rights, the lobbying network set up by Douglass
and Downing during the Johnson administration continued to operate
behind the scenes. Downing had worked with Douglass to lobby President Johnson and organized the Black conventions alongside him. It
was in the supposedly private spaces like restaurants, including the one
Downing managed for the House, that he learned how power worked.
From that perch, Downing formed the relationships he used to bring the
message of the Black conventions to those who held power and formal
office. Those insights let Downing see the importance of a civil rights
bill that integrated supposedly private spaces like restaurants. As he put
it, restaurants were "a creature of the state" and therefore if the federal

government allowed segregation to spread in these places, that meant "the state does the discriminating."[57] Downing therefore rebutted the Democrats who argued that integration was purely "social" and not political. Downing also convened a Black convention to support passage of the bill, and then passed a statement from that convention to Representative Elliott, who read it on the House floor. The restaurateur who had used the informal spaces of public life to acquire influence now used his power to advocate for the passage of a bill that would assure other Black people access to those same places.[58]

After years of debate, in February, Congress passed the Civil Rights Act of 1875. Democrats could not defeat the bill, though they watered it down, weakening the government's enforcement power. Its original educational provision preventing school segregation was also lopped off. But its core remained—speeding up integration and codifying the idea that equal treatment based on race must be the nation's law.

Grant had initially sought distance from the kind of "social equality" embodied in the bill. Now, two years after his skeptical second inaugural address, he signed, on March 1, 1875, the civil rights bill into law. Once again, his views had evolved, this time at the behest of the constitutional constituency that had twice helped to cement his election.[59] The president was accountable to Black people, and they prodded him to acknowledge their political power, which he did by signing a bill that gave these Americans the right to stand side by side with whites in society.

After Grant signed the bill, one attendee of a Black convention of journalists on August 4, 1875, claimed that now "colored people [have] all the rights they would ever get" and added that courts could be counted upon to enforce them.[60] While it might have seemed to some then that the struggle for Black equality had succeeded, the victory proved fleeting.

★ ★ ★

DOUGLASS HAD BEEN HUNTED BY BUCHANAN as he defended a widely dismissed reading of the Constitution that made Black people equal members of "We the People." Later, returning from exile in Canada and England, Douglass watched as his ideas became reflected in the most famous speech ever delivered about constitutional democracy, the Gettysburg Address. The speech still represents a vision of the Constitution born again as a document centered on equality, not slavery. By the time Grant left office, the Constitution had been amended to reflect the idea of Black political equality that Douglass had long championed. And as the congressmen who argued forcefully for the Civil Rights Act of 1875 dramatically illustrated, equality meant more than the vote. It demanded an end to the badges of inferiority placed on Black Americans' social structures. By the end of Grant's administration, the long-standing debate about how citizens should judge their presidents had tilted. Douglass's views about the racial equality he saw promised in the preamble were initially dismissed by both abolitionists and slavery advocates who saw the document as proslavery. Now, Douglass's philosophy of equal citizenship opposed to racial subordination was etched into the Constitution, and explicitly found a presidential defender in Grant.

Every president of this era can be judged by where they stood with Douglass, the visionary who persuasively argued how *Dred Scott* should be reversed. Every president during this period had to contend with Douglass—whether he was chasing him, like Buchanan; deliberating with him, like Lincoln; throwing him out of the president's mansion, like Johnson; or hiring him, like Grant. Douglass's example shows how a constitutional constituency can call a president to account, and how such a constituency can reclaim from courts and public officials a democratic meaning of the Constitution.

Lincoln embraced Douglass, moving the country toward a democratic Constitution, although stopping well short of it. Johnson's opposition to Douglass and Black equality showed that recovery is often not linear, as Johnson served a political constituency that saw white supremacy, not democracy, at the core of the Constitution. As much as Douglass stood for a democratic ideal of what it meant to interpret the Constitution, white supremacist visions, such as Johnson's, always threatened progress toward a democratic interpretation.

After Johnson, Grant seemed to bring Johnson's presidency to disgrace, as laws devoted to Black equality came to define American politics.[61] However, Johnson's ideas had their revenge through a Supreme Court and an electorate that shared his opposition to Black political equality. In the 1870s and 1880s, a series of Supreme Court decisions narrowed the meaning of the Fourteenth and Fifteenth Amendments and thus undermined the recovery of the democratic ideals for which Douglass and Grant had fought.[62] In *United States v. Cruikshank*, the court eviscerated the power of the federal government to protect the civil rights of Black people, ruling that key federal powers granted by the Enforcement Acts were unconstitutional. It reasoned that the Fourteenth Amendment gave Congress the power to limit only governmental violations of civil rights, not violence perpetrated by non-governmental actors such as the Klan. The Supreme Court followed up with the Civil Rights Cases of 1883, striking down the Civil Rights Act of 1875. The court ruled that "social equality" could not be legislated. As they put it, the Fourteenth Amendment gave Congress the power only to regulate governmental violations of equality, not violations by private businesses. Essentially the court took the side of former Confederate leader Stephens. The court's final blow to the Grant legacy of multiracial democracy, at least until the next cycle of crisis and recovery, came in 1896 when in *Plessy v. Ferguson* it advanced the doctrine of "separate but equal," granting segregation legal cover.

These cases were decided alongside the Republican party's abandonment of civil rights. Grant left office in 1877. The election to replace him, between Samuel Tilden and Rutherford B. Hayes, was one of the closest in history. Neither Tilden nor Hayes had won enough electoral votes to win office, and so the House of Representatives set to its constitutional task of selecting the winner. To avert a crisis, Hayes was awarded victory through a backroom deal on the condition he end Reconstruction and pull back the federal government's military commitment in the South. Shortly thereafter, the segregation regime known as Jim Crow sprang into being and grew.

Douglass lived to see his legacy undone. Rather than despair, however, he looked for others to whom he could pass the baton of the constitutional constituency he had fought for. In Ida B. Wells, a journalist, he saw a person more than worthy of it. Before they met, he read and admired her reports on the growing evil of whites lynching Black people. She described this phenomenon of extrajudicial killing with the phrase "lynch law," which highlighted the lawlessness of the violence with irony. Douglass emulated her, publishing his own piece using the phrase in the title. And when he received a letter from a friend looking for Black activists to tour England, he passed the invite to Wells. The handoff was perhaps best symbolized when he visited her Chicago office, where she was writing for a newspaper. Wells pointed out the oyster restaurant across the street but noted it was segregated. Such segregation would have been illegal under the Civil Rights Act of 1875, but now it was protected under the rulings of the Supreme Court. Undeterred, Douglass, according to Wells, "in his vigorous way, grasped my arm and said 'Come, let's go there.' "[63] Inside, as Wells told it, "The waiters seemed paralyzed over our advent, and not one of them came forward to usher us to a table. Mr. Douglass walked up to the nearest table, pulled out a chair, seated me, then took a seat himself."

The year was 1893, and Douglass had passed the torch to Wells, demanding a seat in a restaurant that would exclude them as the nation inched toward its next crisis, which would come in the twentieth century.

SECTION III

EQUAL PROTECTION

The Long March against Second-Class Citizenship

CHAPTER 8

Woodrow Wilson versus Trotter and Wells

Nationalizing White Supremacy

THE WINNER OF THE 1912 ELECTION WAS AN UNLIKELY POLITICAL STAR. A PROFESSOR TURNED university president, Woodrow Wilson catapulted into prominence as a leading scholar of the Constitution, authoring several well-received studies of American history and government, and lecturing prolifically.[1] Later, he parlayed his academic reputation into the New Jersey governorship. Wilson captivated America with his intellectualism and idealism, a bespectacled professor who would bring America into the twentieth century by, according to him, representing all Americans. Wilson drew contrasts with his opponents President William Taft, the Republican nominee, and former president Teddy Roosevelt, the Bull Moose choice, who both promised to break up or regulate the "trusts" (or monopolies) to fight inequality. While Wilson also campaigned on limiting big business, he sought to pass economic reforms that would encourage competition and prevent monopolies from forming in the first place.[2] But did Wilson's vision of "open gates of opportunity for all" Americans include Black Americans?[3] Wilson's soaring campaign

174 | EQUAL PROTECTION

promises were enough to garner some Black support as he declared to Black people explicitly that on racial issues he would "see justice done them in every matter."[4]

Wilson's declaration for racial progress resounded with dramatic panache, precisely because it contrasted with the federal government's complete abandonment by 1912 of any commitment to protect civil rights. The end of Grant's presidency in 1877 had brought a rapid unraveling of the progress that Lincoln and Douglass had catalyzed. For one, the Republicans' crowning achievement—the Civil Rights Act of 1875, intended to transform American society—was in effect for just eight years: the Grant-signed law meant to codify the "equality of all men before the law" was declared unconstitutional by the Supreme Court in 1883. The court's reasoning came from Fourteenth Amendment's guarantee of "equal protection," which the court—against the intentions of the congressional Republicans who crafted it in 1866—reinterpreted to apply only to government action, thus barring antidiscrimination provisions in private settings like businesses, restaurants, hotels, and theaters.[5]

That dramatic rewriting of history paved the way for several landmark court cases that led America into the Jim Crow era. The most infamous of these cases was caused by an incident in 1892 when a mixed-race man named Homer Plessy boarded a railroad car in Louisiana. Plessy sat in a car labeled "whites only"—a violation of Louisiana's Separate Car Act—and was arrested. Plessy's case reached the Supreme Court in 1896. The statute mandated in its railroad cars "equal but separate, accommodations for the white and colored races." Plessy's lawyers argued that the Separate Car Act was unconstitutional because it violated his right to freedom from the "badges of slavery" under the Thirteenth Amendment and denied him equal protection of law under the Fourteenth Amendment. However, the court rejected both of those arguments, finding that the Act was a "reasonable" use of Louisiana's "police powers" to regulate the health, safety, and morals of the population. It found that separate facilities were not a "badge of slavery" and that equal protection did not mandate "social equality." As the court put it, "If one race be inferior to the other socially, the Constitution of the United States cannot put them upon the same frame." That opinion would legitimate the doctrine of "separate but equal," holding that segregation was consistent with the demands of the post–Civil War amendments—the same amendments passed as a bulwark against white supremacy and the subordination of Black people.[6] With the *Plessy v. Ferguson* decision, the court went beyond the Civil Rights Cases of 1883, which had gutted the power of the federal government to limit so-called private discrimination. In *Plessy*, it turned the meaning of "equal protection" on its head. Its work unfinished, the court turned to destroying the Fifteenth Amendment, and with it, Douglass's dream of a universal right to vote. In 1898, the justices examined Mississippi's poll tax, literacy test, and other obstacles invented to prevent Black people from registering, ruling in *Williams v. Mississippi* that these methods did not technically discriminate based on race and were thus legal.[7]

These rulings ushered in a wave of new laws, mostly across the South, that again relegated Black Americans to second-class status. Under this "Jim Crow" regime, Southern states segregated parks, schools, drinking fountains, bathrooms—essentially all public facilities. Mississippi instituted all-white primaries, literacy tests, poll taxes, and grandfather clauses to curtail the Black vote, while also allowing fraud and violence at the polls. Other Southern states followed Mississippi's lead. Black intellectuals and leaders looked on agog as a generation of progress, bitterly won on the battlefield and in the voting booth, washed away before their eyes.

As if to bring the betrayal full circle, this regression was largely overseen by the party of Grant and Lincoln. In 1876, the presidential election was tightly contested, and neither the Republican nor Democratic candidate earned enough electoral votes to win the presidency. The House established an electoral commission to determine the victor, and the presidency was awarded to the Republican, Rutherford B. Hayes, after he agreed to something like a negotiated settlement with Southern Democrats, although no agreement was explicitly recorded: from now on, the federal government would abdicate the responsibility of ensuring racial justice.

Hayes withdrew the federal troops guarding Southern statehouses where Black representatives served, and he largely ended the use of the military to bring about Reconstruction. In the vacuum, Southern Democrats tightened their hold on state government and began legislating the segregationist policies that would define the former Confederacy for the next several decades.

This settlement took a fierce hold on American politics. In 1901, during Theodore Roosevelt's first year in office, the Republican president invited Booker T. Washington, the prominent civil rights leader and Roosevelt's advisor on racial issues, to dine in the White House. The uproar was deafening; the interracial gesture reverberated across the South and threatened Roosevelt's national standing.[8] While Roosevelt continued to make symbolic gestures to support Black Americans, including appointing Black people to federal positions,[9] he was careful after that incident never to brook controversy—and Washington never dined at the White House again. Between the courts, the states, and now the presidency, Black Americans understood that the wheel had turned. Black leaders of Douglass's generation could at least appeal to one party for equal rights. Now, in the twentieth century, disdain for Black equality was a cause that enjoyed robust bipartisanship among those allowed to participate in American politics.

One person who watched the downfall of the Republican Party with a bitter eye was William Monroe Trotter. Trotter took an unusual route to politics. Born into a wealthy political family in 1872 and raised in the mostly middle-class white neighborhood of Hyde Park, Boston, Trotter attended Harvard, becoming the school's first Black Phi Beta Kappa inductee, and was poised to inherit a small fortune. Motivated by the employment discrimination he faced despite his elite education, Trotter turned to activism.[10] In 1901, Trotter founded the *Guardian*, a newspaper that garnered a following among an unlikely readership given his upper-class background: working-class Black people, often from the South or the Caribbean.[11] His goal for the paper was to "hold a mirror up to nature," to forcefully report on and condemn the racism that pervaded every aspect of American life. The *Guardian* was printed in the same building where abolitionist William Lloyd Garrison had published the *Liberator*.[12]

Trotter was skeptical of Booker T. Washington. He viewed Washington's approach, which claimed to favor gradual progress and sought influence within the Republican Party, as complicit in the two parties' support of white supremacy and their abandonment of the Fourteenth and Fifteenth Amendments. On July 30, 1903, Trotter's anger boiled over. Accompanied by working-class supporters, the "Trotterites," he confronted Washington at a public meeting at the AME Zion Church in Boston, where he attempted to ask Washington why he supported a party that was allowing Jim Crow laws to spread nationwide and why Washington didn't fight back.[13] Washington's allies had Trotter removed and pushed for criminal charges of inciting a riot. Washington later referred dismissively to Trotter and the Trotterites as a "few flies."[14] But Trotter's fame grew, as he offered a radical alternative to Washington, because he was willing to call out the Republican Party's betrayal—even if it distanced him from the political elite.

Ida B. Wells shared Trotter's opposition to Washington—and his concern about Washington's expanding influence. During a 1902 meeting of the National Afro-American Council, this concern came to a head. Wells served as the organization's corresponding secretary and had sought to transform it into a movement for civil rights. However, during the course of the meeting, Wells was aghast to discover that Booker T. Washington had installed allies to take over the organization. Believing that his philosophy was at odds with her work on lynching, she resigned, joining Trotter in resisting that leader.[15]

During the same meeting, Wells reported on the racial violence she argued had destroyed Reconstruction; she documented 2,658 Black people who had been lynched since 1885.[16] Her report reflected years of journalistic research on the murders of Black people in the form of vigilante violence that was meant to intimidate Black people from demanding their rights, including voting. Against those who framed lynching as a response to sexual violence by Black people, Wells documented that many of the cases included no such accusation, and even when they did, the vast majority were unfounded. The issue was personal: Wells faced lynching threats in retaliation for reporting on Black murder in her newspaper, the *Memphis Free Speech*. Wells popularized the phrase "lynch law" to capture this era of anti-Black vigilantism—an era enabled by the Supreme Court's refusal to enforce the Fourteenth Amendment and the legislation meant to give it bite.

Reporting and activism were not Wells's first foray into defending civil rights. In 1883, Wells was a twenty-year-old schoolteacher in Woodstock, Tennessee.[17] On September 15, she took the 4 p.m. train from her Memphis home. Wells approached the first car and saw it filled with men, some drinking, and no women. Bypassing the car, she sat in the rear car, seeking a less rowdy atmosphere. As the train reached its first stop, the conductor said he would not take her ticket in that car and ordered her to move to the front coach, which was intended for Black passengers. The indignity of the conductor's demand sparked a life of activism. Wells refused to get up as the conductor and two white passengers grabbed her. She resisted, "holding on to [her] seat" as they tried to pull her away. The conductor and the passengers dragged her out of the car and ripped her dress, almost tearing one sleeve off. Long after the event, Wells held on to her train ticket as inspiration.[18] She sued and won at trial. On appeal, the Tennessee Supreme Court ruled against her, ruling that the conductors were not discriminating on the basis of Wells's race, but sending her to a seat that was "alike in every respect."[19] Her loss presaged the Supreme Court's ruling in *Plessy* a decade later, foreshadowing the era of legalized segregation. Wells's defeat highlighted the limits of courts in protecting the Fourteenth and Fifteenth Amendments.[20]

Wells's reporting complemented Trotter's radical penchant to confront moderates who failed to see the dire state of civil rights. The two changed the course of Black activism and defined the mission of constitutional recovery of the Reconstruction amendments. In 1905, Trotter traveled to the Canadian side of Niagara Falls, and in Ontario he joined with twenty-nine Black leaders to discuss the future of civil rights. The organization they created, called the Niagara Movement, represented a formal rebuke to the accommodationist approach of Washington. Its core principle was to revive the promises of the Thirteenth, Fourteenth, and Fifteenth Amendments—explicitly demanding bold legislation to codify racial equality, just as Grant and Douglass had done.[21] Present in Ontario was another Washington critic, W. E. B. Du Bois, who played a seminal role organizing the meeting (and who would later use the principles of the Niagara Movement as the basis to help found the National Association for the Advancement of Colored People). Wells, too, later promoted the Niagara Movement. The organization would not focus on litigation. Instead, they would use political activism to pursue the promises of equal protection and the right to vote. In theory, they had law on their side, but Wells's experience suing for her rights and the disaster of *Plessy* had shown her and her fellow activists that courts alone could not be relied on to recover the Constitution. Activists needed to demand it.

Trotter, Wells, and their Niagara compatriots watched carefully as Woodrow Wilson rose to prominence. Wilson, a Democrat, had made vague statements supporting civil rights while running for governor of New Jersey in 1910. Trotter saw a need to distance Black activism from the Republican party, and so he supported Wilson's campaign, hoping that if Black people rallied behind him, Wilson might make the Democratic Party the vehicle to recover the post–Civil War constitutional amendments that Republicans had abandoned.[22] Wilson remained vague about his commitment to civil rights while welcoming Trotter's support. As the presidential election of 1912 approached, Trotter and fellow activists won a private meeting with Wilson.[23] There, the candidate expressed his personal opposition to "race and color prejudice," and said he would "observe the law in its letter and spirit." Trotter endorsed him for president.

Wilson seemed to vindicate Trotter's decision when he wrote an open letter to a Black church leader saying he supported "not mere grudging justice" for Black people, "but justice executed with cordial liberality and good feeling." Black Americans, Wilson went on, "may count upon me for absolute fair dealing and for everything by which I could assist in advancing the interests of their race in the United States."[24] Wells did not endorse Wilson, but she showed an openness to Trotter's strategy of distancing the Republican Party by not explicitly endorsing Taft (or Roosevelt), despite having formed a local Republican club in 1910.[25]

Wilson won the three-way 1912 presidential race with 42 percent of the popular vote and a resounding 82 percent of the electoral college votes. Many Black voters bucked their usual Republican allegiance, with an estimated one hundred thousand voting for Wilson (in the places where they could vote).[26] But Trotter's hope in Wilson proved tragically wrong. Far from becoming Trotter's hoped-for expositor of a second Reconstruction, Wilson segregated federal institutions, significantly backsliding on earlier progress. And he used the presidency to normalize—indeed, nationalize—a revisionist history that made white superiority the nation's identity. The effect was to send the country into a constitutional crisis so pernicious it would not be fully undone for fifty years.

Constitutional crises have played out in different settings and at varying cadences in American history: a threat to free speech was stopped by editors and allied presidents; a battle among presidents over constitutional personhood fomented the Civil War and Reconstruction. The presidency of Woodrow Wilson caused a different kind of crisis. The damage he occasioned cut wide and deep in mainstream American political culture through the twentieth century. His white supremacist ideology completely rebuked the multiracial democracy that Frederick Douglass had envisioned, instantiating a disavowal of the constitutional rights of Black people. Unlike Adams, however, Wilson did not reject the ideal of democracy or its centrality to the Constitution. Instead, Wilson, one of the nation's leading constitutional experts, conceived of American constitutional democracy as compatible with, even requiring, racial hierarchy. At the top of that racially ordered democracy, Wilson thought, was a president charged with pursuing efficiency and reducing what he termed the ill of "friction."

To understand the crisis of democracy that Wilson began, consider a memory implantation metaphor inspired by the *Twilight Zone* television series. Imagine a dystopian tale in which an enemy civilization replaces the memories of peaceful Earthlings. With these fabricated memories, the Earthlings warmly remember the malevolent invaders as friends and liberators. The invasion is completed not through violence but an insidious and false deception. This matches the crisis of the Wilson presidency. Although the Confederacy had long ago laid down its arms, Wilson, through rhetoric and executive action, galvanized and nationalized a core element of its mission, reanimating white superiority as a fundamental American principle. Wilson brought that idea mainstream appeal: in the White House, throughout the federal government and its growing executive agencies, in the legal structure of the nation's capital, into classrooms, and on the silver screen. Like Henry Ford with the automobile, Wilson produced white supremacy at scale, reshaping the country's understanding of the Constitution and of itself. Wilson did not invent white supremacy. But he modernized, popularized, and nationalized it.

During Wilson's presidency, communities throughout the country built monuments to the Confederacy, and the end of his second term would see the worst spasm of nationwide racial violence experienced in decades. These events were linked to Wilson's vision for the country, which was expressed in a revisionist history of the nation's past and a racialized hierarchy for its future.

Countering Wilson's insidious vision would require a new kind of democratic constitutional constituency, one that would incorporate a variety of civil rights organizations and leaders over multiple generations. The decades-long movement to recover a racially inclusive notion of "We the People" recruited a diverse cast of characters—including newspaper editors and journalists such as Trotter and Wells, a young lawyer from the Howard University School of Law who fought the white law school that denied him admission, and a savvy economics PhD who persuaded members of a presidential committee to seek to reclaim the democratic understanding of the Fourteenth Amendment's guarantee of "equal protection."

★ ★ ★

TROTTER'S ENDORSEMENT OF WILSON in the election of 1912 did not cause the constitutional crisis over equal protection; Wilson might have won without Trotter's help. Still, Trotter was quick to correct course. Trotter and Wells spent the rest of their lives battling Wilson's modernized white supremacy and its threat to democracy. Before their ideas would gain traction, they found themselves in an all-out battle with the university-president-turned-US-president.

Neither Trotter nor Wells—nor much of America—realized that Wilson had spent his academic career building a philosophy that would bring white supremacy roaring into the twentieth century.

The origins of this philosophy and the counterrevolution that Wilson occasioned began at Princeton University, where Wilson served as a professor and president for twenty years. In largely overlooked archival documents currently housed at Princeton University, Wilson laid the intellectual architecture for how white supremacy would become embedded in American life in the twentieth century.

All presidents bring their political ideas into the White House. However, Wilson's intellectual background sets him apart from other presidents. At the apex of his academic career, Wilson was one of the premier constitutional thinkers of his day. He is the only president to hold a PhD, much less be a university president. He authored dozens of books, articles, and lectures on American history, politics, and law, while lecturing to the children of America's wealthiest, most powerful families.[27] At Princeton, Wilson developed an overarching theory of politics and the Constitution—one which takes on extreme importance as the basis for his nationalization of white supremacy as president. Wilson the president can be fully understood only through Wilson the professor.

Wilson began teaching at Princeton in 1890, just as Jim Crow was taking form in the American South. At Princeton, Wilson's teaching illustrated his approach to politics. Two classes in particular stand out: the first was on constitutional law, where Wilson's lectures narrowed the meaning of the post–Civil War amendments to almost nothing.[28] In the second, on comparative law, Wilson lauded Germany's and Prussia's aspirations to political and cultural efficiency. The two courses worked together, in a way: by minimizing Reconstruction in constitutional law, Wilson opened the door to nationalizing ideas like segregation and anti-pluralism, which in turn supported the efficiency he championed in comparative law. These ideas were not simply the musings of a crank professor; they were imbibed by hundreds of white, male Princetonians, who carried them into elite American institutions.

The ideas in these lectures were preserved by a Princeton librarian shortly after Wilson was elected president of the United States. Undergraduate students in Wilson's classes had jotted down the live ruminations of their professor in black, leather-bound notebooks. The collection of these notebooks, maintained in the Princeton University archives, has never been publicly described or examined.[29]

The notebooks reveal a young professor's obsession with Prussian political theory. This obsession may seem odd from the *president* who fought Germany in World War I, and who drenched his wartime politics in anti-German xenophobia. But much earlier, *Professor* Wilson's interest in Germany was that of an admiring scholar.

That interest began when Wilson was a political science student at Johns Hopkins working toward his PhD, which he received in 1886. Wilson attended lectures about how history could be theorized in systematic terms that describe a progressive improvement of the human condition. He became absorbed by the philosophy of Georg Hegel, the famous nineteenth-century German philosopher who influenced a range of thinkers on the right and left, including Karl Marx.[30] In Hegel's works, personal freedom was framed as a *national* ideal—only achieved when each individual fit a hierarchy that served the larger whole. Hegel's ideas from the early 1800s aligned with an idea emergent in intellectual life in the early 1900s: applying biological principles to social and political conditions. Wilson (like many of his classmates) began to view individuals as cells or cogs within a living organism, which he analogized to the nation. As Wilson's worldview solidified, he came to believe the individual rights described in the Constitution, championed by Jefferson and Madison, were not immutable triumphs, but were instead subservient to transcendent ideals of national order and societal hierarchy.[31]

These ideas came to Wilson from his professor and mentor, Herbert Baxter Adams. Born in Massachusetts and one of the first Americans to receive a PhD from a German university, Adams brought Hegel's German idealism to Johns Hopkins. In Adams's seminars, Hegelian ideas of national glory merged with an account of white America's origins in Germanic tribes—the "Saxon" in Anglo-Saxon. Specifically, Adams advocated the pernicious doctrine of "Teutonic germ theory," which held that American institutions back to the Puritans had biological origin in their Saxon roots. The brilliance of the founders, he argued, came from these Teutonic roots. Those who developed America's constitutional institutions were "letting their race habits and instincts have natural play."[32] Some of Adams's students justified slavery based on this theory, including Thomas Dixon, whose later novel, *The Clansman*, inspired the infamous film *The Birth of a Nation*, portraying the history of the Ku Klux Klan as a heroic struggle against the excesses of Reconstruction. In Adams's lecture hall, Dixon and Wilson forged a friendship that continued for decades, later paying off enormously for Dixon.

As a Princeton professor, Wilson demonstrated how the ideas he encountered at Johns Hopkins suffused his thoughts on American government. What Hegel called "freedom," Wilson transformed into an Americanized "liberty"—a concept that defined Wilson's lectures and was repeated frequently in his students' notebooks from his constitutional and comparative law seminars, and also in his class on the principles of government. To Wilson, people commonly mistook liberty for license, or the ability to act with minimal restraints, which Wilson thought invited anarchy. Instead, he explained, liberty meant order—the absence of chaos.[33]

One Princeton student captured Wilson's thinking particularly vividly: "A free people is a people not subject to the arbitrary choices of its rulers," Wilson is supposed to have said. Nothing radical there. Then Wilson added a crucial qualification: that liberty was reflected in "a people whose interests and whose individual rights somehow get rewarded with a good deal of system and without serious *friction*."[34] This quote illuminates the wider political philosophy developed in Wilson's lectures and academic writing: true liberty was a condition that emerged only in a national system lacking "friction"—and was defined by efficiency in its affairs. Such a system focused on productivity by reducing impediments to society's goals, like the "friction" of social conflict, especially racial violence and class conflict. The maximum state of friction was anarchy, at which stage society broke down completely. Thus, friction was the enemy of liberty—and in Wilson's view, the path for creating good government meant waging a permanent war on friction. Since liberty was the absence of friction, equality was secondary: if hierarchy created efficiency and minimized friction, it should be preferred over equality; and as such, breaking down hierarchies that had enabled efficiency would not only be foolish (paid at the steep cost of social friction) but indeed wrong. Because a society's hierarchies were natural, they reflected cohesion—and a society that enjoys cohesion enjoys less friction.[35]

Ominously, Wilson thought the beneficial nature of this hierarchy applied to voting, where Wilson told students there should be "equality in suffrage . . . up to the point where all are equal in capacity to judge."[36] It was hardly a leap from this conception of liberty, equality, and hierarchy to Wilson's regressive views on race. Wilson took race as a proxy[37] for the ability to "judge." In what he called his "formula," for assessing an individual's merits, race stood as a good predictor of the quality of judgment based on his observance of "fact and performance"—with whites being more apt at judging than Black people.[38]

Wilson didn't just preach these views in his classroom. He popularized them in his writings, including *A History of the American People*, a sweeping five-volume history written for popular consumption and praised by premier historians for its readability; it was lauded by one prominent academic, a fellow student of Herbert Baxter Adams, as "brilliant in style."[39] In these works, Wilson retold the story of Reconstruction from a decidedly white supremacist perspective. He described the postbellum era as chaotic and approaching anarchy, blaming the Grant administration for changes that resulted in a loss of true liberty for Americans. According to Wilson, expanding franchise and political power to Black people was a disaster for a society that should have sought to avoid inefficiency, and the "ignorance and credulity" of Black people "made them easy dupes" for opportunistic Republican politicians.[40]

Wilson's writings at times rewrote history. Describing Reconstruction as a time of "fear, demoralization, disgust, and social revolution," Wilson derided Grant's and the Republicans' aim for a more equitable society as furthering "the dominance of the negroes in the South." (In fact, the goal was to create equality between Blacks and whites, inviting democracy into the South for the first time.) In perhaps his most audacious factual inversion, Wilson even lamented the loss of the franchise, not for Black people—murdered by the thousands in Louisiana and Kansas in opposition to Grant's campaign—but for former Confederates. To these true victims, Wilson reasoned, Reconstruction "shut white men of the older order out from the suffrage even."[41]

In the case of the Ku Klux Klan, Wilson's rewritten historiography was even more egregious. While not outright justifying their crimes, Wilson painted the Klan as a rational, even noble, response to chaos and anarchy—like an immune system gone haywire to attack a virus.

The Klan, Wilson wrote in one volume, would "protect the southern country from some of the ugliest hazards of a time of revolution." While Wilson acknowledged that the Klan was "lawless" and "brutal," leading a "reign of terror," the unmistakable conclusion of Wilson's history is that the ends largely justified the means: whites in the South, Wilson wrote, "had triumphed, and there was at least an end of chronic revolution." The Klan's lawlessness, which included potentially thousands of extrajudicial killings, was made marginal by Wilson, a stance rich in irony for this great abhorrer of anarchy. To Southern Black people, of course, the restorer of law and order wasn't Nathan Bedford Forrest, the first grand wizard of the Ku Klux Klan, but President Grant, whose Department of Justice had thwarted the anarchy the Klan created in the South. Wilson, however, disparaged Grant, painting him as a corrupt imbecile—a characterization that most historians agree today is false, but a portrayal that nevertheless stuck. By framing the Klan as restorers of order, Wilson rewrote anarchy as tranquility, making lies sound truthful and murder respectable—an account as Orwellian as it gets.[42]

Wilson's revisionist history took aim at the Fourteenth and Fifteenth Amendments, which were explicitly designed to topple the hierarchy he lauded as essential to American order and efficiency. Wilson dealt with these Reconstruction amendments by invoking something he was supposedly skeptical of when it came to the superiority of the national government: the supremacy of states' rights. Wilson could have pointed to Supreme Court precedents like *Plessy* to undercut the significance of the amendments. Instead, he went further, purporting to explain the underlying truth that those cases enshrined. It was the states, per notes from his students, that had "control [of] the whole range of civil and religious rights, the education of the people, [and] the regulation of the suffrage"—a de facto truth in the era of lynch law. However, incredibly, Wilson went further, lecturing that "the post-bellum amendments confer the suffrage on no one."[43] That argument is remarkable. By inflating the power of the states, Wilson essentially erased the amendments that had imbued the national government with the responsibility of protecting equality and voting rights—a stance that is all the more remarkable as it came from a future president who would simultaneously defend a new national role for the federal government in promoting economic growth.

With his rising national reputation, Wilson was selected as president of Princeton University in 1902, providing him a platform to put his racial paternalism into full effect. In 1909, a Black student named G. McArthur Sullivan wrote to the university asking to be admitted. Wilson replied dismissively. "I regret to say that it is altogether inadvisable for a colored man to enter Princeton." Wilson's secretary recommended that Sullivan go to a Southern school (or perhaps Brown, since it was Baptist).[44] Wilson's spurious logic here is worth noting. Rather than simply refuse to admit Black students, Wilson claimed to be doing Sullivan a favor: a Black student would simply cause too much friction, which would hurt Sullivan and the white Princeton students. This was a position that foreshadowed his later justifications of segregation as beneficial to Blacks and whites alike.

Wilson's views were therefore not merely a product of his time; rather it was Wilson himself who helped forge the views that his time would later typify, leading a wider academic movement that nationalized white supremacy, efficiency, and disparaging Reconstruction. In a perverse mirror image to Lincoln at Gettysburg helping the country reimagine its founding, Wilson's cynical writings cast an illusion over Reconstruction, eviscerating the memory of the country's "second founding" in favor of a new national ideal based on racial hierarchy. At this juncture, Wilson was still just a university president—even if an influential one—and so his influence had practical limitations. When he became president of the United States, however, he gained the opportunity to put his theories into action at a grand scale.

★ ★ ★

IN 1910, WOODROW WILSON TRADED the Princeton presidency for the New Jersey governor's office. He didn't stay long. After breaking with Democratic Party bosses to pursue a reform agenda, and making just enough vague statements to indicate support of civil rights, he won the presidency of the United States in the election of 1912, aided by an estimated 30 percent of the Black vote—won with the help of William Monroe Trotter—the largest percentage ever for a Democratic presidential candidate.[45] Wilson also benefited from a Republican Party split by former president Theodore Roosevelt's Bull Moose party challenge to President Taft.

Once elected, Wilson's academic work guided his presidency. He idealized a robust central government—the model in Wilhelm's Prussia—which was a departure from American federalism. On Wilson's view, the president would singularly helm this massive ship of state. This was in contrast to the more traditional view of the presidency as defined by constraints. Indeed, in the decades following Reconstruction, America had elected a string of "forgettable" presidents who viewed the job as a minimalist, almost ministerial occupation, as it was severely constrained by the Constitution. But in his 1908 book *Constitutional Government in the United States*, Wilson described the Constitution as "elastic"—a document that conferred immense presidential power if one chose to take it. In his writings, Wilson declared that "the president is at liberty, both in law and conscience, to be as big a man as he can."[46] While the president could not exactly usurp the roles of the other branches, Wilson thought it fine if "Congress be overborne by [the president]" due to his popular support. For the same reason, he thought that the impeachment of Andrew Johnson was a "political" attack on the presidency done "in passion, not in cool judgment."[47] As Wilson saw it, Johnson's attempts to destroy Reconstruction were not a threat to democracy but a president using his legitimate powers. To Wilson, the most important consideration—far more important than whether the president was constitutionally well-behaved—was that the president "must stand always at the front of our affairs."[48]

In emphasizing this lead role, Wilson offered a new justification for the presidency. Unlike Washington, who saw the president as constrained by the Constitution, Wilson believed the president, as the only public official elected by all the people, had a unique independent mandate to pursue policies in all the people's interest: the president is "the representative of no constituency, but of the whole people. When he speaks in his true character, he speaks for no special interest."[49] That role as the sole representative of the entire populace empowered the president to act as a first among equal branches of government. In Wilson's view, a president like Johnson could fight the democratic rights of minorities in the name of democracy, claiming to act on behalf of the people who elected him. That is why Johnson could be a hero in his telling, while Douglass's allies were villains.[50]

In the White House, Wilson adhered with remarkable precision to these views, making sweeping changes to government. He expanded the federal government's power in the economy, creating the Federal Reserve System to manage the nation's money supply. He expanded the press office, holding 159 news conferences during his two terms.[51] And he used that office to appeal directly to the American people, rallying them to support his legislative agenda and pressure their congressional representatives to enact it. Most significantly, he greatly increased the size of the federal government, implementing the early rudiments of a Prussian-like administrative state, whose bureaucracy and sweep, in his view, would supply the necessary order and rigor to bring America into the modern age.[52]

Wilson's mammoth ambitions ran into an inevitable conflict. When Wilson took office, African Americans enjoyed a prominence in the federal workforce that they had almost nowhere else in American life. Since Reconstruction, Black Americans held a variety of positions across the federal government, mostly in Washington, DC.[53] By 1907, Black workers made up 11 percent of federal employees in Washington, from secretaries to scientists. For example, Trotter's father had been a recorder of deeds in the first Grover Cleveland administration.[54] Such a prolific contribution by a supposedly inferior race posed a major obstacle to Wilson's plans of expansion. A radically enlarged government simply could not afford to countenance the notion of African Americans as equal partners, because Black and white employees working side by side, on Wilson's view, created the kind of friction that could invite anarchy.

Thus, Wilson presided over one of the largest setbacks to racial progress in a generation: he resegregated the federal workforce. This he did stealthily—knowing better than to announce the decision at a press conference—by making the policy unofficial, thus giving his administration plausible deniability. The opportunity came when Wilson's postmaster general, Albert Burleson, just one month into his term, proposed a plan to deal with the "intolerable" condition of whites and Blacks working together. In a cabinet meeting, he voiced his disgust about arriving in Washington and discovering the two races sharing bathrooms and drinking glasses.[55] As Secretary of the Navy Josephus Daniels recalled, Burleson was "anxious to segregate white and negro employees in all Departments of the Government." Secretary of the Treasury William McAdoo, sitting nearby, heartily agreed.[56] Wilson remained quiet. Then he spoke words at once cryptic to the public yet instantly understood by the cabinet: while no Black people should lose their positions, the government could be reorganized in whatever way would make the least "friction."[57] In 1913, without a direct order from Wilson, the segregation of the federal government quietly commenced.

Throughout 1913, segregation became gradually unmistakable in Washington. One by one, cafeterias, workplaces, and bathrooms became segregated in practice, but with no flashing signs announcing the change.[58] The cultural change required to enforce this regime was a separate undertaking. Black federal employees suddenly found themselves subject to more menial jobs, worse working conditions, or openly discriminatory managers. Protests often led to retaliation, such as denied promotions.[59] For many Black employees, the experience of segregation was as sudden and obvious as enjoying an integrated cafeteria one day and being relegated to a separate back room the next.

Because no formal policy for this revolution existed, the Wilson administration offered pseudo-denial and deflection—treating the obvious and ongoing segregation as a kind of bureaucratic mystery. When the newspaper editor Oswald Garrison Villard challenged Wilson, Wilson first deflected responsibility to his cabinet. Then he appeared to defend the policy, describing the need to reduce "friction," and insinuating that the policy was a way to keep Black employees out of harm's way.[60] Unsurprisingly, Wilson faced continued pressure. He finally stated that he did "approve of the segregation," but subsequently vowed to a Black delegation, led by Trotter, that he would investigate it. In Wilson's warped worldview, segregation did not necessarily imply discrimination.

Trotter watched with something close to astonishment. As Wilson rose, Trotter had too, transforming readers of his newspaper into a constituency to lobby the federal government to restore the Reconstruction amendments. Trotter had founded the National Independent Political League, which was devoted to fighting for legislation to guarantee voting rights, documenting efforts to use lynching to disempower Black people, and lobbying for a new federal anti-lynching law. The organization was an alternative to the newly formed National Association for the Advancement of Colored People, which both Trotter and Wells came to find too complacent.[61]

Soon into Wilson's term, Wells and Trotter knew they needed to fight the shadow segregation in the federal government. The NAACP was mostly silent on the matter, which Trotter suspected was attributable to the NAACP's then largely white leadership.[62] Wells, who had fought in the courts against segregated public spaces within the states, was not going to ignore segregation as Wilson implemented it federally.

Trotter saw Wilson's spread of segregation as a personal betrayal. Wilson was going beyond the neglect of civil rights that defined past Republican presidencies. He was undoing a bedrock principle underlying the Reconstruction amendments that held that Black people were equal citizens, not to be subject to racial subordination under law. Indeed, Wilson was changing the fundamental understanding of the second founding, erasing the commitment to civil rights that defined its amendments and meanwhile actively expanding segregation.

Trotter and Wells teamed up to respond to Wilson's betrayal. They understood the imperative to sound the alarm to Black activists, while also seeking to convince Wilson to undo his stealth segregation. When Trotter's NIPL appealed to Wilson for a meeting, they found the White

House receptive. In fall 1913, Trotter collected more than twenty thousand signatures from people opposed to Wilson's segregation.[63] These were the voices of the constituency Trotter and Wells sought to represent at the White House.

Armed with the petition, Trotter and Wells, joined by five other Black NIPL leaders, went to the White House. On November 6, 1913, the group sat face-to-face with the president.

Trotter began. Speaking from a prepared memo, Trotter was unsparing in assessing Wilson's actions. The president, he announced, was failing his campaign promises to Black people. "This segregation," Trotter explained, "denies equal freedom and equal opportunity to employees of African descent as compared to all others." He continued: "Never before was race prejudice and race distinction made official under our National Government, never before incorporated in a National Government policy." Still, Trotter shrewdly crafted an out for Wilson—cleverly embracing Wilson's insistence that his cabinet was responsible. "The inauguration of this policy therefore can be attributed to no cause but the personal prejudice of your appointees in the Executive Branch of the Government." Now that Wilson had been made aware of the policy's effects, the enlightened president could nobly undo the mistakes of his underlings: "We cannot believe that after this concrete evidence of its offensiveness to your Afro-American fellow citizens, you will permit this mistaken policy to continue."[64]

Wilson could have run with Trotter's entreaty. Instead, he stalled, demurring that "I do not think that the spirit of discrimination has been shown in any essential matter." He added that he was "slowly making myself familiar with the matter with the hope that I shall see my way clear to do the right thing all along the line." Trotter continued to press Wilson for specific assurances. Wilson resisted, offering only a conclusory statement that "I assure you it will be worked out."[65] Wells, the only woman present, according to her biographer, was "decidedly the second fiddle." She played along with the idea that Wilson hadn't been behind the policy, claiming that the delegation was there only to bring the matter to his attention.[66]

Wilson's assurance amounted to little; the segregation of the federal workforce proceeded. Twelve months after this meeting, Trotter and five allies secured a second meeting with Wilson. This time, Trotter was more aggressive. He reported details of the ongoing segregation, focusing on the "degrading" facts of segregated bathrooms and being "herded" to separate tables in cafeterias.[67] "Only two years ago you were heralded as perhaps the second Lincoln," Trotter said, appealing to Wilson's ego, but also betraying a hint of personal hurt. He said, "What a change segregation has wrought!"[68]

Now, Wilson went on offense, using his favorite formulation to defend the policy and dropping the pretense that he was caught unaware about the government segregation. His cabinet's policies were "seeking not to put the Negro employees at a disadvantage," but rather "seeking to make arrangements which would prevent any kind of friction between the white employees and the Negro employees." Trotter had a retort for the ages: "No, Mr. President, there cannot be any friction with regard to going into a public toilet." Wilson continued to absolve himself of responsibility. "It is going to take generations to work this thing out," he lamely replied. Then, offering the picture of audacity, Wilson shifted responsibility for the suffering caused by his policies onto his interlocutors. "My question would be this," Wilson then asked the group: "If you think that you gentleman, as an organization, and all other Negro citizens of the country, that you are being humiliated, you will believe it." But, Wilson counseled, "If you should take it in the spirit in which I have presented it to you, it wouldn't have serious consequences."[69] The real problem, Wilson offered, was Black Americans allowing themselves to be humiliated. Ominously, this reasoning echoed the logic of *Plessy* in 1896, which said that if Black Americans found segregation outrageous, it was because "the colored race chooses to put that construction upon it."[70] This famous line from *Plessy* had an earlier origin in Wells's case against the railroad from the incident in 1883, where the court had blamed Wells for interpreting the requirement that she leave the train car as a racist insult. Now, in 1914, the president was repeating this white supremacist principle—that Black people were wrongly viewing segregation as an assertion of their inferiority.

Trotter immediately addressed Wilson's gaslighting as racial paternalism: "We are not here as dependents. . . . We are here as full-fledged

American citizens, vouchsafed equality of citizenship by the federal Constitution." But Wilson's condescension was not the only thing disturbing to Trotter; so was the intellectual kinship Wilson's argument shared with *Plessy*. It was now clear to all, Trotter announced, that Wilson believed "separation itself is not wrong, is not injurious, is not rightly offensive to you." Trotter ended by emphasizing fact over feeling: "You hold us responsible for the feeling that the colored people of the country have—that is an insult and an injustice; but that is not in accord with the facts, Mr. President."[71] Trotter's point presaged the 1954 decision in *Brown v. Board of Education* by several decades: segregation was "inherently unequal."

At meeting's end, the two sides had reached a stalemate. Wilson, smoldering, accused Trotter's group of trying to exact political "blackmail."[72] Trotter, in the spirit of Frederick Douglass, vowed to take his case to the people. With that, Wilson abruptly ended the meeting, and had the delegation removed from the building. Later, to his aides, Wilson pledged to never again take a meeting with Trotter. Trotter made good on his promise. The story appeared on the front page of the *New York Times* and other papers across the country.[73] The dustup was a thunderclap moment for a new chapter of activism. From here on, as Trotter and Wells would loudly argue, the Constitution was in exile. Like Douglass before them, Trotter and Wells had to marshal a defense of constitutional rights not through courts but through a constitutional constituency. Wells had not attended this second meeting with Wilson, but she was invited to address the National Equal Rights League, sounding now a much less conciliatory tone: "No president again would ever dare to offer us such insults as we [have] suffered . . . and thus [we will] teach them to fear our vote."[74]

The break with Wilson and the cry for independence sounded by Wells would usher in a new democratic constitutional constituency that opposed second-class citizenship for Black Americans, demanding equal protection and the right to vote. It would thus echo Douglass's goals from an earlier era. But this twentieth-century democratic constitutional constituency could now appeal to explicit guarantees of these rights in the Thirteenth, Fourteenth, and Fifteenth

Amendments. While Douglass's view of the Constitution had been seen as quirky, a minority view, now his victories gave ballast to this new century of constitutional constituents. And while, like Douglass's constituency, this new constituency would fight through multiple presidencies and a variety of organizations, its methods would become more varied. In addition to publications and conventions, it would employ civil disobedience, public advocacy through a civil rights committee, and skillful use of new media. It would also draw from professions as varied as journalism, law, economics, and the pulpit. Ultimately, it would combine constitutional demands with a mass movement of public protests that brought the inequities endured by Black Americans to television screens across the country, triggering the cultural shift needed to facilitate lasting political change. And it would refuse to be defined by one political party, opposing a Democratic president who resisted the call for equal protection and joining with others who responded to it. The confrontation with Wilson echoed Douglass's with Andrew Johnson nearly five decades earlier. Unlike Douglass, however, Trotter and Wells would not have even one political party as their purported ally. And litigation would be for naught during the Supreme Court's *Plessy* era. But the confrontation with Wilson had clarified the depth of the crisis they faced. The sitting president and Democratic Party leader was a declared enemy of equality and proponent of segregation. With each branch of government undercutting the recovery of the post–Civil War amendments, the goal of multiracial democracy was under assault—and this assault was just beginning.

★ ★ ★

WHILE THE UNITED STATES WAS undergoing a generational retrogression in segregating the federal government and nation's capital—it was also experiencing the birth of modern American culture. After the first voice broadcast[75] was aired in 1906, a strange new technology—radio—was born, which exploded in popularity by the end of Wilson's presidency, knitting the country together. Meanwhile, publishing tycoons were rap-

idly expanding in such ways that allowed Americans to experience public discourse and events in unison; by 1910, William Randolph Hearst's
newspapers and magazines alone reached nearly three million readers.[76]

The most powerful tool forging this singular American culture was
cinema. At the start of Wilson's presidency, small numbers of Americans crowded into "nickelodeons," located in storefronts, paying a
nickel to see a short amusing movie.[77] By 1920, millions had sat through
full-length feature films in the nation's many "movie palaces." The film
industry held up a mirror in which Americans for the first time could
look at themselves, and in turn shaped identities in the process. Wilson
capitalized on this zeitgeist, resulting in what scholar Jeffrey Tulis has
called the "rhetorical presidency."[78] One of Wilson's predecessors, Teddy
Roosevelt, had coined the term "bully pulpit" to describe the president's
informal power to marshal public support for his ideas and policies.
Wilson took the bully pulpit concept a step further when he utilized
all the levers of mass culture, not simply the news, to keep the president
permanently atop the national discourse.[79]

Wilson attempted to influence politics by shaping cultural opinion
through the press office. Although it was created by Theodore Roosevelt, Wilson pioneered its modern use, holding the first presidential
press conference in the Oval Office.[80] According to one scholar, he acted
like a professor, dictating what reporters should write, an ambition made
easier by the fact that many present were former Princeton students.[81]

Wilson's frequent use of the bully pulpit to shape national opinion
makes his near-total silence about lynching so telling. Despite frequent
appeals from the NAACP, Trotter, and Wells, Wilson, like his predecessor Taft, said nothing about the national crisis of lynching for almost
his entire presidency. In two pamphlets written in 1892, Wells had documented 241 instances of extrajudicial killings of Blacks by whites up to
that point.[82] In 1912, the year Wilson was elected, sixty-two documented
were cases. In the eight years of Wilson's presidency, the crisis continued. Spasms of organized or spontaneous violence by white supremacist groups spread across the country, aiming to instill fear and terror in
Black communities, causing an average of more than fifty documented
lynchings per year.[83]

Trotter had supported Wilson's campaign in part because he believed him to care about the injustice of this violence. It is clear now how wrong Trotter was. Wilson's lecture notes indicated that he believed a federal law opposing lynching would be unconstitutional. We can see why: any such law would be based on Congress's power to enforce the Fourteenth Amendment, which for Wilson was essentially toothless. Wilson's silence on lynching fit a pattern of silence established by Taft. But, as evidenced by Wilson's response to a popular film that was largely a paean to extrajudicial killings, Wilson went beyond leaving racial violence to the states—he was fomenting it nationally.

Woodrow Wilson would not call himself an ardent defender of the Klan. His academic work criticized the group's lawless methods of enforcing racial hierarchy, including its "brutal crimes" that made society "infinitely more disturbed than defended." And yet, Wilson's complaint was with the Klan's methods—not their goals. To Wilson, racial hierarchy was worth preserving. The Klan was merely forced into existence by the "intolerable burden of governments sustained by the votes of ignorant negroes"[84]—an extraordinary conceit that seemed to make Black people responsible, indirectly, for their own murders. When the Klan used intimidation to keep Black people from the polls, Wilson thought their ends at least partially justified the means: if the federal government insisted on mixing the races, inviting friction, it was inevitable someone would step in. Although he abhorred violence—he helped create an international League of Nations to avert it—Wilson nevertheless idealized a legalized form of racial order.

This was the intellectual soft spot that the author Thomas Dixon maximally exploited. After Johns Hopkins, where Dixon and Wilson studied under the racist Henry Baxter Adams, Dixon came into fame for books and essays that attacked both Black people and Reconstruction.[85] One of Dixon's most famous works was *The Clansman*, published in 1905, which lionized the Ku Klux Klan as a heroic counterinsurgency in the tradition of the Teutonic Knights, while depicting Black people in the South as degenerates, sexually depraved, and power hungry. After selling over a million copies, *The Clansman* was turned into a play, where it toured across the country.[86] The play's success caught the attention of

D. W. Griffith, the soon-to-be eminent film director, son of a former Confederate officer, who was looking for a subject to apply his revolutionary techniques in narrative filmmaking. In 1914, Griffith and Dixon collaborated to turn *The Clansman* into a feature film, *The Birth of a Nation*.

The film, premiering in February 1915, depicts American history through an unabashedly white supremacist lens. Its title cards say the Civil War was started by a president who disregarded state sovereignty. Enslaved persons before the war are depicted as happy. And the film's second half is even more noxious. Reconstruction is recounted as a time when Blacks dominated whites and raped and married white women against their will. The plot recounts a mostly Black South Carolina legislature legalizing interracial marriage while representatives eat chicken, laugh on the legislature's floor, and eye white women in the balcony viewing area with lust. A Black lieutenant governor then tries to use the law to nonconsensually marry a white Southern woman, an act that motivates the main character to begin the Ku Klux Klan to save her and others like her from a "Black Empire."[87] A crucial part of the film involves a lynching in retaliation for an attempted sexual assault. The dead Black body is then thrown at the door of the lieutenant governor. Called "racial pornography" by film critic Vincent Brown, *The Birth of a Nation* defends the Klan and lynching, which are portrayed as a necessary counter to Black sexual violence.[88] The very title, *The Birth of a Nation*, refers to a concluding scene in which the Klan stops Black people from voting and allows white supremacy to be reclaimed. By the end, Northern and Southern whites overcome sectionalism to unite under the Klan's banner against the supposed threat of Black dominance. *The Birth of a Nation*, to Dixon and Griffith, is the death of Reconstruction and the Fifteenth Amendment.

The similarities between Wilson's version of American history and that peddled by Dixon and Griffith is no coincidence. *The Clansman* and *The Birth of a Nation* drew explicitly from Wilson's work, *A History of the American People*. Three title cards from the film quote Wilson criticizing Black equality and speaking approvingly about the Klan. One reads, "The white men were roused by a mere instinct of self-preservation . . . until at last there had sprung into existence a great

Ku Klux Klan, a veritable empire of the South, to protect the Southern country." Another describes a determination by Republicans to "put the white South under the heel of the black South." A third meant to bolster the depiction of irresponsible Black rule describes the "insolences" of Black officeholders.

These quotes credited to Wilson were edited to omit Wilson's critiques of the Klan,[89] demonstrating Griffith's intent to capitalize on the implied endorsement of the president. Dixon met with Wilson on February 3, 1915, and proposed that the president screen the film in the White House. The screening would dramatically boost Griffith's efforts to get the film greenlit by censorship boards, which in some regions had banned the play. Griffith would use the screening to claim the film was endorsed by Wilson. And he noted that he had essentially used the president's academic work to ensure the film's accuracy, a claim the national censorship board later backed.[90] On February 18, 1915, *The Birth of a Nation* was shown in the East Room of the White House to cabinet members and their families; also in attendance were Griffith and Dixon, Wilson's daughter, Margaret, and his personal physician.[91] Wilson reportedly left silently after the film ended. His copy of the printed program was found crumpled, leading one historian to speculate he might have left in anger. But, clearly, he was not angry: Wilson offered the White House as a forum of prestige for Griffith to push his history, and he never objected to the inclusion of his quotations, even as the film was shown around the country.[92]

Trotter knew the danger posed by *The Birth of a Nation* and sought to have it banned by organizing protests and litigation in the courts. Years earlier, in his hometown of Boston, Trotter had successfully closed a performance of *The Clansman* by appealing to the mayor.[93] Now, however, the production company's attorney, John Cusick, successfully resisted attempts to censor the film by arguing that the film was educational, noting the White House screening.[94]

Griffith condemned the attempts to ban the film as an attack on free speech, later writing a pamphlet about the dangers of censorship.[95] But that claim ignores the fact that censorship then was common to prevent disorder. Indeed, within a few years, the Supreme Court's "clear and present danger" rule for the First Amendment explicitly allowed for censorship of work that would bring unrest. Trotter was simply seeking parity with how other security threats were treated. As he saw it, the threat of anti-Black violence from the film was real and imminent, standards that even the modern Supreme Court has invoked in disallowing some speech that might spark riots.

Trotter's censorship board battles were unsuccessful, and so he turned to direct protest. On April 17, 1915, Trotter joined five hundred men in Boston outside the Tremont Theatre to protest the screening of the film. Trotter and several men entered the lobby to buy tickets so that they could protest inside when he and five others were arrested for planning to disrupt the film.[96] Undeterred, the next day Trotter and other activists spoke out against the film, convening over one thousand supporters at Faneuil Hall. On April 19, Trotter led a march to the governor's office, this time with some two thousand supporters.[97] Trotter even joined forces with former foes such as Booker T. Washington and the NAACP in protesting film screenings nationwide.[98]

Trotter protested *The Birth of a Nation* because he partly feared it would stir white supremacist violence. On Thanksgiving in 1915, with the Atlanta premiere just eleven days away, William Joseph Simmons traveled to Stone Mountain, an area on the outskirts of the city, and burned a cross. On opening night, Simmons marched with his group down Peachtree Street, covered in white sheets.[99] Simmons claimed to be launching the second iteration of the Ku Klux Klan, reviving it for the first time since the Grant Administration had destroyed it. But, since the movie had been released previously in other cities, and advertisements abounded in Atlanta, it seems likely that Simmons was as much copying the film's portrayal of the Klan as he was trying to imitate the original iteration. Simmons's launch proved effective. By the mid-1920s, the Klan would recruit nearly five million members and commit grievous violence.[100] If anything, Trotter had understated the danger of the film. But less well understood is Wilson's involvement. If the second iteration of the Klan was made in the image of *The Birth of a Nation*, it partly owed its origins to the twenty-eighth president, whose work had inspired it and who gave it the imprimatur of the White House.

In November 1916, as Wilson sought reelection, his party sought to flip crucial Midwestern congressional districts. Representative William Rodenberg, a Republican from East St. Louis, Illinois, was particularly vulnerable. Seeking to tarnish his reputation, local Democrats and Democratic-aligned newspapers accused him of helping Black voters move to his district and paying them to vote Republican, saying he was "colonizing" East St. Louis by "importing" Black people from Republican strongholds to form a Republican "Black Belt" from which to win reelection. The *East St. Louis Journal*, a Democratic Party organ, also claimed to have done an investigation showing that 1,500 "colonized" Black people planned to "swell Rodenberg's Black Belt vote." Part of the plan, according to the *Belleville News-Democrat*, was to buy Black votes for two dollars, leading one resident to ask, "Why do the colored voters sell their votes so cheap?"[101]

Wilson openly stoked the conspiracy about colonization on election eve. He sent a telegram to his campaign headquarters, which was distributed throughout the nation's newspapers, that began expressing optimism about winning, but ended on a more disturbing tone. He warned of "conscienceless agents of the sinister forces working in opposition to progressive principles and popular government" who might "resort in their desperation to industrial coercion or to the evil and insidious practices of a decade and more ago."[102] By a decade ago, Wilson was referring to the supposed origin of the colonization process.[103]

In November of 1916, the Department of Justice gave official credence to the conspiracy theory by making false claims about it being widespread in East St. Louis and nationwide.[104] The assistant attorney general running the investigation recklessly claimed that more than three hundred thousand Black people in three states had been co-opted into the scheme. Another DOJ statement claimed that sixty thousand Black people were brought north in the few months prior to the election. The Democratic papers were eager to print these lies.

Tensions rose during a strike in the summer of 1917. An all-white union had walked out of a munitions factory in East St. Louis, and when Black workers took their place union-aligned journalists spewed venom at the Black strike breakers. Skirmishes began when a white worker was supposedly robbed by a Black man. Then, on July 1, 1917, a white man shot into Black homes from his truck. Black residents retaliated, and the violence cascaded. The result was one of the worst massacres against African Americans since the Civil War. Over three days it was estimated that more than one hundred Black people were murdered by whites, and another nine whites were estimated killed. Six thousand were driven from their homes.[105]

Days after the riot, Ida B. Wells traveled to East St. Louis to document what happened. She focused on four women who had lived through the massacre. One told Wells how every Black person the white mob saw was shot and beaten. Another, whose house had been torn apart and burned, said she saw her white neighbor wearing her clothing after the massacre.[106] Wells also advocated on behalf of one of the Black residents who was being scapegoated for the violence.

The DOJ could have prosecuted those who were responsible. But such prosecutions would have undermined Wilson's philosophical opposition to federal civil rights protection. Specifically, the DOJ could have used the Enforcement Act of 1871, also known as the Ku Klux Klan Act, to seek justice against racially motivated murders. But Wilson would not be swayed. Through his attorney general, he claimed that the federal government had no jurisdiction to even investigate the massacre. Wells pointed to the Ku Klux Klan Act to counter that point, but her efforts failed to convince the president. Wilson's constitutional theory suggested why he found the Ku Klux Klan Act unconstitutional: per his Princeton lectures, he held that the Fourteenth and Fifteenth Amendments created no new powers of the federal government.

Despite the inaction of the Department of Justice, Congress held hearings about the events in East St. Louis. Representative Rodenberg testified about the horrors, saying, "It is impossible for any human being to describe the ferocity and brutality of that mob. In one case, for instance, a little ten-year-old boy, whose mother had been shot down, was running around sobbing and looking for his mother, and some member of the mob shot the boy, and before life had passed from his body they picked the little fellow up and threw him in the flames."[107]

Wells, unsuccessful in convincing Wilson to prosecute, turned to lobbying him to support a new anti-lynching bill. Her bill made it to the House but never to Wilson's desk, and Wilson remained silent until July 1918, when he finally issued a statement. He called every lynching a "blow at the heart of ordered law and humane justice," adding that lynchers betray democracy and undermine the country's promotion of moral values abroad. He "earnestly and solemnly" begged citizens to "actively and watchfully . . . make an end of this disgraceful evil."[108] Yet the statement was classic Wilsonian evasion. On the one hand, anyone reading the statement would think Wilson abhorred the violence. On the other, Wilson's solution, to ask everyday Americans to stop the lynching, was a far cry from Wells's demand for federal prosecutions of racial violence against Black people. Wilson resisted that option for his entire presidency. This resistance was consistent with his willingness to expand the federal government's reach in almost every matter except civil rights.

★ ★ ★

WORLD WAR I, and the aggressive nationalism Wilson encouraged at home, added a new dimension to the civil rights struggle for Trotter and Wells. At home, the war spurred the passage of the Espionage Act of 1917 and the Sedition Act of 1918. Not since the Alien and Sedition Acts under the Adams presidency had there been federal laws banning disloyal speech, but Wilson saw them return. Trotter's allies, including a young A. Philip Randolph, a critic of Wilson and the war, and later a co-organizer of the March on Washington in 1963, were prosecuted. Randolph fled federal authorities after being charged with distribution of "seditious material"—an article criticizing Wilson—under the Espionage Act.[109]

On the world stage, Wilson called himself a defender of democracy, advocating for a League of Nations—an international organization to promote global cooperation and prevent future wars—to make the world safe for democracy. "The beauty of all democracies is that every voice can be heard, every voice can have its effect," Wilson said, making the case for the League, which was "what America has always fought for."[110]

The hypocrisy was staggering, especially to Trotter and Wells, who could not understand how Wilson would make the world safe for democracy abroad while attacking it at home. Despite watching allies prosecuted under the Sedition Act of 1918, they continued their criticism—even doubled down. Trotter and Wells took their activism to the world stage. When Wilson made his case internationally, so would Trotter and Wells.

Wells and Trotter had reason to think that highlighting Wilson's hypocrisy might pressure him to reverse course, as it was a strategy that had worked for women's suffrage. At the start of his tenure, Wilson had adamantly opposed a constitutional amendment to guarantee women the vote. Later, under major pressure from the suffrage movement, he flipped. On June 7, 1918, Wilson wrote to the president of the International Woman Suffrage Alliance explaining his change of position: "I agree without reservation that the full and sincere democratic reconstruction of the world for which we are striving... will not have been completely or adequately attained until women are admitted to the suffrage." Wilson noted that "the war could not have been fought without" women and that it was time to show the nation's "gratitude" by granting suffrage.[111]

That change happened because of a mass movement. In 1913, a white suffrage activist named Alice Paul organized a march down Pennsylvania Avenue on the day before Wilson's inauguration. Four years later, Paul, alongside her fellow activists, began picketing the White House, where she was arrested for obstructing traffic. Paul deliberately sought out publicity, seeing that since women contributed to the war effort so significantly, Wilson would look like a hypocrite for demanding so much of them while giving so little. In prison, she began a hunger strike and was sent to solitary confinement, garnering more publicity. Finally, under this onslaught, the president relented, announcing his newfound appreciation of the link between democracy and women's contributions, and becoming an adamant supporter of national women's suffrage.

Wells had supported the constitutional amendment that would guarantee women the right to vote, but she worried that without a national recommitment to civil rights, it might protect only white women. Fueled by that concern, she and a pair of allies organized a group devoted to Black female suffrage in Illinois, The Alpha Suffrage Club. She represented the Alpha Club in the Illinois contingent of Paul's 1913 protest at Wilson's inauguration.[112] When Wells arrived, leaders of the march told her that the procession needed to be Whites-only. The danger of an integrated march was that it might undermine support for female suffrage by white supremacist Democrats, who were supporters of Wilson. Wells refused to leave. She joined the white Illinois delegation, and made sure she was included in a photo of the now-integrated delegation.

When Wilson shifted his position to support the suffrage movement in 1918, Wells didn't back off her criticism; she deepened it. Wilson's "sincere democratic reconstruction" did not apply to the equal citizenship of Black men and women, she thought. Just as Paul had, she aimed to use his hypocrisy of preaching democracy abroad while denying it at home to change his mind on civil rights.[113]

In January 1919, Wilson planned a peace conference in Versailles, France, to negotiate the end of World War I. In the gathering of delegates representing more than thirty countries, Wilson planned to push his proposed League of Nations.[114] Wilson also pushed his Fourteen Points, which proposed postwar principles for organizing international affairs. To Trotter and Wells, Versailles presented an irresistible opportunity. Right before the Versailles meeting, Trotter organized a Liberty National Colored Congress for World Democracy, convening civil rights organizers to strategize in Washington.[115] The conference chose eleven delegates to travel by boat to Versailles, including Trotter and Wells. Initially, some objected to sending Trotter because he was so controversial and had fought publicly with the president. But Wells prevailed, arguing that excluding Trotter would be "allow[ing] President Wilson to select our delegates."[116] Trotter had two goals. If the delegation were allowed entry, they would demand that the concerns of African Americans were addressed in the once-in-a-lifetime peace process. If they were refused, then the delegates would picket the conference, causing international embarrassment to Wilson and highlighting the American president's hypocrisy to the world.

The White House quickly caught on to the plan. When the delegation applied for passports to travel to France, the War Department refused to grant passports to any Black individuals, except W. E. B. Du Bois and the president of the Tuskegee Institute.[117] Wilson and his administration suppressed dissent at home, and he certainly sought to avoid it abroad at perhaps the most important peace conference in history. Trotter was undeterred. He hatched a plan to travel to Versailles secretly without a passport. Known for his handlebar mustache, Trotter shaved it off to avoid recognition. Needing to arrive without a passport, he decided to pose as a cook on a ship traveling to France—rapidly learning culinary skills in a crash course from a friend, Mary Gibson, and becoming skilled enough in the kitchen to join a French ship, *L'Ancore*,[118] sailing to Le Havre, a port city about 125 miles outside Paris. On arrival, the captain would not let staff disembark. But Trotter volunteered to deliver the mail on shore, and instead of returning to the ship he boarded a train to Paris.[119]

When Trotter turned up in Versailles, ready to request an audience with Wilson and his delegation, he found the treaty already drafted and in Germany's hands. Ever persistent, Trotter sent his delegation's agenda to the negotiators while ginning up support in the local press.[120] One idea coming from the deliberations of the civil rights organizers was an addendum to Wilson's Fourteen Points, the principles he had laid out to guide the peace settlement after World War I. Trotter's delegation proposed a "Fifteenth" Point calling for an end to worldwide race discrimination.[121] Their demand included no less than "the elimination of civil, political, and judicial distinctions based on race or color in all nations for the new era of freedom everywhere."[122] Although Wilson did not meet with him, Trotter managed to have his proposal read by the secretary of the League of Nations, Sir Eric Drummond, who viewed it sympathetically, a fact that surely frustrated Wilson, who had sought to keep Trotter as far from Versailles as possible.[123]

Trotter wasn't the only one to criticize the League of Nations and the treaty. After returning from Versailles, Wilson embarked on a twenty-two-day speaking tour to turn public opinion in his favor. The bias he had built behind ivory tower walls, and the racism he encoded in talk of "friction," became more explicit, exposing his white supremacy and anti-pluralism during a summer rife with anti-Black massacres. On September 25, 1919, Wilson took the stage in Pueblo, Colorado, before a crowd of three thousand at Memorial Hall. Before he turned to politics, Wilson began by dedicating the new hall to those who had sacrificed in World War I. Even though African Americans, Italian Americans, Jewish Americans, and Irish Americans had died in large numbers in the war, Wilson trampled on their memory by alluding to a common slur at the time, "hyphenated-Americans," to distinguish between those with roots in this country and those without. This was not the Teutonic germ theory propounded by Herbert Baxter Adams in full, but his rhetoric painted Anglo-Saxons as the true loyal Americans. Wilson said, "There is an organized propaganda against the League of Nations and against the treaty proceeding from exactly the same sources that the organized propaganda proceeded from which threatened this country here and there with disloyalty." Then he went further: "I want to say—I cannot say too often—any man who carries a hyphen about with him carries a dagger that he is ready to plunge into the vitals of this Republic. . . . If I can catch any man with a hyphen in this great contest I will know that I have got an enemy of the Republic." Wilson continued: "It is only certain bodies of foreign sympathies, certain bodies of sympathy with foreign nations that are organized against this great document which the American representatives have brought back from Paris." The gauntlet was laid down. Any American, especially a hyphenated American, that threatened the League was a disloyal American, an ally of our enemies.[124]

Wilson's assault on "hyphenates" was not new for him. As early as 1916 he used the term, which disparaged Irish Americans, German Americans and all groups who identified with nations or ethnic groups beyond the United States. Black Americans feared that the term and its xenophobia would apply to them, because those like Trotter who spoke out against Wilson were accused of being corrupted by foreign powers, specifically communist Russia. Wilson allies indicated that Black dissent would give way to contentment only if, as Representative James

Byrnes of South Carolina said, "the Bolsheviki of Russia ... will leave [Black people] alone."[125] Such rhetoric echoed earlier accusations against Germany that it had stoked Black dissent during the war.

In 1919, when asked to testify before the Senate Committee on Foreign Relations as representatives of the National Equal Rights League about their anti-racism amendment to the League of Nations, Trotter and his ally, Allen Whaley, focused on the accusations of Black loyalty to foreign powers. Bluntly, Whaley said, "I am not hyphenating the black man, because he is a real American."[126] Trotter argued that demanding an anti-racism amendment was not disloyalty to America, and indeed it was necessary lest Black people be left as the only unrecognized people in a global democracy. Only if their rights were recognized on the international stage would the threat of violence at home be averted. That was no abstract threat. Trotter said, "Mr. Chairman, the oppression of colored Americans by their fellow white Americans is getting to the point where unless the governmental authorities, State and National, take hold of the situation and put their feet down firmly against this continuance, you nor I nor none of us can be assured that our own dear land shall be the land of peace, shall be without violence, shall be without insurrection and shall be without war."[127] Whaley reiterated that the anti-racism amendment could serve as a "sign that the country wants to put down mob violence and put down the lynching of black men, and black women, and black children in the Southland."[128]

Despite Trotter's warnings, the rhetoric painting Black people as disloyal continued from a close Wilson ally with deadly consequences. Charles Hillman Brough, sometimes called "another Wilson,"[129] had studied economics, history, and jurisprudence at Johns Hopkins under Herbert Baxter Adams. He also attended a series of lectures that Wilson gave there.[130] After working as a professor, Brough followed in Wilson's footsteps by trading academia for a governor's mansion, this time in Arkansas. Wilson and Brough were Democratic Party allies, sharing the belief that disloyal outsiders threatened American security. Brough, like Wilson, linked Black protest to foreign interference in US affairs. Brough and Wilson had been set to speak together in Little Rock, Arkansas. But Wilson canceled, having collapsed in Pueblo, Colorado following a speaking engagement on September 25, 1919. Instead of glowing in the aftermath of hosting a president, Brough spent that week bringing paranoid fantasies to life.[131]

On October 1, Brough received three urgent telegrams informing him about labor unrest in the town of Hoop Spur. He became increasingly paranoid, fearing Arkansas faced an insurrection by Black radical agitators. The paranoia exploded on September 30,[132] when, outside the Hoop Spur church, a white man died in a scuffle between Black union members and whites attempting to disrupt their meeting. Brough used the death to demand federal intervention to quell what he said was a coming insurrection. The arrival of federal troops did not stop the violence, and white mobs murdered at least two hundred Black people. Later, in an official report, Brough declared that he and the troops were heroes for quelling a looming insurrection. Though the accounts of the event are vague, some reports indicate that the troops participated in the massacre. At a minimum, federal troops stood by during the slaughter, then contributed to a cover up. Brough's official story was the basis for prosecuting twelve Black men for murdering three white people. Each of the accused were convicted in an Arkansas trial court. One wrote to Wells. Overcoming fears for her life, Wells traveled to Arkansas, dressing as a sharecropper to avoid detection.[133] In a published pamphlet, Wells drew on her investigation to report on the events. Her conclusions were vindicated by the Supreme Court, which eventually overturned the convictions.[134]

Another journalist, Walter White, field secretary for the NAACP, traveled to Arkansas, where through an interview in the governor's office he revealed Brough's motives for covering up the massacre. Brough would likely never have granted an interview to a Black journalist. But White's light complexion let him pose as a white journalist. The governor, convinced by the ruse, told White that he had sent the military to fight foreign powers leading a Black insurrection in the state. Publications such as the NAACP's *The Crisis*, Brough claimed, were sowing discord in Arkansas. That interview almost never saw the light of day, as White barely escaped Arkansas alive. After speaking with the governor, White went to the Hoop Spur area and interviewed residents of Elaine,

Arkansas, a town where much of the violence had occurred. Word got out that a Black journalist in town was "passing" as white. Fearing for his life, White fled, taking the railway out of town that troops had arrived on several days before. The conductor told him he would miss the "fun." What fun? White asked. The men of the town were out to lynch a Black journalist.

In addition to these events in Arkansas, whites in Washington, DC, started riots that summer, killing multiple Black people. Many of those who rioted in DC were military members. President Wilson, responsible for governance in the capital, failed to call out the military for several days. Historians attribute many of the lost lives to this failure to act.[135]

Wells's and White's stories of the tragedy in Elaine became crucial documentary evidence of the "Red Summer."[136] The term Red Summer was first used to convey the blood spilled in Hoop Spur, Elaine, DC, and other places throughout the nation in 1919 from white supremacist violence against Black people. It has also come to stand for the accusations of Black loyalty to "Red" Russia. It is true that Wilson did not urge the murder of Black Americans. But his rhetoric—such as hyping fears of disloyal outsiders and "hyphenated" Americans in 1919, and ginning up the conspiracy about "colonization" in the 1917 election—helped stoke it. And when that violence is understood in the context of his textbook lectures and his actions in resegregating the federal workforce, it becomes clear that Wilson had sown the seeds for that violence, all while claiming to support stability. Ironically, in the name of avoiding friction between the races, Wilson spawned the outpouring of Black blood.

★ ★ ★

WILSON MODERNIZED WHITE SUPREMACY BY rewriting the past. As a professor, a university president, and America's president, Wilson found myriad ways to distort American history, leaving out past struggles for racial justice and relentlessly pointing to an efficient future in which racial hierarchies would be solidified under a Constitution that prized an expanded federal government. In Wilson's history, Reconstruction was a moment of constitutional destruction, not recovery. It should then come as little surprise that Wilson found common cause with a political constituency that included states-rights Southerners nostalgic for the Confederacy. In fact, Wilson's own approach to white supremacy went well beyond these Southerners' attachment to their provincial "way of life." He transformed it into a national credo. Wilson told this account through his lectures and textbooks, then with Dixon and Griffith through popular media. The merging of a modern ideology of white supremacy and modern technology spread these ideas into mainstream American thought. Wilson presided over a cancer that spread first to the nation's brain, then to its heart, and soon to its blood. By the end of the Wilson presidency, white supremacy and Black second-class citizenship were thoroughly ingrained in American politics. Wilson hadn't just threatened multiracial democracy; he killed it for a generation.

However, Wilson's blatant betrayal of civil rights, and his conflicts with Wells and Trotter, helped plant the seeds of recovery. During the Red Summer, the NAACP added one hundred thousand members, a recognition that Wilson brought urgency to the struggle for civil rights. Nevertheless, those seeds of recovery seemed dormant as Wilson's anti-pluralism and racist programs took root in the mainstream of both political parties. In the 1920s, segregation spread throughout the country. Meanwhile, Congress passed the most restrictive immigration law in its history, the Johnson-Reed Act. Despite such dire times for multiracial democracy, the recovery of that ideal would come eventually. In contrast to previous recoveries from assaults on democracy, this battle for a racially inclusive ideal of "We the People" was slower. So mired in the erasure of the ideal of multiracial democracy were all three branches of government that citizens would have to work for decades to reclaim it.

And in 1934, the year of Trotter's death, in a small Baltimore law office at the desk of Thurgood Marshall and in the city solicitor's office in Philadelphia where Sadie Alexander worked, that movement began to bud.

CHAPTER 9

Harry Truman and Sadie Alexander

To Secure these Rights Once More

IN 1944, PRESIDENT FRANKLIN ROOSEVELT, KNOWING HE WAS DYING BUT BELIEVING AMERICA needed consistent leadership, decided to seek an unprecedented fourth term in office.[1] Roosevelt campaigned on "experience" as opposed to his opponent's "immaturity."[2] With World War II raging in Europe and the Pacific, with more than eleven million Americans serving in the military,[3] the stakes were especially high for any running mate he might choose, as that person might need to replace the dying president. Taking no political chances, Roosevelt dumped his controversial vice president, Henry Wallace, shaking up the Democratic ticket. The decision changed the course of civil rights in the twentieth century.

A former agriculture secretary in the progressive mold, Vice President Wallace was despised by Southern Democrats for his outspoken support of civil rights.[4] In 1944, Roosevelt was focused on winning the war, not waging a battle at home. His advisors persuaded him to enlist a compromise candidate, one more acceptable to pro-segregation Southern Democrats. Just before the Democratic National Convention, they put their plan into motion. After a fight at the convention, with Wallace's supporters angling to keep him as vice president, a junior senator from Missouri, a Democratic loyalist with a thin record and thinner name recognition, Harry S. Truman, emerged as the new vice-presidential candidate.

Truman was born in 1884 in the small town of Lamar, Missouri. He spent most of his youth in the nearby town of Independence. Twenty years earlier, during the Civil War, many of Missouri's citizens had fought for the Union, and its largest city, St. Louis, was a hub of Black culture and industrialization. Independence, however, might as well have been in the Deep South. Truman's grandparents had been Kentucky slaveowners, part of what Truman recalled as "a violently unreconstructed southern family." Truman's parents despised Lincoln and valorized Confederate guerrilla leaders. The worst racial epithets in the American lexicon were commonplace in their household.[5] When a reporter went to gather material about Truman, Truman's sister told him "Harry is no more for n***** equality than any of us."[6]

In 1944, Roosevelt's health declined rapidly, preventing him from doing much electioneering. Truman, sixty, became the face of the campaign. It became what Truman later called the easiest campaign of his life, with the country hesitant to change course during the war.[7] African Americans chose in large numbers to stick with the Democrats and the New Deal, a shift from the Republican Party that had begun with Roosevelt's 1932 victory and coalesced by 1936.[8] Southern Democrats, mollified by the choice of Truman, fell in line. Roosevelt cruised to a resounding and historic fourth term, winning 53 percent of the vote, three million votes more than his Republican opponent, Thomas Dewey.[9]

Five months after the election, Roosevelt died from a massive cerebral hemorrhage.[10] Truman, the only modern president who did not graduate college, and still barely known to the country, was now tasked with leading the United States through World War II and shaping the postwar global order. That evening in the White House, before he was sworn in as the thirty-third president, Truman sought to console a widowed Eleanor Roosevelt. She shocked him by asking what she could do for him. After all, she cracked dryly, "You are the one in trouble now."[11]

In fact, trouble was brewing for Truman not just abroad, but also at home. Many Southern Democrats were growing increasingly concerned over one issue: civil rights. Now that Truman was president, what did he plan to do, if anything, with his newfound power? Cautiously, Southerners in Congress remained hopeful that the new president shared their racial outlook. Traveling aboard Roosevelt's funeral train as it meandered from Georgia to DC, Senator Burnet Maybank of South Carolina reassured a fellow Southerner: "Everything's going to be all right," he murmured. "The new President knows how to handle the n******."[12]

Black Americans' economic and political prospects had seen little improvement since Woodrow Wilson left office more than two decades earlier. As the federal government grew,[13] the persistent segregation within its ranks hurt even more lives. Within the Black community, a debate raged, prefigured by Trotter's initial decision to support Wilson for president.[14] Some Black leaders argued that with Roosevelt, the opportunities for Black people presented by the New Deal outweighed the racial discrimination that often accompanied it. Supporting that side were the gains Black people made in some New Deal programs of the 1930s, including the job training and education made possible through the GI Bill of 1944, and FDR's assembling of Black advisors and directors, such as Mary McLeod Bethune, to form his "Black Cabinet."[15] Some scholars credit FDR with creating a new model of economic citizenship that included Black people and reformed much of the feudalism that had defined the postwar Southern economy.[16] At the urging of civil rights leaders and Roosevelt's Black Cabinet, programs such as the Civilian Conservation Corp (CCC) and the Works Progress Administration (WPA) employed hundreds of thousands of Black workers to build Black schools and community centers, teach adult education and work training classes, and facilitate art projects. These programs transformed the infrastructure of the rural South and taught thousands valuable reading, writing, and job skills.[17] Roosevelt in many ways continued the progressive national role in the economy initiated by Wilson, whom he admired. But, unlike Wilson, Roosevelt was not personally ideologically committed to white supremacy. FDR's accession to the racist structure of the New Deal was likely a pragmatic deferral to Southern Democrats in Congress to keep his coalition together. Still, despite his refusal to support broad civil rights legislation advocated by the NAACP and other civil rights groups,[18] FDR issued an executive order enacting a limited ban on discrimination in government defense contracts.[19]

One of the most sophisticated voices in the debate over how Black people fared during the New Deal was Sadie Alexander, the first Black woman to earn a PhD in economics[20] and a staunch Roosevelt critic. Alexander called out the racial segregation and inequality that accompanied the New Deal and the myriad ways it harmed African Americans. In an analysis that decades later would be confirmed by political scientist Ira Katznelson,[21] Alexander pointed to the implicit ways that New Deal programs excluded African Americans. The Social Security Act, she noted, "exempts persons employed as domestic servants or in agriculture," work done disproportionately by African Americans.[22] The centerpiece of the New Deal, the National Recovery Act, Alexander said, "might well bear the nomenclature Negro Reduction Act,"[23] arguing that it increased unemployment among African Americans and increased the racial pay gap, with higher wages attracting white workers to jobs traditionally done by Black workers. Alexander concluded, "Roosevelt never had in mind the security of the American Negro."[24] Katznelson later substantiated Alexander's thesis by showing that minimum wage and unionization laws central to the New Deal had loopholes that excluded work traditionally done by Black people.[25] Furthermore, the Federal Housing Administration often denied loans and mortgages to Black people who tried to buy a home in majority-white areas. These loans and mortgages were, however, given to similarly qualified white people.[26] In agriculture, Southern administrators of federal programs denied benefits to Black people.[27] Black Americans did experience some economic gains during the New Deal from rising overall prosperity; but overall, as Alexander said in one 1935 speech, the New Deal had been a "raw deal."[28]

"Raw deal" was also a phrase that Walter White, promoted from adventuring journalist to the executive secretary of the NAACP,[29] employed in bluntly assessing Roosevelt's civil rights record.[30] By 1945, as Truman took office, there was little indication that the segregated economic arrangements that defined the New Deal would change. But White was determined that America should finally see a recovery of the democratic promises of the Fourteenth and Fifteenth Amendments and an end to Black people's second-class citizenship. To accomplish that, White sought to place civil rights atop Democrats' domestic agenda. President Truman could be persuaded, White believed, if the abuse of Black veterans was publicized nationally.[31] By the end of World War II, thousands of Black soldiers had returned from overseas, after having liberated countries in which they often enjoyed a higher status than they had in the American cities they had left to join the war. In 1946, one of these returning Black serviceman was Isaac Woodard. At twenty-three, Woodard left South Carolina to join the war effort, serving with distinction in the Pacific theater and rising to the rank of sergeant.[32] When he returned home, Woodard was optimistic about his prospects in an American society that might treat Black people differently now that they had served their country in such large numbers. Instead, he found something very different. On the bus home to South Carolina, Woodard got into an argument with the driver after requesting to use the restroom. When they arrived at the next stop in Batesburg, South Carolina, the chief of police Lynwood Shull arrived. He dragged Woodard off the bus and beat him senseless, blinding him for life.[33] Later, a local judge found Woodard guilty of drunk and disorderly conduct despite no evidence to support those charges.[34] The NAACP succeeded in hunting down Shull to legally prosecute him, and when he was acquitted at trial by an all-white jury, the audience burst into applause.[35]

For Black soldiers returning from the war, such as Woodard, the American South was still a war zone. Stories like Woodard's were not uncommon in 1946, which was a particularly violent year in Southern history. That summer, a Georgia mob shot and killed two Black couples.[36] The perpetrators never faced punishment. In Mississippi, a group of Black soldiers were kicked off a truck and viciously attacked.[37] Local justice was often elusive.

Believing Woodard should be a national symbol of race-based discrimination, Walter White invited him to his Washington office. White called the meeting a "poignant memor[y]" that he would never forget.[38] Woodard, blinded, reached for White's hand "in the manner of one feeling his way in the darkness of a strange place." He told White that he had seen him speak during the war, noting, "I could see *then*."

White sought to take the specific injustice Woodard suffered and use it to remove the nation's blinders to the denial of African Americans' constitutional rights to equal democratic citizenship. In the summer of 1946, together with labor, education, and religious leaders, the NAACP created a National Emergency Committee Against Mob Violence.[39] Its leadership prepared for an all-out public relations battle. White organized religious leaders to preach about the need for civil rights, urged union leaders to use their political clout to shine a spotlight on the issue, and pushed NAACP members to lobby Congress.[40] He also sought to harness the power of Black consumers, urging them to pressure newspapers they read to devote more coverage to anti-Black violence.[41] White believed that if the NAACP could marshal the nation's sympathy, they could use it to turn the gears of Congress. White's strategy, however, historically had a persistent hitch: the president.

White took the reins of the NAACP in 1930. During his leadership, the NAACP had repeatedly sought a meeting with the president. Roosevelt initially refused but agreed in 1934 at the urging of First Lady Eleanor Roosevelt, who joined the organization that year.[42] During the meeting the president revealed his indifference to civil rights, refusing to publicly support an anti-lynching bill, stating that it would cost him politically and that he believed it may be unconstitutional—a belief reminiscent of Wilson's anemic understanding of the Fourteenth Amendment.[43] The NAACP's primary political victory during the Roosevelt administration came when White joined forces with A. Philip Randolph, who led one of the country's largest Black unions, the Brotherhood of Sleeping Car Porters.[44] White and Randolph threatened to organize a march in Washington, DC, to demand civil rights and an end to the racial inequality in the government and defense industries.[45] In response, Roosevelt hastily agreed to an executive order that banned discriminatory employment practices among government contractors,[46] an important but limited victory given that much of the New Deal remained segregated. Eleanor lobbied her husband to do more, including to pass an anti-lynching law. In a private letter, she once told White that she had personally appealed to Roosevelt about making lynching a federal crime—but that Roosevelt still refused, in part because he thought the Constitution provided limited power to the federal government to undo local injustice.[47]

After the Roosevelt administration's failure on civil rights, Truman's ascendance to the presidency offered little hope, and the first year of his administration started poorly. The NAACP believed that the FBI had neglected Woodard's attack. In scathing letters to Truman's attorney general, Tom Clark, a young NAACP lawyer named Thurgood Marshall wrote acidly that the FBI's failure was part of a "one-sided" pattern, in which they worked harder to solve crimes against white people than Black people.[48]

In the aftermath of Woodard's assault, the NAACP prepared to do battle with the Truman administration. Leaders of the National Emergency Committee Against Mob Violence demanded a meeting with the president. Given Truman's reputation, they expected a hostile response; instead, he granted the meeting and welcomed them to the White House in September 1946. White and five other delegates from the National Emergency Committee joined Truman.[49] White took the lead. He told Truman about the blinding of Woodard, using it as a way into a wider discussion of the epidemic of lynching throughout the country. White observed that "the president sat quietly, elbows resting on the arms of his chair and his fingers interlocked against his stomach as he listened with a grim face."[50] Truman later described what it felt like as he heard the stories of the Black soldiers' assault: "[My] stomach turned.... Whatever my inclinations as a native of Missouri might have been ... I [decided to] fight to end evils like this."[51] When Truman finally spoke, his first remark was to admit his own ignorance. "My God," the president ruminated, "I had no idea it was as terrible as that!"[52] Truman pledged that he would join forces with White, the NAACP, and the National Emergency Committee to reshape national opinion on civil rights and recover the national government's role in protecting them. It was the beginning of the rebound from Wilson's assault on multiracial democracy—and the end of backsliding on the guarantee of civil rights enshrined in the Reconstruction amendments, a fact painfully endured by Black Americans.

★ ★ ★

IN THEIR MEETING, Truman agreed on the need for federal action—a simple presidential promise the NAACP had waited over years to hear—and a strategy. Addressing the group, Truman declared, "We've got to do something." They then turned to how. Truman and White agreed that the most important task was to galvanize public opinion to combat white supremacy. Truman said, "The president can do nothing unless he is backed by public opinion."[33] That assessment fit well with White's public awareness campaign on the need for a new civil rights agenda. Now, in broad terms, the president had pledged to support that plan.

Truman suggested that public opinion could best be swayed by a panel of citizens representing the entire society who would study the state of civil rights and make recommendations about how to protect them.[54] Today, a blue-ribbon commission to "study" an issue is often how progress gets stymied, not catalyzed. Not so in 1946. Then, the extent of America's civil rights failures was much less widely acknowledged among whites—a measure of just how poorly the federal government had handled civil rights, and how effectively Wilsonian-style history had helped bury the constitutional vision of Reconstruction. There were, for example, no robustly publicized national databases on hate crimes, nor detailed psychological studies on segregation's impact on children.[55] Basic fact-finding was a necessary first step before the nation could recover its commitment to civil rights. More generally, if the ostensible risk of "friction," which Wilson used as a justification for nationalizing segregation, was no longer to be the default federal policy, then Americans had to learn why that philosophy was flawed.[56]

The next day after the meeting with White, Truman wrote to Attorney General Clark, informing him that he was "very much alarmed at the increased racial feeling all over the country." The solution would "require the inauguration of some sort of policy"—as opposed to having the Department of Justice adjudicate new incidents on a case-by-case basis. To ensure that his staff understood his seriousness, Truman told his assistant, "I am very much in earnest on this thing and I'd like very much to have you push it with everything you have."[37]

On December 5, 1946, Truman issued Executive Order 9808 establishing the President's Committee on Civil Rights. Its goal was to "inquire into and to determine whether and in what respect current law-enforcement measures and the authority and means possessed by Federal, State, and local governments may be strengthened and improved to safeguard the civil rights of the people."[38] The first section of the order detailed the fifteen members of the committee, who came from areas of expertise that spanned from academia and business to labor and law. Walter White had consulted with Truman on the composition of the committee. To successfully galvanize public opinion, White thought, required they recruit leaders from the "establishment" business world, who would show broad national support toward civil rights. White had heard of remarks that Charlie Wilson, the CEO of General Electric, had made about the crisis of civil rights. He suggested that this CEO should serve on the committee, and Truman agreed.[59] White was also encouraged by the presence of the two Black members of the committee: Channing Tobias and Sadie Alexander, both allies of the NAACP.[60]

Tobias, a member of the NAACP board of trustees, was in the room with White and Truman when the commission was conceived.[61] He was skeptical, worried that forming a commission would be an excuse for doing nothing.[62] White assuaged Tobias by making him the association's formal representative on the committee, its eyes and ears, giving the NAACP a window into the proceedings.[63] Tobias had given the keynote address at a major conference on race in Finland in 1926 and had met Gandhi in 1937 as a delegate to the YMCA world conference in India; he could speak to how poorly America's civil rights record was perceived abroad.[64]

Sadie Alexander, an economist and lawyer from Philadelphia, was the only woman on the commission. Alexander was focused on how the federal government's abandonment of civil rights had been destructive for African Americans economically and legally. In her work as an economist, she had detailed the disastrous economic and health outcomes for African Americans,[65] and had spoken out about discrimination in the New Deal. She also became an expert on civil rights and earned a law degree from the University of Pennsylvania,[66] joining husband Raymond Pace Alexander in defending Black people who were falsely accused of crimes or who had suffered discrimination, at times collaborating with the NAACP's lead attorney, Thurgood Marshall.[67]

Racial discrimination was not just something Alexander analyzed objectively. Alexander had grown up in Philadelphia and Washington, DC, in a family of accomplished Black professionals.[68] In the 1910s, at the almost all-white University of Pennsylvania,[69] she thrived academically, but Penn was far from welcoming. At lunch, she took her meals in the library lobby because the dining room was for whites only. Off campus, Philadelphia offered ample episodes of discrimination. On a double date at a whites-only theater with her future husband and another Black couple, an employee approached the couples to tell them to leave. When they loudly began to speak French and Spanish, confounding the employee, he remarked that he would allow them to stay because they were not "n******."[70] Alexander recounted this story often as she reflected on a society that had forgotten the legal guarantees of the Constitution and excluded Black people from the new federal commitment to create employment.[71] As a member of the civil rights committee, Alexander would use the skills she had honed as an economist and lawyer to show the all-male group of commissioners how America treated women and other Black people in the 1940s.

For all White and Truman's optimism, however, Alexander and Tobias had their work cut out for them. Charlie Wilson, the commission's chair, interrupted Truman's inaugural speech to the commission, in a way that seemingly tried to lower the expectations, interjecting, "We will do our best to work something out," and that we "hope it will be helpful."[72] Truman saw the mission of the committee differently. Right after Wilson's interlude, Truman said he was "alarmed at certain happenings around the country," and that he wanted to exercise maximum national authority in fighting for civil rights. "I want the Attorney General to know just exactly how far he can go legally from the Federal Government's standpoint." He then conveyed a thinly veiled message to

Southern Democrats, mimicking the states-rights arguments of South-erners: "I don't think the Federal Government ought to be in a posi-tion to exercise dictatorial powers locally," he said. "But there are certain rights under the Constitution of the United States which I think the Federal Government has a right to protect."[73] Truman's remarks tele-graphed his desire for a commission to produce a major report.

★ ★ ★

THE NAACP HAD SET THE STAGE for a new agenda in civil rights. But in the months leading up to White's meeting with Truman, an internal battle had deter-mined the future of its own strategy, with huge implications for national policy. In 1935, the vice dean of Howard University School of Law, Charles Hamilton Houston, left academia to serve as the NAACP's first general counsel.[74] He had a straightforward strategy: if *Plessy* demanded separate but equal, he would bring suits that made "equal" so expensive to implement that even the officials who believed *Plessy* was sacrosanct would abandon it. In one notable case, Houston represented a student suing the University of Missouri's law school, which excluded Black peo-ple, to demand that the state either create a genuinely equal law school for Black students or allow integration at Mizzou.[75] Following Houston's logic, the NAACP did not seek a direct attack on *Plessy* in court. Instead, states' failure in even adhering to *Plessy* could motivate tangible prog-ress on integration.[76] The NAACP strategy was to overturn separate but equal and end segregation incrementally—by showing that the country had never even delivered the bare promise of a separate but equal society.

By 1947, Houston's legal department had been replaced by a more ambitious team, the NAACP Legal Defense Fund, led by a former Houston student, Thurgood Marshall. Marshall began to seek more "complete support" throughout the NAACP for an "all-out attack on segregation."[77] By 1948, the board of directors at the NAACP took Mar-shall's side, pledging to fight only for an end to segregation, not for more equal segregated facilities.[78]

Marshall's vision of reversing *Plessy* was now the NAACP's official mission. Marshall wanted to move fast in dismantling the *Plessy* precedent, abandoning the gradualism of his teacher, Houston. For Marshall, the commitment was not just about convincing courts to reverse the rightly reviled case. Marshall pressed the idea that segregation inherently entailed subordination—echoing the aggressive approach of the Grant era.[79] And like the Reconstruction leaders before him, Marshall chose to make the case that separate was inherently unequal not just in court but in national public opinion.[80]

In letters to the editor published in newspapers throughout the country, Marshall challenged writers and editorial boards in public debate. In a Texas paper, he asked why newspapers should be protected under the First Amendment, but Black people weren't protected under the Fourteenth, charging, "Do you believe that you're obliged only to believe in certain provisions of the constitution?"[81] Marshall was almost as aggressive with local affiliates of the NAACP who balked at the new strategy, making clear to Roy Wilkins and other NAACP leaders that these officials should embrace an "all-out attack on segregation."[82]

Marshall had brought the NAACP to see reversing *Plessy* as the new mission of the organization. It was up to Sadie Alexander to bring that policy to the presidential commission. The NAACP had formed a growing constituency for restoring civil rights. Marshall installed a more aggressive legal strategy. Now Alexander would try to harness the power of that constituency and its newly declared agenda to bury *Plessy*. She aimed to begin that process by bringing to the committee's attention the deep flaws of *Plessy*, and eventually convince the president to adopt the constitutional agenda of the Civil Rights Movement as his own. It was a historic opportunity after Wilson's odious treatment of Alexander's predecessors, Trotter and Wells. And whereas Roosevelt had been indifferent to civil rights, representatives of the Civil Rights Movement were now invited to help set the president's agenda. It was a moment that, like Lincoln's consultation with Frederick Douglass, provided an opportunity to influence a president's thinking. Indeed, Truman's openness to the findings of the committee suggested that he might see this constituency as his own, just as Grant had done in the previous century.

However, before Alexander could make the case for a report that announced the need to reverse *Plessy*, she needed to educate the commissioners on the daily indignities of separate but equal doctrine. At the committee's early meetings, members often stayed and met at the whites-only Statler Hotel in Washington, DC. The White House had to secure an exception to allow Alexander and Tobias to stay at the hotel.[83] A later committee event at the integrated campus of Dartmouth inspired Alexander to write to a white committee member about the camaraderie that was built outside the segregated hotel where she and Tobias were tolerated only as an exception: the trip to Hanover, New Hampshire, made it "possible for each of us to know each other better." "After all," she added, "the great problems in the world, in my opinion are largely because we do not know each other."[84] At Dartmouth, Tobias and Alexander could stand as equals with their fellow committee members as opposed to being second-class at the Statler.

Early in the committee's formation, Alexander and Tobias got a sense of the challenges they would face with their white colleagues. One battle concerned the commission's staff of researchers and lawyers, which was initially entirely white. The commission then agreed to hire one—and only one—Black researcher. Alexander supported Cecil Poole, a Harvard-trained lawyer, but the commission hired someone else without consulting Alexander or Tobias.[85] Frustrated but focused on their larger goal, Alexander worked to ensure that civil rights organizations would testify before the commission—especially those who knew the evils of segregation intimately.[86] Drawing on the legal minds of the National Urban League and the NAACP—including her ally Marshall—would help Alexander shape the committee's report.[87]

In April 1947, Alexander invited Marshall to appear before the committee. There, Marshall propounded one of the most influential constitutional arguments of the twentieth century. Reading from prepared remarks, Marshall argued that the preservation of American democracy required the destruction of *Plessy*. The Thirteenth, Fourteenth, and Fifteenth Amendments, he said, "were intended to raise the negro from the status of a slave to that of a free and equal citizen." The ratification of these amendments, Marshall continued, signaled "that the ultimate responsibility of accomplishing this task could only be handled by a national government which was free from the prejudices and provincial notions of racial superiority."[88] That this guarantee was "purely academic and unreal is undoubtably the greatest indictment of our American democratic form of government."[89]

Furthermore, Marshall argued, the Supreme Court's rulings in *Plessy* and related cases didn't merely undermine the legal guarantees of American democracy; they created, in the minds of many Black Americans, a deeply rooted skepticism about the very existence of American democracy. But Marshall knew this skepticism could be dramatically changed. He encouraged the committee to imagine a new ending to America's story and urged them to see their work as rewriting the country's history, which had veered so badly off course in *Plessy*, under Wilson and in decades after. In effect, Marshall said, the commission could be part of the movement to recover the Constitution by recommending actions consonant with a broad reading of the Reconstruction amendments: "There is no word in our Constitution that requires segregation—not one word any place," Marshall said. "The meaning of the whole Constitution is that there shall be complete and absolute equality." He closed unequivocally: "You can not have equality with segregation."[90]

Perhaps in a show of respect to her colleagues, Alexander cross-examined Marshall. "The Supreme Court hasn't said so," Alexander noted in response to Marshall's contention that the Constitution requires equality and rejects segregation. How could the committee presume to say integration was required, after the Supreme Court and five decades of case law sanctioned separation?[91] Furthermore, how could they go against such ingrained Supreme Court precedent, armed only with a new and largely untested legal theory? Marshall's response was lawyerly; he distinguished *Plessy* from segregation in education, noting the steady movement toward desegregating education by several states' courts. More important than his lawyerly response was the wider context of the hearing: Marshall was subtly telling the committee that the Supreme Court did not own the Constitution or have final say on its meaning; the post–Civil War amendments existed independently of anything the justices had written, and it was up to the committee to declare that the principle of *Plessy* was wrong and that the Constitution barred segregation.[92]

Marshall's testimony[93] that the committee could go beyond the Supreme Court was a guiding light in the creation of its final report. Truman had asked that the committee push for civil rights as far as the law allowed. If not for the work and insights provided by Marshall and Alexander, that push might have meant pursuing Houston's strategy of demanding separate but truly equal facilities within the *Plessy* framework. But as the committee began its final task—writing the report—it reached an extraordinary conclusion: no matter what the Supreme Court had said, the principle of separate but equal was wrong and must be reversed through federal government action.[94] Here, the president had a large role to play. According to the committee, the executive branch should end segregation immediately in the federal government and the military, as this was where the president could act without congressional approval or a court order.[95] FDR had forbidden federal contractors from discrimination in hiring, but he had left in place segregation among federal employees throughout the executive branch. The committee urged that Truman go beyond FDR and issue an executive order to desegregate the federal government. Such action would show the country that separate had no place in society.

For Alexander, a broader recovery of the post–Civil War amendments also required robust legislation from Congress. Initially, the committee recommended legislation that would end segregation in "public accommodations" such as hotels and restaurants, much like the civil rights bill of the preceding century had done. Alexander thought that did not go far enough. She also wanted the commission to recommend the end of segregation in the institution that had shaped her life more than any other: education. She thus pursued education reforms along the lines George Downing had pushed the previous century. The federal government doesn't have direct power over public education, which is administered by the states. Still, Alexander thought states could be pressured to end segregation if the federal government created the right incentives. Ever the economist, Alexander argued Congress should condition federal funds to states on the desegregation of public schools.[96]

These bold ideas seemed to have the president's backing. In June 1947, the NAACP convened its annual conference in Washington, DC. There, Alexander's coalition received an unexpected boost from Truman himself, who addressed the group.[97] Standing on the steps of the Lincoln Memorial, Truman declared, "It is more important today than ever before to ensure that all Americans enjoy these rights. When I say all Americans, I mean all Americans." That introduction set the tone for a no-holds-barred address. Truman explained that fighting for civil rights was not about "protection of the people against the Government, but protection of the people by the Government." He described a new vision, one in which the government was "a friendly, vigilant defender of the rights and equalities of all Americans." No longer could the country idly appease its "slowest state" or "most backward community"—a thinly veiled slight against the South. Instead, Truman declared, "Our National Government must show the way."[98] Truman's address was mentioned on the front page of the next day's *New York Times*[99]—and it signaled to the committee members that he was still all in on their mission.

The speech put wind in the sails of the committee's more progressive members. Still, there was resistance to Alexander's bolder ideas, especially among the committee's Southern contingent. They thought Alexander's proposals were too radical, especially in education,[100] fearing Southerners would see them as overly intrusive. Alexander had won several key allies to her conditional funding plan, including the committee's two Jewish members, Morris Ernst and Roland Gittelsohn.[101] Other members remained staunchly opposed. One member proved to be a key player: Franklin Delano Roosevelt Jr.—the thirty-two-year-old son of the ex-president and Eleanor Roosevelt. Roosevelt Jr. was a moderate. In an initial vote the day after Truman's speech,[102] he sided with the Southern contingent, opposing the proposed denial of funds to segregated states and objecting to a recommendation that states pass fair educational practice laws, leaving the committee deadlocked on both questions.[103]

But FDR Jr. showed a capacity to adapt. Although his father had been too cautious to wade into civil rights, his mother was outspoken for Truman's more aggressive approach. Eleven years after her private letter to White, the former First Lady served on the NAACP's board.[104] She was particularly fond of Marshall and likely was excited by the prospects of the committee endorsing his vision.[105] She had looked on from the stage[106] while Truman delivered his speech to the NAACP. Over the summer, Eleanor spoke with her son and talked the sense into him that only a mother—and perhaps only Eleanor Roosevelt—could. Duly chastened, Roosevelt Jr. changed his vote when the committee formally addressed the state funding and public education questions in September.[107] Now with the support of a bare majority, Alexander's ideas, including a condemnation of *Plessy*, and the plan to end school segregation using congressional carrots and sticks, would be formally recommended to President Truman, and be reported to millions of Americans who would read it. In September, the commission sent their updated report to the printers.

On October 30, 1947, the committee showed the draft to Truman. Titled "To Secure These Rights," the report's four sections ran 178 pages. It catalogued in exhaustive detail the humiliations and terrors of daily life for Black Americans: lynching and mob law; police brutality; involuntary servitude as punishment; the violent denial of voting rights; and discrimination in employment, education, housing, health care, and public services. Then it issued a categorical rebuke to both segregation and the larger racial order of the United States. Without "social institutions that will guarantee equality of opportunity to all men," it argued, the promise that "all men are created equal as well as free" could never be realized. In far too many instances, the commission wrote, America continued to violate that principle.[108]

On the question of segregation, the report's rebuke was firm: segregation must end. Reflecting the hidden role of Alexander's strategy, the report addressed *Plessy* directly. The decision that had invented "separate but equal" was wrong, both in its application and in its very logic. In practice, "it is almost always true that while indeed separate, these facilities are far from equal." Segregation "brands the Negro with the mark of inferiority and asserts that he is not fit to associate with white people." And a "law which forbids a group of American citizens to associate with other citizens in the ordinary course of daily living creates inequality by imposing a caste status on the minority group." Echoing the influence of Marshall, the report declared the Constitution's Reconstruction-era amendments should be read to "guarantee to all persons a full and equal status in American society."[109] It was up to the federal government, the commission declared, to make that guarantee real again.

To do that, the commission rejected previous half-hearted efforts to make progress on civil rights by relegating protection to the states. Just like the war against the Axis powers or the highway system that would soon connect all of America, the commission emphatically declared civil rights the job of the federal government: "The national government of the United States must take the lead in safeguarding the civil rights of all Americans." So long as the Constitution was the law of the land, the federal government has the "power . . . to protect the rights essential to national citizens in a democratic nation."[110]

The report last turned to its recommendations, in which each branch of government had a responsibility to guarantee civil rights. All three branches had contributed to segregation and discrimination, and each had to be unerringly committed to their eradication. In particular, the commission urged the White House to bulk up the civil rights section of the Department of Justice, and to establish a permanent United States Commission on Civil Rights in the White House. They also called for the end of segregation in the federal government and across the military. When it came to Congress, the commission demanded sweeping anti-lynching legislation, the elimination of poll taxes, consequences for police brutality, and perhaps most drastically, prohibiting any federal funds to public or private agencies that engaged in segregation. Finally, the report called on public officials and the courts to interpret the three post–Civil War amendments as they were intended, safeguarding strong protections for the equal rights of all citizens. The logic of *Plessy* could no longer be part of any branch of government's thinking. American segregation had to be eradicated.[111]

On the surface, the commission's report was a set of recommendations to the president. In reality, it was a road map for recovering a Constitution that had been abandoned since the demise of Reconstruction.

In December 1947, "To Secure These Rights" was published for the American people to read. Among civil rights groups, its publication was a triumph. An astonished Roy Wilkins, then editor of NAACP's official magazine, *The Crisis*, called the report "almost a duplication of the program of the Association."[112] Even the name of the report evoked one of Thurgood Marshall's earlier speeches to the NAACP, in which he had described "the legal attack to secure civil rights."[113]

If the drafting and ratification of the Constitution was the country's first founding, and the enactment of the Reconstruction amendments the second, this moment had the potential to be a third. However, a third founding could not just be written on paper. It had to gain widespread support, which meant an aggressive promotion of its values, especially by government officials. President Truman had asked for recommendations. Now he had them. The spotlight fell on the man from Missouri. If there was any hope of recovering the equal protection promised by the amended Constitution, Truman had to act—and act big.

★ ★ ★

ON FEBRUARY 2, 1948, less than two months after "To Secure These Rights" was published, Truman delivered a special message to Congress.[114] In it, he detailed the ways his administration would fundamentally reshape the government to fully protect the civil rights of all Americans.

Truman's message began by reiterating a core American value: "We believe that all men are created equal and that they have the right to equal justice under law." Addressing the nearly all-white Congress,[115] he spoke as frankly as he had before the NAACP about the country's failure to realize that value. "We shall not, however, finally achieve the ideals for which this Nation was founded so long as any American suffers discrimination as a result of his race." Referencing the committee report, he noted the "serious gap between our ideals and some of our practices. This gap must be closed." Closing this gap would require significant action by the federal government just as the committee had urged. In fact, many of his recommendations mirrored those in the report, calling for strong anti-lynching legislation, bills to protect the right to vote, a permanent commission on civil rights, fair employment practice legislation, and an end to discrimination in interstate transportation facilities.[116] While he did not call on the courts, his declaration embodied a vision of the Constitution inconsistent with *Plessy*'s logic and supportive of strong action for equality. And he was preparing to do even more.

On July 26, 1948, the White House aimed squarely at reversing the nationalization of white supremacy that had been ushered in by Woodrow Wilson. In Executive Order 9980, Truman enacted a "policy of fair employment throughout the Federal establishment, without discrimination because of race, color, religion, or national origin," ending legalized segregation in the federal government with the stroke of his pen. Unlike Wilson, who had pled ignorance about the inner workings of the vast executive branch, Truman also created a Fair Employment Board to monitor and enforce the progress of integration. With this single act, *Plessy* was dealt a significant blow.

Executive Order 9981, however, would become even more famous. In fewer than 450 words, Truman ended segregation in the military.[117] The US Navy, Army, and Air Force were ordered to desegregate "rapidly," and an advisory committee on equality in the armed services was born. In some ways, by targeting one of America's most culturally conservative institutions, it was Truman's boldest action. For Truman, the order was also the most personal, given that his conversion to the cause of civil rights was prompted by Walter White's dramatic description of the assault on Isaac Woodard. It was also a direct blow to the grand theories of German efficiency that Wilson had peddled—and the notion that the military needed segregation to avoid "friction."[118]

Not content with formal actions alone, Truman attempted to shape public opinion. In August, Truman received a letter from Ernie Roberts, an old friend and a Southerner, who told Truman to abandon his civil rights program and urged the president to "let us let the South take care of the N******."[119] In reply, Truman sent Roberts a note illustrating the evils that Black people faced in the South. He told Roberts that the South was "eighty years behind the times" and that as president he would fight for equality of opportunity even if it cost him reelection. Along with the letter, Truman sent a document that he thought would change Roberts's mind: a copy of "To Secure These Rights." Two weeks later, Roberts wrote back to Truman, saying that the committee's report was so thorough, its findings so shocking—and its argument so understandable—that Roberts's position had shifted. Roberts empha- sized the enormity of the task of changing the South's practices, and still advised slow action, but he now agreed with Truman that the fed- eral government had to act.[120] In a way, Truman hadn't persuaded Ernie Roberts at all; Sadie Alexander had.[121]

Truman hadn't just taken steps practically unheard of in the pre- ceding seventy years—he had done it in an election year. The American political consensus was rocked by Truman's blizzard of actions. So was the South. Southern Democratic politicians viewed Truman's actions as a direct assault on their so-called "way of life."[122] Truman's actions made his political advisors nervous; they feared a Southern rebellion that could swing the presidency to his Republican rival, Thomas Dewey, even if Dewey was seen as a civil rights progressive for his time.[123] But Truman had two convictions. First, he had a bread-and-butter view of postwar liberal democracy; if the economy was strong, and government was seen as looking out for the basic needs of most Americans, then many white Americans would accept action on civil rights—most of them didn't actually interact with Black people in their daily lives. Second, he could live with a strong stand for civil rights costing his votes. As Truman put it in his letter to Ernie Roberts, if supporting civil rights "ends up in my failure to be reelected, that failure will be in a good cause."[124]

Truman's decision at first appeared catastrophic. At the Demo- cratic National Convention, delegates from Alabama and Mississippi walked out, crying, "You shall not crucify the South on this cross of civil rights."[125] By October 1948, Dewey was the heavy favorite.[126] On Election Day, Truman suffered an enormous defection among Southern Democrats so incensed by racial grievance they supported a rich New York Republican over a hardscrabble Midwestern farmer—presaging a seismic change in partisan alignment that cemented in the coming decades. Taking votes away from Truman was the governor of South Carolina, Strom Thurmond, a virulently segregationist Democrat, who mounted a third-party campaign devoted to thwarting civil rights.[127]

But to the shock of virtually everyone in politics, Truman's wisdom was revealed: with the help of African American voters,[128] Truman won the election—the first time he was on the ballot as president.[129] (The shocker was famously immortalized by a photograph of a grinning Truman holding a copy of a prematurely printed newspaper headline: "DEWEY DEFEATS TRUMAN.")[130]

The remainder of his presidency could have been a culmination of the strong civil rights achievements he won in his first term. Instead, there were no major breakthroughs. But that doesn't mean nothing was done. Truman's second term included the far less visible work of implementing his proposals and executive orders—a crucial task even if it garnered few headlines.[131] But between 1948 and 1953, the task of integration had begun, and soon Black soldiers and white soldiers would fight side by side in Korea, the first widespread integrated armed effort since the battles of the Civil War.[132]

Truman's transformation did not occur in a vacuum. It was done at the behest of an organized democratic constitutional constituency, headquartered at the NAACP Legal Defense Fund and steered by citizen-scholars such as Thurgood Marshall and Sadie Alexander. While these two crucial figures in the struggle for a democratic understanding of equal protection took up the mantle of earlier figures such as Trotter and Wells, their methods differed. Surprisingly, they were invited to advise a president who by his own family's accounts had once adhered to the Democratic Party's policy of white supremacy. That president's appointment of Wells and her coordination with Marshall played a pivotal role in recovering the democratic ideal of equal protection. At this stage, Alexander and Marshall continued the tradition of the newspaper editors and Douglass by effecting change through prevailing on recovery presidents rather than courts. Thanks to their work and Truman's, the 1950s would become a very different decade than the previous one, with "To Secure These Rights" setting a clear standard against which future presidents would be judged.

CHAPTER 10

Dwight D. Eisenhower, John F. Kennedy, Lyndon Johnson, and Martin Luther King Jr.

The Road to Recovery

WITH SADIE ALEXANDER'S LEAD AND THURGOOD MARSHALL'S HELP, TRUMAN AND THE President's Committee on Civil Rights had initiated a constitutional recovery. However, Marshall had reason to be skeptical when the former Supreme Allied Commander in Europe during World War II, Dwight D. Eisenhower, assumed the presidency in 1953. From Marshall's position, Eisenhower's record on civil rights was mixed, at best. Marshall had spent years writing letters to Eisenhower and his staff during the war, urging him to address the NAACP's concerns about racial discrimination in the military. Eisenhower never responded.[1]

Yet Eisenhower's support was about to become crucial to the future of civil rights. In 1951,[2] Marshall quietly filed a new lawsuit, the culmination of his long-term strategy to undo "separate but equal." The case, now known as *Brown v. Board of Education*, aimed to strike at the heart of *Plessy*. In the aftermath of the rebuff of *Plessy* by the President's Committee on Civil Rights and Truman's wholehearted endorsement of the report it produced, Marshall decided that it was time to seek victory in court.

The significance of the case was clear. Overturning public school segregation would be a major and shocking achievement. But alone, it might not account for much—if lacking presidential support, it would amount to little more than a paper victory, particularly if states and local governments refused to follow a court ruling. Eisenhower's support would be indispensable. Marshall was skeptical that given Eisenhower's indifference to civil rights, as illustrated by those unanswered letters, he would act as president to enforce civil rights.

Of course, before he could consider how Eisenhower would enforce the end of segregation, Marshall had to win in court. That possibility seemed within reach when in 1953, Fred Vinson, chief justice of the Supreme Court, and likely opponent of desegregation, died of a heart attack.[3] Marshall was encouraged when Earl Warren, California's Republican governor, was nominated to be chief justice. There were some reasons for concern, given that Warren had willingly carried out FDR's executive order to intern Japanese Americans during World War II.[4] Marshall traveled to California to meet with allies and California Supreme Court judges to find out, as he put it, "what the hell [Warren] was all about." One judge assured him that Warren would be an ally, and offered a guarantee: "If he doesn't do right, call us up and we'll come and kick his ass."[5]

In 1952, the Supreme Court heard a first round of oral arguments in Marshall's case but decided in June 1953 to order a second.[6] One lawyer on Marshall's team was a Howard Law professor, Spottswood Robinson. A decade earlier, one of Robinson's law students, Pauli Murray, suggested in Robinson's class that it was time for a "frontal assault" to reverse *Plessy* in the court. Murray's classmates responded with "astonishment" and "hoots of derisive laughter."[7] Ever confident, she bet Robinson ten dollars that *Plessy* would be overturned within twenty-five years. Now, a decade later, Robinson, strategizing with Marshall, distributed a paper Murray had written outlining a strategy to show that separate was inherently unequal, relying on social science research demonstrating the pernicious effects of segregation.[8] To make this case, Marshall recruited two psychologists, Mamie and Kenneth Clark, who had developed expertise in education and integration.[9] The Clarks had earlier designed studies in which Black children were given the choice of white dolls and Black dolls. The subjects chose the white dolls in large numbers. Children as young as three years old decided that the Black dolls looked "bad" while the white dolls were a "nice color."[10] The Clarks were able to convincingly link these perceptions to segregated education, demonstrating segregation's devastating effects on the self-esteem of Black children.

But Marshall needed more than the best evidence to win. Eisenhower's support would be crucial. Instead of approaching the president directly, Marshall received the help he needed when Eisenhower deferred to Attorney General Herbert Brownell's professional judgment to write a legal brief in the case.[11] Eisenhower preferred to keep his position on segregation private and take no official stand on the case. But Brownell pointed out if the Supreme Court requested that the administration weigh in, they couldn't refuse; Eisenhower had to choose.[12]

Eisenhower was conflicted—his views complicated by his personal feelings on race. In February 1954, Eisenhower invited Warren to a "stag dinner," along with other well-connected Washington politicos, where Eisenhower seated Warren near John Davis,[13] the *pro*-segregation attorney in *Brown v. Board of Education*. After the dinner, Eisenhower took Warren aside, a conversation Warren recounted in his memoirs. "These are not bad people," Eisenhower reportedly said. "All they are concerned about is to see that their sweet little girls are not required to sit in school alongside some big overgrown Negroes." (A professor to whom Warren told the story said Warren's book sanitized the quote, saying Warren told him Eisenhower had used the phrase "big black bucks."[14])

Before it heard oral arguments, the Supreme Court asked the Eisenhower administration to weigh in officially.[15] In response, the Department of Justice submitted its legal brief, which narrowly focused on the court's questions. It determined that, although the legislative history of the Fourteenth Amendment was inconclusive on the issue of racial segregation in public education, the amendment's original purpose was to secure "full and complete equality before the law and to abolish all legal distinctions based on race or color."[16] It also determined that courts could rule on segregation in schools, opening the door to reversing *Plessy*. The brief went on to acknowledge, however, that *implementing* integration could pose problems.[17] The brief was classic Eisenhower: restrained, morally clinical, and hewing as closely to the facts as possible.

On May 17, 1954, the nine justices assembled at the Supreme Court bench. Facing[18] a packed audience of court-goers and reporters, the court announced its decision in *Brown v. Board of Education*. Warren, reading his opinion from the bench, added the word *unanimously* to the famous holding: "We conclude, [unanimously], that in the field of public education the doctrine of 'separate but equal' has no place. Separate educational facilities are inherently unequal."[19] The audience audibly gasped. Marshall and his team had done it: *Brown* ruled that the *Plessy* doctrine of "separate but equal" was unconstitutional in public schools. Soon, the logic of *Brown* moved beyond schoolhouses, as the court extended its holding to other places of accommodation like beaches and golf courses.[20]

The opinion was designed to make a public case for desegregation. It included social science data from the Clarks that showed the feelings of inferiority segregation imposed on Black students. And it paired this scientific appeal with moral rhetoric, decrying the injustice of institutionalized racial subordination. When Warren wrote, "Separate educational facilities are inherently unequal,"[21] it was like he was quoting Marshall's life's work and endorsing Murray's legal strategy. It was also a vindication of William Monroe Trotter—who had stood in the Oval Office in 1914 and told Woodrow Wilson that segregation was the work of white supremacy. Moreover, the opinion was a rebuke of past court decisions—and past presidents who had endorsed and implemented them. By the court's logic—though not stated so explicitly—presidents as recent as Wilson and FDR had violated the Equal Protection Clause with their segregationist policies. Marshall had successfully brought the arguments of Trotter, Wells, Murray, and Alexander before the most powerful court in the country.

That legal victory still needed the president's support. Even by the time of the ruling, Eisenhower's support for implementation remained in doubt. It seemed Eisenhower might not go along at all: in private, he told a staff member that the "decision was wrong."[22] Two days after the ruling, Eisenhower responded with the weakest of statements: "The Supreme Court has spoken and I am sworn to uphold the constitutional processes in this country; and I will obey."[23] Marshall wasn't blind to what the president's statement meant. At a celebration party, Marshall told his NAACP colleagues a cold truth: "I don't want any of you to fool yourselves, it's just begun, the fight has just begun."[24]

That fight centered on the timeline for implementation. Solicitor General Simon Sobeloff drafted a legal brief for the new case about implementation, which Brownell had to clear with a wary Eisenhower, who still had given little public indication of supporting *Brown*.[25] On November 20, 1954, Eisenhower discussed the draft with some of his top legal brass. In one part, it read, "Racial segregation in public schools is unconstitutional and will have to be terminated as quickly as possible." It was a basic statement of a forceful position. Eisenhower scratched out one word, "possible," and replaced it with "feasible." Subtle but significant, the change turned a moral demand into one tempered by pragmatism or perceived political risk.[26] When the brief was submitted, Marshall made a difficult but shrewd decision not to criticize the president publicly. In drafting a public statement, Marshall told an aide to "pick out a couple of paragraphs and say I agree with them," giving appearance to the public that Marshall and Eisenhower were allies.[27]

Conciliatory public statements by Marshall and the NAACP Legal Defense Fund could not paper over the differences between them and the Supreme Court. That became clear when in May 1955, the Supreme Court issued *Brown II*, adjudicating how fast the states must desegregate their public schools. That ruling hewed closer to Eisenhower's vision than Marshall's, announcing that students must be admitted to public schools "on a racially nondiscriminatory basis with all deliberate speed."[28] In a story that Marshall would often recount, his secretary went to the dictionary to try to understand the ruling's meaning. "I'm looking at *deliberate*," she said, "and the first word of similarity for *deliberate* is *slow*. Which means 'slow speed.' "[29] It was a partial win for Eisenhower. He could let the court make its original bold ruling without committing the White House to bold executive action. Marshall had scored a historic victory in the first *Brown* case. But when it came to implementation, he was hamstrung. His conciliatory approach had fallen short.

★ ★ ★

DESPITE THE UNDENIABLE VICTORY IN *BROWN*, the foot-dragging of *Brown II* meant that much of Southern life stayed segregated. Integration would not be achieved through a Court decision alone. This was especially true in Montgomery, the capital of Alabama. In this context, on December 1, 1955, Rosa Parks ignited a yearlong civil rights struggle to integrate the city by refusing to give up her seat on the bus. Parks was not the first Black woman there to face arrest for maintaining her seat. Claudette Colvin, a high school student and member of the NAACP youth council, of which Parks was an advisor, had done so earlier that year. On December 5, the Monday after Parks's arrest, the boycott of the Montgomery public bus system officially kicked off.

Martin Luther King Jr., newly elected to lead the Montgomery Improvement Association, ascended to national prominence as the boycott's leader. He shaped the protest as a reclaiming of constitutional rights, declaring on the first night at the Holt Street Baptist Church to a crowd of five thousand, "We are not wrong ... if we are wrong, the Supreme Court of this nation is wrong. If we are wrong, the Constitution of the United States is wrong. If we are wrong, God Almighty is wrong."[30] King faced threats of violence, including the bombing of his personal residence while his wife and baby were home.[31] In February, just weeks after the bombing, King was in Nashville preaching at Fisk University, when mass indictments came down for the 115 leaders of the boycott, including himself.[32] Alabama, using a 1921 statute that outlawed boycotts, was trying to intimidate and detain the movement's organizers. His father and inner circle urged him not to return to Montgomery. But King Jr. had other ideas.

Beside himself at his son's decision to return, King Sr. had a close confidant place a call to Thurgood Marshall.[33] Marshall promised to use the entire weight of the NAACP's Legal Defense Fund to defend King Jr. In the Montgomery courtroom,[34] things looked bleak. The judge in this nonjury trial, arch-segregationist Eugene Carter, found King Jr. guilty.[35] But Marshall artfully used the adverse decision to show in federal court that the protestors, not the segregationists, were on the Constitution's side. Advising lawyers on the ground, Marshall made sure the cases of King, Rosa Parks, and a third group of protestors including Colvin, Aurelia Browder, and Mary Louise Smith were appealed on grounds that *Brown* had repudiated segregation. In *Browder v. Gayle*, the Supreme Court affirmed a lower court decision that effectively reversed *Plessy v. Ferguson*, a ruling that integrated the Montgomery buses and ended the need for the boycott.[36]

As crucial as Marshall's support was in court, the vanguard of constitutional change was shifting from the courtroom to King's vision of protest, a change that harkened back to how Trotter and Wells had envisioned citizens reclaiming the document. Marshall did not think that the leadership of the Civil Rights Movement should move from litigation to law-breaking. Out of the public eye, King and Marshall squared off over civil disobedience. Marshall told King he believed the quest for civil rights was a matter of law, so disobeying a law, even an unjust one, betrayed its aims.[37] King disagreed. He was a student of the theologian Thomas Aquinas and an advocate of natural law. For Aquinas and King, an "unjust law [was] no law at all." So civil disobedience could be justified as a movement for "higher law," synonymous with morality and authored by God.[38] Layered within that philosophical disagreement was a tactical one. When law student Harris Wofford approached Marshall about the possibility of an American Civil Rights Movement based on Gandhi's principles of civil disobedience, Marshall rebuffed him.[39] But King embraced Gandhian tactics, agreeing with Wofford that in Montgomery and the South, what liberated Indian citizens from colonial rule could liberate American citizens from segregation.[40]

In King, Marshall saw a threat. Persuading Eisenhower to fully implement *Brown* was a delicate process, and he worried that the increasing visibility of King's civil disobedience could derail it, alienating the law-and-order president. Marshall's premise for bringing Eisenhower on board was that the law now required integration. But King openly defied the law and might give the president a way of further retrenching his support for implementing *Brown*.

The press eagerly covered the tension between Marshall and King. When asked by a reporter if protest could help implement *Brown*, King replied affirmatively. Marshall was taken aback. Their private dispute was now in the newspaper. Marshall told a reporter bluntly that King was not an expert on school desegregation, and one reporter thought that Marshall saw King like a "boy on a man's errand."[41] His implication was clear: law was rational, to be left to trained adults to further civil rights; King was immature, acting out, and undermining the victory Marshall had won in court.

This debate took on new urgency as white supremacists fought implementation of *Brown*. In early 1956, Southern congressmen drafted the Southern Manifesto, a racist screed masquerading as a states' rights document critiquing "a clear abuse of judicial power." It said that *Plessy* was based on "elemental humanity and commonsense," and explicitly lauded states that had opted to "resist forced integration by any lawful means." The manifesto framed *Brown* as judge-made law violating the Constitution. Since 1896, they noted, "separate but equal" had been widely accepted by courts and Congress. Throughout the country, especially in the South, calls to impeach Chief Justice Warren for judicial activism erupted.[42]

Privately, Marshall blamed Eisenhower, viewing the backlash as a consequence of the president's lack of support for *Brown*. Eisenhower had equivocated, extolling the need to "understand the southerners as well as the Negroes," and suggesting that there were "extremists on both sides."[43] According to law professor James Simon, Eisenhower thought the law should be obeyed, "but he also called for understanding of the white South where both custom and law had been turned upside down. Law alone, [Eisenhower] said repeatedly, could not change people's hearts or minds."[44] On September 6, 1956, Marshall

242 | EQUAL PROTECTION

wrote to Eisenhower: "My Dear President Eisenhower," he began, "surely, you do not mean to equate lawless mobs with federal courts as 'extremists.' "[45]

Marshall wanted to keep his dispute with Eisenhower private; King employed a different approach. Two years after *Brown II*, integration was moving lethargically. Eisenhower needed to be called out publicly. King began to organize a march on Washington to pressure the president to act. Rather than help, Marshall privately called King a "first rate rabble rouser," disapproving the plan and strategy. An FBI memo reported the remarks, and according to one historian, might have reinforced the Eisenhower administration's disapproval of the march.[46] The march instead became a more subdued "prayer pilgrimage." And the planned protest about failing to implement *Brown* morphed into a "celebration" of the anniversary of the case. Still, King's speech at the event cemented him as the leader of the Civil Rights Movement. King argued that legal victories, like in *Brown*, would ring hollow unless Black people garnered enough political power to demand implementation. Speaking of *Brown*, King said, "Give us the ballot, and we will quietly and nonviolently, without rancor or bitterness, implement the Supreme Court's decision of May seventeenth, 1954."[47] Calls of "yes" and "that's right" accompanied this line and others that employed the signature phrase, "give us the ballot."

Whether due to King's public protest or Marshall's private cajoling, Eisenhower became more supportive of civil rights, sending proposed legislation to Congress that resulted in the Civil Rights Act of 1957. Central was its Section III, which would outlaw segregation in public accommodations, including hotels and restaurants. The provision would therefore revive the ban on segregation in public accommodations that the court had struck down in the Civil Rights Cases of 1883. Section III would also empower the Justice Department to seek the help of federal judges to enforce that ban, as it granted the executive branch strong enforcement powers to enforce civil rights.[48] But Section III was intolerable to the Southern Democrats like Richard Russell, who rejected the integration and enforcement provisions out of hand, saying, it would "force a commingling of white and Negro children."[49]

King pushed back, arguing for the strongest version of the bill and met with Vice President Richard Nixon to lobby for it.

The Senate majority leader, a Texas Democrat named Lyndon Baines Johnson, had other ideas. His desire to hold the party together and nurture his presidential ambitions drove Johnson to seek a compromise bill that appeased Northern liberals without losing all Southern conservatives. That meant weakening the bill. Johnson worked to get rid of Section III and its mechanism for outlawing segregation in public accommodations. Johnson also sought to erode the power it gave the Justice Department and courts to enforce voting rights by requiring any voting enforcement be subject to the veto of local juries, which, as he reminded Southern segregationists, would often be all white. Johnson ultimately shepherded through the Senate an anemic bill, which Nixon derided on the Senate floor as a "vote against the right to vote."[30]

Eisenhower faced a question: Sign the weak bill or veto it? King wrote to Nixon to encourage Eisenhower to sign the bill. "I feel that civil rights legislation is urgent now, and the present limited bill will go a long way to insure it. So it is my hope that the President will not veto the bill."[31] The bill was signed into law by President Dwight D. Eisenhower on September 9, 1957.

King had now taken his place at the center of the Civil Rights Movement, focusing on restoring the Constitution through legislation and executive action. Still, his efforts had fallen short of his hopes. The defeat of the stronger bill confirmed for King that Walter White and Truman had been right all along: the president can do little without public opinion.

★ ★ ★

DESPITE MARSHALL'S ATTEMPTS TO have Eisenhower defend *Brown* publicly, the president refused. By winter 1957, he had made no definitive statement supporting *Brown*. But if Marshall's and King's entreaties couldn't prod Eisenhower into taking a side, Orval Faubus was about to do exactly that. The governor of Arkansas, Faubus was a vehement segregationist, and he interrupted *I Love Lucy* on local television to announce his mobilization of the Arkansas National Guard to prevent "blood [running] in the streets" at Central High School after *Brown*.[52] Not content with slowing integration, Faubus demanded none. In August 1957, a federal judge in Arkansas ordered the implementation of a desegregation plan, including admitting Black students to Central High School in Little Rock beginning that fall. Faubus saw a cynical chance to become the political face of Southern resistance. On Labor Day, Faubus declared that *Brown* violated Arkansans' "constitutional rights," and that the federal court's decision to integrate lacked any "authority." Taking the law into his own hands, he ordered the Arkansas National Guard to uphold law and order (by, ironically, refusing to abide by a legal court ruling).[53] On September 4, some 270 armed members of the Arkansas National Guard circled the school to block the entry of the nine Black enrollees. Reports abounded of racist mobs who planned to harass any Black people near the school.[54] Faubus had started a direct confrontation, pitting federal law against state resistance.

Furious, Marshall and NAACP lawyers sought an injunction against Faubus. They also demanded federal intervention.[55] Eisenhower, meanwhile, refused to come to the aid of Marshall or the students. On September 3, the day before the confrontation, Eisenhower had suggested in a press conference that he thought federal intervention inexpedient, saying, "now, time and again, a number of people—I, among them—have argued that you cannot change people's hearts merely by laws."[56] Nevertheless, despite lacking the president's backing, the Black students arrived at Central High School the next day. They were surrounded by harassing masses who were virulently opposed to the integration and used racist language. Some in the crowd called for the teenagers to be lynched.[57]

Eisenhower sent a telegram to Faubus that read, "When I became President, I took an oath to support and defend the Constitution of the United States. The only assurance I can give you is that the Federal Constitution will be upheld by me by every legal means at my command."[58] Despite the missive, Eisenhower still desperately wanted to avoid public confrontation. He came up with a compromise. On vacation in Newport, Rhode Island, he summoned Faubus to make a deal. On September 14, Faubus arrived, and the conciliatory commander tried to resolve the crisis with a personal appeal. Eisenhower suggested that Faubus could keep the troops in place but clarify they were there to "obey the Courts," not oppose segregation. He worried about how the public would perceive a "trial of strength between the President and a Governor" because the president would have to win, and Eisenhower "did not want to see any Governor humiliated."[59]

Adding further pressure to Faubus, on September 20, thanks to the NAACP's persistence, a federal judge ordered Faubus to remove the troops. Faubus, irate, announced, "Now begins the crucifixion."[60] Within hours, he appeared on national television to announce the withdrawal of the Arkansas National Guard and the deployment of the Little Rock Police Department. He also pleaded for Black students not to attend Central High School. When those students showed up on Monday, hell awaited. Over one thousand angry, "hysterical" protestors, joined by the Ku Klux Klan, tormented the students, advocating violence and assaulting Black reporters present.[61] The students were hurried out a side door into police cruisers and sped away, just hours after entering.

Eisenhower, the risk-averse compromiser, needed to act. Marshall's frustrations boiled over. In an April 1957 interview, he had lampooned Eisenhower, saying he had not "done anywhere near what he could have done." Eisenhower should have encouraged Southerners to support *Brown*, and used "the full influence of his position as president to bring about a peaceful solution of this problem." Eisenhower talked often of his duty to uphold the law; Marshall evoked a higher one. "Moral leadership should come from the top executive of the government," he said. "It's his responsibility, and he can't duck it."[62] Marshall, the best-known civil rights lawyer in the country, was calling Eisenhower a failure.

Eisenhower was feeling the force of Marshall's critique. From the archives, a scrap survives with Eisenhower's thoughts and doodles. In the top left corner, he drew a plane, perhaps a military plane, as he considered intervention. He wrote in script, "troops-not to enforce integration but to prevent opposition by violence to order of court," and below, "in Arkansas . . . president can stand by . . . or he can carry out his oath of office."[63] Even in Eisenhower's most decisive moment, he emphasized to himself that he was not defending or implementing *Brown* but standing by the rule of law as interpreted by courts. That was where Marshall had hoped to bring the president, recognizing that he would never be integration's staunchest moral defender, but believing he could take notice of his oath.

On September 23, 1957, Eisenhower signed Proclamation 3204, "command[ing] all persons engaged in such obstruction of justice [in Little Rock] to cease and desist therefrom, and to disperse forthwith," in order to ensure the Black students of Central High School could attend their school.[64] The order's language was, characteristically, restrained, making no mention of segregation or its moral evil. But his actions one day later were anything but restrained. Conditions were so dangerous in Little Rock that Eisenhower signed Executive Order 10730 authorizing the secretary of defense to enforce the prior day's proclamation with the United States Army and Air Force. The order was used to send the 101st Airborne Division into Little Rock[65]—the same military division General Eisenhower had commanded in the Battle of the Bulge to protect democracy abroad was now charged with defending the rule of law at home.[66] With federal troops outside Central High School, the students arrived and, under military protection, made it to class.

Finally, after the students had entered, Eisenhower publicly addressed the nation, explaining why he had aided the Little Rock Nine (as the Black students came to be known). "The very basis of our individual rights and freedoms" rests on the president enforcing court decisions, he explained. Eisenhower forcefully condemned "mob rule" and the actions of "demagogic extremists" who instigated violence. There were aspects of Eisenhower's reluctance when he expressed "sadness" for the action he was "compelled . . . to take." But the tone and message were clear. Disobeying legal mandates would not be tolerated. The president, when pushed, would make school integration real.[67]

The speech was imperfect in many ways. Eisenhower spoke at length and with understanding about the difficulties Southerners faced changing their way of life, while still refusing to defend racial equality. But it was the action that accompanied the words that made the speech historic. Long hesitant to commit his office to civil rights enforcement, in Little Rock Eisenhower finally took action to legitimize the court's ruling in *Brown* and realize the promise of integrated education. Although his stated view of the Constitution was deferential to courts, here he took aggressive, independent action to enforce the Constitution's guarantee of the rule of law. Eisenhower's unexpected intervention breathed new life into the promise of equal protection.

Eisenhower's actions seemed to vindicate Marshall's approach to civil rights: courts, not presidents, decided the law; and when presidents followed the Constitution, they listened to what the judicial branch ruled. But even after the ostensible conclusion to the crisis, the Little Rock school board and superintendent sought to reverse course, arguing that the "tensions, bedlam, chaos and turmoil in the school" should be grounds for delaying the integration plan for two-and-a-half years and sending the Black students back to segregated schools.[68] In *Cooper v. Aaron*, the court rejected these claims and the finding of the district court, issuing a statement that offered a strong rebuke to Faubus and a defense of Marshall's view. "The interpretation of the Fourteenth Amendment enunciated by this Court in the *Brown* case is the supreme law of the land, and Art. IV of the Constitution makes binding on the States 'any Thing in the Constitution or Laws of any State to the Contrary notwithstanding.'"[69] Furthermore, the court warned, "No state legislator or executive or judicial officer can war against the Constitution without violating his solemn oath to support it."[70]

King, too, was vindicated in Little Rock. His public pressure likely influenced Eisenhower, and his nascent movement supporting *Brown* counterbalanced the public opinion that was resistant to it. Moreover, King had illuminated a problem with Marshall's solely legal approach: it did not work for integration. When Eisenhower left office in January 1961, only 6 percent of Black students attended integrated schools.[71] Reflecting on the period and his relationship with King, Marshall would see things very differently than he had before, calling him a "great" leader, perhaps finally understanding their approaches as complementary.[72]

★ ★ ★

IN NOVEMBER 1960, Martin Luther King Jr. was in trouble. On prime-time national television, King debated James Kilpatrick, a leading constitutional thinker of Southern segregationists and popular editor of the *Richmond News Leader.* The program was "The Nation's Future," on NBC; the topic was the student lunch counter sit-ins spreading through the South that aimed to integrate public accommodations.[73] The program was being broadcast on ninety-eight stations nationwide.[74] The audience was composed of civil rights groups, conservative groups, and mayors representing the American Municipal Association Convention.[75] Kilpatrick refused to speak to King directly, aiming his remarks at the moderator. He also refused to acknowledge King's titles—reverend or doctor—calling him "Mr. King."[76]

Even King could not deny the obvious: Kilpatrick was winning the argument. King was not a natural debater. At times, he looked flustered against his well-practiced opponent, a professional polemicist. Kirkpatrick's argument was beguilingly simple: government integration of private businesses had *already* been deemed unconstitutional by the Supreme Court in the 1870s and 1880s. In *Cruikshank* in 1876, and the Civil Rights Cases of 1883, the court determined that the Equal Protection Clause applied strictly to *government* action. The aim of the lunch counter sit-ins, on the other hand, was to integrate *privately owned* facilities: hotels, restaurants, theaters—the public accommodations owned by private proprietors where Black people had been excluded for decades. Albeit for opposite purposes, Kilpatrick used a Marshall-esque approach to argue against King: the court decided the Constitution, not citizens, and the provisions proposed in the new civil rights act had already been deemed invalid. Furthermore, he said the protestors' behavior was "a boorish exhibition of what seems to me plain bad manners in crashing into a place where they are not welcome."[77]

King tried a rebuttal. His argument rested on natural law theology, which King had studied for his PhD. Segregationist laws, he argued, were unjust, and therefore inherently unlawful. King quoted Aquinas: "An unjust law is no law at all," and "when we find an unjust law, I think we have a moral obligation to take a stand against it, and I think these local laws that have been set up are unjust." Kilpatrick pounced. King's prescription was a recipe for "anarchy." King's view made it seem like any law could be disregarded, at any time, if thought to be unjust.

That was a caricature of King's views, which enshrined nonviolence, not anarchy, as the backbone of civil disobedience: just as civil disobedience required peaceful protest, it also required accepting the punishment. After briefly dwelling on this point, King returned to natural law. Thomas Jefferson had invoked natural law to write the Declaration of Independence. In invoking Jefferson, King was now on Kilpatrick's turf. Jefferson wrote the Declaration to start a revolution; did King wish to overthrow the government? Kilpatrick noted that Jefferson fiercely supported state's rights—precisely what Southern segregationists defended, meaning "Jefferson, whom you seem to admire a good deal," opposed King's position.

Following the debate, King was despondent. He knew he'd lost, and worse yet, so did his hopeful followers. One leader of the Student Nonviolent Coordinating Committee deemed King "no match" for Kilpatrick.[78] Few doubted King's intellect or persuasive capacity. Instead, what King lacked—as he himself suspected—was a political vocabulary to respond, one that didn't derive from ancient European theologies.

While King mulled over this problem, John Herriford, an undergraduate at the University of Minnesota who had watched the debate, wrote to King, dismayed by King's performance.[79] Natural law, he argued, was too "vague" a concept for defending civil rights legislation. Then he shared a compelling suggestion. To convince a nation to change its constitutional understanding of race, King should infuse his moral theory with the anti-tyranny principle found in the framers' writings and the Constitution. Kilpatrick had done just that when he invoked Jefferson to cast civil rights as an impingement on freedom. Herriford flipped Kilpatrick's argument on its head: the constitutional problem with segregation was that it was tyrannical, and it therefore violated what the Constitution was created to avoid. Instead of relying on Aquinas's principle that an unjust law is no law, King should instead argue that "an unjust law is one in which the minority is denied basic rights given to the majority."[80] King eagerly replied, asking for permission to use the phrase. Herriford responded that no one needed permission to use the framers' ideas. Like Douglass and Lincoln before him, King then wrapped himself in the ideas of the framers and the founding documents to appeal for social and political equality.

King's notes show him wrestling with Herriford's ideas. A lesser thinker would have dismissed a letter from an undergraduate. But like many brilliant minds, King took criticism seriously, no matter the source. Herriford was right that relying too heavily on Aquinas was a mistake; whereas looking to the original Constitution would be key to countering Kilpatrick. King had long turned to the Reconstruction amendments as part of the political and legal campaign which repudiated *Plessy*. But King now realized he could also draw from the eighteenth-century slave owners who wrote the Constitution. King's handwriting on Herriford's letter reveals his thinking: "It takes from the opponent a weapon that he has always used as a weapon aimed over the head of the negro."[81] King did not need to abandon his natural law argument to invoke the framers; he could argue from both the perspective of natural law and the anti-tyranny principle.

King used this newly formulated approach to highlight the unconstitutionality of segregation and disenfranchisement. He also used it to justify civil disobedience to reclaim constitutional rights. In 1963, the centennial of the Emancipation Proclamation, with promises from President John F. Kennedy for a new civil rights bill but no congressional action, King turned his attention to Birmingham, Alabama, a city King called "probably the most thoroughly segregated city in the United States."[82] The choice of locale was strategic: King understood that Bull Connor, Birmingham's notorious sheriff, was likely to attack demonstrators, perhaps violently. This would put the brutality of segregation on national display, and King could use the city's unjust repression to highlight his new defense of civil disobedience.

Civil rights organizers petitioned the city for a permit to march. They were denied. A defiant King marched anyway on April 12, 1963. That same day, he and others were arrested for violating the permit ordinance. King was thrown into the local jail, where he spent eight days before receiving bail. Over that week, King drafted one of the most seminal statements about the Constitution ever written. The guards refused to allow King stationery. Instead, he scribbled his thoughts on a newspaper, scratching arrows to direct his editors where to look next.[83] At first, King invoked natural law, as he had before. But now he supplied an argument about the stakes: the issue was whether America would have a democratic Constitution or a tyrannical one. "An unjust law is a code that a majority inflicts on a minority that is not binding on itself." That code, he continued, was one in which the minority "had no part in enacting or creating because they did not have the unhampered right to vote."[84] King created a bridge from the founding idea of "no taxation without representation" to an understanding of constitutional democracy in which segregation had no place. Segregation was not just a moral wrong, but a constitutional wrong, undemocratically imposing burdens upon a minority, without ever having involved them in the system that created the law.

Over the next few months, King's scrawled manifesto was published widely in periodicals such as the *Christian Century, Christianity and Crisis*, the *New York Post*, and *Ebony* magazine, and was often titled, "Letter from a Birmingham Jail."[85] It received instant acclaim. King had found the political vocabulary that had been missing in his 1960 debate against Kilpatrick. The letter grounded the moral principle at stake in the Constitution. In short order, he took this potent combination nationally. Four months after his arrest, at the March on Washington, King stood before the Lincoln Memorial, and told Americans, "I have a dream." Before that famous refrain, however, King stated the basis for his dream: The "magnificent words" of the Constitution, the "promissory note to which every American was to fall heir."[86] These documents, King said, permitted him, and every American, to conceive of his dream. King brought foreword the moral force within the country's founding, just as Lincoln had at Gettysburg. Within hours of the speech's broadcast, even skeptics seemed to acknowledge the potency of King's argument. Later that day, the once-vacillating President Kennedy, who had not still fully supported a civil rights bill, invited King to the Oval Office. "I have a dream," Kennedy said, standing to greet King.

While it took Frederick Douglass decades to see a president invoke his ideas, King had achieved the feat in a matter of hours.

Another iteration of King's argument about tyranny appeared at the Supreme Court, too. In 1960, King had been arrested after being indicted for perjury by an Alabama grand jury. The case itself came about when his supporters placed an advertisement in the *New York Times* that criticized the police in Montgomery. Some claims were false, leading the city's police commissioner, L. B. Sullivan, to sue the *New York Times* and King's supporters for libel. When it decided the now-famous case, *New York Times Co. v. Sullivan*, the Supreme Court could have restricted itself to a narrow interpretation of libel law. Instead, it deployed a soaring, broad-minded defense of constitutional democracy, linking King to Madison and Jefferson in their resistance to the Alien and Sedition Acts. Jefferson and Madison, the court said, had resisted the acts as an exercise of their constitutional right to criticize the government, just as the protest movements were doing with segregation. For the first time in two centuries, the Alien and Sedition Acts were repudiated by the Supreme Court, writing, "Although the Sedition Act was never tested in this Court, the attack upon its validity has carried the day in the court of history."[87] The case affirmed an idea central to King's philosophy: tyranny could come not just from an oppressive monarch like King George, but also from domestic officials acting as mini-monarchs, such as John Adams or L. B. Sullivan, shutting down people's rights to resist.

King had thus changed the debate—from an argument on baroque theories of natural law to one drawing on the Constitution. He had twice been core to controversies at the Supreme Court, prompting the court to recognize the centrality of citizen protest against public officials, marking anti-tyranny as an animating principle of American government. King was on solid ground invoking Jefferson against states' rights arguments like those made by Kilpatrick. But as important a role as King played in case law, the principles of his Constitution still had to be fought for in the streets. In King's embrace of the founding principles of the Constitution, he would galvanize a protest movement, mobilizing masses of people into a democratic constitutional constituency.

★ ★ ★

LYNDON JOHNSON'S WORK WATERING DOWN the 1957 civil rights bill suggested the Civil Rights Movement could not trust him. So, as Johnson was sworn in on Air Force One on November 22, 1963, hours after an assassin's bullet struck President Kennedy, movement leaders had reason for concern. But James Farmer, the director of the Congress on Racial Equality, believed the new president might be an ally. Around when Johnson began working on the 1957 bill, he reportedly started telling the same motivational anecdote "over and over—with his customary vividness." The story involved his cook Zephyr Wright and her husband driving from Texas to Washington, DC, and being denied restaurant service, and needing to "squat in the road to pee" because she could not use whites-only bathrooms. Johnson would end by emphasizing, "That's just bad[,] that's wrong." For Johnson, this story "became a staple of his conversations at Georgetown dinner tables—and other venues as well." Anyone who knew Johnson, knew that his mind was set on getting real civil rights protections for Black Americans.[88]

King remained skeptical about LBJ's supposed conversion to the civil rights cause, but he did not doubt the president's pragmatism. That certainty was enough for King to try to work with Johnson on new civil rights legislation. Johnson, soon after he was sworn in, unsuccessfully tried to call King. King soon returned the call. Put through by Johnson's secretary, the president answered with characteristic ebullience. King opened by stressing the priority of civil rights saying, "I think one of the great tributes that we can pay . . . President Kennedy is to try to enact some of the great, progressive policies that he sought to initiate."[89] Johnson wanted something broader. Yes, Johnson would support a civil rights bill, but he expected King to support his economic agenda too, as economic justice was also part of the movement for civil rights. "I will have to have you-all's help, I never needed it more than I do now," Johnson relayed. Implicit in the request was a demand for loyalty. If they were to work together, Johnson expected King to restrain his public statements and criticism. FBI director J. Edgar Hoover protested the alliance by proclaiming that King's close advisor, Stanley Levison, was a known communist. Johnson, however, knew he needed King's support, and he rebuffed Hoover's warning, though he did defer to Hoover in the matter of keeping FBI wiretaps on King.

The first test of King's willingness to withhold criticism came as the civil rights bill languished in committee. This bill banned segregation in public accommodations, going further than the deal Johnson brokered in 1957. House Rules Committee chair Howard W. Smith and a cadre of Southern segregationist senators, led by Richard Russell, Strom Thurmond, Richard Byrd, William Fulbright, and Sam Ervin, sought to bury it.[90] When King, appearing on *Meet the Press*, was asked why he was not protesting the bill's lack of progress, King demurred; it was time to let Johnson work his legislative magic. When the bill stayed stuck in committee, Johnson called *Washington Post* publisher Katharine Graham, urging her to report on congressional laziness, specifically how congressmen were taking vacations amid what was supposed to be a debate about a historic civil rights bill. The tactic, combined with the threat of a discharge petition, which would move the bill out of the House Rules Committee, worked. The *Post* embarrassed Chairman Smith, who returned from being "out on [his] farm," tail between his legs, and let the bill reach the floor.[91]

Southern segregationist representatives, including Smith, however, had one last ploy to kill the bill. In a bid to make it unpopular, Smith proposed amending the bill to ban discrimination on the "basis of sex" in employment. A coalition of Southern segregationists joined him to support the poison pill amendment. Other conservatives sought to paint the amendment, and thus the whole bill, as ridiculous: Representative Emanuel Celler mocked gender equality by saying when his wife told him to do something he always responded, "Yes, dear."[92] When the amendment passed, Johnson and King simply swallowed the supposedly poisonous pill, pushing hard for both its anti-segregation and anti-sexist provisions.

The bill faced its biggest challenge in the Senate. There it stared down a sixty-day debate. The arguments eerily mirrored those by James Kilpatrick. Senator Robert Byrd of West Virginia, a former high-ranking Klan official, spoke for more than fourteen hours on the Senate floor.

Byrd claimed the bill was unconstitutional because the Supreme Court in the *Civil Rights Cases* already rejected mandated integration in privately owned businesses. Months earlier, Senate Majority Whip Hubert Humphrey had anticipated Byrd's arguments. According to Humphrey, the court had been wrong in the *Civil Rights Cases*. Humphrey said it was time to correct the mistake: "We simply have to face up to this question: are we as a Nation ready to guarantee equal protection of the laws as guaranteed in the United States Constitution . . . [as] each American knows that the promises of freedom and equal treatment found in the Constitution and the laws of this country are not being fulfilled for millions of our Negro citizens and for some other minority groups."[93]

Humphrey's argument won. On July 2, 1964, Johnson signed the Civil Rights Act of 1964 into law. King was given one of the signing pens, along with Zephyr Wright. Shortly after, King campaigned for Johnson's reelection, which he won handily with 61.1 percent of the vote. Five days before LBJ's second inauguration, King called the president. Their tone was cooperative. Johnson stated that voting rights were a priority, and he asked King to demonstrate its necessity by finding instances in which Black people had faced discrimination at the polls. King readily agreed. After so much fraught confrontation between the people and presidents for decades, true cooperation seemed at hand—for now.[94]

King didn't reveal it to Johnson, but he already had a strategy that would prove monumentally effective. He moved his organization in the Southern Christian Leadership Conference to Selma, Alabama, using that city as a base of operations to pressure Johnson into supporting voting rights. King's earlier restraint had been strategic; now, another approach was needed, one that embraced the idea for presidents to pursue constitutional restoration, public opinion, and a protest movement must demand it. On March 7, 1965, state troopers attacked voting rights protestors—led by a younger civil rights leader, John Lewis, the head of Student Nonviolent Coordinating Committee (SNCC)—with force. The violence was so severe that Lewis's skull was fractured, and others were left bloodied and concussed. This violence perpetrated by the state shocked the nation, and the event became known as Bloody Sunday. King used the incident to intensify the pressure on Johnson. Quickly, two days later, King planned a second march to Birmingham over the same bridge where Lewis had been beaten. This march would rebuke both the local police who sought to stop it and the president who was failing to deliver on the promised voting rights bill.

The president now saw betrayal, and he sent former Florida governor LeRoy Collins to Alabama to meet with King. On the morning of March 9, Collins and John Doar, the head of the Civil Rights Division at the Justice Department, informed King that a federal district court judge from Alabama, Frank Johnson, had signed an injunction against the march. The news came despite King's attorneys petitioning Johnson to authorize the march the day before.[95] King and his advisors met to deliberate. Legal advisor Harris Wofford told him that that while the movement had benefited from civil disobedience, this situation was different: King had always defied state and local court order; this time, a *federal* judge had denied the permit, the same branch charged with enforcing *Brown*. But Wofford misunderstood King's view of civil disobedience: the Constitution's anti-tyranny principle held regardless of whether any court recognized it. It was a principle for citizens to demand through civil disobedience when public officials, including federal judges, ignored it. For King, while federal courts were sometimes useful, they had no monopoly on constitutional meaning. On the morning of the march, King spoke to the crowd, insisting it would continue, no matter the court order, since the Constitution still authorized it: "We march in the name of the Constitution, knowing the Constitution is on our side. The right of the people peaceably to assemble and petition the government for a redress of grievances shall not be abridged. That's the First Amendment."[96]

King led his marchers down the streets of Selma. Approaching the middle of the Edmund Pettus Bridge, where previous marchers had been attacked on Bloody Sunday, they faced a line of troopers. Suddenly the troopers opened their line, allowing marchers to pass. At the last moment, King decided not to move forward toward the capital in Montgomery. Wofford later learned King had promised not to break the terms of the injunction. King had led a march "toward" Montgomery, but not "to" it, so had not technically violated the order. This parsing allowed him to show fidelity to the law while arguing in his speech and demonstration that no court, even a federal court, had a monopoly on constitutional interpretation.

For King, civil disobedience had a moral and a constitutional justification. It was also meant to teach America about rights lost which needed to be reclaimed. The message was received after Selma: 48 percent of Americans supported the demonstrators.[97] And more Americans ranked civil rights as a priority (26 percent), second only to Vietnam (29 percent). While Johnson at first saw King's planned march as a betrayal, with public opinion shifting the president recognized that King had done what he had asked in their phone conversation: galvanize public opinion. As Richard Goodwin, Johnson's speechwriter, explained, Johnson realized after Selma that on the voting rights bill "there was no other side . . . Blacks had been marching for the right to vote. They'd been beaten up in the streets."[98]

On March 15, 1965, eight days after Bloody Sunday and six days after King's second march, Lyndon Johnson addressed a special session of Congress, focusing on the need to pass the Voting Rights Act. His speech was viewed on television by more than seventy million Americans.[99] His speech, given to a packed House chamber, was an ode to King's movement, much like Lincoln's Gettysburg address had been an ode to Douglass's. Following King, Johnson invoked an anti-tyranny principle that King had developed in his correspondence with Herriford, equating the fight for the bill with the eighteenth-century demand to "Give me liberty or give me death." Said Johnson, "Our fathers believed that if this noble view of the rights of man was to flourish, it must be rooted in democracy. The most basic right of all was the right to choose your own leaders." Johnson then tied the framers to the modern Civil Rights Movement, implicitly vindicating King's tactics by echoing the movement's most famous words "Their cause must be our cause too," he said. "Because it is not just Negroes, but really it's all of us, who must overcome the crippling legacy of bigotry and injustice. And we shall overcome."[100]

Southern segregationists took the speech, and especially these words, as a rebuke. They were right to do so.[101] King watched the speech from Selma with aides. He was known for never shedding tears through all his hardship. But at this moment he broke, crying tears of victory when he heard Johnson.[102]

Johnson's strong support boded well for the bill, but King was not done advocating. He needed to change the understanding of America's lawyers before a bill could be guaranteed. On April 21, 1965, King spoke to the New York State Bar Association to defend civil disobedience, a topic mainstream lawyers would not obviously embrace. Before a likely skeptical audience, King spoke carefully, encouraging the role of lawyers in the Civil Rights Movement to redeem "the hundred-year-old dishonored pledge of the Fifteenth Amendment."

King's real purpose was to convince the audience that lawyers and courts were secondary figures in the fight for civil rights, behind citizens engaged in civil disobedience. To make his point, he needed to destroy the myth that *Brown* was the end of the struggle, rather than the beginning. King brought social science data to prove that the ruling had done virtually nothing for integration, a charge confirmed three decades later by political scientists. He said the "sad statistics are so clear: in the South, not more than 2 percent of all Negroes in Southern schools attend classes with white students." True integration would come, he argued, not only from courts or lawyers, but from a political moment using extralegal means to vindicate the Constitution. Here, King compared himself to the revolutionaries of the Boston Tea Party—"pretty good company," as he put it. King won the crowd. The organizer, a former judge who had coined the term New Deal, told King that the New York State Bar Association had signed on to promote Congress's voting rights bill.[103]

On August 6, 1965, Johnson signed the Voting Rights Act, a sweeping law with provisions aimed to end the barriers that were keeping Black voters from the polls. With the bill's signing, James Kilpatrick's reading of the Constitution seemed to face a fatal blow. Still, King was not complacent. He continued to defend his anti-tyranny principle until his last moments on earth. Three years later, on April 4, 1968, King was in Memphis to protest for fair wages for janitors. The city had won an injunction against King, but he rallied supporters in a nearby temple to demonstrate anyway. The night before the march, King prepared them for civil disobedience and invoked the words enshrined by Madison in the First Amendment, proclaiming its central anti-tyranny principle: "Somewhere I read of the freedom of assembly. Somewhere I read of the freedom of speech. Somewhere I read of the freedom of press. Somewhere I read that the greatness of America is the right to protest for right. . . . And so just as I say, we aren't going to let dogs or water hoses turn us around, we aren't going to let any injunction turn us around."[104] As he spoke, James Earl Ray, an outspoken volunteer for George Wallace's segregationist campaign, which Kilpatrick advised, plotted King's assassination. The next day, Ray killed King.[105]

★　★　★

JUST AS PRESIDENTS OF THE nineteenth century could be judged by where they stood with Frederick Douglass, the presidents of the twentieth century can be judged by where they stood with a bevy of leaders who were devoted to recovering the constitutional guarantee of equal protection that was lost after the Grant presidency. Trotter, Wells, White, Alexander, Marshall, and King were citizen readers of the Constitution who saw the nationalization of segregation and the spread of white supremacy and violence as the constitutional crisis it was. They sought to combat it by influencing presidents, whether through criticism or alliance.

Unlike previous periods of obvious crises, part of what defined the twentieth century's crisis of presidents and courts who read constitutional "equal protection" to be compatible with segregation, was the silence of many white people who accepted that understanding. Americans might have sided with Adams over the newspaper editors, or they may have sided with Buchanan over Douglass, but they did so with the awareness that a deep constitutional conflict was at the center of their politics. In contrast, Wilson's crisis of nationalizing white supremacy went unnoticed by many white Americans, because he did it surreptitiously. When Trotter and Wells insisted that Wilson's policies ushered in a constitutional crisis by nationalizing segregation, by spreading hate through the culture with works like *The Birth of a Nation*, and by prioritizing the avoidance of racial "friction" over seeking racial equality, many white Americans shrugged. But that indifference would change as King took the baton, brilliantly extolling the meaning of the Constitution in his Montgomery speech, then refining it after the debate with Kilpatrick until his mature understanding of the document, grounded in an anti-tyranny principle, animated one of the most important presidential speeches in history.

The groundwork for King's movement was laid much earlier by the NAACP and much lesser-known citizen readers of the Constitution, in particular Walter White and Sadie Alexander. Their chief victory lay in convincing former racist Truman to embrace the report by the President's Committee on Civil Rights that outlined a plan for constitutional recovery. Eisenhower would never become a full-fledged supporter of civil rights, but the public pressure on him from King and Marshall would ensure he at least—in his role as an enforcer of the rule of law— supported *Brown*, a minimal but important intermediary step on the road to recovery. During LBJ's presidency, a massive constitutional constituency was led by King, who convinced a president that breaking the law could be synonymous with recovering the lost ideal of equal protection—the culmination of work done by less celebrated figures.

Throughout the twentieth century, these constitutional constituency leaders demanded an understanding of the Fourteenth Amendment's equal protection guarantee that prohibited second class citizenship and segregation, thus refusing to accept the Supreme Court's interpretation of the document and the obligations it placed on presidents. Instead, these citizens invoked their own right to read the Constitution by and for the people, and used their interpretation to hold presidents to account.

It is perhaps the most serious constitutional misunderstanding of our time that *Brown* is seen as the sole moment where the theory and practice of separate but equal was soundly defeated. That misconception ignores the much more significant role of constitutional constituencies in reclaiming equal protection on behalf of the people. Still, to say the importance of *Brown* has been exaggerated is not to say it played no role at all. *Brown* bolstered the arguments of citizen interpreters like Trotter, vindicating their understanding of the Equal Protection Clause. The case clarified why Truman, in desegregating the military and the federal government, was not just acting morally but was fulfilling a constitutional duty. And it became a central tool in King's constitutional theory and rhetoric, as he rallied Congress and presidents to pass the laws that more effectively ushered in integration. The Civil Rights Act of 1964, using the proposal Sadie Alexander had fought to include in "To Secure These Rights," effectively offered carrots and sticks to Southern states to desegregate. That largely unsung technical provision succeeded where the courts had failed. That Alexander's role in constitutional history is relatively unknown while Chief Justice Warren's is widely celebrated speaks to the need to rethink how constitutional rights are reclaimed.[106] The victory in reversing segregation should not be attributed solely to nine Supreme Court justices, but rather to the activists who were willing to call out the crisis of segregation starting in the 1910s.

One counterargument to seeing that citizen recovery efforts were at the core of the Civil Rights Act of 1964 might be to point to how the Supreme Court ultimately upheld the act. In *Heart of Atlanta Motel, Inc. v. United States*, the justices ignored whether the Equal Protection Clause gave Congress the power to pass the act. Instead, they found the act's footing in Congress's jurisdiction over interstate commerce. So a skeptic might claim the act was not legislation related to the Fourteenth Amendment at all. That would repeat the mistake of overstating the importance of *Brown*. The Supreme Court is not the final arbiter of constitutional meaning. Lyndon Johnson, congressional supporters, and most of all the long line of leaders of constitutional constituencies pushing for the integration bill did see the act as resurrecting equal protection. It is to them, rather than to the courts, that we as modern readers of the Constitution should look for in understanding the constitutional significance of the Civil Rights Act of 1964. Even if the nineteenth-century case striking down the original civil rights legislation was never formally reversed by the Supreme Court, Johnson's "We Shall Overcome" speech signified how the principle beneath that decision was overturned in the hearts of the American people.

King is sometimes caricatured as having been overly optimistic about the future of race in the United States, and his supporters as naive about the need for an ongoing civil rights struggle. But King had no such illusions that passing two monumental laws ended the struggle. When speaking at the New York State Bar Association, he was asked if after the passage of the Voting Rights Act, civil disobedience would no longer be necessary. King answered emphatically that it would continue to be necessary so long as there were unjust laws. The guarantee of voting rights would not end injustice, and that meant civil disobedience must be invoked in an ongoing struggle to protect civil rights.

That the modern Supreme Court has retrenched many of the rights won by the constitutional constituency spanning roughly the first seventy years of the twentieth century does not mean their efforts were for naught. It is a reminder that constitutional rights throughout American history are won by citizens prevailing upon the political branches, not by courts proclaiming them out of thin air. The decisions by the court to eviscerate voting rights in *Shelby County v. Holder* in 2013, undoing much of the Voting Rights Act, and its efforts to end de facto segregation in its *Parents Involved in Community Schools v. Seattle School District* decision in 2007, thwarting efforts to end school segregation not just in the South but in the North, repeat a pattern of past Courts undermining constitutional constituencies. But the court's decisions are not the final say about constitutional meaning. That must come from citizens seeking to reclaim rights that are continually undermined by the political branches. The decisions of the court are calls to action. The push and pull of crisis and recovery has no simple end.

SECTION IV

THE RULE OF LAW

The Battle for Presidential Accountability

CHAPTER 11

Richard Nixon versus Daniel Ellsberg and Grand Jury One

Criminality in the Oval Office

WE CAN TAKE HEART IN THE EXAMPLES OF THE DEMOCRATIC CONSTITUTIONAL RECOVERIES examined so far. They show that, even when presidents use their power to attack democracy, and even when those presidents commit to ideologies at odds with democracy, "We the People" can recover a Constitution devoted to self-government. In these examples, citizen readers and the constitutional constituencies they galvanized on behalf of democracy often won out over presidents and courts, using moral sense, rhetorical savvy, political skill, and extraordinary persistence.

The crisis caused by Richard Nixon, however, is different. Nixon's crimes, and the response to them by American institutions, show that recovery of democratic principles is *not* inevitable, especially when those institutions are assaulted by a president. Though beginning five decades ago, the impact of this final crisis of democracy and the Constitution remains with us today.

The crisis of the Nixon presidency and its threat to democracy did not come out of the blue. It was predicted, eerily, by Patrick Henry,

the anti-Federalist and Revolutionary War hero, at America's founding. Henry argued that a fatal flaw in the office of the presidency made
the proposed constitutional system vulnerable not merely to crisis,
but collapse. At the Virginia Ratifying Convention in 1788, Henry
argued the vast powers granted to the president—serving as the singular head of the executive branch and commander in chief of the
military—rendered the nation vulnerable to a criminal occupying
America's highest office. Such a president, Henry predicted, would
realize that his powers could be deployed to aid and abet his criminal
ambitions. Henry took care to note that such a president could, in theory, be checked by a criminal investigation. But facing the prospect of
criminal charges, the president would simply rely on his constitutionally granted powers to thwart the prosecutors; and if the prosecutors
did not back down, the president could simply collapse the system,
demanding the full powers of a monarch. Henry's warning called to
mind a concern raised at the constitutional convention that "the prerogative of pardon . . . was too great a trust. The President may himself
be guilty" and those guilty of a crime "might be his own instruments."
The presidency was a loaded gun and its ostensibly benign powers
might be used for ill.

"If [the president] be guilty," Henry told the convention, then his
criminal proclivities meant that he wouldn't hesitate "to make one bold
push for the American throne." Henry predicted this president would
succeed, because the army—already accustomed to saluting the president as commander in chief—"will salute him [as] monarch . . . and
assist in making him king." Citizens would surely try to resist such an
attempted coup. But Henry asked his fellow convention-goers, "What
[power] have you to oppose this force? What will then become of you
and your rights? Will not absolute despotism ensue?"[1]

If Washington's second inaugural address is the guide to how "We
the People" can use the Constitution to hold a president in check,
then Henry's speech stands as its antithesis. It explains how a laudable
attempt to enforce the Constitution against a criminal president might
bring about the collapse of constitutional democracy itself.[2]

Pro-ratification speakers rebutted Henry's critique. They tried to show why a criminal president would not be above criminal justice and would face prosecution like any other person. At North Carolina's first ratifying convention, James Iredell (a future Supreme Court justice) declared that if a president "commits any crime, he is punishable by the law of his country."[3] James Wilson told the Pennsylvania ratifying convention that a president does not enjoy "a single privilege or security that does not extend to every person throughout the United States"— marking the "genius of the system."[4]

The debate between Patrick Henry and his pro-ratification foes continues to rage. Was Henry correct that any attempt by the "people" to criminally indict a president would collapse the constitutional system? Or were Wilson and Iredell correct, when they argued that a criminal president would be indicted, just like any other guilty person—subject to trial, prosecution, and even imprisonment?

In 1973, Richard M. Nixon was Henry's warning come to life. As Adams had done, Nixon employed a self-serving constitutional vision that allowed him to persecute his critics. And as in past crises, a group of citizen readers of the Constitution worked courageously to check Nixon's power. The mostly unknown members of Grand Jury One tried to expose Nixon's violations of the criminal law. They challenged his claims of "executive privilege"—his justification for keeping his actions secret and his presidency immune from criminal investigation and prosecution. A leaker who sought to reveal the administration's secrets also challenged Nixon, in an effort to tame an executive branch that he knew firsthand threatened American democracy. That challenge to the president would so enrage Nixon it unleashed a criminal conspiracy from the Oval Office.

Previous cycles of crisis and recovery were etched out in clear—if slow-going—victories by constitutional constituencies. The crisis of Watergate, however, is different. Citizens challenged Nixon's monarchical idea of the presidency. Even so, the structure of the executive branch that allowed Nixon to flout the law largely still exists. The truth is, we have never fully recovered from the Nixon presidency.

★ ★ ★

ON JUNE 30, 1971, President Nixon learned that the Supreme Court had dealt him a humiliating blow. In *New York Times Co. v. United States*, the court ruled that the *Times* could continue to publish a damning and embarrassing secret history of the Vietnam War known as the Pentagon Papers. The Papers, initially provided to the *Times* by an anonymous leaker, showed (among other things) that Nixon's promises that the Vietnam War was winnable were deceptive—from the start, the war was defined by a series of military failures hidden from the American people.

In an effort to stop the publication, Nixon's Justice Department had sought an injunction, arguing that the *Times* had violated the Espionage Act. It argued that this act, signed into law by Woodrow Wilson in 1917, trumped the First Amendment's guarantee of free speech. Nixon's team also argued that the threat to the "security of the United States" from publishing the documents ought to supersede the paper's First Amendment right to freedom of the press.[5] In ruling against Nixon, the court wrote that it could imagine "no greater perversion of history" than Nixon's claim that the president enjoyed a sphere of power not limited by the First Amendment. And it added that the limit on state power by the protections of a free press was intended to prevent "any part of the government from deceiving the people and sending them off to distant lands to die of foreign fevers and foreign shot and shell."[6] In other words, any power the president enjoyed to protect national security was limited by the First Amendment; the *Times* could publish the documents.

Nixon was livid. Inside the Oval Office, with his chief of staff, H. R. Haldeman watching, Nixon raged against the defeat, which he took personally. He seethed against the leaker, whom he derided as an enemy of the American people, and whose actions, emboldened by the court, could set a dangerous precedent. He bristled with antisemitic slurs, later ranting against the "Jews" who "dominated" the *Times* and *Washington Post*, which had also published excerpts of the papers. In characteristic fashion, Nixon wanted payback. "Do you think, for Christ sakes, the *New York Times* is worried about all the legal niceties?" Nixon asked contemptuously, suggesting that his enemies weren't fighting fair. "We're up against an enemy, a conspiracy. They're using any means," Nixon said. "We are going to use any means. Is that clear?" Haldeman said he understood.[7]

Then Nixon doubled down on directing a crime. Two weeks earlier, on June 17, 1971, Nixon had ordered his staff to break into the Brookings Institution, a left-leaning think tank in Washington, DC.[8] The news that he had lost the Pentagon Papers case gave urgency to the order. But his staff hesitated to complete the break-in, so on July 1, Nixon again emphatically ordered the crime. "Did they get the Brookings Institute raided last night?" he asked. "I want the Brookings Institute safe cleaned out."[9]

Inside the safe at Brookings, Nixon believed, there were more classified papers, this time possibly detailing his private thoughts and misdeeds during the Vietnam War. Some historians speculate that he was particularly incensed by the possibility of more papers at Brookings because they might reveal that his campaign had secretly sought to prolong the war by undermining peace talks during what is known as the Chennault Affair, and had bombed the neutral country of Cambodia along the Ho Chi Minh Trail.[10] It goes without saying that a private citizen has no authority to order a break-in of a private building and loot their safe. But Nixon thought the rules of private citizens didn't always apply to him. He believed the office accorded him special powers, especially around national security. The powers of the presidency, he believed, authorized him to do what average people could not—even order a burglary—if it meant protecting the nation.

Nixon had given the original order to burglarize Brookings to Haldeman and his national security advisor, Henry Kissinger. Kissinger tried to reason with Nixon. If the Brookings Institution had no right to possess the papers because of Nixon's executive privilege, then the president should go to federal court to have the papers seized legally. Nixon scoffed back at Kissinger's remark, demanding the documents "on a thievery basis."

The Supreme Court's ruling had shown that any damaging information in that safe could be published in the nation's papers. As he skulked in the Oval Office, Nixon ordered Haldeman: "Get in and get those files. Blow the safe and get it."[11]

As it happens, the break-in at the Brookings Institution never took place. When word of the plot reached John Dean, who served as the White House counsel in the Nixon administration, he called off the plan.[12] But from the Brookings scheme, another plot was hatched. In July 1971, Nixon's staff created the Special Investigations Unit—more commonly known as the Plumbers. The nom de guerre reflected the SIU's core mission: to seal up leaks and, more dramatically, to silence the leakers.

As the country soon learned, the Pentagon Papers had been leaked by Daniel Ellsberg. His background suggested someone groomed to enter the highest reaches of governmental power. He received an officer's commission as a lieutenant in the US Marines, where he led a platoon. He also earned a PhD in economics from Harvard. As an employee of the State Department, he then was assigned to work in Vietnam, where he began to form his assessment of the failure of American policy there. Ellsberg then moved from government to the RAND Corporation, a think tank closely aligned with the American military and foreign policy establishment, where he had worked earlier in his career. Assigned the task of writing a top-secret history of the war, Ellsberg began to have doubts about American policy in Vietnam, which grew into full-fledged opposition to the war.

Ellsberg embodied what Nixon viewed as the primary threat to his presidency. Nixon later called him a disloyal "punk" who revealed the secrets of the Oval Office to the public, thus threatening to pierce the veil of secrecy that protected the nation itself. The nation was at war. Ellsberg, by airing the country's dirty laundry, was giving comfort to America's enemies, Nixon thought.

On September 3, 1971, the Plumbers, led by former CIA operative E. Howard Hunt and former FBI agent G. Gordon Liddy, both of whom worked in the White House, and which included Cuban Americans Bernard Barker, Felipe DeDiego, and Eugenio Martinez, who claimed they were told this was a legitimate government operation, broke into the private office of Ellsberg's psychiatrist, Lewis Fielding.[13] While Hunt kept tabs on Dr. Fielding and Liddy patrolled the area in a rental car, the other three crowbarred open Fielding's four-drawer filing cabinet, seeking anything that might discredit or embarrass Ellsberg in public.[14] Discrediting Ellsberg became the central mission of the Plumbers, and an obsession of Nixon's. "I just say that we've got to keep our eye on the main ball. The main ball is Ellsberg. We've got to get this son of a bitch," Nixon told Attorney General John Mitchell in June 1971. "We can't be in a position . . . of allowing the fellow to get away with this kind of wholesale thievery, or otherwise it's going to happen all over the government."[15]

In May 1972, the Plumbers escalated their operations against Ellsberg. This time, they sought to, as Ellsberg later put it, "totally incapacitate" him—a vague and sinister euphemism. On May 3, a gathering was to take place on the steps of the Capitol in Washington, where Ellsberg and other anti-war activists would gather for a dramatic reading of an anti-war play. The Plumbers planned to start a riot, then physically attack Ellsberg, making the assault appear like an accident in the free-for-all chaos. To deflect the Capitol police's attention from Ellsberg and the attack, they planned a counterdemonstration, organized by nineteen-year-old college student Roger Stone, according to Watergate prosecutor Nick Akerman, who later investigated the Nixon administration for its crimes against Ellsberg. With Stone was another Plumber, Frank Sturgis, a former marine later arrested in the Watergate break-in.[16]

As the play was recited at the Capitol that day, Sturgis and others moved toward Ellsberg, intending to assault or murder him, Akerman said in a 2021 interview. A scuffle ensued on the steps and attackers could not get through the crowd, so Ellsberg escaped unharmed. As Akerman put it, "It was going to be a physical attack. Everything [in the plot] happened, but they couldn't get close enough." Though the plot was foiled, it revealed how far Nixon's Plumbers would go to shut down perceived enemies who threatened government secrets. Speaking to me in 2021, Akerman said, "These guys weren't doing [these crimes] in a vacuum. It was done because of Nixon."[17]

Nixon's treatment of Ellsberg was typical among his political enemies. Nixon ordered his staff to draw up an Opponents List (commonly referred to as an enemies list), containing the names of journalists, protest leaders, and Democrats, seeking to discover "how we can use the available federal machinery to screw our political enemies."[18] At another juncture, he told Haldeman, "Please get me the names of the Jews. You know, the big, Jewish contributors of the Democrats . . . Could we please investigate some of the cocksuckers?"[19] His hatred of the whistleblower, Ellsberg, reflected his general disdain for dissenters. That hatred sometimes mixed with his antisemitism. "Hoffman's a Jew," Nixon told Haldeman, referring to famed anti-war protestor Abbie Hoffman. Nixon continued, "About half of these [protestors] are Jews."[20] A conversation on May 5, 1971, with Haldeman spoke to his desire to suppress protest or worse. When Haldeman proposed they recruit "thugs" to physically attack protestors, Nixon responded positively, adding that they should get "guys who'll go in and knock [protestors'] heads off."[21]

Suddenly, Patrick Henry's nightmare was no longer hypothetical. Nixon rejected the idea that a president was subject to criminal law, rebooting Adams's quasi-monarchical conception of the presidency. Like Adams, Nixon, too, thought the president was separate and above ordinary citizens because of his unique office. As Nixon put it: "There are certain inherently governmental activities, which, if undertaken by the sovereign in protection of the interest of the nation's security are lawful, but which if undertaken by private persons, are not."[22]

Nixon's crimes weren't merely the product of impulses; they were carefully considered expressions of a vision of the Constitution similar to that of John Adams. Adams had argued that, as a sovereign entity, a president could not be prosecuted due to his role in the constitutional system. Under this view, if a president were subject to ordinary judicial processes, that would necessarily mean his or branch of government could not be coequal with the judiciary because the president would be subject to control by judges and juries. Nixon doubled down on this view. Like Adams, Nixon thought his immunity from criminal law stemmed from his duties as commander in chief. He succinctly captured this view when he famously told television interviewer David Frost: "When the president does it, that means that it is not illegal."[23]

Many viewers thought that line was absurd. Frost replied by commenting that Nixon's view would technically give him the right to commit murder. But Nixon's statement was not offered carelessly. It reflected a deliberate understanding of the office of the president. As Nixon explained to Frost, again echoing Adams, "If the President, for example, approves something because of the national security, or . . . because of a threat to internal peace . . . then the President's decision in that instance is one that enables [those following his orders to do so] without violating a law." Both Adams and Nixon were called paranoid by their contemporaries. But Nixon embraced it as a virtue. "Call it paranoia," Nixon told Frost, "[b]ut paranoia for peace isn't that bad."[24]

For Nixon, the commander in chief power let the president shut down opponents—domestically and abroad. That power traditionally gave the president total discretion to conduct a war on foreign soil; so, too, amid domestic strife, thought Nixon, could the president shut down dissent at *home*. Oddly enough, Nixon drew from Abraham Lincoln to support this view, paraphrasing him to Frost: "Actions which otherwise would be unconstitutional, could become lawful if undertaken for the purpose of preserving the Constitution and the Nation."[25]

Frost retorted that Lincoln presided over a war at home, not in Vietnam. Nixon disagreed. For him, the battle at home over Vietnam *was* a civil war, one that triggered the president's emergency powers, giving him prerogative to use otherwise criminal means to shut down dissent. "This nation was torn apart in an ideological way by the war in Vietnam, as much as the Civil War tore apart the nation when Lincoln was President," Nixon told Frost. Regarding his number one enemy, Ellsberg, Nixon said, "I didn't want to discredit the man as an individual. I couldn't care less about the punk," he said. "I wanted to discredit that kind of activity which was despicable and damaging to the national interest."[26]

★ ★ ★

NIXON CALLED ELLSBERG THE "most dangerous man in America" and used the powers of the presidency to quash him. But Ellsberg became a symbol of anti-Nixon resistance, a status he earned from leaking the Pentagon Papers and the targeting he endured as a result. Yet Ellsberg was more than the target of the president's rage. His reasons for leaking the papers reveal a constitutional understanding opposite to Nixon's. If Nixon sought to revive Adams's monarchical presidency, Ellsberg inherited the democratic resistance to that idea, following the likes of Duane, Douglass, and Wells. If Nixon had revived Adams's war on dissent, Ellsberg revived the idea of a presidency accountable to the people, and the renewal of Washington's call to challenge a president.

As a former Washington insider who had defected from the establishment, Ellsberg had originally supported the Vietnam War. Like his former boss, Secretary of Defense Robert McNamara, he saw winning in Vietnam as essential to combating aggression. But after traveling to Vietnam as a State Department official in the Johnson administration, Ellsberg witnessed firsthand what he saw as a failed policy. Though disheartened about the war, Ellsberg remained in elite circles and sought to end it through internal discussion.

In 1969, on the RAND team tasked with evaluating the government's Vietnam policy, Ellsberg concluded that the war was a failure in execution and purpose. The North Vietnamese posed no threat to American interests; there was no set of "dominos" that would fall if the war were lost, as multiple presidential administrations had argued. Furthermore, the North had not acted aggressively toward the South. Perhaps most profoundly, Ellsberg saw evidence that, despite the promises of American presidents, the United States and South Vietnamese could never win outright.

After the report was finished, it was sent to the White House for evaluation. Ellsberg hoped President Nixon would see the need to end the war. Nixon instead doubled down. Ellsberg learned from a close friend, an aide to Henry Kissinger, that Nixon would likely escalate the war, while falsely telling the public he was ending it. The aide, Mort Halperin, told Ellsberg that Nixon was also considering using a tactical nuclear weapon in Vietnam, thinking it might end the conflict. Indeed, tapes from 1972 released in 2002 revealed Nixon replying to Kissinger, who had been outlining various strategies, "I'd rather use the nuclear bomb."[27] In an interview weeks before his death in 2023, Ellsberg told me about why his fear that Nixon would use a nuclear weapon was alone "sufficient" for him to leak the Pentagon Papers. Ellsberg had helped craft the documents outlining America's nuclear strategy, so he knew the topic well. And when he had security clearance at Brookings, he saw cables from General Westmoreland in 1968 that made him believe a nuclear strike was a real possibility. But it was Halperin, a true insider, who convinced him the chance of going nuclear was significant. Ellsberg pressed Halperin on "whether he had seen documentation or just was surmising the danger."[28] When Halperin responded he had documentary evidence, Ellsberg knew he had to act. But how?

In August 1969, Ellsberg was visiting San Francisco for an anti-war conference hosted by the War Resisters League. As peace activist Randy Kehler, recently indicted for refusing to cooperate with the draft board and facing a soon-to-be-served prison term, spoke to the crowd, it dawned on Ellsberg what he should do. Kehler argued that the path to stopping the war involved breaking the law to save the Constitution. Ellsberg connected Kehler's argument to those of King and Gandhi. As Ellsberg put it, civil disobedience was required to change the nation's course—even if it meant going "to prison to say that this war was wrong."[29]

That fall, Ellsberg, joined on one occasion by his thirteen-year-old son and ten-year-old daughter, used a Xerox machine at his friend's girlfriend's office to copy the secret history of the war that he had stowed in his office safe.[30] In total, he copied seven thousand pages. Ellsberg tried to persuade congressional leaders to investigate the secret history of the war for themselves. His attempt fell on deaf ears. Frustrated and out of options, he delivered the papers to the *Times*.

Attorney General John Mitchell investigated the leak and obtained four affidavits, including one from Ellsberg's ex-wife, who perhaps turned him in to protect their children who had helped him with copying. She told investigators that Ellsberg had cut off the tops of the documents marked Top Secret (Ellsberg's ten-year-old daughter had been assigned that specific task.)[31] Ellsberg's decision to leak the documents enraged Nixon, because it challenged his vision of the presidency. Ellsberg meanwhile had revitalized the tradition of citizens holding presidents to account through direct action, not just during Election Day. In

Ellsberg's view, Nixon's actions had become so hidden that there was no way for Americans to understand the policy being carried out in their name. The only way to fight back against Nixon's aggrandized presidency was for an insider like himself to take secret information and put it in the people's hands, since "This is a self-governing country. We are the government." Nixon, in contrast, thought the "Executive Branch *is* the government," Ellsberg wrote.[32] Leaking the Pentagon Papers was a direct reminder of the people's sovereignty, in stark contrast with what Ellsberg understood to be Nixon's belief that "I am the state." The stakes could not be higher. Ellsberg explained to me that Nixon was "tak[ing] foreign policy out of the hands of the population," making America "not a democracy."[33]

Ellsberg's challenge to the executive branch prompted Nixon to reassert power. He vowed to pursue Ellsberg as an enemy and to shut him down, along with anyone else who challenged his authority. I pressed Ellsberg on why he thought Nixon pursued him so vigorously, especially since the Pentagon Papers were about previous administrations. On reflection, Ellsberg thought Nixon knew that he, Ellsberg, possessed other documents that would more directly damn him. Indeed, Ellsberg had helped craft an official nuclear strategy document that Nixon feared he would release, making the president look like Dr. Strangelove. Nixon's fears were not misplaced. Ellsberg had those documents and considered releasing them. Finally, Ellsberg suggested that Nixon might have thought he had evidence of Nixon's secret dealing with the North Vietnamese, urging them not to make peace until he took office. This is perhaps why Nixon so desperately wanted to raid the Brookings safe, as this was where Ellsberg and Halperin might be storing such prized information.[34] Those were Ellsberg's speculations about Nixon's motives, and were surmises by the person who Nixon so opposed that he brought a regime of criminality in the White House to try to silence.

But Nixon, for all his criminality, might never have been held to account were it not for a band of citizens, a group of anonymous residents living in Washington, DC. Though occupying the same city as Nixon, their neighborhoods—impoverished and crime-ridden—were a world apart from the Oval Office. They were the opposite of Washington insiders. But metaphorically, they would break through the White House's gates, challenging not just Nixon's idea of executive privilege, but his notion of the presidency. If Ellsberg fired the warning shot about Nixon's threat to democracy, Grand Jury One was the cavalry coming to save it.

★ ★ ★

GRAND JURY ONE WAS COMPOSED OF twenty-three anonymous American citizens who were residents of Washington, DC. Together, they reflected the demographics of their city. At least fourteen were Black.[35] At least thirteen were women. They came from various working- and middle-class worlds. Ethel Peoples was a janitorial worker at a local hospital. Elayne Edlund worked as a legal secretary in a private law firm. Howard Evans was a postal clerk. The jury's foreman, Vladimir Pregelj, was an immigrant from Yugoslavia, hired as an expert researcher in international trade by the Library of Congress.[36]

Grand juries are convened to decide whether to criminally indict those accused of crimes. Jurors are chosen among the local population, often sit for months at a time, and are usually presented with a plethora of possible indictments by prosecutors. A grand jury's proceedings are intensely secret, with criminal penalties for revealing them; the mere identities of grand jurors are rarely made public. When these grand jurors received their notice to serve, none could have imagined they would change the course of American history. At first, Grand Jury One heard routine burglary cases. But on June 17, 1972, an extraordinary break-in happened. A group of suspects, later revealed as the Plumbers, were arrested for breaking into the Democratic National Headquarters at the Watergate office complex.

Some fifty years later, I spoke to Ethel Peoples from her home in DC. Seemingly surprised to hear from an academic so many years after Watergate, Peoples returned my call in the midst of the COVID-19 pandemic in 2021 at 10 p.m. Jovial and ready to chat, Peoples told me that few, if any, of her family or friends knew at the time the role she had played in forcing Nixon to resign.[37] Early in the investigation, it was obvious to Peoples that she was in the midst of important events. In the early days of Grand Jury One, a bus took the grand jurors to the hotel where they were sequestered from the public. A group of reporters—what Peoples called "a mob of newspaper men"—followed the bus, trying to learn what had happened that day. All her life, she had been cleaning up after doctors and nurses, watching as they made life-or-death decisions. Now, she was being asked to hold the most powerful people in the country accountable. Federal grand juries, including Grand Jury One, are independent of the executive branch, and they represent a constitutionally established people's check on abuses of power. But the attorneys assigned to work with grand juries in the federal system are Department of Justice employees working under the attorney general, who in turn work for the president. To assess the merits of an indictment, the grand jurors, working with lawyers assigned to assist them, can subpoena witnesses and conduct interviews.

In the fifty years after Watergate, a slow drip of public disclosures has made clear how central a role Grand Jury One played. Between June 1972 and March 1974, Grand Jury One subpoenaed numerous White House staffers in an effort to discover whether the break-in was ordered by White House officials, including the president. By April 1973, the grand jury had heard testimony from former Attorney General John Mitchell, who said that he never approved the Watergate break-in. But Mitchell was lying under oath, making him guilty of perjury. The burglar James McCord, testifying truthfully in the hopes of being granted immunity, had already told a Senate committee that Mitchell knew the plan.[38]

The grand jury interviews were fraught with racial and class conflict. Nixon aide Patrick Buchanan, who later ran for president pushing white nationalism, implied Nixon's overwhelmingly white staff resented being interviewed by Black jurors, whom he suspected were motivated by partisan anti-Nixon politics. "Only a single member of that 23-member grand jury was a Republican," complained Buchanan, in a *Times* column at the height of the crisis in June 1974, in an attempt to publicly disparage the grand jury as the investigation heated up. Buchanan added, "Seventeen of the 23 were black—members of a racial minority that voted, nationally, upwards of 10 to 1 against the President, a minority whose political leaders have rapidly characterized Richard Nixon and his Administration as bigoted and racist."[39]

Despite the racist attitudes and hostility from Nixon staffers, the grand jury pressed on, building pressure on the president. Nixon himself felt increasingly threatened by the investigation, which he regarded as a usurpation of his constitutional powers—namely, his "executive privilege." He saw the grand jury, like Ellsberg, as political enemies that violated his constitutional prerogative of secrecy and the privilege to do what he needed in the nation's interest. On March 21, 1973, Nixon met with White House Counsel John Dean to devise a plan to halt the investigation. Dean told Nixon that the grand jury would likely indict members of the senior staff, including Mitchell. Nixon wanted to know why the presiding judge, John Sirica, was not doing a better job controlling the grand jury, complaining, "I thought he was a hardliner judge."[40]

Since pressuring Sirica was not an option, Nixon needed another plan. Dean suggested that the president try ending the proceedings of Grand Jury One and replacing them with a more pliant group and a new, loyal prosecutor. Nixon was receptive. "We could use Petersen," Nixon said, referring to one of his assistant attorneys general. Dean agreed, calling Henry Petersen a "soldier"—but feared that Petersen was so loyal that the reason for appointing him would be obvious.[41] But the men were in general agreement: with a savvy loyalist installed as special prosecutor, the grand jury could be controlled.

Nixon had tried to influence grand juries before to attack his enemies, so it was natural for him to do it again to defend himself. Notably, after he lost the Pentagon Papers case, Nixon told Attorney General Mitchell to ensure Ellsberg was indicted by a grand jury. "We've gotta get this son of a bitch," said Nixon. "I was talking to somebody over here yesterday, I mean one of our... the PR types, and they're saying, 'Well, maybe we ought to drop the case if the Supreme Court doesn't, uh, sustain and so forth.' And I said, 'Hell, no. I mean you can't do that.'"[42] Even though his theories of executive privilege were rejected by the Supreme Court, Nixon thought he could use a grand jury to indict his enemy. On these orders, Mitchell indeed ensured that Ellsberg was indicted by a federal grand jury for violating the Espionage Act, the same law that the Supreme Court refused to say favored Nixon in the Pentagon Papers case. (The charges against Ellsberg were later dismissed.) Now it was Dean's turn to ensure that another federal grand jury acquiesced to the president. If federal grand juries could be used as a sword to take down opponents, they could also be a shield to protect Nixon from prosecution.

If the plan failed, Dean and Nixon had a backup plan: To "just hunker down," said Dean, fighting the investigation "at every corner, every turn... don't let people testify, cover it up is what we're really talking about."[43] As Nixon later told David Frost, he didn't view this moment as criminal obstruction of justice. By covering up Watergate, Nixon believed he was protecting the nation's interest, actions that fell within his presidential prerogative. It is worth noting that this new iteration of "executive privilege" went well beyond what Nixon had claimed when trying to stop the Pentagon Papers. There, the existence of an ongoing war was at least connected to his claim of war powers. But in Watergate, despite the fact that he was not acting pursuant to his commander in chief powers, Nixon convinced himself that the same logic applied: an attack on him as the "sovereign" was really an attack on the nation. This was why, as he saw it, he could legally cover up the crimes of Watergate, even though it would be a crime if anyone else did it.

Grand Jury One, by contrast, had a far more democratic understanding of the presidency. Guided by this alternate vision, they took down the wall of secrecy that Nixon called executive privilege. On July 16, 1973, a Nixon aide named Alexander Butterfield was called before a Senate committee investigating Watergate in parallel to the grand jury. Butterfield testified that all of Nixon's Oval Office conversations were taped, using a secret taping system with microphones in his desk and fireplace. Immediately, the grand jury foreman, Vladimir Pregelj, and his fellow jurors knew they had to demand the tapes, and immediately, because they knew that Nixon would try to claim executive privilege. While the Supreme Court had forbidden executive privilege in the Pentagon Papers case, the grand jury's effort to overcome executive privilege in the president's private conversations was more significant. The tapes contained the intimate conversations of the president and his closest advisors. Grand Jury One was asserting its own power, an action that resists the common characterization that a grand jury is merely a rubber stamp for prosecutors. And they rejected the idea that they were mere finders of fact. Instead, these grand jurors, by demanding to hear the tapes, claimed the right to be constitutional interpreters in a broader sense—and in so doing reshaped the relationship between the people and the president. Not since the early nineteenth century had a jury claimed subpoena powers over a president.[44]

On July 27, 1973, Judge Sirica convened the members of Grand Jury One, in public, before the press. The move was highly unorthodox. By doing so, he was publicly revealing the names of the jurors. Yet Sirica thought the moment called for a public recognition of the power of the grand jury to enforce the law, even against the president, with the press there to document it. The *New York Times* described the foreman Vladimir Pregelj as a "46-year-old Yugoslav refugee who has worked for the Library of Congress since 1957. A bachelor, he lives on Capitol Hill."[45] Pregelj was "dressed in muted but mod clothing." Nineteen other jurors, including Elayne Edlund, were also mentioned by name. One by one in front of the press, Judge Sirica asked the jurors if they objected to a subpoena of the audio tapes from President Richard Nixon's recordings, which might describe a Watergate cover-up. Not a single one of the twenty-three jurors objected.[46]

One of the few living members of Grand Jury One is Priscilla Woodruff, who still lives in DC. I asked her what it was like when, at age thirty, she voted to subpoena the president. "When you do stuff, you can't get away with it," she replied flatly. Demanding the tapes was just common sense. Woodruff was appealing to a basic principle: a president did not have fundamentally different rights than any other citizen.

On August 29, 1973, Judge Sirica ordered Nixon and his staff to turn over the White House tapes to his court. Judge Sirica's opinion, and the appeal that upheld it, stands as a fundamental defense of the grand jury's constitutional understanding, and a rebuff of Adams's and Nixon's theories. Sirica emphasized that in the American constitutional

282 | THE RULE OF LAW

system, the grand jury holds sovereign power to investigate on behalf of the people. Nixon was wrong to claim that he was the "sovereign," and thus immune from investigation. Sirica was moved by the grand jury, describing in his autobiography, "Here was the grand jury made up of ordinary citizens from the District of Columbia, some of them poor people, telling the president of the United States, the most powerful man in the world, to turn over the tapes."[47] After initially refusing to turn over the tapes, Nixon complied once Sirica's order was affirmed by the appeals court.

Although he turned over the tapes, Nixon initiated his plan with Dean: curbing the grand jury by instituting a loyalist special prosecutor. Since his appointment as special prosecutor in May 1973, Archibald Cox, a professor at Harvard Law School, had worked aggressively with Grand Jury One to investigate the possible crimes committed by Nixon and his staff. Cox was not the "soldier" Nixon wanted. Rather than serve Nixon's desire to curb the grand jury, Cox had emboldened them— including to seek the tapes. On Saturday, October 20, 1973, Richard Nixon ordered Attorney General Elliot Richardson to fire Cox. Richardson refused and resigned immediately. Nixon then ordered Deputy Attorney General William Ruckelshaus, now the acting attorney general, to fire Cox. He refused and stepped down in protest, too. Solicitor General Robert Bork, now the newest acting attorney general, complied with Nixon's order, firing Cox.

The sequence of rapid resignations, which became known as the Saturday Night Massacre, was Nixon's attempt to use his power as sovereign to control the grand jury—regardless of what any court said. Special Prosecutor Cox was a member of the Department of Justice. As the head of the executive branch, Nixon claimed the power to fire him and any other functionary.

Suddenly, the fate of Grand Jury One was uncertain. Abstractly, the courts had declared a right to investigate the president. But practically, it was uncertain if investigations would continue. On October 23, Sirica assembled the grand jurors to discuss the crisis.[48] He assured them that they were still empaneled, and that they should continue their work; Nixon did not have the power to fire *them*. Cox's employees in the special prosecutor's office were also confused as to whether they still had jobs, so they continued to go to work—thwarting Nixon's attempt to shut them down. As convinced as he was of his power to fire Cox, Nixon still cared about public opinion. And polls showed Nixon's approval numbers dipped to 27 percent after the Saturday Night Massacre, the lowest of his presidency, which had reached nearly 70 percent before the Watergate investigation.[49] Increasingly, it became clear that the investigation could not be halted without political upheaval.

In November 1973, Acting Attorney General Bork appointed a new special prosecutor, Leon Jaworski. Perhaps in Jaworski, Nixon would find the loyalist he sought. Unlike Cox, Jaworski had voted for Nixon. And unlike Cox, he was not an expert on constitutional law, and so was perhaps more likely to defer to the president.

But the more Nixon sought control over Grand Jury One, the more they demanded independence. On January 30, 1974, Pregelj challenged the president in a letter sent to the White House, insisting the president conduct an in-person interview. Pregelj began by acknowledging the proposal by the president's lawyer that the president might answer "written questions, without an opportunity for direct questioning by any Juror." Pregelj dismissed that out of hand. That "would not only be unsatisfactory but might well fall short of the Grand Jury's duty to the public." Pregelj told Nixon in writing, "We believe we are justified in requesting that any testimony taken by the Grand Jury from you be taken under conditions substantially comparable to those upon which we have insisted in the case of all other witnesses."[50] Pregelj's letter was met by dead silence, highlighting a contrast between two divergent ideas of the presidency. Nixon insisted upon secrecy and the president's ability to stand above the criminal process. Pregelj, in contrast, treated the president as any other citizen suspected of a crime, with his role as foreman giving him power to address the president not as a subject of his sovereign will, but as a citizen juror with the power to hold him to account. Pregelj, like the newspaper editors who challenged Adams, found himself in a battle with a president over the meaning of the Constitution.

The letter was only a small taste of things to come. Grand Jury One grew bolder, defying the new special prosecutor that Nixon hoped would reign them in. Indeed, when the group convened for a private meeting away from the gaze of Jaworski, they conducted a straw poll on whether to indict the president on criminal charges related to Watergate. The moment was not reported until almost a decade after it occurred because of grand jury secrecy rules. Nothing like it had occurred in American history. Enthusiasm in the room for the indictment was palpable. Discussion ensued. Surveying the consensus, one of them asked for a show of hands.[51] Would the members of this federal grand jury vote to indict President Richard Nixon, charging him with the crimes of bribery and obstruction of justice? Founders like James Wilson and President Adams long ago opined on whether a sitting president could be indicted. Now these residents of Washington, DC, were bringing the debate to life. As the hands came into the air, it was clear which side Grand Jury One would take. The decision to indict the president was unanimous. Elayne Edlund even said, "Some of us raised both hands."

Among the artifacts of the moment is a secret draft of the four-count indictment of Richard Nixon prepared by Peter Rient,[52] one of the prosecutors assisting the grand jury. Count one alleged bribery, obstruction of justice, and obstruction of a criminal investigation. Count two alleged unlawful interference with a witness. Count three alleged obstructing a federal investigation.[53] Count four alleged additional interference with an investigation through bribery. The initial vote and the indictment dramatically rejected Nixon's (and John Adams's) view of the broad immunities of sitting presidents. The indictment began "the Grand Jury charges" and went on for six pages to lay out the supporting facts. An unofficial vote had taken place. The indictment was drawn up. It was time to move forward.[54]

But when word got to Leon Jaworski that the Grand Jury had taken the unofficial vote to indict the president, he was livid. Jaworski ordered the grand jury reassembled and confronted them. He told the jurors that it was unclear whether the Constitution allowed a sitting president to be indicted while in office, repeating Adams's view (and an Office of Legal Counsel memo that had been drafted months earlier by Assistant Attorney General Robert Dixon).[55] The members of the grand jury had won the right to *investigate* the president. But an *indictment* of a president was a different matter. If Grand Jury One moved forward with the indictment, he warned, it would risk disabling the executive branch, and with it, the government.[56]

Jaworski then proceeded to invoke the most dramatic reason the grand jury should not indict. As Harold Evans, the postal clerk, recalled: "Mr. Jaworski gave us some very strong arguments why he shouldn't be indicted, and he gave us the trauma of the country and he's the commander in chief of the armed forces and what happens if he surrounds his White House with his armed forces?" As Evans remembered, Jaworski continued to push the point. Such a move would be illegal, no doubt. But given the power of the presidency, no branch would have the ability to enforce the indictment if the president resisted with force. The implication was clear at that moment: American democracy would be no more. Jaworski summarized the danger of a self-coup as Evans described it through a rhetorical question: "Would the courts be able to act?"[57] Such a standoff would reveal the raw power of the presidency. Almost two centuries after Patrick Henry warned of the threat that an indicted president could use his office to collapse the republic, Jaworski used that same possibility to dissuade the grand jury from indicting Nixon. Just as Henry warned, the grand jurors were being told that an indictment would trigger a claim that the president was like a monarch. Jaworski essentially asked the grand jury what Henry had asked the ratifying convention: *What [power] have you to oppose this force?*

Things were at an impasse. Jaworski then pulled a power move, trying to reign in the grand jury. In normal federal criminal procedure, the power to indict lies with the grand jury. However, only the prosecutor can sign the indictment. Jaworski told the members of the grand jury that if they indicted, he would refuse to sign it—leaving the jury without a prosecutor to try the case.

The standoff required resolution. Jaworski and his counsel, attorney Philip Lacovara, then around thirty years old, met privately to discuss what to do. Speaking to me in 2021, Lacovara reflected on the two-part approach Jaworski had suggested to Grand Jury One. First, if the grand jury agreed to postpone the indictment, Jaworski could help them transfer their evidence to Congress to aid their ongoing investigation and possible impeachment of the president. If the information helped bring about an impeachment and conviction, *then* Jaworski told them, they could still indict Nixon since he would no longer be a sitting president. One obstacle remained. It was a criminal violation to share grand jury information with any other outside entity. But grand juries, Lacovara suggested to Jaworski, still retained the right to share information with other grand juries. Using this loophole, Lacovara argued that Grand Jury One could legally transmit their evidence to the House Judiciary Committee, which, during impeachment proceedings, functionally operates as a constitutional grand jury, sending its indictment to the Senate for trial. It was a novel argument at the time, Lacovara recalled—one never affirmed by a Supreme Court. But it was worth testing, especially if it meant avoiding the indictment of a sitting president, and Nixon possibly calling in the National Guard to surround the White House.

Second, Lacovara suggested to Jaworski that they could offer the grand jury aid in continuing to criminally investigate the president during his impeachment, readying the case for an eventual indictment. To show the grand jury the commitment of the special prosecutor's office to an eventual prosecution of Nixon, Lacovara and Jaworski offered to name Nixon as an unindicted co-conspirator in the criminal case that they were bringing against John Mitchell, the former attorney general. That label would make it clear Nixon had committed a crime. Jaworski presented the two-part plan to Pregelj and the grand jury, who agreed.[58]

On March 1, 1974, Grand Jury One set part one in motion, when it provided to Judge Sirica a "road map" to Nixon's crimes. Judge Sirica then provided the documents to the House Judiciary Committee on behalf of the grand jury. The grand jury had backed off indicting the president. But they used the process of impeachment to demonstrate that Nixon's crimes made him unworthy of holding office. Later grand juries took inspiration from Grand Jury One and sent similar road maps to Congress in the impeachments of presidents Clinton and Trump.

As Congress headed toward Nixon's impeachment, the second part of Jaworski's plan moved forward. The grand jury named Nixon as an unindicted co-conspirator in their indictment of John Mitchell and other staffers. It was that case which prompted the final and most famous battle over executive privilege. Some White House tapes had been handed over, evidence the grand jury used in determining the guilt of Mitchell and Nixon. But other tapes had been withheld on grounds of executive privilege. Lacovara and Jaworski—now honoring the commitment they had made to the grand jury—sought Supreme Court review of the tapes. Rather than trying to stymie the grand jury, Jaworski sought to make it clear, at least for now, that the president was not above the law.

Lacovara saw the importance of the name of the case in making that point. "Who in 2021 would care about *United States v. Mitchell*?" So taking advantage of a procedural maneuver that would allow them to rename the case—*United States v. Nixon*—they made it clear that "It was the American people challenging the president in their demand for more tapes," Lacovara said.[59]

As a result of *United States v. Nixon*, sixty-four more recorded conversations were ordered to be turned over to Judge Sirica.[60] In turn, the tapes were passed to Congress. Hidden in the audio of these tapes was the "smoking gun"—in which Dean and the president discussed covering up Watergate, and the president can be heard approving the bribery of the Watergate burglars in return for their silence. By July 1973, 71 percent of Americans watched some part of the Watergate hearings, which were fueled in large measure by the information provided by Grand Jury One. Republicans and Democrats in Congress made known that they supported impeachment. Relying on the road map and the smoking gun, the Judiciary Committee voted 27 to 11 to impeach Nixon on charges that he "prevented, obstructed and impeded the administration of justice" and the committee voted 28 to 10 that he abused power by "violating the constitutional rights of citizens, impairing the due and proper administration of justice," a charge that applied to the Ellsberg break-in. A third committee vote approved the charge that he had refused to honor Congressional subpoenas.[61] The evidence of the cover-up was irrefutable. Now facing a credible vote by Republican and Democratic members of the Senate to convict, Nixon resigned on August 8, 1974, stating his desire to avoid embroiling the country in an impeachment trial. He called his resignation "self-impeachment."

Even after he left office, the crisis continued. Nixon sought to bring to his home in San Clemente, California, a treasure trove of evidence that would be relevant if the grand jury were to indict him.[62] Congress intervened, passing the Presidential Recordings and Materials Preservation Act, requiring Nixon's papers and the tapes of the Oval Office conversations to be turned over to the National Archives, where they remain today.

Even still, the main battle over the indictment had just begun. Jaworski called Lacovara into his office to discuss whether Nixon might be subject to further investigation. Complicating matters were the rumors that the new president, Gerald Ford, planned to pardon Nixon. If the pardon came with a grand jury indictment, there might be a new constitutional crisis with competing demands from the grand jury and the president. Lacovara and Jaworski needed more information to see how fast the grand jury should act if they were to indict Nixon. Lacovara and Jaworski agreed that Jaworski would meet with Ford's chief of staff, Al Haig, to see if the pardon was imminent. But Lacovara was shocked when, on September 8, 1974, soon after Jaworski's meeting with Haig, Ford announced a "full, free, and absolute" pardon for any crimes committed by Nixon during his presidency. In an effort to ascertain what Ford planned to do regarding any potential pardons, it is possible that Jaworksi hastened the pardon by alerting the president's chief of staff to the possibility of the grand jury pursuing the indictment further.

Incensed, Pregelj fired off a letter to Jaworski. Claiming that the pardon was a betrayal of the grand jury, he asked Jaworski to find a way to challenge the president's authority. All along, the grand jury had pushed for the indictment. They had backed off only temporarily because of the complications of indicting a sitting president. But now that Nixon was no longer in office, the relevance of Jaworski's objection that there might be a constitutional bar to an indictment had evaporated. No principled or legal reason existed to deny the grand jury the power to indict Nixon. And the notion for which the grand jury had fought—supposedly affirmed in *United States v. Nixon*—was that the president was not above the law. Pregelj's letter made painfully clear that the grand jurors now felt that principle had been undermined by Ford's pardon.

Juror Elayne Edlund wrote directly to President Ford in a final protest. She wrote: "In the summer of 1972, as a member of the Watergate Grand Jury, I told one of the prosecutors outside the grand jury room that truth may be buried 90 times over, but it will still rise up, even if it takes 2 years or 6 years. Prior to Sunday, I believed it had taken 2 years, now I believe it may take 6 years, but it will prevail."[63]

Lacovara showed sympathy with the grand jury. He publicly announced his intention to resign in protest. The pardon, he said, was a betrayal of everything that the grand jury and the special prosecutor's office had worked toward—accountability and justice for Nixon's crimes.

The journalist I. F. Stone also backed the grand jury. Pardons, he pointed out, were valid under the Constitution "except in cases of impeachment." The structure of the Constitution was meant to block a president from evading criminal accountability, he argued.[64] Ford, by pardoning Nixon in matters related to his impeachment, was usurping the rule of law—the very idea for which the grand jury had fought, and the premise of the entire constitutional system.

These arguments, though made with passion, landed with a thud. Despite his agreement with the grand jury, and despite Lacovara's protests, Jaworski backed Ford's decision to pardon Nixon as constitutional beyond legal challenge: the special prosecutor served within the Department of Justice, and that meant that the president's decisions were binding on that office. With the Nixon special prosecutor now backing up the president, Ford succeeded in stopping the grand jury's effort to prosecute Nixon. There would be no prosecution for obstruction or bribery.

Other criminal investigations of Nixon halted, too. Akerman, the Justice Department prosecutor, could not pursue an indictment of Nixon for attempting to assault Ellsberg, for ordering the break-in at the psychiatrist's office, or for other offenses, such as Nixon's possible attacks on protestors or tax fraud, and of course for Watergate. Now, because of the pardon, the public still knows little about Nixon's crimes beyond the break-in. Jaworski returned to Texas. Grand Jury One dispersed, the members returning to their lives in Washington. They had played a major role in forcing Nixon's resignation. But now Nixon's successor had tamed them. Rather than being prosecuted as Grand Jury One had demanded, Nixon was left to live the life of a statesman, publishing books and opining on government affairs until his death in 1994. He died in the hospital after a stroke at home, his two daughters at his side, a president—not a convicted criminal.

★ ★ ★

DESPITE EDLUND'S INSISTENCE IN HER LETTER to Ford that justice would eventually be done, the story of Grand Jury One left an ambiguous legacy. If a future president, similarly criminally minded as Nixon, were elected, could his or her criminal ambitions be curbed? Could a new prosecutor and grand jury stop such a president? Would Patrick Henry's and Leon Jaworski's warning about an attempted self-coup become reality? Could a constitutional democracy survive such a crisis? Understood properly, Nixon's presidency and resignation is not a study in the strength of our institutions. It is an illustration of their vulnerability and the prescience of Henry's warning. A future president unwilling to "self-impeach" and determined to use the power of the office to further criminal ambitions might destroy the constitutional system itself.

Why had a democratic constitutional constituency not risen up in the aftermath of Nixon's criminal presidency to demand once and for all that a chief executive who violated the law would be tried and, if convicted, sentenced to prison like any other person? In previous crises, citizens galvanized around the idea of a recovery. But this time was different. An answer might be found in the framers' warnings about the dangers of even supposedly benign presidential powers. As Governor Randolph made clear and Henry made even more vivid, the danger of a criminal president was that he could use his vast powers to destroy democracy itself. In this case, the pardon of Nixon allowed his vast crimes to be swept under the rug despite the initial outcry against them. Jefferson had used the pardon in a laudatory way to wipe away the convictions of the editors targeted by Adams—and the notion that a president could outlaw dissent. But this time, what Hamilton referred to as the "benign prerogative" of the pardon would become democracy's Achilles' heel. Ford's pardon wiped away from the public view not only the crimes of Watergate but also Nixon's multifaceted criminal attack on Ellsberg and other political opponents. As a result of this pardon, there would be no public trial of Nixon around which citizens could rally. There would also be no way to enact the grand jury's democratic constitutional vision for handling a criminal president: impeachment, removal, indictment, and eventual imprisonment. Citizens such as Ellsberg and the grand jurors had done their part to defend democracy and could have become the standard bearers for a new constitutional constituency devoted to a rule of law above which no person, not even a president, would stand. But the pardon power, a vestige of the British monarchy, nipped in the bud the constitutional constituency and recovery that could have grown from a public trial.

The outcry about the pardon, which likely contributed to Ford's loss to Jimmy Carter in 1976, suggests that the public was well aware of the need to rein in presidential power. However, Ford still succeeded in not only protecting his former boss from the force of law; as a result, the Nixon presidency provided a template that future criminal presidents could follow to avoid true accountability for their crimes. Ford sacrificed his own presidency in a misguided effort to move the country forward, but in the process, he failed to contend with the dangers of the presidency that his predecessor brought into clear relief. Ford's pardon may have been motivated by the belief that Nixon's crimes were an aberration not likely to be repeated, but a future president's actions would give the lie to this belief, showing just how prescient Henry's warning was.

CHAPTER 12

Coda

Our Current Crisis

IN MID-JUNE 2017, DON MCGAHN, PRESIDENT TRUMP'S WHITE HOUSE COUNSEL, WALKED INTO HIS West Wing office,[1] for what he believed would be the last time. McGahn packed his papers, then called his chief of staff, Annie Donaldson, to say he was resigning. Without divulging details—seeking to protect Donaldson from criminal liability—he said the president had asked him to do something unethical, perhaps illegal, involving the Mueller investigation, and he had refused. That night, McGahn called White House Chief of Staff Reince Priebus to explain: "The president wants me to do some crazy shit."

Robert Mueller was appointed May 17, 2017, by Deputy Attorney General Rod Rosenstein as a special counsel to investigate accusations that the Russian government had influenced the 2016 presidential election. The appointment was prompted by Trump firing FBI director James Comey, who had been investigating contacts between Trump campaign officials, including George Papadopoulos, and associates of Russian president Vladimir Putin. Rosenstein oversaw the investigation after Attorney General Jeff Sessions recused himself because his role in Trump's campaign presented a potential conflict of interest. A team of fifteen attorneys pursued the case. Like Cox and Jaworski decades before, Mueller worked within the office of the attorney general, part of the executive branch. As Nixon had done with Cox, Trump tried to use his staff to control an investigation into his wrongdoing.

Specifically, the "crazy shit" related to two phone calls from President Trump. Trump had learned that Mueller's investigation had widened beyond his initial probe. Obstruction of justice—for impeding Mueller's investigation, specifically for working with his son, Don Jr., to fire Comey—was on the table, which was an offense Trump could commit even if he committed no underlying crime regarding Russia.

Trump's tweets were possible evidence of obstruction. For instance, on May 12, Trump seemingly threatened Comey: "James Comey better hope that there are no 'tapes' of our conversations before he starts leaking to the press!" After Mueller's investigation commenced, Trump increased his attacks on the investigator. On June 15, Trump called the investigation "the single greatest WITCH HUNT in American political history—led by some very bad and conflicted people!" The next day, June 16, in reference to Rosenstein, Trump tweeted, "I am being investigated for firing the FBI Director by the man who told me to fire the FBI Director!"[2]

President Trump was determined to do more than tweet. In mid-June, he called McGahn and ordered him to fire Mueller, contriving a conflict of interest, since Mueller had disputed a bill as a member of Trump's Virginia golf club. As Trump said, "You gotta do this. You gotta call Rod."[3]

McGahn, trying to placate Trump, told him he would investigate. But he was torn between loyalty and knowing there was no inappropriate conflict, which he thought "silly." McGahn had personally investigated the so-called conflict at the golf course, finding only Mueller's polite request for a refund when he ended his membership. Days later, Trump called McGahn back to reiterate: "Mueller has to go. . . . Call me back when you do it."[4] As McGahn later told Mueller's investigators, the phone calls evoked the Saturday Night Massacre.

Not long before, Trump's plan to fire Mueller wouldn't have just been unethical—it would have been impossible. The reason was a law that created an office of an "independent counsel," which reigned for two decades after Watergate and kept this kind of presidential mischief largely in check. That law came in 1978, when Congress passed and President Carter signed the Ethics in Government Act, which included a provision creating an "Independent Counsel." Its goal was to upend the previous system of investigating presidential wrongdoing, where a prosecutor like Cox was technically a servant of the executive branch— and thus could be fired at any time by the president. It was precisely this system that enabled the Saturday Night Massacre. Under the new statute, courts reviewed any attempt to fire an independent prosecutor and could reject such attempts that were without good cause. Moreover, the new law stipulated that although the attorney general called for an appointment of an independent prosecutor, the appointment was made by a panel of judges independent from the president. Purely political or self-interested firings of an "independent prosecutor" were illegal.

Through several administrations, the law functioned to provide checks on wrongdoing, bringing public attention and prosecutions of White House staff and allies. About twenty independent counsels were appointed during the Carter, Reagan, Bush, and Clinton administrations. The law achieved its core purpose: not once did any of those presidents even attempt to fire an independent prosecutor. Indeed, presidents largely respected independent counsel investigations. During Lawrence Welsh's investigation of the Iran-Contra scandal under Reagan, which involved accusations that Reagan officials used illegal arms sales to Iran to fund a rebel group in Nicaragua, the president publicly welcomed the investigation in a speech to the nation. This was the opposite of Nixon's approach to Cox. A constitutional challenge to the law that came before the Supreme Court in 1988 failed. Only one justice dissenter, Justice Antonin Scalia, declared that it unconstitutionally usurped the supposed presidential prerogative over federal prosecutions.

But the strong reign of the Independent Counsel Act came to a screeching halt under Bill Clinton. During his campaign, Clinton praised the law. And in 1994 he signed its renewal. Attorney General

Janet Reno said, "It is my firm conviction that the law has been a good one, helping to restore public confidence in our system's ability to investigate wrongdoing by high-level executive branch officials."[5] But Clinton changed his tune once the law interrupted his presidency. In August 1994, Ken Starr was appointed independent prosecutor to investigate an allegedly corrupt land deal known as Whitewater. Starr decided there was insufficient evidence of criminal acts regarding Whitewater. But during his investigation he came across a different possible avenue for prosecution: in a lawsuit against Clinton for sexual harassment by Paula Jones, a former Arkansas state employee, Clinton might have committed perjury when he denied under oath having had an affair with White House intern Monica Lewinsky. When Starr asked Clinton again under oath about whether he had "sexual relations" with Lewinsky and whether he had lied about it in testimony, he denied it. Clinton admitted to an "inappropriate relationship," but denied having "sexual relations," trying to imply that oral sex was not covered by that phrase.[6] Unconvinced by Clinton's evasive argument, Starr concluded that Clinton committed perjury both in the Jones lawsuit and his own investigation. Starr also investigated whether Clinton obstructed justice by ordering his secretary Betty Currie to retrieve gifts he had given Lewinsky to hide their relationship. Clinton also repeatedly invoked "executive privilege" in an effort to not turn over documents—reviving the Nixon-era concept of unchecked presidential authority that predecessor presidents had nearly entirely abandoned, with Reagan and Bush, for example, invoking it only for their subordinates. Despite Clinton's appeal to executive privilege, the investigations continued.[7]

As Cox and Jaworski had done during Watergate, Starr worked with a grand jury. Once again, citizens from Washington, DC, were faced with whether to indict the president. Freda Alexander was a lifelong resident of DC and a proud Clinton voter. She enthusiastically approved of his appointment of minorities to cabinet positions.[8] But despite supporting the president in 1992, as foreperson of the grand jury in 1998 she started doubting the president's integrity. Alexander believed Clinton was guilty of perjury when he repeated that he never had "sexual relations" with Lewinsky, saying, "I took offense to it. I consider myself a normal human being and I think oral sex falls within the definition of sexual relations."[9] Despite Alexander's conclusion, Starr convinced the grand jury to follow the road map developed by the Watergate grand jury, forgoing indictment, and instead aid in the impeachment process. With the grand jury, Starr issued a report to Congress, which became the basis for Clinton's impeachment on December 19, 1998.

Despite two Republican presidents complying with independent prosecutors, many Republicans disliked the law. They thought it an overreaction to Watergate that stifled the office of the presidency. Robert Bork, who carried out the Saturday Night Massacre, led the fight, giving speeches defending his firing of Cox and railing against the law meant to prevent its repeat, suggesting there had been no crisis in Cox's firing and that the law was itself the crisis.[10] Justice Scalia's lone dissent against the law provided an intellectual framework for opposition to it, forming the basis for the "unitary executive" theory that held that a president needed to have the power to fire any criminal investigators of his or her wrongdoing. After Clinton's impeachment, many Democrats, long supportive of the law, saw eye to eye with Scalia and Bork. Believing Starr had abused his authority, they bemoaned that an independent counsel could harass a president—their president—with impunity. In 1999, as Clinton's first term was ending, the Independent Counsel Act was scheduled to expire. It had been renewed thrice. But after Clinton's impeachment, few defenders remained. On June 30, the Independent Counsel Act expired.[11]

Almost two decades later, the Independent Counsel Act would have made firing Mueller impossible. There was no legitimate "cause" for Trump to fire him. Like Nixon, Trump just wanted to thwart an investigation into his wrongdoing. But with the Independent Counsel Act off the books, the judiciary had no clear mandate to stop it—and McGahn had no clear basis to refuse.

McGahn was familiar with Watergate and saw its connection to Trump's order. He saw himself as Attorney General Elliot Richardson, and Mueller as Archibald Cox. As a legal matter, however, McGahn agreed with Bork—who had followed Nixon's orders, and who argued that under the Constitution, a president had complete control over prosecutions within the executive branch. Like Bork, McGahn believed Nixon's order was a legal command, but unlike Bork he believed it unethical. Similarly—without an Independent Counsel Act to prevent otherwise—McGahn concluded Trump *could* fire Mueller, but he feared that doing so would start the new Saturday Night Massacre. McGahn regarded Cox as the hero of Watergate, not Bork. McGahn did not want to be Saturday Night Massacre Bork.[12] As history appeared to be repeating, McGahn wanted to be on its right side. Doing so, and resisting Trump's order, would not be costless. For one, it meant risking a break with the Federalist Society, the powerful conservative legal organization that had propelled McGahn's career. But that afternoon, he went to the West Wing to pack his bags.

★ ★ ★

THE NEXT DAY, Reince Priebus spoke with McGahn and convinced him not to resign. McGahn also followed his advice and never acted on Trump's order. Curiously, Trump never again pressed McGahn to fire Mueller. Perhaps Trump concluded that another route might be more effective, which was to order his former campaign manager Corey Lewandowski to instruct Jeff Sessions to reverse his recusal so that he could interfere with Mueller's investigation. But Lewandowski balked and attempted to pawn the job off on another official. Those around the president later said Trump decided the political risks were too great to follow through with the firing.

The accounts of these firing orders were included in Volume II of Mueller's report to Congress. In excruciating detail, the report shows how Trump tried his own version of the Saturday Night Massacre. Without the principled refusal of McGahn—a Richardson, instead of a Bork—Mueller's probe would have been quashed.

As Mueller saw it, however, his investigation could only go so far. Mueller never prosecuted Trump for obstructing justice because, according to Department of Justice policy from the Nixon administration—issued a month before the Saturday Night Massacre, and later endorsed by Clinton's Office of Legal Counsel—presidents could not be criminally indicted while in office—a view to which Mueller thought himself bound. In his report to Congress, Mueller cited the Clinton memo, clarifying that it forbade him from criminally charging President Trump, even if Trump could be indicted for obstruction after his term.

Meticulously, Mueller detailed ten instances of Trump's possible attempts to obstruct justice. His report painstakingly demonstrated that Trump had "corruptly" interfered with the investigation, a necessary element of obstruction of justice. But as staffer Andrew Weissmann explained, the report implied but did not state when Trump was guilty: When Trump was "not guilty of certain crimes, we said so; and when he was, we were silent."[13]

The parallel to Nixon's Saturday Night Massacre was resoundingly clear. But this time, as far as we know, there was no grand jury demanding an indictment of the president. There would be no serious outcry about the attempted firing; no dip in the president's favorability ratings; no revelations by staffers testifying before the nation, as there had been with John Dean; and no series of resignations by attorneys general, like Richardson and Ruckelshaus. To the contrary, Trump's willingness to fire Mueller eviscerated the investigation: as Weissmann explained, they were reticent to indict because they feared that Trump would fire Mueller: "This sword of Damocles affected our investigative decisions, leading us at certain times to act less forcefully and more defensively than we might have."[14]

There is another crucial reason that the public still misunderstands Mueller's findings: Attorney General William Barr, a loyal Trump factotum, pushed a false narrative about the Mueller report. When Barr was allowed to review a privileged, nonpublic version of the report, he held a press conference, announcing that "the evidence developed during the Special Counsel's investigation is not sufficient to establish that the President committed an obstruction-of-justice offense."[15] But that was Barr's conclusion, not Mueller's. And the statement implied that the Mueller report said something it did not. Mueller scolded Barr for sowing "public confusion" about the report. Still, the damage was done. Barr's press conference obscured the reality that Mueller had demonstrated criminal violations by the president. As a result, Volume II of Mueller's report is overlooked.

In such scenarios, there is another avenue for political accountability: Congress could consider impeachment. Behind closed doors,
leaders in Congress debated whether Mueller's report offered sufficient
grounds to impeach over the obstruction. Members of the House Judiciary Committee argued that the parallels to Watergate required such
an impeachment,[16] though that view was rejected by House Speaker
Nancy Pelosi and most congressional Democrats.

Instead, Congress impeached the president on a different matter:
Trump's attempt to pressure the president of Ukraine, Volodymyr Zelensky, to investigate the son of Trump's campaign rival, Joe Biden. In
July 2019, Trump offered a deal to Zelensky. If he worked with Trump
ally Rudolph Giuliani to investigate Hunter Biden's allegedly corrupt
involvement with a Ukrainian company, among other things, Trump
would pledge military support for Ukraine, including continuing aid
already pledged by Congress. One article of impeachment accused
Trump of "abuse of power" regarding the phone call; a second charged
him with obstructing Congress's investigation by repeatedly invoking
executive privilege to evade subpoenas.

The Ukraine impeachment hearings did not galvanize voters. Fewer
than 5 percent of Americans watched them on television; during the
Watergate hearings, an estimated 80 percent tuned in. A matter about
the fate of the then-obscure European country seemed anything but
relatable. Neither did the public seem particularly outraged about
Trump's quid pro quo. With just one dissenter, Republicans voted to
acquit Trump, whose approval ratings remained steady.

Would this first impeachment trial have gone differently if the
charges included the obstruction of justice outlined in Mueller's report?
Maybe not. But a broader impeachment would have gone further to
show that Trump, like Nixon, was guilty of criminal acts—and presidents should face criminal accountability just like other citizens.
Instead, Trump and Barr framed Mueller's report as an exoneration.

Ironically, Trump owed a debt of thanks to Bill Clinton, along
with the Democrats who opposed his impeachment. It was Clinton,
not Trump, who conceived of rallying a political base to resist and discredit a grand jury investigation and impeachment. Trump here fol-

lowed in Clinton's footsteps, not Nixon's. Nixon had faced a grand jury determined to indict and a House Judiciary Committee that rallied the American people. Trump, like Clinton, defeated his impeachment.

Following Trump's impeachment, Senator Susan Collins announced that Trump had been taught a "lesson" by the impeachment, presumably to respect the Constitution.[17] Far from it. Having survived impeachment, Trump learned the opposite lesson—that he could use presidential power to advance almost any scheme, no matter how illegal. A path had been cleared for an even greater crisis. It proved precisely the one Patrick Henry predicted.

★ ★ ★

ON JANUARY 6, 2021, at 1:10 p.m., Trump concluded a "Stop the Steal" rally on the Ellipse, a fifty-two-acre park located a mile and a half from the Capitol. The rally capped an almost two-month long effort by the Trump campaign to stop Congress from certifying Joe Biden's election as president, as the Constitution required. Trump spoke for more than an hour, while the joint session of Congress progressed. This rally was meant as a protest of what Trump falsely claimed was a stolen election. He said, "If you don't fight like hell, you're not going to have a country anymore," and "We're going to the Capitol." During the speech, Trump claimed that Vice President Mike Pence, as the presiding official of the certification, could "do the right thing" and refuse to accept the votes sent by state officials. To Trump, "If Mike Pence does the right thing, we win the election. . . . We're supposed to protect our country, support our country, support our Constitution, and protect our Constitution." At the end of the speech, he urged supporters to "walk down Pennsylvania Avenue" to the Capitol.[18] Following those remarks, Trump's supporters stormed the building in an effort to stop the electoral college certification from proceeding. Subsequently, about 140 officers from the Capitol police and the Washington, DC, metropolitan police were injured in the riot in the Capitol Building.[19]

As Select January 6th Committee co-chair Bennie Thompson put it, the speech "summoned a mob," inciting a violent attack on the Capitol. Many in the crowd saw the speech as a presidential invitation to insurrection. One man interviewed by the FBI said he participated because "President Trump said to do so."[20] Stephen Ayres, who pleaded guilty to criminal "disorderly conduct" for illegally entering the Capitol, also saw Trump's speech as a directive, remarking, "We basically just followed on what [Trump] said."[21] The events of January 6 left five people dead. One was a police officer who passed away of a stroke after battling the mob. Four responding officers took their own lives in the months following (at least one of them had reported being traumatized by the riot). Dozens of Capitol police officers were injured, among them an officer crushed in a door while trying to thwart the mob and another who was dragged and beaten outside the building.[22]

Once inside the Capitol building, the mob sought to violently stop representatives from certifying the election, some of them chanting menacingly "Where are you, Nancy?" (meaning House Speaker Nancy Pelosi). Some members of the House huddled in the balcony of the House Chamber, fearing for their lives.[23]

Amid this violence, the attempted attack on Vice President Pence most directly struck at the centuries-old tradition of a peaceful transition of power. As the crowd surged into the building, chanting, "Hang Mike Pence," his Secret Service detail believed an attack on him was imminent. Some agents called their families to say goodbye for what they believed was the last time. Trump watched Fox News from the dining room next to the Oval Office as these events unfolded. He saw reports of the mob chanting to kill his vice president. Eerie images of a gallows erected outside the Capitol were shown across media networks. According to an aide to Chief of Staff Mark Meadows, when White house lawyer Pat Cipollone urged Meadows to ask Trump to intervene, Meadows replied that Trump "thinks Mike [Pence] deserves it. He doesn't think they're doing anything wrong." Similarly, when Minority Leader Kevin McCarthy pleaded with Trump to send the National Guard, he sided with the insurrectionists, remarking, "Well, Kevin, I guess these people are more upset about the election than you are."[24]

The prospect of killing the vice president is horrific on its own. Less known is that if Pence had been killed, the constitutional requirement to certify the election of the new president under the Twelfth Amendment would have been thrown into turmoil, perhaps letting the insurrection succeed. Under the Twelfth Amendment, the vice president must certify the election. If Pence had died, no vice president could be appointed without the president's nomination and approval of Congress, an unlikely scenario given the circumstances. Absent a vice president to certify electoral votes, no one knows what would've happened. Perhaps the election would have been decided by the House, with each state delegation having one vote, a process that could have propelled Trump's election, given the Republican majority of state delegations. The role of the vice president was fundamental at that moment, and the threat to his life was a dire threat to American democracy.

Before January 6, 2021, the transition of power shepherded by the electoral count had never been violently obstructed. Speaker Pelosi called the events "unprecedented" and a major documentary about the day uses that word as its title.[25] But while "unprecedented" rightly characterizes the unique violence of January 6, scheming to disrupt the certification process was not unprecedented. The truth is, January 6 reflects a more urgent truth we must confront as Americans: the power of the presidency has always been a loaded gun, one that threatens American democracy itself. Patrick Henry's warning has always been relevant.

★ ★ ★

TRUMP'S EFFORT TO SUBVERT THE election results was not the first time a president's party plotted to exploit the loopholes of the Electoral College in an attempted coup. Allies of President John Adams sought to keep him in power in an eerily similar fashion, under which a committee of Federalists would refuse to certify electoral votes cast for Adams's opponent, thereby choosing the president themselves. Newspaper editor William Duane exposed the plot, accusing Adams and his party of planning a coup. His reporting foiled the plan.

Trump's scheme, therefore, was not entirely new. Like Adams, Trump came to believe there were few, if any, constraints on presidential power; Trump once said Article II gave him the power "to do whatever I want." And like Adams, Trump understood the vulnerability of the Electoral College. But unlike in 1799, the crisis of January 6 lingers. Dealt his defeat, Adams retired peacefully to Massachusetts. Trump, however, continues falsely to claim the election was stolen, and that Biden governs illegitimately as president. The ex-president commands a large constituency willing to believe this lie. Almost a year into his term, only 63 percent of the American people believed that Biden was the rightfully-elected president.[26]

January 6 reveals Trump's parallels with Wilson, too. Many insurrectionists flew Confederate flags on January 6, and Trump catered to those waiving them. He said to the crowd in his speech on the Ellipse, "We signed a little law. You hurt our monuments, you hurt our heroes, you go to jail for ten years, and everything stopped. You notice that? It stopped. It all stopped."[27] On January 6, 2021, for the first time in history, the Confederate battle flag was proudly carried inside the Capitol. Like Wilson, Trump used his bully pulpit to advance false claims of voter fraud, which was tinged with racist imagery. Beyond Wilson, Trump expanded its power exponentially by using social media to speak directly to his supporters.

There is yet another dimension to the constitutional threat posed by January 6 that makes recovery a profound challenge: people who claim to be "citizen readers" of the Constitution, but who serve an anti-democratic ideology. Converging on the Capitol that day were citizens who superficially resemble the constitutional constituencies profiled throughout this book. Like Duane, Douglass, Trotter, and Alexander, they appealed to the Constitution to support their efforts. Their reading of the document, however, is not a democratic one that challenges tyrannical presidents, but a monarchical one that empowers them.

Stewart Rhodes is one of these corrupted readers. Rhodes served in the military and graduated from Yale Law School in 2004, when he received a prestigious clerkship for a judge on the Arizona Supreme Court. But Rhodes became radicalized by 2009 when he founded a group, the Oath Keepers, which organized former military and law enforcement members under the pretense of upholding their constitutional oaths. The group's aim became to keep Trump in power at all costs. Shortly after the election, Rhodes amplified Trump's lies, claiming Joe Biden "was not duly elected,"[28] and because he was not legitimately elected, Oath Keepers should "refuse to acknowledge that anything he does is constitutional." Rhodes was criminally prosecuted for his plan to disrupt the certification of electoral votes, convicted, and sentenced to eighteen years in prison and thirty-six months of supervised release. Rhodes cast himself as devoted to constitutional restoration. But while the constitutional constituencies we have examined fought for democratic rights that would constrain future presidents of any party, Rhodes sought to empower one specific former president. In doing so, Rhodes pushed a constitutional meaning that would amplify the danger the presidency has always posed. Rhodes and his ilk are the foot soldiers of Patrick Henry's prophecy. They—like the white supremacist supporters of Andrew Johnson, or even the Ku Klux Klan—believed they supported the Constitution while supporting the leaders who threatened it.[29]

During the Nixon era, the prosecutor Leon Jaworski eerily presaged January 6. He told Grand Jury One that indicting Nixon could trigger a self-coup. Even though Nixon "self-impeached," his threat to democracy was perceived to be so strong that the special prosecutor made it a critical reason not to prosecute him, despite the grand jury wanting to do so.

As much as Patrick Henry's warning predicted the threats to democracy carried out by the presidents here profiled, past responses to those presidents offer hope for the future of democracy. The newspaper editors of the eighteenth century, Frederick Douglass's abolitionist movement, and the NAACP each began as small groups who fought against great odds. Their leaders faced prosecution, exile, and humiliation. The recoveries they led may appear inevitable, but only in retrospect. Given their modest beginnings, their victories show us that a new constitutional constituency could emerge in the face of threats to democracy. The patterns of the past, however, provide no guarantees about the future. The recoveries led by citizens after the threats from Adams, Buchanan, Johnson, and Wilson contrast with the Nixon presidency, where Daniel Ellsberg and Grand Jury One fought for accountability but never saw full justice. These examples show there is no ironclad guarantee of recovery; instead, they show the need for citizens' vigilance and readiness to take up the mantle of democracy even when it seems hopeless. Considering that Frederick Douglass spent 1859 being chased from this country, and within a decade saw the passage of the Reconstruction amendments, we can see that even at moments of despair, triumph might be around the corner.

Skeptics might claim that such a constitutional constituency can no longer emerge due to obstacles like partisanship or a fragmented media. But constitutional constituencies have surmounted intense partisanship (even violence) and contended with similarly fragmented media. Douglass's newspaper had a distribution only in the thousands; the newspaper editors of the eighteenth century brought their case against Adams with similar numbers of subscribers. Now, as then, the same communication tools that transmit hate and lies can also be used to restore democracy and recover from crisis.

Some might argue, however, that a new constitutional constituency seeking democratic restoration would be stymied by the Supreme Court, where rulings like *Dred Scott* or *Plessy* have been the norm, and *Brown* the exception. Still, however, the constitutional constituencies of the past often emerged in opposition to the court and justices like Roger Taney and Samuel Chase. Even if the current Court is hostile to an emergent constitutional constituency, the past offers hope that such a constituency might still prevail.

Finally, some may claim that antidemocratic ideology is too strong a force in American political culture to be overcome. But consider the extraordinary ideas held by past presidents who stood against democracy and who were ultimately defeated. Adams saw the president's role as that of a quasi-monarch and rejected popular sovereignty. Buchanan attempted to expand slavery nationally, violating the promise of a multiracial democracy. Johnson sought to make the end of slavery brought about by Thirteenth Amendment consistent with a belief in white supremacy. Wilson tried to build a national racial hierarchy. And Nixon claimed that his crimes were legal. That these presidents were elected shows that while their ideas might seem backward today, at the time they were widely accepted. Indeed, many contemporary legal experts agreed with them, dismissing those who read the document democratically as novices. Justice Samuel Chase sat in judgement of what he regarded as rogue newspaper editors, disregarding their First Amendment claims. Wilson echoed the segregationist ideas of the Supreme Court as he threw William Monroe Trotter out of the White House. Although many were appalled by Nixon's crimes and claims to be above the law, legal scholars like Robert Bork championed his views during and after his terms.

Our current moment is also marked by profound antidemocratic threats. But the examples throughout this book make clear that while our democratic Constitution is vulnerable, committed citizens can save it. We should be heartened by the fact that in the face of antidemocratic presidents, citizens resisted and often succeeded in restoring democratic meaning to the Constitution. In the first four instances of presidents who threatened democracy, Adams, Buchanan, Johnson, and Wilson, citizens' democratic understanding of the Constitution prevailed, at least for a time. And even though the fifth, Nixon, escaped legal accountability and left the presidency dangerously immune from prosecution, citizens stopped him from serving, which was a partial victory.

Speaking before her death, Watergate juror Elayne Edlund remarked, "No matter how many decades, it matters [that] justice must be done."[30] She was referring to the justice due to Richard Nixon, who she and other jurors fought to indict, and was a call to justice that never occurred. Despite our failure to adequately respond to Watergate, it is still possible to make good on her demand. The Constitution is not self-executing. It will not provide democratic rights and presidential accountability to the people on its own. Instead, "We the People" must continually demand that our presidents honor democracy and the promise of the preamble. We fail to honor Edlund's call—and that of Washington's second inaugural address—at our peril.

ACKNOWLEDGMENTS

THIS BOOK HAS BEEN A TEAM EFFORT THROUGH THREE DRAFTS. I THANK MY AMAZING RESEARCH assistants, each of whom made significant contributions at different stages of the project. I began working very closely with Aidan Calvelli developing sample chapters that combined biographies of the presidents studied in this book with their constitutional thinking; his revisions were crucial in this early effort. I then turned to writing a largely reimagined second draft. At this stage, Ben Wofford provided research assistance, made extensive edits, and helped me to conceptualize a more engaging structure for each chapter. As I turned to a final draft, Chris Woods came on board. He pushed for more in-depth research, particularly on Daniel Ellsberg, which led me to reach out to that crucial figure in American history and ultimately interview him, as it turned out, months before his death. Jackson Vail from *The New Yorker* then did a careful job fact-checking the full manuscript, with an assist again from Aidan Calvelli.

I have also benefited greatly from comments and conversations with colleagues as I worked on this project. Russ Muirhead and Nancy Rosenblum provided crucial feedback on the entire final draft. Eric Beerbohm, David McNamee, and James Morone were helpful sounding boards throughout. Andrew Kent pushed me to do a better job of seeing the point of view of crisis presidents. Conversations with Jan-Werner Müller helped me to develop what became the main thesis of the book. Early conversations with George Kateb and Stephen Macedo made me believe that I had a point to make and a story to tell at the intersection of political theory and American political development. Helen Aslanides provided crucial encouragement and mentorship. I benefited from conversations with Melvin Rogers about the topics in this book and from the participants in the COVID-era Martin Luther King Jr. online reading group, in particular Meena Krishnamurthy and Brandon Terry. In addition, this project has benefited from conversations with and comments from Steven Calabresi, Emily Zackin, Aziz Huq, Jeffrey Howard, Isabel Baird, and Kevin McGravey. Much of my thinking in this book started as two review essays in academic journals about popular constitutionalism. In particular, I learned a great deal from engaging with Elizabeth Beaumont's *The Civic Constitution*. I also thank my editors at W. W. Norton, including Quynh Do and Nneoma Amadi-obi, who helped me to shape and refine the project.

In addition to generous colleagues, I am lucky to be surrounded by a loving and supportive family. My wife, Alli, listened to me read the entire third draft to her out loud, commenting along the way about how to make the prose stronger and the argument tighter. My seventeen-year-old daughter, Sophie, discussed points over meals, bringing her knowledge of American history and her keen insight to bear. I also thank Susan Brettschneider, Eric Brettschneider, Robert Klopfer, John Weisz, Lane Brettschneider, Caroline Desjardins, Kim Brettschneider, Pat Heppell, Alex Heppell, and Myer Heppell for their love and support.

Just as this book was going to proofs, my family faced the enormous loss of my mother-in-law, Virginia Weisz. Jenny, as we called her, was passionate about history because she saw in it lessons for our current politics. She was a fierce defender of civil rights and focused her career as an attorney on championing the rights of children. She feared the rise of Trump and Trumpism but believed in the power of committed citizens to overcome it. I dedicate the book to her memory.

NOTES

INTRODUCTION

1. Blight, David. *Frederick Douglass: Prophet of Freedom*. (Simon & Schuster, 2018.)
2. See, e.g., Skowronek, Stephen. *Presidential Leadership in Political Time: Reprise and Reappraisal*. (University Press of Kansas, 2020.) For another account of recurring crises in American democracy, see Lieberman, Robert and Mettler, Suzanne. *Four Threats: The Recurring Crises of American Democracy*. (St. Martin's Publishing Group, 2020).
3. For a defense from the founding era of the singular executive, see Hamilton, Alexander. *Federalist No. 70*.
4. Hamilton, *Federalist No. 70*.
5. Henry, Patrick. "Speech in the Virginia Convention," June 5, 1788, in *The Debates in the Several State Conventions on the Adoption of the Federal Constitution*, ed. Jonathan Elliot (J.B. Lippincott Company, 1891), 3:168-183.
6. Robert Dahl makes this point. Dahl, Robert. *How Democratic is the American Constitution?* (Yale University Press, 2001.)
7. See, e.g., Juan Linz and Arturo Valenzuela, ed. *The Failure of Presidential Democracy*. (Johns Hopkins University Press, 1994.)
8. Wood, Gordon. *The Radicalism of the American Revolution*. (Vintage Books, 1993.)
9. Reed Amar, Akhil. *The Central Meaning of Republican Government: Popular Sovereignty, Majority Rule, and the Denominator Problem*, 65 U. COLO. L. REV. 749, 761 (1994).
10. Sometimes overreaching is done in the name of democracy, as leaders claim to have the right to authoritarian policies because they were elected, a claim that confuses populism with self-government. See Brettschneider, Corey. "Popular Constitutionalism Contra Populism." University of Minnesota Law School, *Constitutional Commentary* 30 (2014): 81–88; Muller, Jan-Werner. *What is Populism?* (University of Pennsylvania Press, 2016.)
11. "Second Inaugural Address, 4 March 1793," Founders Online, National Archives. https://founders.archives.gov/documents/Washington/05-12-02-0200.
12. "From George Washington to Lewis Nicola, 22 May 1782." Founders Online, National Archives.
13. This point is in contrast with the ideas present in Ackerman, Bruce. *We The People*. (Harvard University Press, 1993.) There, Ackerman equates change at the behest of the population as a whole, with the masses demanding action. Constitutional constituencies, in contrast, are smaller, acting on behalf of the sovereign people.
14. I thank Aziz Huq for this formulation.
15. National Archives and Records Administration. "William Lloyd Garrison and the Constitution." Prologue: Quarterly of the National Archives and Records Administration. https://www.archives.gov/publications/prologue/2000/winter/garrisons-constitution-1.
16. Chemerinsky, Erwin. *We the People: A Progressive Reading of the Constitution for the Twenty-First Century*. (Picador, 2018.)
17. For a recent version of the argument that the Constitution did not protect slavery as originally conceived, see also, Wilentz, Sean. *No Property in Man*. (Harvard University Press, 2018.)

CHAPTER 1: JOHN ADAMS VERSUS COOPER, BACHE, AND DUANE:
A PRESIDENT'S ATTEMPT TO SHUT DOWN THE OPPOSITION

1. Przeworski, Adam. *Crises of Democracy.* Cambridge University Press, 2019, 33–35.

2. "Treasury Department Building, Washington: June—August 1800." Buildings of the Department of State, Office of the Historian.

3. "13 South Fifth Street, Philadelphia November 1797—May 1800." Buildings of the Department of State, Office of the Historian.

4. See, e.g., Fruchtman Jr., Jack. *The Political Philosophy of Thomas Paine.* (Johns Hopkins University Press, 2011.)

5. See, e.g., Morone, James. *Republic of Wrath.* (Basic Books, 2020.)

6. "John Adams' Diplomatic Missions." *American Experience,* PBS, 2019.

7. See, Wood, Gordon. *Friends Divided: John Adams and Thomas Jefferson.* (Penguin Press, 2017.)

8. Carlson, Peter. "Encounter: John Adams' Bow to King George III." *HistoryNet* 7 (August 2017).

9. "John Adams Diplomat to France." Boston Tea Party Ships and Museum, September 23, 2019; see also, Ruppert, Bob. "How John Adams Almost Undermined the French Alliance." *Journal of the American Revolution* (July 7, 2015).

10. See, Nelson, Eric. "Flipping His Whigs: A Response to Gordon S. Wood." Essay posted online; see also, Wood, *Radicalism.*

11. Nelson, *Flipping His Whigs.*

12. Feikert-Ahalt, Clare. "Sedition in England: The Abolition of a Law from a Bygone Era." *Library of Congress Blogs* (2012).

13. "John Adams to John Quincy Adams, 2 January 1793." Founders Online, National Archives. https://founders.archives.gov/documents/Adams/04-09-02-0213.

14. "Timothy Pickering." George Washington Presidential Library.

15. "To Alexander Hamilton from Timothy Pickering, 25 March 1798," Founders Online, National Archives.

16. Wood, *Friends Divided*; see also, Morone, *Republic of Wrath.*

17. Kurtz, Stephen G. "The French Mission of 1799–1800: Concluding Chapter in the Statecraft of John Adams." *Political Science Quarterly* 80, no. 41(965): 543–57.

18. "John Adams to Abigail Adams, 4 December 1796." Founders Online, National Archives.

19. DiCanio, Teddi. "Alien and Sedition Acts: 1798." JRank Law Library.

20. McCullough, David. *John Adams.* (Simon & Schuster, 2002), 618; Congressional Globe website. 5th Congress, 2nd Session, 2163–64.

21. See, e.g., "John Adams," *Encyclopedia Britannica*; McCullough, *John Adams,* 505. McCullough claims that Adams saw the laws as "war measures"; See, e.g., Ryerson, Richard Alan. "Like a Hare before the Hunters." *Proceedings of the Massachusetts Historical Society,* Third Series 107 (1995): 16–29, at 17.

22. Solomon, Stephen. "James Madison's Report to the Virginia House of Delegates, 1800." History Speaks, First Amendment Watch, 2018.

23. Formisano, Ronald. *For The People: American Populist Movements from the Revolution to the 1850s.* (University of North Carolina Press, 2008.)

24. Thomas Paine, "Letter to George Washington from Thomas Paine, 30 July 1796." Cited in Bird, Wendell. *Criminal Dissent: Prosecutions under the Alien and Sedition Acts of 1798.* (Harvard University Press, 2020.)

25. Smith, Jeffery. *Franklin and Bache: Envisioning the Enlightened Republic.* (Oxford University Press, 1990), 149.

26. Scherr, Arthur. "Inventing the Patriot President: Bache's 'Aurora' and John Adams," *The Pennsylvania Magazine of History and Biography* 119, no. 4 (October 1995): 369–99.

27. Bird, *Criminal Dissent*.

28. Callender, James. *The Prospect Before Us* Vol. 2, pt. 2. (Printed by M. Jones, S. Pleasants, Jun., and J. Lyon, 1800), 57.

29. "9 Insults That Make the Presidential Campaign Seem Civilized," *Merriam-Webster*.

30. "From John Adams to Benjamin Rush, 22 April 1812." Founders Online, National Archives.

31. Mitchell, Stewart, ed. *New Letters of Abigail Adams, 1788–1801*. (Houghton Mifflin Harcourt Publishing Company, 1947.)

32. Bird, *Criminal Dissent*.

33. Ibid., 219.

34. Rachlin, Robert D. "The Sedition Act of 1798 and the East-West Political Divide in Vermont." Vermont Historical Society. Vermonthistory.org/journal/78/VHS7802Sedition-Act1798.pdf.

35. Neumann, Caryn E. "Matthew Lyon." Free Speech Center, The First Amendment Encyclopedia.

36. "Samuel Chase Impeached." Federal Judicial Center. https://www.fjc.gov/history/timeline/samuel-chase-impeached.

37. See, e.g., Shugerman, Jed. *The People's Courts: Pursuing Judicial Independence in America.* (Harvard University Press, 2012.)

38. See, Pasley, Jeffrey. *The Tyranny of Printers: Newspaper Politics in the Early American Republic.* (Charlottesville, VA: University of Viriginia Press, 2001.)

39. Bird, *Criminal Dissent*, 5,425; see also, Little, Nigel. " 'Great Gulf of All Undone Beings': William Duane's Radicalism in a Global Context." *Eighteenth-Century Ireland* 21 (2006): 107–24.

40. Bird, *Criminal Dissent*, 5, 437.

41. Smith, James Morton. "The Aurora and the Alien and Sedition Laws, Part II: The Editorship of William Duane." The Pennsylvania Magazine of History and Biography, Penn State University Libraries, 77, no. 2 (April 1953): 123–55.

42. Adams, Charles Francis. *The Works of John Adams, vol. 9 (Letters and State Papers 1799–1811).* (Boston: Little, Brown and Co., 1856).

43. Smith, "The Aurora."

44. Ibid.

45. Ibid., 148–51.

46. Ibid., 153.

47. "To Thomas Jefferson from Thomas Cooper, 23 March 1800." Founders Online, National Archives.

48. Smith, "The Aurora," 146. (Emphasis original.)

49. Smith, James Morton. "President John Adams, Thomas Cooper, and Sedition: A Case Study in Suppression." *Journal of American History*, 42, no. 3 (1955): 438–65.

50. Smith, "President John Adams," 440–41, 446.

51. Lehman, Forrest K. "Seditious Libel' on Trial, Political Dissent on the Record: An Account of the Trial of Thomas Cooper as Campaign Literature." *The Pennsylvania Magazine of History and Biography* 132, no. 2 (2008): 117–39.

52. Cooper, Thomas. *An Account of the Trial of Thomas Cooper of Northumberland; on a Charge of Libel against the President of the United States.* Printed by J. Bioren. Evans Early American Imprint Collection, 1800.

53. Lehman, " 'Seditious Libel' on Trial," 119.

54. Cooper, *An Account of the Trial.*
55. Volokh, Eugene. "Thomas Cooper, Early American Public Intellectual." *New York University Journal of Law and Liberty* (2009): 372–81.
56. Bird, *Criminal Dissent,* 7, 126.
57. Cooper, *"An Account of the Trial of Thomas Cooper."*
58. Ibid.
59. "Thomas Jefferson to Joseph C. Cabell, 1 March 1819." Founders Online, National Archives.
60. Madison, James. *Papers 12:196–209.* 8 June 1789.

CHAPTER 2: THOMAS JEFFERSON AND THE EDITORS' CAMPAIGN: THE RECOVERY BEGINS

1. "To James Madison from Thomas Jefferson, 5 April 1798." Founders Online, National Archives.
2. "James Madison's Ciphers." Library of Congress.
3. "To James Madison from Thomas Jefferson, 5 April 1798." Founders Online, National Archives.
4. "To James Madison from Thomas Jefferson, 16 January 1799." Founders Online, National Archives.
5. "To James Madison from Thomas Jefferson, 22 November 1799." Founders Online, National Archives.
6. Bird, *Criminal Dissent,* 146.
7. "Biography: Abigail Adams." *American Experience,* PBS.
8. "Abigail Adams to Mary Smith Cranch, 7 April 1798." Founders Online, National Archives.
9. See, e.g., "From Thomas Jefferson to Benjamin Franklin Bache, 22 April 1791." Founders Online, National Archives.
10. "Thomas Jefferson to Spencer Roane, 6 September 1819." Founders Online, National Archives.
11. "Resolutions Adopted by the Kentucky General Assembly, 10 November 1798." Founders Online, National Archives.
12. Ibid.
13. See e.g., "From Thomas Jefferson to James Madison, 30 January 1799," Founders Online, National Archives. https://founders.archives.gov/documents/Jefferson/01-30-02-0460.
14. Ibid.
15. Ibid.
16. Wineapple, Brenda. "Our First Authoritarian Crackdown." *The New York Review,* July 2, 2020.
17. James Madison, "Report on the Virginia Resolutions," January 1800, in *The Writings of James Madison,* vol. 6, 385-401. (Forgotten Books, 2018.)
18. See Larson, Edward. *A Magnificent Catastrophe: The Tumultuous Election of 1800, America's First Presidential Campaign.* (Simon & Schuster, 2008.)
19. Halperin, Terri Diane. *The Alien and Sedition Acts of 1798.* (Johns Hopkins University Press, 2016.)
20. Bradburn, Douglas. "A Clamor in the Public Mind." *William and Mary Quarterly,* Third series, vol. 65 (2008): 599.
21. Ibid.
22. Ibid. Generally, see the good discussion by Bradburn on the language of constitutional interpretation used by citizens protesting the acts.
23. Ferling, John. *Adams v. Jefferson: The Tumultuous Election of 1800.* Oxford University Press, 2005.

24. Dunn, Susan. *Jefferson's Second Revolution: The Election Crisis of 1800 and the Triumph of Republicanism.* (Houghton Mifflin, 2004), 167–68.
25. Ferling, *Adams v. Jefferson,* 136.
26. Halperin, *Alien and Sedition.*
27. "From Thomas Jefferson to James Madison, 26 April 1798." Founders Online, National Archives; see also, "From Thomas Jefferson to James Madison, 12 May 1800." Founders Online, National Archives.
28. Ferling, *Adams v. Jefferson,* 140.
29. Ibid., 136.
30. See Larson, *Magnificent Catastrophe.*
31. Fleming, Thomas. "Verdicts Of History IV: 'A Scandalous, Malicious, and Seditious Libel.'" *American Heritage* 19, no. 1 (1967).
32. Dunn, *Jefferson's Second Revolution,* 169.
33. Ibid.
34. Larson, *Magnificent Catastrophe,* 134.
35. Ibid.
36. Dunn, *Jefferson's Second Revolution,* 169.
37. Larson, *Magnificent Catastrophe,* 135.
38. "To James Madison from Thomas Jefferson, 9 November 1800." Founders Online, National Archives.
39. Larson, *Magnificent Catastrophe,* 154.
40. Halperin, *Alien and Sedition.*
41. Lepore, Jill. "Party Time: Smear Tactics, Skulduggery, and the Début of American Democracy." *The New Yorker* (September 10, 2007).
42. Ferling, *Adams v. Jefferson,* 155–56.
43. Dunn, *Jefferson's Second Revolution,* 110.
44. See, e.g., Ferling, *Adams v. Jefferson,* 153.
45. "Matthew Lyon. Vermont's Spitting Irishman." *New England Historical Society.*
46. Thomas Jefferson. "First Inaugural Address." The Avalon Project, Yale Law School, March 4, 1801.
47. Ferling, *Adams v. Jefferson,* 205.
48. For the letter best describing Jefferson's departmentalism, see, "From Thomas Jefferson to Spencer Roane, 6 September 1819." Founders Online, National Archives.
49. Shesol, Jeff. "When Presidents Think about Defying the Courts." *The New Yorker* (February, 2017).
50. "From Abigail Smith Adams to Thomas Jefferson, 25 October 1804." Founders Online, National Archives.
51. "From Thomas Jefferson to Abigail Smith Adams, 11 September 1804." Founders Online, National Archives.
52. Bird, *Criminal Dissent,* chs. 8–9.
53. "From Thomas Jefferson to Joseph H. Nicholson, 13 May 1803." Founders Online, National Archives.
54. Ibid.
55. "Samuel Chase: The Samuel Chase Impeachment Trial." J Rank Law Library.
56. See, Whittington, Keith. *Constitutional Construction: Divided Powers and Constitutional Meaning.* (Harvard University Press, 2001), 21–71.
57. Whittington, Keith. "Should the House Impeach If the Senate Won't Convict?" *Lawfare*

Journal (May 8, 2019). Also see, Bailey, Jeremy. *Constitutionalism, Conflict, and Consent: Jefferson on the Impeachment Power.* (Cambridge University Press, 2008.)

58. Bird, *Criminal Dissent*, location 8632; see also, "From Thomas Jefferson to Thomas McKean, 19 February 1803." Founders Online, National Archives.

59. *People v. Croswell*, 3 Johns. Cas. 337 N.Y. (1804).

CHAPTER 3: JAMES MADISON AND HANSON: PROTECTING SPEECH DURING WAR

1. "On This Day, the British Set Fire to Washington, D.C." *National Constitution Center*, August 24, 2023.

2. "Thomas Jefferson: Jefferson's Library." *Library of Congress*, 2019.

3. "A Most Magnificent Ruin: The Burning of the Capitol during the War of 1812." Architect of the Capitol, August 1, 2023.

4. Pitch, Anthony. "The Burning of Washington." The White House Historical Association website, 2019.

5. "On This Day, the British Set Fire to Washington, D.C."

6. Pitch, "The Burning of Washington"; "On This Day, the British Set Fire to Washington, D.C." National Constitution Center, 2019.

7. "Flight of the Madisons." The White House Historical Association.

8. Heidler, David S., and Jeanne T. Heidler. "War of 1812." *Encyclopædia Britannica*, 14 Sep. 2023.

9. "Summer 1812: Congress Stages Fiery Debates over Whether to Declare War on Britain." National Park Service.

10. Bickam, Troy. *The Weight of Vengeance: The United States, the British Empire, and the War of 1812.* (Oxford University Press, 2017, 185.)

11. Iggulden, Emily. "The 'Loyalist Problem' in the Early Republic: Naturalization, Navigation and the Cultural Solution, 1783–1850." "Master's Theses and Capstones," University of New Hampshire, 2008, 89.

12. See, e.g., Rubin, Zoe. " 'The Tories of 1812': Decoding the Language of Political Insults in the Early Republic." Written for: *Creation of the American Politician.* https://docslib.org/doc/6731752/the-tories-of-1812-decoding-the-language-of-political-insults-in-the-early-republic; "To James Madison from the Republican Citizens of York County, District of Maine, 10 September 1812 (Abstract)." Founders Online, National Archives.

13. Adams, Henry. *History of the United State of America during the First Administration of James Madison.* (Charles Scribner's Sons, 1918), 400.

14. Lyon, Jacquelynn A. "The Pen and the Petticoat: Gendered Slander Against Dolley Madison in the Early American Republic." Undergraduate Thesis, University of Colorado Boulder, 2017.

15. "A New Nation Votes." New Nation Votes, American Antiquarian Society.

16. Dielman, Louis, and William Marine. *The British Invasion of Maryland, 1812–1815.* (Heritage Books, 2009), 7.

17. Ibid., 8.

18. "Baltimore Residents Riot against Antiwar Dissenters." National Park Service.

19. Hannum, Patrick H. "James McCubbin Lingan, an American Story." *Journal of the American Revolution* (April 2019).

20. "Baltimore Residents Riot against Antiwar Dissenters." National Park Service.

21. "An Exact and Authentic Narrative of the 2nd Baltimore Riot (1812)." The Public Domain Review.

22. Poole, Robert M. "Light Horse- Harry Lee: Overreaching Hero of the Revolution." *History-Net* (August 8, 2017).
23. Gilje, Paul. "The Baltimore Riots of 1812 and the Breakdown of the Anglo-American Mob Tradition." *Journal of Social History* 13, no. 4 (1980): 547–64; see also, "To James Madison from Henry Lee, 15 January 1813." Founders Online, National Archives.
24. Gilje, "Baltimore Riots."
25. "To James Madison from James Monroe, 4 August 1812." Founders Online, National Archives.
26. Hickey, Donald. *The War of 1812: A Forgotten Conflict.* (University of Illinois Press, 2012.)
27. Nelson, Eric. *The Royalist Revolution: Monarchy and the American Founding.* (Harvard University Press, 2014); Feldman, Noah. *The Three Lives of James Madison: Genius, Partisan, President.* (Random House, 2017.)
28. Read, James H. "James Madison." *Free Speech Center.* September 19, 2023.
29. Madison, James. "Federalist No. 10," in *The Federalist Papers*, by Alexander Hamilton, John Jay, and James Madison. Accessed at *Founders Online*.
30. Madison, James. "First Inaugural Address," March 4, 1809, accessed at *Miller Center*.
31. See, e.g., "To James Madison from the Republican Citizens of York County, District of Maine, 10 September 1812 (Abstract)." Founders Online, National Archives.
32. "To James Madison from the Citizens of Natchez, Mississippi Territory, 29 July 1812 (Abstract)." Founders Online, National Archives.
33. "To James Madison from Elbridge Gerry, 15 August 1812." Founders Online, National Archives.
34. *The Institutes of Justinian.* Printed for P. Byrne, 1812, 631.
35. Ibid., 630.
36. "Gerry to Dearborn, 2 Sept. 1811." *Maine Historical Society.* For the idea that Gerry supported restrictions on Federalist printers, see, Morison, Samuel. *The Life and Letters of Harrison Gray Otis.* (Houghton Mifflin Company, 1913), 57.
37. "To James Madison from William Pinkney, 5 July 1812," Founders Online, National Archives.
38. Lewis, Jan Ellen. "Defining the Nation: 1790 to 1898," in *Security v. Liberty* (New York: Russell Sage Foundation, 2008); see also, Wittes, Benjamin and Singh, Ritika. "James Madison, Presidential Power, and Civil Liberties in the War of 1812," in *What So Proudly We Hailed: Essays on the Contemporary Meaning of the War of 1812*. Washington, DC: Brookings Institution Press, 2012. I would like to acknowledge Wittes for his contribution to my thinking on Madison's respect for free speech and civil liberties throughout this chapter.
39. "To James Madison from Henry Dearborn, 15 August 1812." Founders Online, National Archives.
40. Hickey, *The War of 1812.*
41. Custis, George Washington Parke. *An Address Occasioned by the Death of General Lingan.* (Bradford & Read, 1812.) https://archive.org/details/addressoccasioneoocust/page/n1/mode/2up
42. *Interesting Papers Relative to the Recent Riots at Baltimore.* Philadelphia, 1812.
43. "To James Madison from James Monroe, 4 August 1812." Founders Online, National Archives.
44. "To James Madison from James Monroe, 4 August 1812." Founders Online, National Archives; see also, Gilje, *The Baltimore Riots.* Noting the militia was Federalized; see also,

Frank A. Cassell. "The Great Baltimore Riot of 1812." *Maryland Historical Magazine* 70 (1975): 241–59.

45. "To James Madison from John Armstrong, 4 September 1814." Founders Online, National Archives; see also, McKenney, Thomas Loraine. "Reply to Kosciusko Armstrong's Assault Upon Col. McKenney's Narrative of the Causes that Led to General Armstrong's Resignation of the Office of Secretary of War in 1814." (W. H. Graham, 1846), 18, 27.

46. "To James Madison from John Armstrong, 4 September 1814." Founders Online, National Archives.

47. Ibid.

48. "Madison's March 4, 1813: Second Inaugural Address." Miller Center, University of Virginia. Accessed October 20, 2016.

49. "Andrew Jackson and the Militia Tradition." Military History, Erenow.

50. "Battle of New Orleans." History website, August 9, 2022.

51. Stagg, J. C. A. *Mr. Madison's War: Diplomacy and Warfare in the Early American Republic, 1783–1830*. (Princeton University Press, 1983.)

52. "Military Despotism! Arbitrary Arrest of a Judge." Library of Congress; see also, Warshauer, Matthew. "Andrew Jackson and the Legacy of the Battle of New Orleans." Wiley Online Library, 2013.

53. "To James Madison from John Dick, 10 March 1815." Founders Online, National Archives. For the controversy surrounding whether Dick was actually arrested, see, Pic, Sara. "Jackson's Bodyguard: Lawyers Who Fought in the Battle of New Orleans." Law Library of Louisiana.

54. "From James Madison to James Monroe, 9 April 1815." Founders Online, National Archives.

55. See, e.g., "To James Madison from Alexander J. Dallas, 12 May 1815." Founders Online, National Archives; see also, Wegmann, Mary Ann, et al. "The Old Federal Courthouse: Present Day Andrew Jackson Hotel." New Orleans Historical; see also, Deutsch, Eberhard. "The United States Versus Major General Andrew Jackson." *American Bar Association Journal* 46, no. 9 (September 1960), *JSTOR*, http://www.jstor.org/stable/25721288: 946, 966.

56. For a reference to the drafting process, see, "To James Madison from Alexander J. Dallas, 1 August 1815." Founders Online, National Archives.

57. For the final letter Dallas sent Jackson with this message, see, "Alexander James Dallas to Andrew Jackson." Library of Congress.

58. "To James Madison from Alexander J. Dallas, 13 April 1815." Founders Online, National Archives.

59. "Worcester v. Georgia." *Encyclopædia Britannica*, 2019.

60. "Future President Andrew Jackson Kills Charles Dickinson in a Duel." *History* (July 28, 2019).

61. "From James Madison to James Monroe, 19 October 1797." Founders Online, National Archives.

62. "'The Hunters of Kentucky': A Popular Song Celebrates the Victory of Jackson and His Frontier Fighters over the British, 1824." History Matters.

63. "Slavery at Monticello FAQs." *Thomas Jefferson Foundation*. https://www.monticello.org/slavery/slavery-faqs/.

64. Feldman, Noah. "James Madison's Lessons in Racism." Opinion, *The New York Times*, October 2017; see also, Spies-Gans, Paris Amanda. "James Madison." Princeton & Slavery, *Princeton*, 2009; and Gordon-Reed, Annette and Peter Onuf. *"Most Blessed of the Patriarchs": Thomas Jefferson and the Empire of the Imagination*. (Liveright, 2017.)

65. *The Appeal* was censored widely throughout the South. Possession of any book brought capi-

tal punishment for enslaved people in multiple states. Georgia made it punishable by death to circulate any material calling for a slave revolt, an obvious reference to Walker's work. Other states fined those who held copies, or even put a bounty on Walker's head. Southern newspapers frequently refused to talk about slavery at all. Slaveholders therefore could use their own voices and free speech to bolster support for slavery, all the while punishing those who disagreed. Walker's demand for equal treatment was so threatening to the power of slaveholders throughout many states that they simply dispensed with free speech for Whites and Blacks alike. For a comprehensive account of Walker, censorship, and free speech see Kennedy, Randall. "Randall Kennedy on American Slavery: American Censorship." Banned Books Week, YouTube video, September 30, 2019; see also, Eaton, Clement. "A Dangerous Pamphlet in the Old South." *The Journal of Southern History* 2, no. 3 (1936): 323–34.

66. Kennedy, "American Censorship."

CHAPTER 4: JAMES BUCHANAN VERSUS FREDERICK DOUGLASS: A FAKE NEUTRALITY

1. *The Liberator* blog. Boston Public Library, July 26, 2018. https://www.bpl.org/blogs/post/the-liberator/.
2. "American Anti-Slavery Society." *Encyclopædia Britannica*, July 28, 2016.
3. Garrison, William Lloyd. "The First Issue of 'The Liberator.'" Bartleby, accessed 2015.
4. Brain, Jessica. "The Abolition of Slavery in Britain." *Historic UK*, June 12, 2019.
5. Representative John Quincy Adams, upon passage of this gag rule, immediately objected, arguing that it violated the Constitution's Speech and Debate Clause. "Am I gagged?" he asked, incredulous that the House would not recognize him. See, "John Quincy Adams and the Gag Rule." Bill of Rights Institute.
6. O'Neill, Aaron. "United States: Black and Slave Population 1790–1880." Statista, February 12, 2020.
7. Browne, Patrick. "The Garrison Mob of 1835, Boston." Historical Digression, March 1, 2016.
8. "A Covenant with Death and an Agreement with Hell." Massachusetts Historical Society.
9. "Abolitionists and the Constitution." Constitutional Rights Foundation.
10. Massachusetts Historical Society, "Covenant with Death."
11. Blight, *Prophet of Freedom*, 98–99, 100.
12. Ibid., 100.
13. "Abolitionists: Frederick Douglass." Gilder Lehrman History Online, Digital History.
14. Blight, *Prophet of Freedom*, 100.
15. Ibid., 189.
16. Spooner, Lysander. *The Unconstitutionality of Slavery.* (Bela Marsh, 1845.)
17. Blight, *Prophet of Freedom*, 190.
18. See, e.g., Spooner, *The Unconstitutionality of Slavery.*
19. *The North Star*, vol. I, no. 37, 1848. Smithsonian Learning Lab.
20. Blight, *Prophet of Freedom*, 191.
21. "Frederick Douglass Project Writings: Change of Opinion Announced." Frederick Douglass Project, River Campus Library, University of Rochester, 2018.
22. As quoted in Masur, Kate. *Until Justice Be Done: America's First Civil Rights Movement, from the Revolution to Reconstruction.* (Norton, 2021.)
23. Blight, *Prophet of Freedom*, 217.
24. Ibid., 214.
25. See Masur, *Until Justice Be Done*, 244.

26. "Proceedings of the Colored National Convention, Held in Rochester, July 6th, 7th, and 8th, 1853." Colored Conventions Project Digital Records.

27. Ibid.

28. Masur, *Until Justice Be Done*, 246.

29. Ibid., 246–49.

30. "James Buchanan Inaugural Address." Miller Center, University of Virginia. Accessed October 20, 2016.

31. "Presidential Series: James Buchanan." National Guard.

32. Weatherman, Donald. "James Buchanan on Slavery and Secession." *Presidential Studies Quarterly* 15, no. 4 (1985): 797–98.

33. Ibid., 798.

34. Kelley, Ellen. "Everything Wrong with the Buchanan Administration." Libertarianism, 2021.

35. "Frederick Douglass Paper." Library of Congress, September 26, 1856.

36. Urofsky, Melvin. "Dred Scott Decision." *Encyclopaedia Britannica*, September 10, 2018; see also, "Harriet Robinson Scott." Historic Missourians.

37. Morone, James. *Republic of Wrath: How American Politics Turned Tribal, From George Washington to Donald Trump.* (Basic Books, 2020.)

38. Auchampaugh, Philip. "James Buchanan, The Court and the Dred Scott Case." *Tennessee Historical Magazine* 9, no. 4 (1926): 235–36.

39. See Fehrenbacher, Don. *The Dred Scott Case: Its Significance in American Law and Politics.* (Oxford University Press, 2001), 307–12; see also, Auchampaugh, "James Buchanan."

40. Weatherman, "James Buchanan."

41. "Robert Cooper Grier to James Buchanan." February 23, 1857. https://digitallibrary.hsp.org/index.php/Detail/objects/2281.

42. See, Farber, Daniel. "A Fatal Loss of Balance: Dred Scott Revisited." *Pepperdine Law Review* 39, no. 1 (2011).

43. Buchanan, "James Buchanan Inaugural Address."

44. *Scott v. Sandford*, 60 U.S. 19 How. 393 (1857).

45. "Acts of Congress Held Unconstitutional in Whole or in Part by the Supreme Court of the United States." Justia US Law.

46. Ibid.

47. Frederick Douglass, "Speech on the Dred Scott Decision." May 1857. https://www.utc.edu/sites/default/files/2021-01/fddredscottspeechexcerpt2018.pdf.

48. Ibid.

49. Douglass, Frederick. "The Dred Scott Decision." Speech delivered before the American Anti-Slavery Society, New York, May 14, 1857.

50. "The Frederick Project Writings: The Dred Scott Decision." Frederick Douglass Project: University of Rochester, 2018.

51. Douglass, Frederick. "The Dred Scott Decision." Speech delivered before the American Anti-Slavery Society, New York, May 14, 1857.

52. *Scott v. Sanford* (1857).

53. U.S. Const. art. IV, § 2, cl. 3.

54. Douglass, Frederick. "The Constitution of the United States: Is It Pro-Slavery or Anti-Slavery?" BlackPast, March 15, 2012.

55. Douglass, "Dred Scott Decision."

56. Wilentz, Sean. *No Property in Man: Slavery and Antislavery at the Nation's Founding.* (Harvard University Press, 2018), 1009.

57. Douglass, "Dred Scott Decision."
58. Ibid.
59. Ibid., 44.
60. *Scott v. Sanford* (1857).
61. Ibid.
62. Douglass, "Dred Scott Decision," 40.
63. Ibid.
64. "Proceedings of a Convention of the Colored Men of Ohio, Held in the City of Cincinnati on the 23d, 24th, 25th and 26th Days of November, 1858." Colored Conventions Project Digital Records, 1858.
65. "New England Colored Citizens' Convention, August 1, 1859." Colored Conventions Project Digital Records, 1859.
66. Douglass, "Dred Scott Decision."
67. "Purged Away with Blood." American Battlefield Trust, October 16, 2018.
68. "Kansas Constitutions." Kansas Historical Society. August 2018. https://www.kshs.org/kansapedia/kansas-constitutions/16532&lang=en.
69. See Graber, Mark. "The Nonmajoritarian Difficulty: Legislative Deference to the Judiciary." *Studies in American Political Development* 7, no. 1 (1993): 35–73; see also, Mettler, Suzanne, and Lieberman, Robert. *Four Threats: The Recurring Crises of American Democracy.* (St. Martin's Press, 2020.)
70. Blight, *Prophet of Freedom*, 295–96.
71. Douglass, Frederick. *Narrative of the Life of Frederick Douglass, an American Slave.* (Dover Publications, 1995), 217.
72. Blight, *Prophet of Freedom*, 298.
73. Ibid., 294–98; see also, Tsai, Robert. *America's Forgotten Constitutions: Defiant Visions of Power and Community.* (Harvard University Press, 2014.); Tsai, *America's Forgotten Constitutions*; see also, Douglass, Frederick. "The Constitution and Slavery." March 16, 1849.
74. Blight, *Prophet of Freedom*, 298, 301.
75. Ibid., 290–305; also, "John Brown's Raid on Harpers Ferry." History.
76. Blight, *Prophet of Freedom*, 305–6.
77. "Buying Frederick Douglass's Freedom, 1846." Gilder Lehrman Institute of American History.
78. Blight, *Prophet of Freedom*, 290–305.
79. Frederick Douglass, *Life and times of Frederick Douglass, Written by Himself.* (Boston, De Wolfe & Fiske Co., 1892), 224–25; see further letters for details of fear of escape: "Letter #111: Transcription." Frederick Douglass Project, University of Rochester.
80. Douglass, *Life and Times*, 231.
81. For an example of a lecture, see Douglass, "The Constitution and Slavery." See also, Douglass "The Constitution of the United States: Is It Pro-Slavery or Anti-Slavery?"
82. Ibid.; This article claims the widespread franchise had been achieved by Jackson's election: Feller, Daniel. "Andrew Jackson: The American Franchise." Miller Center, University of Virginia, October 4, 2016.
83. Blight, *Prophet of Freedom*, 325–26.
84. Ibid., 321.
85. Frederick Douglass, "What to the Slave is the Fourth of July?" 1852. https://nmaahc.si.edu/explore/stories/nations-story-what-slave-fourth-july.
86. Douglass, "Speech on the Dred Scott Decision."

CHAPTER 5: ABRAHAM LINCOLN AND FREDERICK DOUGLASS:
THE TRANSFORMATION OF A PRESIDENT
1. Douglass, *Life and Times*. At 5441.
2. Blight, *Prophet of Freedom*, 459. Also see Douglass, *Life and Times*, 5432.
3. Douglass, Frederick. "Frederick Douglass Project Writings: The President and His Speeches." Frederick Douglass Project, University of Rochester.
4. Blight, *Prophet of Freedom*, 322.
5. Ibid., 323.
6. "Letter from Abraham Lincoln to Albert Hodges, April 4, 1864." The American Presidency Project (hereinafter APP). https://www.presidency.ucsb.edu/.
7. "Abraham Lincoln to Mary Speed, September 27, 1841." APP.
8. "Congressman Abraham Lincoln's Draft of a Bill to Abolish Slavery in the District of Columbia, January 1849." U.S. Capitol Visitor Center, 2019.
9. Lincoln, Abraham. "Speech on the Dred Scott Decision"; see also Lincoln, Abraham "House Divided Address." APP.
10. Lincoln, Abraham. "Debate with Stephen Douglas, October 7, 1858." APP.
11. Lincoln, Abraham. "Cooper Union Address, 1860." APP.
12. Lincoln, Abraham. "First Inaugural Address." APP.
13. Lincoln, Abraham. "Letter to Greeley, August 22, 1862." APP. (Emphasis added.)
14. Pinsker, Matthew. "Lincoln's Fremont Problem." History 288: Civil War & Reconstruction.
15. Lincoln, Abraham. "Letter to Albert Hodges, 1864." APP.
16. Lincoln, Abraham. "Letter to Horace Greeley, August 22, 1862." APP. (Emphasis added.)
17. See, e.g., Lincoln, Abraham. "Lyceum Address." APP.
18. Ibid.
19. Johnson, Walter, and Jamala Rogers. "No Excuse for Forgetting Black St. Louis." *STL Today*.
20. O'Neil, Tim. "A Crusading Editor Is Killed Defending the Freedom of the Press." *STL Today*, November 7, 2022.
21. "Elijah Parish Lovejoy." A People's History of Colby College: Activism and Social Justice Since 1813. https://web.colby.edu/activism/stories/lovejoy/.
22. Brands, H. W. "How John Brown Showed America That It's Not Enough to Be on the Right Side of History." *Time*, October 6, 2020.
23. Lincoln, Abraham. "The Perpetuation of Our Political Institutions." Address delivered to the Young Men's Lyceum of Springfield, Illinois, January 27, 1838.
24. Lincoln, "Speech on the Dred Scott Decision."
25. Blight, *Prophet of Freedom*, 323.
26. Freeman, Joanne. "Timeline of the Civil War." The Library of Congress, 2015.
27. Stephens, Alexander. "Cornerstone Speech." American Battlefield Trust, May 11, 2017.
28. "The Generals and Admirals: John C. Frémont (1813–1890)." Mr. Lincoln's White House, The Lehrman Institute.
29. Blight, *Prophet of Freedom*, 353.
30. Frederick Douglass, "The President and His Speeches." *Douglass' Monthly*. September, 1862.
31. Ibid.
32. Douglass, Frederick. "The Reasons for Our Troubles." Frederick Douglass Project, University of Rochester.
33. Bulla, David W. "Abraham Lincoln and Press Suppression Reconsidered," *American Journalism* 26, no. 4 (2009): 11–33.

34. Sheppard, Si. *The Partisan Press: A History of Media Bias in the United States.* (McFarland, 2007), 160.

35. Holzer, Harold. *Lincoln and the Power of the Press: The War for Public Opinion.* (Simon & Schuster, 2014.)

36. After 1863, the suspension of habeas corpus was lawfully justified by an Act of Congress. The Habeas Corpus Suspension Act gave the president authority to suspend the writ, though it also limited when the suspension applied and allowed some prisoners to be released. 12 Stat. 755 (1863); see, Samuels, Shirley, ed. *The Cambridge Companion to Abraham Lincoln.* (Cambridge University Press, 2012), 200.

37. The Digital Scholarship Lab and the National Community Reinvestment Coalition, "Not Even Past: Social Vulnerability and the Legacy of Redlining," *American Panorama*, ed. Robert K. Nelson and Edward L. Ayers.

38. See, Hutchinson, Dennis. "Lincoln the Dictator," *South Dakota Law Review* 55, no. 284 (2010).

39. Curtis, Michael. "Lincoln, Vallandingham, and Anti-War Speech in the Civil War." *William and Mary Bill of Rights Journal* 7 (1998).

40. "July 4th Message to Congress." Miller Center, University of Virginia. Access October 20, 2016. (Emphasis added.)

41. Lincoln, Abraham. "Letter to Albert Hodges." Abraham Lincoln Online, 2018.

42. Douglass, "Reasons for Our Troubles."

43. Stauffer, John. *Giants: The Parallel Lives of Frederick Douglass and Abraham Lincoln.* (Hachette Book Group, 2008); see also, Masur, Kate. "The African American Delegation to Abraham Lincoln: A Reappraisal." *Civil War History* 56, no. 2 (2010): 117–44.

44. Lincoln, Abraham. "Address on Colonization to a Deputation of Negroes." August 14, 1862. Collected Works of Abraham Lincoln.

45. "Martin Delany." *Encyclopaedia Britannica*, 2019.

46. Blight, *Prophet of Freedom*, 372. See also, Douglass, "The President."

47. Ibid., 415.

48. See, e.g., Douglass, Frederick. "The Slave's Appeal to Great Britain." Accessed at: *Traditions of the Ancestors.* https://www.tota.world/article/1103/.

49. Lincoln, Abraham. "Emancipation Proclamation," January 1, 1863. APP.

50. Stauffer, *Giants*, 233.

51. Douglass, Frederick. *The Complete Autobiographies of Frederick Douglass.* Simon and Schuster (May 20, 2013), 290.

52. Ibid., 291.

53. Ibid.

54. "Frederick Douglass on the 'Mission of the War.'" *The New York Times*, January 14, 1864.

55. "Frederick Douglass 'the Mission of the War.'" BlackPast, accessed September 19, 2019.

56. "Frederick Douglass on Abraham Lincoln." *The Liberator*, September 16, 1864, 3; see also, Blight, *Prophet of Freedom*, 431.

57. See "The Preachers: John Eaton (1829–1906)." Mr. Lincoln and Friends, The Lehrman Institute.

58. See, e.g., Blight, *Prophet of Freedom*, 435; see also, Stauffer, *Giants*, 267–69. And see also, Larson, Micheal, and John Smith, eds. *Grant, Lincoln and the Freedmen: Reminiscences of the Civil War by John Eaton.* (University of Tennessee Press, 2022), 176.

59. Blight, *Prophet of Freedom*, 436; see also, "Lincoln and Douglass Shared Uncommon Bond." NPR.

322 NOTES TO PAGES 129–139

60. See, e.g., Foner, Eric. *The Fiery Trial: Abraham Lincoln and American Slavery*. (Norton, 2011.)

61. Douglass, *Life and Times*; see also, Blight, *Prophet of Freedom*.

62. Vorenberg, Michael. *Final Freedom: The Civil War, the Abolition of Slavery, and the Thirteenth Amendment*. (Cambridge University Press, 2004), 2606; see also, Miller, Jim. "Frederick Douglass to Theodore Tilton, October 15, 1864." *Civil War Notebook* blog, May 8, 2020.

63. Blight, *Prophet of Freedom*, 437.

64. See, "Frederick Douglass." Mr Lincoln and Freedom, The Lehrman Institute, 2019; see also, Vorenberg, *Final Freedom*, for discussion on Douglass convincing Lincoln to abandon the letter.

65. See "Letter from Frederick Douglass." The Liberator Files.

66. See, e.g., Douglass, *The Dred Scott Decision*. As early as 1861, Lincoln had linked the Declaration and the Constitution in the metaphor of an "apple of gold" adorned in "frame of silver." But it is at Gettysburg that his more full realization of this synthesis begins to reflect Douglass's democratic view. Abraham Lincoln, "Fragment on the Constitution and the Union," January 1861, in Roy P. Basler, ed., *The Collected Works of Abraham Lincoln*, Vol. 4 (New Brunswick, NJ: Rutgers University Press, 1953), 168–69.

67. See Blight, *Prophet of Freedom*, 414; see also, for examples of Douglass and Lincoln overlapping in content, Douglass, Frederick. "Cast Off the Mill-Stone." Frederick Douglass Project, University of Rochester.

68. Lincoln, Gettysburg Address, November 19, 1863. APP.

69. Foner, *The Fiery Trial*, 307. See also, Lincoln, "Second Inaugural Address." APP.

70. See Foner, *The Fiery Trial*.

71. See Vorenberg, *Final Freedom*.

72. Foner, *The Fiery Trial*, 311–17.

73. "Milestone Documents." National Archives, April 9, 2021. (As we will see, although that punishment exception generated no debate at the time, that exception would be used by Southern states to resist emancipation.)

74. For a discussion of "badges and incidents," see, e.g., Vorenberg, *The Final Freedom*; Brandwein, Pamela. *Rethinking the Judicial Settlement of Reconstruction*. (Cambridge University Press, 2011.)

75. "Frederick Douglass Speech on the Thirteenth Amendment." Almost Chosen People, January. 19, 2015.

76. Douglass, *Life and Times*, 273.

77. Ibid., 260.

78. Ibid.

CHAPTER 6: ANDREW JOHNSON VERSUS FREDERICK DOUGLASS: A NEW THREAT IN THE MIDST OF RECOVERY

1. Douglass, *Complete Autobiographies*, 295–96; Wills, Garry. "Lincoln's Greatest Speech." *The Atlantic*, September 1999; "Vice-President Johnson's Address." *The New York Times*, March 6, 1865.

2. Varon, Elizabeth R. "Andrew Johnson: Life before the Presidency." Miller Center, University of Virginia, October 4, 2016.

3. Johnson, Andrew. "Speech on Harper's Ferry Incident," in *The Papers of Andrew Johnson, Vol. 3, 1858–1860*. Bergeron, Paul, ed. (University of Tennessee Press, 2000.)

4. Levine, Robert. *The Failed Promise: Reconstruction, Frederick Douglass, and the Impeachment of Andrew Johnson*. (W. W. Norton, 2021.)

5. Wineapple, Brenda. *The Impeachers: The Trial of Andrew Johnson and the Dream of a Just Nation*. (Random House, 2019), 45.

6. Foner, Eric. *A Short History of Reconstruction*. (Harper Perennial, 2015), 88.
7. "Civil Rights Act of 1866: An Act to Protect All Persons in the United States in Their Civil Rights, and Furnish the Means of Their Vindication." National Constitution Center.
8. Original minutes of meeting in Syracuse: "Proceedings of the National Convention of Colored Men; Held in the City of Syracuse, N.Y.; October 4, 5, 6, and 7, 1864; with the Bill of Wrongs and Rights; and the Address to the American People." Colored Conventions Project Digital Records. Also mentioned in Blight, *Prophet of Freedom*. Chronological listing of all meetings from this period here: "Conventions by Year." Colored Conventions Project.
9. Ibid., 42.
10. "Convention of the Colored People of New England, Boston, December 1, 1865." Colored Conventions Project Digital Records.
11. Levine, *Failed Promise*, 83.
12. "Transcript, Meeting between President Andrew Johnson and a Delegation of African-Americans, White House, February 7, 1866." House Divided, Dickinson College.
13. Blight, *Prophet of Freedom*, 474. See also, Bergeron, Paul. *The Papers of Andrew Johnson Vol. 10: February–July 1866*. (University of Tennessee, 1993), 48.
14. As quoted in Blight, *Prophet of Freedom*, 475.
15. Douglass, *Complete Autobiographies*, 302–4.
16. Levine, *Failed Promise*, 94; Bergeron, *Papers, Vol 10*, 48.
17. "Letter from Charles Sumner to George William Curtis, 13 April, 1864" in Palmer, Beverly Wilson, ed. *The Selected Letters of Charles Sumner*, Vol. 2. (Northeastern University Press, 1990), 233. I would like to thank Michael Vorenberg for calling this source to my attention.
18. Levy, Pema. "How a Three-Word Phrase Sabotaged Black Voting Rights, and How They Can Be Reconstructed." *Mother Jones*, 2021.
19. "Freedmen's Bureau Acts of 1865 and 1866." United States Senate, January 12, 2017.
20. "Veto of the Civil Rights Bill." Teaching American History, 2013.
21. U.S. Constitution, Fourteenth Amendment. (Emphasis added.)
22. See, "Andrew Johnson." *American Heritage*.
23. Blight, *Prophet of Freedom*, 483.
24. See, Douglass, Frederick. "What the Black Man Wants." Frederick Douglass Project, University of Rochester; see also, Blight, *Prophet of Freedom*.
25. Douglass, Frederick. "Reconstruction." *Atlantic Monthly* 18 (1866): 761–65.
26. "Report on the National Convention of Colored Men, Washington D.C., January 10, 1867." Colored Conventions Project Digital Records. Good overview of conventions and Douglass role here: Robinson, Stephen. "The Black Convention Movement and Black Politics in Nineteenth-Century America." Black Perspectives, African American Intellectual History Society.
27. "Address and Resolutions of the National Equal Rights League Convention of Colored Men, Held at Washington, D. C., January 10th, 11th and 12th, 1867." Library of Congress.
28. Ibid.
29. "Andrew Johnson: Campaigns and Elections." Miller Center, October 4, 2016.
30. "'An Absolute Massacre': The New Orleans Slaughter of July 30, 1866." National Park Service.
31. Levine, *Failed Promise*, 118.
32. Quoted and recounted in the articles of impeachment against Andrew Johnson, online at "Impeachment Trial of President Andrew Johnson, 1868." United States Senate.
33. Wineapple, *Impeachers*, 5–8.

34. Gates, Henry Louis. "The Truth behind '40 Acres and a Mule.'" The African Americans: Many Rivers to Cross, PBS, September 18, 2013.
35. Ibid.
36. Andrew Johnson, "Executive Order—General Orders: 145." Online by Gerhard Peters and John T. Woolley, APP.
37. "Committee of Freedmen on Edisto Island, South Carolina, to the Freedmen's Bureau Commissioner [October 20 or 21, 1865]"; see also, "the Commissioner's Reply, October 22, 1865"; see, "the Committee to the President, October 28, 1865." Freedmen and Southern Society Project. University of Maryland. https://history.umd.edu/research/projects-archives/freedman-southern-society.
38. See, e.g., Bostick, Douglas. A Brief History of James Island: Jewel of the Sea Islands. (The History Press, 2008), see chapter 12.
39. Wineapple, Impeachers, 211–12.
40. Ibid., 235.
41. Cong. Globe, 40th Cong, 2d Sess. 1340 (1868) (statement of Rep. Bingham).
42. This material and interpretation of "technicalities" is from Levine, Failed Promise, 210.

CHAPTER 7: ULYSSES GRANT AND THE DOUGLASS CONSTITUENCY: SECURING THE RIGHT TO VOTE AMID VIOLENCE

1. "'Our ticket, Our Motto: This is a White Man's Country; Let White Men Rule.' Campaign Badge Supporting Horatio Seymour and Francis Blair, Democratic Candidates for President and Vice-President of the Unites [sic] States, 1868." The New York Public Library Digital Collections, 1868.
2. Chernow, Ron. Grant. (Penguin Press, 2017), 621.
3. Ibid., 620–21; see also, Foner, Eric. Give Me Liberty!: An American History, Volume 5. (Norton, 2004); and Wineapple, Brenda. Ecstatic Nation: Confidence, Crisis, and Compromise, 1848–1877. (Harper Perennial, 2014), 448.
4. Douglass, Frederick. "The Work Before Us." The Independent, 1868.
5. "Address of the Colored Men's Border State Convention to the People of the United States, Baltimore, August 5–6, 1868." Colored Conventions Project Digital Records.
6. Ibid.
7. Christensen, Matthew. "The 1868 St. Landry Massacre: Reconstruction's Deadliest Episode of Violence." Theses and Dissertations, University of Wisconsin Milwaukee, 190.
8. Ibid.
9. "Grant, Reconstruction and the KKK." American Experience, PBS, 2019.
10. "Camilla Massacre." New Georgia Encyclopedia; "White Mobs Ambush Black People in Georgia in Mass Lynching." Equal Justice Initiative.
11. "Presidential Election of 1868." Library of Congress.
12. "Ulysses S. Grant & the 15th Amendment." National Parks System, 2016.
13. Cramer, Michael John. Ulysses S. Grant: Conversations and Unpublished Letters. (Forgotten Books, 2018), 65.
14. Chernow, Grant, 583.
15. Ibid., 586; See also, "Grant, Reconstruction, and the KKK."
16. Cramer, Ulysses S. Grant, 66.
17. Chernow, Ron. "What a Simple Pen Reminds Us about Ulysses S. Grant's Vision for a Post-Civil War America." Smithsonian Magazine, November 2017.
18. Douglass, Frederick. "We Welcome the Fifteenth Amendment May 12–13, 1869." The Speeches of Frederick Douglass: A Critical Edition. (Yale University Press, 2018.)

19. Lutz, Alma. *Created Equal: Elizabeth Cady Stanton, 1815–1902.* (John Day, 1940), 46.
20. O'Brien, C. C. "'The White Women All Go for Sex': Frances Harper on Suffrage, Citizenship, and the Reconstruction South." *African American Review* 43, no. 4 (2009).
21. Du Bois, W. E. B. (William Edward Burghardt), 1868–1963. *The Souls of Black Folk; Essays and Sketches.* (A. G. McClurg, 1903); see also, Levine, *Lost Promise.*
22. "Proceedings of the National Convention of the Colored Men of America: Held in Washington, D.C., on January 13, 14, 15, and 16, 1869." Colored Conventions Project Digital Records.
23. "Proceedings of the Colored National Labor Convention: Held in Washington, D.C., on December 6th, 7th, 8th, 9th and 10th, 1869." Colored Conventions Project Digital Records.
24. "Black-American Representatives and Senators by Congress, 1870–Present." US House of Representatives: History, Art & Archives.
25. Blight, *Prophet of Freedom,* 721.
26. Grant, Ulysses. "State of the Union Address." The American Presidency Project (APP).
27. "Joseph Hayne Rainey." Black Members of Congress, U. S. Government Publishing Office (GPO).
28. "The Enforcement Acts of 1870 and 1871." United States Senate, May 21, 2018.
29. Ibid.
30. "Proceedings of the State Convention of the Colored Citizens of Tennessee, Held in Nashville, Feb. 22d, 23d, 24th & 25th, 1871." Colored Conventions Project Digital Records.
31. Ibid.
32. "Memorial of a committee appointed at a meeting of Colored citizens of Frankfort, Ky., and vicinity, praying the enactment of law for the better protection of life." *Colored Conventions Project.* https://omeka.coloredconventions.org/items/show/539.
33. Ibid.
34. "The Enforcement Act of 1871," 17 Stat. 13.
35. "The Ku Klux Klan Act of 1871." History, Art & Archives, United States House of Representatives Historical Highlights, 2019.
36. See, e.g., Shugerman, Jed. "A New Civil Case Powerfully Opens a New Front against Trump for Russia Conspiracy." *Take Care* blog.
37. Gillette, William. *Retreat from Reconstruction 1869–1879.* (Louisiana State University Press, 1982), 43; see also, Trickey, Erick. "The 150-Year-Old Ku Klux Klan Act Being Used against Trump in Capitol Attack." *The Washington Post,* February 18, 2021.
38. See, e.g., "The South Carolina Ku Klux Klan Trials of 1871–1872." Federal Judicial Center, 2022.
39. See, e.g., Brands, H. W. "Grant Takes on the Klan." HistoryNet, August 7, 2017.
40. "Proceedings of the Southern States Convention of Colored Men, held in Columbia, S.C., commencing October 18, ending October 25, 1871." Colored Conventions Project. https://omeka.coloredconventions.org/items/show/543.
41. See, e.g., "New National Era (Washington, D.C.)." March 23, 1871. Library of Congress.
42. Wang, Xi. *Trial of Democracy: Black Suffrage and Northern Republicans, 1860–1910.* (Athens: University of Georgia Press, 1997), 103.
43. Speech reprinted in Douglass's newspaper: *New National Era;* see also, e.g., Blight, *Prophet of Freedom,* 524.
44. Chernow, *Grant,* 746.
45. Ibid., 705–6.
46. Ibid., 627–28, 641–42.
47. "U.S. Grant and the Colored People." Library of Congress.
48. Foner, Eric. *Reconstruction: America's Unfinished Revolution, 1863–1877.* (Harper & Row, 1988.)
49. Chernow, *Grant,* 759–60.

50. Grant, Ulysses S. "Second Inaugural Address," March 4, 1873. Accessed at *National Parks Service*. https://www.nps.gov/articles/000/president-ulysses-s-grant-s-second-inaugural -address-march-4-1873.htm.
51. "Landmark Legislation: Civil Rights Act of 1875." United States Senate, April 2019.
52. Ibid.
53. Du Bois, W. E. B. *Black Reconstruction in America. 1860–1880*. (The Free Press, 1935), 594.
54. Congressional Record, House of Representatives, 43rd Congress, 1st Session. At 378–82; see also, "Civil Rights Act of 1875." United States House of Representatives.
55. "Speeches of African-American Representatives Addressing the Civil Rights Bill of 1875." Neglected Voices, New York University.
56. Congressional Record, House of Representatives, 43rd Congress, 1st session, vol. 2, 407–11; available at A Century of Lawmaking for a New Nation: U.S. Congressional Documents and Debates, 1774–1875, http://www.memory.loc.gov/cgi-bin/ampage.
57. Downing's efforts are documented here: McPherson, James M. "Abolitionists and the Civil Rights Act of 1875." *The Journal of American History* 52, no. 3 (1965). See also, "George T. Downing (1819–1903)." BlackPast, October 23, 2017; see also, Downs, Gregory, and Kate Masur. "The World the Civil War Made." (University of North Carolina Press, 2015); see also, Davis, Hugh. " 'We Will Be Satisfied with Nothing Less': The African American Struggle for Equal Rights in the North during Reconstruction." (Cornell University Press, 2011.)
58. " 'The Bulwark of Freedom': African-American Members of Congress and the Constitution during Reconstruction." United States House of Representatives.
59. See "Civil Rights Act of 1875." United States House of Representatives. See also, Chernow, *Grant*, 811.
60. "Convention of Colored Newspaper Men Cincinnati, August 4th, 1875, Wednesday A. M." Colored Conventions Project Digital Records.
61. Tulis, Jeffrey, and Nicole Mellow. *Legacies of Losing in American Politics*. (University of Chicago Press, 2018.)
62. *United States v. Cruikshank*, 92 U.S. 542.
63. Wells-Barnett, Ida B. *Crusade for Justice: The Autobiography of Ida B. Wells*. (University of Chicago Press, 1972), 102.

CHAPTER 8: WOODROW WILSON VERSUS TROTTER AND
WELLS: NATIONALIZING WHITE SUPREMACY
1. See, e.g., Wilson, Woodrow. *A History of the American People*. (Harper and Brothers, 1902.)
2. "Progressives and the Era of Trustbusting." Constitutional Rights Foundation, 2019.
3. "The New Freedom (1913)." National Constitution Center, 2023.
4. "Letter from Bishop Walters to Woodrow Wilson, November 16, 1912." W. E. B. Du Bois Papers. University of Massachusetts Amherst (hereinafter Du Bois Papers).
5. *Civil Rights Cases*, 109 U.S. 3 (1883).
6. *Plessy v. Ferguson*, 163 U.S. 537 (1896).
7. *Williams v. Mississippi*, 170 U.S. 213 (1898).
8. "Teddy Roosevelt's 'Shocking' Dinner with Washington." NPR, March 14, 2012. For a reference to the intensity of the blowback to Washington's invitation, see, "Niggers in the White House." Theodore Roosevelt Center, Library of Congress Manuscript Division, 2019.
9. See, e.g., Frusciano, Thomas Joseph. "Theodore Roosevelt and the Negro in the Age of Booker T. Washington, 1901–1912." Graduate Student Theses, Dissertations, & Professional Papers, University of Montana, 1975, 194.

10. Greenridge, Kerri. *Black Radical: The Life and Times of William Monroe Trotter* (Liveright, 2019). xiv.

11. Greenridge, *Black Radical*, 60–62.

12. Ibid., xi.

13. Ibid., 106–9.

14. Ibid. 109; see also, Giddings, Paula. *Ida: A Sword Among Lions*. (Amistad, 2009), 450.

15. Giddings, *A Sword Among Lions*, 437.

16. Giddings, *Ida*, 437. Modern accounts have found a similar number of lynchings. The Equal Justice Institute, for example, documented 4,400 racialized lynchings between Reconstruction and World War II. "Lynching in America." *Equal Justice Initiative*, 2019.

17. "Ida Wells-Case," *Digital Public Library of America*.

18. Wells-Barnett, *Crusade for Justice*.

19. Fowler, Russell. "Ida B. Wells at the Tennessee Supreme Court." Tennessee Bar Association.

20. Wells, Ida B. "Lynch Law in America." Accessed at Digital History, 1900.

21. Christensen, Stephanie. "Niagara Movement (1905-1909)." BlackPast, May 17, 2019.

22. Lunardini, Christine A. "Standing Firm: William Monroe Trotter's Meetings with Woodrow Wilson, 1913–1914." *The Journal of Negro History* 64, no. 3 (1979): 244–64.

23. Greenridge, *Black Radical*, 184–85.

24. "Woodrow Wilson and the Negro Question." Bill of Rights Institute.

25. Giddings, *Ida*, 489.

26. Akina, John. "Woodrow Wilson & the Black Vote in 1912." Global Black History, January 17, 2021.

27. Ambar, Saladin. "Woodrow Wilson: Life before the Presidency." Miller Center, University of Virginia, August 29, 2017; see also, Cooper, John Milton. "Woodrow Wilson: The Academic Man." *The Virginia Quarterly Review* 58, no. 1 (1982): 38–53.

28. Papers of Woodrow Wilson Project Records, call #MC178, Public Policy Papers, Department of Special Collections, Princeton University Library. (Hereinafter Wilson Project Records.)

29. Ibid.

30. See, e.g., Newman, Simon P. "The Hegelian Roots of Woodrow Wilson's Progressivism." *American Presbyterians* 64, no. 3 (1986): 191–201.

31. "Obedience to the Law," Wilson Diary, Wilson Project Records.

32. Berkowitz, Peter. "The Roots of the Elite Left's Attack on Freedom." Real Clear Politics.

33. "Obedience to the Law," Wilson Diary, Wilson Project Records. This distinction which is at the core of Wilson's philosophy is most prominently found in "Locke's Second Treatise on Government."

34. "Hillard's Notes," Papers of Woodrow Wilson Project Records, call #MC178, Public Policy Papers, Department of Special Collections, Princeton University Library, 7.

35. "Hillard's Notes," "Wilson Project Records," 7.

36. Ibid.

37. For Wilson, gender was another proxy. He wrote, "Teaching women about politics is like teaching stone masons about fashion." Yet he also wrote that his young students at the women's college Bryn Mawr "have begun their work finely." The ambivalence in his judgment stands out less than his generalizations. Individuals have varying capacities, but it is important to find rough indicators of ability, like gender. That view carried over in Wilson's views on race and suffrage. See also, Rogal, Samuel J. "From Pedagogue to President: Thomas Woodrow Wilson as Teacher-Scholar." *Presidential Studies Quarterly* 24, no. 1 (1994): 49–56.

38. "The Formula," Wilson Project Records, Box 6, Folder 6.
39. Turner, Frederick J. *A History of the American People*. By Woodrow Wilson, PhD, Litt. D., LL.D. In five volumes. (New York and London: Harper and Brothers. 1902. Pp. xxvi, 350; xix, 369; xvi, 348; xv, 343; xii, 338.)" A review. *The American Historical Review* 8, no. 4 (July 1903): 762–65.
40. Wilson, *A History of the American People*, 46.
41. Ibid., 46, 49, 58, 58.
42. Ibid.
43. "Halsey Notes." Wilson Project Records. Box 5, Folder 4.
44. Woodrow Wilson, draft of a letter to G. McArthur Sullivan, 3 December 1909, in Arthur S. Link, ed. *The Papers of Woodrow Wilson* 15, (Princeton University Press, 1973), 550; see also Link, *Papers*, 19, 557.
45. Meier, August. "The Negro and the Democratic Party, 1875–1915," *Phylon* 17, no. 2 (2nd Qtr., 1956): 173–91.
46. Wilson, Woodrow. *Constitutional Government in the United States* (Columbia University Press, 1908), 32, 34, 39.
47. Wilson, *A History of the American People*, 54.
48. Wilson, *Constitutional Government in the United States*, 44.
49. Ibid., 38.
50. Such thinking about the presidency in my view is rightly labeled populism, not democracy. See Brettschneider, *Popular Constitutionalism Contra Populism*"; also see Muller, *What is Populism?*
51. Hendrix, Steven. "Trump's 'Fake News Awards': Nothing like the First White House Press Conference." *Washington Post*, January 18, 2018.
52. Skowronek, Stephen. *Building a New American State: The Expansion of National Administrative Capacities, 1877–1920.* (Cambridge University Press, 1982), 193–211.
53. Yellin, Eric. *Racism in the Nation's Service.* (University of North Carolina Press, 2013), 16, 25.
54. "James Monroe Trotter." Getting Word: African American Oral History Project, Thomas Jefferson Foundation.
55. Wolgemuth, Kathleen L. "Woodrow Wilson and Federal Segregation." *The Journal of Negro History.* 44, no. 2 (1959): 159.
56. Weiss, Nancy J. "The Negro and the New Freedom: Fighting Wilsonian Segregation." *Political Science Quarterly* 84, no. 1 (1969): 64.
57. Ibid., 64.
58. Yellin, *Racism in the Nation's Service*, 121.
59. Ibid., 114.
60. For an example of "friction" as central to Wilson's politics, see, e.g., Wolgemuth, "Woodrow Wilson."
61. See Greenridge, *Black Radical*, 173.
62. Ibid., 191.
63. Giddings, *A Sword Among Lions*, 528.
64. Lunardini, Christine A. "Standing Firm: William Monroe Trotter's Meetings With Woodrow Wilson, 1913–1914." *The Journal of Negro History* 64, no. 3 (1979): 244–64. https://doi.org/10.2307/2717036.
65. Lunardini, Christine A. "Standing Firm: William Monroe Trotter's Meetings with Woodrow Wilson, 1913–1914." *The Journal of Negro History* 64, no. 3 (1979): 244–64.
66. Giddings, *A Sword Among Lions*, 529.

67. Ibid., 555.
68. Ibid.
69. Ibid.
70. Lunardini, "Standing Firm."
71. Ibid.
72. Ibid, 262.
73. Lehr, Dick. "The Racist Legacy of Woodrow Wilson." *The Atlantic*, November 27, 2015.
74. Giddings, *A Sword Among Lions*, 557.
75. Fung, Brian. "Merry Christmas! 107 Years Ago Tonight, Americans Heard the World's First Radio Show." *Washington Post*, December 24, 2013.
76. Procter, Ben. *William Randolph Hearst: The Early Years, 1863–1910*. (Oxford University Press, 1998), X.
77. "First Nickelodeon Opens." History. November 13, 2009.
78. Tulis, Jeffrey. *The Rhetorical Presidency*. (Princeton: Princeton University Press, 1987.)
79. Ibid.
80. Hendrix, "Trump's 'Fake News Awards.'"
81. Manheim, Jarol B. "The Honeymoon's Over: The News Conference and the Development of Presidential Style." *The Journal of Politics* 41, no. 1 (1979): 55–74; see also, Cornwell, E. E. "The Press Conferences of Woodrow Wilson." *Journalism and Mass Communication Quarterly* 39, no. 3 (1962)" 292–300.
82. "Ida B. Wells and the Campaign against Lynching." Bill of Rights Institute.
83. "Lynching Statistics by Year." Archives at *Tuskegee University Archives Repository*. http://archive.tuskegee.edu/repository/digital-collection/lynching-information/.
84. Wilson, *A History of the American People*, 58.
85. Kirkpatrick, Mary Alice. "Thomas Dixon, 1864–1946 and Arthur I. Keller (Arthur Ignatius), 1866–1924." *Documenting the American South*, University of North Carolina.
86. Faulkner, Ronnie. "The Clansman." NCpedia, 2006.
87. Baldwin, Davarian L. "'I Will Build a Black Empire': The Birth of a Nation and the Specter of the New Negro." *The Journal of the Gilded Age and Progressive Era* 14, no. 4 (2015): 599–603.
88. Brody, Richard. "The Black Activist Who Fought against D. W. Griffith's 'The Birth of a Nation.'" *The New Yorker*, 2017.
89. Benbow, Mark E. "Birth of a Quotation: Woodrow Wilson and 'Like Writing History with Lightning.'" *The Journal of the Gilded Age and Progressive Era* 9, no. 4 (2010): 509–33.
90. Lehr, Dick. *The Birth of a Movement: How Birth of a Nation Ignited the Battle for Civil Rights*. (PublicAffairs, 2017); Powell, Susan. "Boston and the Birth of a Nation: Cradle of the Modern Civil Rights Movement." *North Alabama Historical Review* 1 (2011): 131–42.
91. Benbow, Mark E. "Birth of a Quotation." I am also indebted to Erika Kiss for elucidating the connections and parallels between the movie and the book.
92. Ibid.
93. Shea, Andrea. "Documentary Resurrects Civil Rights Crusader's Battle to Ban 'Birth of a Nation' in 1915 Boston." *WBUR*, NPR, 2017.
94. Powell, "Boston and the Birth of a Nation," 132.
95. Lynskey, Dorian. "How the Fight to Ban *The Birth of a Nation* Shaped the Nascent Civil Rights Movement." *Slate Magazine*, March 31 2015.
96. "'Birth of a Nation' Proceeds." *The New York Times*, April 18 1915.
97. Powell, "Boston and the Birth of a Nation," 136.

98. See, e.g., Rylance, David. "Breech Birth: The Reception to D. W. Griffith's *The Birth of a Nation*." *Australasian Journal of American Studies* 24, no. 2 (2005): 1–20.

99. Clark, Alexis. "How 'The Birth of a Nation' Revived the Ku Klux Klan." History, August 26, 2018; see also, Rice, Tom. "'The True Story of the Ku Klux Klan': Defining the Klan through Film." *Journal of American Studies* 42, no. 3 (2008), 471–88.

100. Rice, "'The True Story of the Ku Klux Klan,'" 471–88.

101. Rudwick, Elliott M. *Race Riot at East St. Louis, July 2, 1917*. (University of Illinois Press, 1964.)

102. "President Thanks All His Workers." *Bridgeport Telegram*. November 6, 1916. Accessed at *Library of Congress:* "World War history: daily records and comments as appeared in American and foreign newspapers, 1914–1926."

103. Giddings, *A Sword Among Lions*, 560.

104. Rudwick, *Race Riot at East St. Louis*, 14.

105. Keyes, Allison. "The East St. Louis Race Riot Left Dozens Dead, Devastating a Community on the Rise." *Smithsonian Magazine*, June 30, 2017.

106. Wells-Barnett, Ida B. "The East St. Louis Massacre: The Greatest Outrage of the Century." (The Negro Fellowship Herald Press, 1917); see also, Giddings, *A Sword Among Lions*, 563.

107. "US House of Representatives Hearings Regarding the Riot at East St. Louis, Illinois." Woodrow Wilson Presidential Library.

108. "President Woodrow Wilson's Proclamation of July 26, 1918, Denouncing Lynching." Amistad Resources.

109. Greenridge, *Black Radical*, 278.

110. "Final Address in Support of the League of Nations." Top 100 Speeches, American Rhetoric.

111. Wilson, Woodrow. "Address to the Senate on the Nineteenth Amendment." APP.

112. See Giddings, *Sword Among Lions*.

113. For a vindication of her concerns see Jones, Martha. *Vanguard: How Black Women Broke Barriers, Won the Vote, and Insisted on Equality for All.* (Basic Books, 2020.)

114. Wilson, Woodrow. "Speeches by Woodrow Wilson: League of Nations." US Embassy.

115. Wells-Barnett, *Crusade for Justice*, 324; Greenridge, *Black Radical*, 257.

116. Wells-Barnett, *Crusade for Justice*, 324.

117. Greenridge, *Black Radical*, 572.

118. Ellis, Mark. *Race, War, and Surveillance: African Americans and the United States Government during World War I.* (Indiana University Press, 2001.)

119. Greenridge, *Black Radical*, 264–66.

120. Ibid., 265.

121. Cohassey, John "Trotter, Monroe 1872–1934." Encyclopedia.com.

122. Giddings, *A Sword Among Lions*, 583.

123. Greenridge, *Black Radical*, 266.

124. Wilson, Woodrow. "The Pueblo Speech." Voices of Democracy.

125. Ellis, Mark. "J. Edgar Hoover and the 'Red Summer' of 1919." *Journal of American Studies* 28, no. 1 (1994): 39–59.

126. United States. Congress. Senate. Committee on Foreign Relations. *Treaty of Peace with Germany: Hearings Before the Committee on Foreign Relations, United States Senate, Sixty-Sixth Congress, First Session on the Treaty of Peace with Germany, Signed at Versailles on June 28, 1919, and Submitted to the Senate on July 10, 1919 by the President of the United States* (Washington, DC, Government Printing Office, 1919), 682.

127. Greenridge, *Black Radical*, 271.

128. United States Congressional Serial Set, Issue 7605, at 682.
129. Cook, Charles Orson. "'The Glory of the Old South and the Greatness of the New': Reform and the Divided Mind of Charles Hillman Brough." *The Arkansas Historical Quarterly* 34, no. 3 (1975). 227–41.
130. Lisenby, Foy. "Charles Hillman Brough as Historian." *The Arkansas Historical Quarterly* 35, no. 2 (1976) 115–26.
131. See, e.g., Cook, Charles. "Arkansas's Charles Hillman Brough, 1876–1935: An Interpretation." *University of Houston ProQuest Dissertations Publishing*, 1980.
132. Stockley, Grif. "The Massacre: What Happened." *UA Little Rock Center for Arkansas History.*
133. Wells-Barnett, Ida B. *The Arkansas Race Riot.* (Hume Job Print, 1920.)
134. See, e.g., Karabel, Jerome. "The Ghosts of Elaine, Arkansas, 1919." *The New York Review of Books*, 2019; see also, *Moore v. Dempsey*, 261 US 86 (1923).
135. Lewis, Tom. *Washington: A History of Our National City.* (Basic Books, 2015).
136. "Red Summer." National WWI Museum and Memorial.

CHAPTER 9: HARRY TRUMAN AND SADIE ALEXANDER:
TO SECURE THESE RIGHTS ONCE MORE

1. Rosenwald, Michael. "FDR Had a Secret as He Sought a Fourth Term in 1944: He Was Dying." *Washington Post*, October 5, 2020.
2. Catledge, Turner. "Roosevelt Nominated for Fourth Term." *New York Times*, July 21, 1944.
3. "Research Starters: US Military by the Numbers." The National WWII Museum, 2000.
4. Greenfield, Jeff. "The Year the Veepstakes Really Mattered." *POLITICO*, July 10, 2016.
5. Leuchtenburg, William E. "The Conversion of Harry Truman." *American Heritage.*
6. McCullough, David. *Truman.* (Simon & Schuster, 2011), location 11086.
7. Casper, Miracle. *Presidential Lost Files: Harry S. Truman.* YouTube video, November 7, 2017.
8. See, e.g., Daphney, Daniel. "How Blacks Became Blue: The 1936 African American Voting Shift from the Party of Lincoln to the New Deal Coalition." Pell Scholars and Senior Theses, Salve Regina University, 2012, 77.
9. "Election of 1944." The American Presidency Project.
10. "The Death of President Roosevelt, April 12, 1945." Publish Policy Institute at Hunter College, Roosevelt House at Hunter College.
11. See McCullough, *Truman*, location 6434.
12. Leuchtenburg, William E. "The Conversion of Harry Truman." *American Heritage* 42, no. 7 (1991): 3; see also Brown, DeNeen. "How Harry S. Truman Went from Being a Racist to Desegregating the Military." *The Washington Post*, July 26, 2018.
13. Holcombe, Randall G. "Federal Government Growth before the New Deal." The Independent Institute.
14. Lehr, "The Racist Legacy of Woodrow Wilson."
15. Katznelson, Ira, and Suzanne Mettler. "On Race and Policy History: A Dialogue about the G.I. Bill." *Perspectives on Politics* 6, no. 3 (2008): 519–37; Ross, B. Joyce. "Mary McLeod Bethune and the National Youth Administration: A Case Study of Power Relationships in the Black Cabinet of Franklin D. Roosevelt." *The Journal of Negro History* 60, no. 1 (1975): 1–28.
16. Purdy, Jedediah. "Bernie Sanders's New Deal Socialism." *The New Yorker*, November 20, 2015.
17. Mettler, Suzanne, *Soldiers to Citizens: The G.I. Bill and the Making of the Greatest Generation.* (Oxford University Press, 2007); see also, Murphy, Mary-Elizabeth B. "African Amer-

icans in the Great Depression and New Deal." Oxford Research Encyclopedias, American History, November 19, 2020.

18. Sparrow, Paul. "Eleanor Roosevelt's Battle to End Lynching." Franklin Roosevelt Presidential Library, February. 12, 2016. https://fdr.blogs.archives.gov/2016/02/12/eleanor-roosevelts-battle-to-end-lynching/.

19. Executive Order—General Orders: 145. APP.

20. Adams, Kimberly. "Why the Words of America's First Black Economist Resonate Today." Marketplace, June 28, 2021.

21. See, e.g., Katznelson, Ira. *Fear Itself: The New Deal and the Origins of Our Time*. (W. W. Norton, 2013); See also, Alexander, Sadie. *Democracy, Race, and Justice: The Speeches and Writings of Sadie T. M. Alexander*, Nina Banks, ed. (Yale University Press, 2021.)

22. Alexander, *Democracy, Race, and Justice*, 101.

23. Ibid., 100.

24. Ibid., 101.

25. Katznelson, *Fear Itself*, 161–63, 170–75, 544–46.

26. Rothstein, Richard. *The Color of Law: A Forgotten History of How Our Government Segregated America*. (W. W. Norton, 2018.) In particular see chapter two. Also see Gross, Terry. "A 'Forgotten History' of How the U.S. Government Segregated America." *Fresh Air*, NPR, May 3, 2017.

27. Pauley, Garth. *The Modern Presidency and Civil Rights*. (Texas A&M University Press, 2001), 18–22.

28. Alexander, *Democracy, Race, and Justice*, 173.

29. "Our History." NAACP, 2021.

30. Hanson, Joyce. *Mary McLeod Bethune and Black Women's Political Activism*. (University of Missouri, 2003), 125.

31. White, Walter. *A Man Called White: The Autobiography of Walter White*. (University of Georgia Press, 1995.)

32. Butler, Kirstin. "Seeing Isaac Woodard." *PBS*, March 25, 2021.

33. Ibid.

34. White, *A Man Called White*, 326.

35. Ibid., 327; see also Butler, *Isaac Woodard*. "Federal Court Jury Acquits South Carolina Officer after Blind Veteran Accuses Him." *The New York Times*, November 6, 1946.

36. Stevens, Matt. "Secrets of 1946 Mass Lynching Could Be Revealed after Court Ruling." *New York Times*, Feb. 12, 2019.

37. McCullough, *Truman*, location 11077.

38. White, *A Man Called White*, 327.

39. Juhnke, William E. "President Truman's Committee on Civil Rights: The Interaction of Politics, Protest, and Presidential Advisory Commission." *Presidential Studies Quarterly* 19, no. 3 (1989): 593–610; at 593.

40. White, *A Man Called White*, 329–30.

41. Ibid., 329–30.

42. Sparrow, "Eleanor Roosevelt's Battle."

43. White, *A Man Called White*, 169; Michaelis, David. "Eleanor Fights Lynching." *American Heritage*.

44. "A. Philip Randolph." AFL-CIO, 2019.

45. "African Americans Threaten March on Washington, 1941." Global Nonviolent Action Database.

46. "Executive Order 8802: Prohibition of Discrimination in the Defense Industry." Franklin D. Roosevelt Presidential Library and Museum, 2019.
47. See "Letter, Eleanor Roosevelt to Walter White Detailing the First Lady's Lobbying Efforts for Federal Action against Lynchings, 19 Mar. 1936." Library of Congress.
48. See, Long, Michael. *Marshalling Justice: The Early Civil Rights Letters of Thurgood Marshall.* (Amistad Press, 2010), 189–90, 192.
49. "End Mob Violence, Truman is Urged; Delegation at White House Also Asks Special Session of Congress to Pass Strong Laws." *The New York Times*, September 20, 1946.
50. White, *A Man Called White*, 330–31.
51. "Harry S Truman and Civil Rights." National Parks Service.
52. Juhnke, "Committee on Civil Rights," 594.
53. Ibid., 593–94.
54. "Executive Order 9808." Harry S. Truman Presidential Library, 2020.
55. One attempt to rigorously catalogue civil rights abuses that predated the commission was Ida B. Wells's *Lynch Law in All Its Phases* (The New York Age Print), published in 1892. Also in 1946, Kenneth and Mamie Clark founded the Northside Center for Child Development in Harlem, where they conducted psychological research on the effects of segregation among young children that would later become famous in *Brown v. Board*.
56. "Brown v. Board and the 'Doll Test.'" NAACP Legal Defense Fund, 2023.
57. "Letter, Harry S. Truman to Attorney General Tom Clark, with Attached Memo to David Niles, September 20, 1946." Truman Presidential Library; see also Baime, A. J. *Dewey Defeats Truman: The 1948 Election and the Battle for America's Soul.* (Mariner Books, 2020), 20.
58. Executive Order 9808.
59. White, *A Man Called White*, 332.
60. Ibid.
61. Nelson, H. Viscount. "Channing H. Tobias (1882–1961)." BlackPast, January. 17, 2007.
62. White, *A Man Called White*, 331.
63. Juhnke, "Committee on Civil Rights," 596.
64. See Nelson, "Channing H. Tobias"; see also, "Channing H. Tobias: 'Defender of Liberties.'" *The Crisis*. NAACP, December 1980, 566–67.
65. See, e.g., Alexander, *Democracy, Race, and Justice*, 65–71.
66. "Sadie Tanner Mossell Alexander, 1898–1989." Penn Libraries, University of Pennsylvania Archives and Records Center.
67. See Mack, Kenneth. *Representing the Race: The Creation of the Civil Rights Lawyer.* (Harvard University Press, 2012); see also Tushnet, Mark. *Thurgood Marshall: His Speeches, Writings, Arguments, Opinions, and Reminiscences.* (Lawrence Hill Books, 2001), chapter 12, pp. 138–43.
68. "Sadie Tanner Mossell Alexander Oral History, October 12, 1977." Temple Digital Collections, Temple University Libraries; see also, "Sadie Tanner Mossell Alexander, 1898–1989." Penn Libraries, University Archives and Records Center.
69. Alexander, *Democracy, Race, and Justice*, 1, 73; "Sadie Tanner Mossell Alexander." West Philadelphia Collaborative History.
70. Alexander, *Democracy, Race, and Justice*, 132–33.
71. Ibid., 132–34.
72. "Remarks to Members of the President's Committee on Civil Rights." Harry S. Truman Presidential Library.
73. Ibid.

74. "Charles Hamilton Houston." Harvard Radcliffe Institute, Harvard University.

75. "Charles Hamilton Houston." NAACP.

76. Mineo, Liz. "The Civil Rights Lawyer Who Paved the Path." *Harvard Gazette*, May 16, 2018.

77. Tushnet, Mark. *The NAACP's Legal Strategy against Segregated Education, 1925–1950.* (University of North Carolina Press, 2005), 115.

78. Tushnet, *The NAACP's Legal Strategy*, 114–15.

79. Ifill, Sherrilyn. "How Thurgood Marshall Paved the Road to 'Brown v. Board of Education.'" *Smithsonian Magazine*, March 10, 2021.

80. See "Grant" chapter.

81. Long, *Marshalling Justice*, 210–15.

82. Ibid., 224.

83. Riehm, Edith S. "Forging the Civil Rights Frontier: How Truman's Committee Set the Liberal Agenda for Reform 1947–1965." Dissertation, Georgia State University, 2012.

84. See "Sadie Alexander to Francis Matthews. July 15, 1947." In *Sadie Tanner Mossell Alexander Papers*, UPT 50 A374S. Penn Libraries, University of Pennsylvania Archives. (Hereinafter *Alexander Papers*.)

85. "Sadie Alexander to Channing Tobia. 1947." *Alexander Papers*.

86. See, e.g., Alexander's letter to Carr pleading for the National Urban League to testify before the committee, "Sadie Alexander to Robert Carr. March 15, 1947." *Alexander Papers*; "Robert Carr to President's Committee on Civil Rights. April 10, 1947." *Alexander Papers*.

87. "Statement of Thurgood Marshall Before the President's Committee on Civil Rights." Record Group 220: Records of Temporary Committees, Commissions, and Boards. *National Archives*. NAID: 239791208.

88. "Committee Meeting: Thursday, April 17, 1947." *Presidents Committee on Civil Rights*. Accessed at: *BlackFreedom*, at p. 101.

89. Ibid., 98.

90. Ibid., 130.

91. Ibid., 130.

92. Ibid., 129–33.

93. Ibid., 129–33.

94. See "To Secure These Rights: The Report of the President's Committee on Civil Rights." Harry S. Truman Presidential Library, National Archives, 166–72.

95. "To Secure These Rights," 168.

96. Juhnke, "Committee on Civil Rights," 603–4; "Committee Meeting: Thursday, June 30, 1947." *Presidents Committee on Civil Rights*. Accessed at: BlackFreedom. at 147–48.

97. "Harry S. Truman NAACP Speech." Voices of Democracy.

98. Ibid.

99. Streator, George. "Truman Demands We Fight Harder to Spur Equality." *The New York Times*, June 30, 1947, p. 1, 3.

100. Juhnke, "Committee on Civil Rights," 603–4.

101. Ibid., 603–4.

102. Ibid., 602.

103. Ibid., 603–4.

104. "Roosevelt, (Anna) Eleanor." The Martin Luther King, Jr., Research and Education Institute, May 31, 2017.

105. Williams, Juan. *Thurgood Marshall: American Revolutionary* (Crown, 2011), 180.

106. Glass, Andrew. "Truman Addresses NAACP, June 29, 1947." *POLITICO*, June 29, 2018;

"President Harry S. Truman Speaks to the Conference of the National Association for the Advancement of Colored People." Truman Presidential Library, National Archives.

107. Juhnke, "Committee on Civil Rights," 604.

108. "To Secure These Rights," 4.

109. Ibid., 82, 79, 82, 81.

110. Ibid., 99, 109.

111. Ibid., 99, 104, 112, 104–13, 79–83, 166.

112. Juhnke, "Committee on Civil Rights," 593.

113. Tushnet, *Thurgood Marshall*, 90, ch. 8.

114. Truman, Harry S. "Special Message to the Congress on Civil Rights." The Gilder Lehrman Center for the Study of Slavery, Resistance, and Abolition, Yale University, April 9, 2015.

115. "Black-American Representatives and Senators by Congress, 1870–Present." US House of Representatives, History, Art & Archives.

116. Truman, "Special Message to Congress."

117. "Executive Order 9981." Harry S. Truman Presidential Library, National Archives.

118. See chapter on Woodrow Wilson.

119. "Correspondence between Harry S. Truman and Ernie Roberts, September 2, 1948." Harry S. Truman Presidential Library, National Archives.

120. "Sadie Alexander to Robert Carr." July 7, 1947. *Alexander Papers.*

121. Ibid.

122. See, e.g., "From Slavery to Segregation." Segregation in America, Equal Justice Initiative, 2018.

123. See McCullough, *Truman*, location 11177, 11868, 11949.

124. "Correspondence between Harry S. Truman and Ernie Roberts."

125. Inskeep, Steve, and Ron Elving. "In 1948, Democrats Weathered Civil Rights Divide." The Democratic Convention, NPR, August 27, 2008.

126. Gosnell, Harold F. *Truman's Crises: A Political Biography of Harry S. Truman.* (Greenwood Press, 1980), 407–9; Topping, Simon. "'Never Argue with the Gallup Poll': Thomas Dewey, Civil Rights and the Election of 1948." *Journal of American Studies* 38, no. 2 (2004): 179–98, 194.

127. "Strom Thurmond, Foe of Integration, Dies at 100." *The New York Times*, June 27, 2003.

128. Topping, "Never Argue," 1.

129. "Election of 1948." APP.

130. Nix, Elizabeth. "'Dewey Defeats Truman': The Election Upset behind the Photo." *History*, November 2018.

131. McCullough, *Truman*; "Harry S Truman and Civil Rights." National Parks Service; Casper, *Presidential Lost Files.*

132. Dahms, Jonathan. "Army Commemorates 60th Anniversary of Armed Forces Integration." U.S. Army, July 24, 2008.

CHAPTER 10: DWIGHT D. EISENHOWER, JOHN F. KENNEDY, LYNDON JOHNSON, AND MARTIN LUTHER KING JR: THE ROAD TO RECOVERY

1. Long, Michael. *Marshalling Justice: The Early Civil Rights Letters of Thurgood Marshall.* (Amistad Press, 2010), 147.

2. "Timeline of Events Leading to the Brown v. Board of Education Decision of 1954." National Archives, August 15, 2016.

3. "Chief Justice Vinson Dies of Heart Attack in Capital; Jurist Succumbs Unexpectedly at Apartment at Age of 63." *The New York Times*, September 8, 1953.

4. White, G. Edward. "The Unacknowledged Lesson: Earl Warren and the Japanese Relocation Controversy." *VQR*, 2019.

5. Williams, Juan. *Thurgood Marshall: American Revolutionary.* (Crown, 2011), 239.

6. "Brown v. Board of Education Timeline."

7. Murray, Pauli. *Song in a Weary Throat.* (Liveright, 2018); see also, Rosenberg, Rosalind. *Jane Crow: The Life of Pauli Murray.* (Oxford University Press, 2017.)

8. Murray, *Song in a Weary Throat*, 329.

9. "Kenneth and Mamie Clark Doll." National Park Service, 2016; Clark, Kenneth B., and Mamie P. Clark. "Emotional Factors in Racial Identification and Preference in Negro Children." *The Journal of Negro Education* 19, no. 3 (1950): 341–50.

10. Severo, Richard. "Kenneth Clark, Who Fought Segregation, Dies." *The New York Times*, May 2, 2005.

11. Simon, James. *Eisenhower v. Warren: The Battle for Civil Rights and Liberties.* (Liveright, 2018), location 2094.

12. Ibid., location 2172.

13. Ibid.

14. Ibid., 179–81, 198.

15. Powe Jr., Lucas. *The Warren Court in American Politics.* (Harvard University Press, 2000), 23.

16. "Supplemental Brief for the United States on Reargument, Brown v. Board," US Reports, October 1953, p. 187.

17. Ibid., 132, 152.

18. "Brown v. Board of Education." National Archives, August 15, 2016.

19. Kluger, Richard. *Simple Justice: The History of Brown v. Board of Education and Black America's Struggle for Equality* (Vintage, 2004), 710.

20. Power Jr., *The Warren Court*, 60.

21. *Brown v. Board of Education of Topeka* 347 U.S. 483 (1954); see also, Williams, *Thurgood Marshall*, 242–44.

22. Williams, *Thurgood Marshall*, 249.

23. Peters, Gerhard, and Woolley, John T. "Dwight D. Eisenhower, The President's News Conference Online." The American Presidency Project.

24. Williams, *Thurgood Marshall*, 247.

25. Kramer, Victor. "President Eisenhower's Handwritten Changes in the Brief on Relief in the School Segregation Cases: Minding the Whys and Wherefores," University of Minnesota Law School, Constitutional Commentary, 1992, pp. 224–27.

26. Victor, "President Eisenhower's Handwritten Changes," 228.

27. Williams, *Thurgood Marshall*, 251.

28. *Brown v. Board of Education II* 349 US 294 (1955). *US Reports.*

29. Williams, *Thurgood Marshall*, 257.

30. Kennedy, Randall. "Martin Luther King's Constitution: A Legal History of the Montgomery Bus Boycott," *The Yale Law Journal* 98, no. 6 (1989): 1000. (Hereinafter, "MLK's Constitution.")

31. Branch, Taylor. *Parting the Waters: America in the King Years 1954–1963.* (Simon & Schuster, 1988), 164.

32. Branch, *Parting the Waters*, 168.

33. Ibid., 176.

34. "State of Alabama v. M. L. King, Jr., No. 7399." The Martin Luther King, Jr. Research and Education Institute, Stanford University.

35. Kennedy, "MLK's Constitution," 1030.
36. Rubinowitz, Leonard. "The Courage of the Civil Rights Lawyers: Fred Gray and his Colleagues." *Case Western Reserve Law Review* 67, no. 4 (2017): footnote 83.
37. Tushnet, *Thurgood Marshall*, 470.
38. E.g., Branch, *Parting the Waters*, 740.
39. Williams, *Thurgood Marshall*, 266.
40. Wofford, Harris. "What I Saw at Selma." *POLITICO*, March 7, 2015.
41. Branch, *Parting the Waters*, 189.
42. Congressional Record, 84th Congress Second Session, vol. 102, part 4, March 12, 1956. (Washington, DC: Governmental Printing Office, 1956), 4459–60.
43. O'Donnell, Michael. "Eisenhower v. Warren: The Battle over Brown." *The Atlantic*, March 9, 2018.
44. Simon, *Eisenhower v. Warren*, 62.
45. Long, *Marshalling Justice*, 345.
46. Branch, *Parting the Waters*, 216.
47. "Give Us the Ballot," in the King Encyclopedia, The Martin Luther King Jr. Research and Education Institute, Stanford University.
48. Stern, Mark. "Lyndon Johnson and Richard Russell: Institutions, Ambitions and Civil Rights," *Presidential Studies Quarterly* 21, no. 4 (Fall 1991): 694; Caro, Robert. *Master of the Senate III: The Years of Lyndon Johnson.* (Vintage, 2003), 870, 892.
49. Caro, *Master of the Senate*, 870, 892.
50. See Branch, *Parting the Waters*, 220.
51. "To Richard M. Nixon," in the King Encyclopedia, The Martin Luther King Jr. Research and Education Institute, Stanford University.
52. "Dwight Eisenhower and the Central High School Crisis," National Parks Service.
53. Simon, *Eisenhower v. Warren*, loc 4711.
54. Ibid., 293.
55. Tushnet, Mark. *Making Civil Rights Law: Thurgood Marshall and the Supreme Court, 1936–1961.* (Oxford University Press, 1996), 257–59; Williams, *Thurgood Marshall*, 286.
56. "Dwight Eisenhower and the Central High School Crisis."
57. Simon, *Eisenhower v. Warren*, 293–95.
58. "Dwight Eisenhower and the Central High School Crisis."
59. Ibid.
60. Ibid.
61. Simon, *Eisenhower v. Warren*, 304.
62. The Mike Wallace Interview, "Lost Thurgood Marshall Interview with Mike Wallace," *ABC News*.
63. "Handwritten notes by President Eisenhower on decision to send troops to Little Rock, September 1957." [DDE's Papers as President, Administration Series, Box 23, Little Rock, Arkansas(2).]
64. "Dwight Eisenhower and the Central High School Crisis."
65. The Posse Comitatus Act, passed under President Hayes, normally prevents federal authorities from using federal troops to enforce domestic law. However, as the Supreme Court would later allude to in *Cooper v. Aaron*, Eisenhower's use of troops. This use of the act was the opposite of how President Wilson used it.
66. Simon, *Eisenhower v. Warren*, 306.
67. "Dwight Eisenhower and the Central High School Crisis."

68. *Cooper v. Aaron*, 358 US 1 (1958).
69. *Cooper v. Aaron*.
70. Ibid.
71. "Brown v. Board of Education." The Presidency In-Depth Exhibits, The Miller Center, University of Virginia.
72. Tushnet, *Thurgood Marshall*, 470.
73. "Debate with James J. Kilpatrick on 'The Nation's Future'," in the King Encyclopedia, The Martin Luther King Jr. Research and Education Institute, Stanford University.
74. "The Congressional Record: Proceedings and Debates of the 87th Congress," 107(12) 15538.
75. "Debate with James J. Kilpatrick."
76. Hustwit, William. *James J. Kilpatrick: Salesman for Segregation*. (University of North Carolina Press, 2013), 111. I also owe credit to Brandon Terry for pointing me to sources on King's embrace of natural law.
77. "Debates with James J. Kilpatrick."
78. Hustwit, *James J. Kilpatrick*; quoting Garrow, David. *Bearing the Cross: Martin Luther King, Jr. and the Southern Christian Leadership Conference* (William Marrow Paperbacks, 2004.)
79. I am indebted to the Martin Luther King Reading Group, and specifically to Brandon Terry, for this material.
80. Papers of Martin Luther King, Volume VII. Accessed at: https://kinginstitute.stanford.edu/publications/papers-martin-luther-king-jr-volume-vii.
81. Ibid.
82. King, Martin Luther. "Letter from Birmingham Jail." The Martin Luther King Jr. Research and Education Institute, Stanford University. April 16, 1963.
83. Branch, *Parting the Waters*.
84. King, "Letter from Birmingham Jail."
85. "Letter from Birmingham Jail."
86. King, Martin Luther Jr. "I Have a Dream." Speech, Lincoln Memorial, Washington, D.C., August 28, 1963. In "The Martin Luther King, Jr. Encyclopedia," edited by Clayborne Carson et al. (Martin Luther King Jr. Research and Education Institute, 2019.)
87. *New York Times Co. v. Sullivan*, 376 US 254 (1964).
88. Caro, *Master of the Senate*, 888–89.
89. "Telephone Conversation #56 between LBJ and Martin Luther King, Jr. November 25, 1963." LBJ Presidential Library.
90. "On This Day, Filibuster Fails to Block the Civil Rights Act." The National Constitution Center, June 19, 2022.
91. Gold, Susan Dudley. "The Civil Rights Act of 1964," (Marshall Cavendish Benchmark, 2011.)
92. Menand, Louis. "How Women Got in on the Civil Rights Act," *The New Yorker*, July 21, 2014.
93. Congressional Record, United States Senate (June 9, 1964) at 13111; Congressional Record, US Senate (March 26, 1964) at 6428.
94. "Conversation with Martin Luther King," White House Secret Tapes, at the Miller Center, University of Virginia, January 15, 1965.
95. Branch, Taylor. *At Canaan's Edge: America in the King Years, 1965–68*. (Simon & Schuster, 2007), 68.
96. Wofford, Harris. "What I Saw at Selma." *POLITICO*, March 7, 2015.
97. Kohut, Andrew. "From the Archives: 50 Years Ago: Mixed Views about Civil Rights but Support for Selma Demonstrators." Pew Research Center, January 16, 2020.
98. Boeri, David. "The Making of LBJ's Historic 'We Shall Overcome' Speech." WBUR, March 14, 2014.

99. Zelizer, Julian. "LBJ and the Speech That Changed America." *The Atlantic*, March 12, 2015.
100. "We Shall Overcome: Lyndon Johnson and the 1965 Voting Rights Act." The White House Historical Association.
101. Taylor Branch, *Pillar of Fire: America in the King Years, 1963–65*. (Simon & Schuster, 1999.)
102. Caro, Robert. "When LBJ Said, "We Shall Overcome." *The New York Times*, August 28, 2008.
103. King, Martin Luther Jr. "The Record of the Association of the Bar of the City of New York: The Civil Rights Struggle in the United States Today." City of New York Bar Association, 1965.
104. King Jr., Martin Luther. "*I've Been to the Mountaintop.*" April 3, 1968.
105. Hustwit, *James J. Kilpatrick.*
106. Murphy, "African Americans in the Great Depression."

CHAPTER 11: RICHARD NIXON VERSUS DANIEL ELLSBERG AND
GRAND JURY ONE: CRIMINALITY IN THE OVAL OFFICE

1. Elliot, Jonathan, ed. "The Debates in the Several States Conventions on the Adoption of the Federal Constitution," (Philadelphia, 1866), 59–60; quoted in Freedman, Eric. "The Law as King and the King as Law: Is the President Immune from Criminal Prosecution before Impeachment?" *Hastings Constitutional Law Quarterly* 20, no. 7 (1992).
2. My thinking in this area is influenced by Freedman, "The Law as King."
3. Elliot, "Debates in the Several States," 109.
4. Ibid., 523. Others defended immunity.
5. *New York Times Co. v. United States*. U.S. Reports. 403 U.S. 713. (1971). Oral Arguments.
6. Ibid.
7. The Secret White House Tapes. Tape 534–002B. July 1, 1971. Miller Center, University of Virginia.
8. "Breaking into Brookings." Miller Center, University of Virginia, May 26, 2017. Nixon reiterated the order on June 30th: "Tapes Show Nixon Ordering Theft of Files." *The New York Times*, November 22, 1996.
9. The Secret White House Tapes. 534–002B. July 1, 1971.
10. Newman, Caroline. "'Blow the Safe and Get It': Listen to Nixon's Response to the Pentagon Papers." *UVAToday*, January 11, 2018; see also, Graff, Garrett M. *Watergate: A New History*. (Simon & Schuster, 2022.)
11. The Secret White House Tapes. Tape 525–001A. June 17, 1971.
12. Fulsom, Don. "Nixon's Darkest Secrets: The Inside Story of America's Most Troubled President." (Thomas Dunne Books, 2012), 8. Fulsom suggests Dean was worried about legal consequences.
13. "The Fielding Break-In 50th Anniversary," Richard Nixon Presidential Library and Museum, September 7, 2021.
14. "The Plumbers." *The New York Times*, July 22, 1973; Edwards, Owen. "The World's Most Famous Filing Cabinet." *Smithsonian Magazine*, October 2012.
15. The Secret White House Tapes. Tape 533. June 29, 1971.
16. Eyewitness account from Ellsberg, see: Kupferburg, Seth, and Richard Sia. "Ellsberg Says Anti-War Moratoriums Delayed Mining of Haiphong for Two and a Half Years." *The Harvard Crimson*.
17. Akerman's documentation, including a memo on the plot to attack Ellsberg are here: "Watergate Special Prosecution Force: Memorandum." Department of Justice. (Hereinafter, *Grand Jury Records*.)
18. Special Assistant George T. Bell, "Exhibit No. 41." *Memorandum*, August 16, 1971. Access in The Final Report of the Select Committee on Presidential Campaign Activities.
19. The Secret White House Tapes. September 13, 1971.

20. *Grand Jury Records*, 17 and 18.
21. Ibid., 16 of PDF.
22. Quote is here: "Excerpts from Interview with Nixon about Domestic Effects of Indochina War." *New York Times*, May 20, 1977.
23. Frost, David, interviewer. "The Frost/Nixon Interviews." Richard Nixon. Part 3. *ABC*, May 19, 1977.
24. Rozell, Mark. "President Nixon's Conception of Executive Privilege: Defining the Scopes and Limits of Executive Branch Secrecy." *Presidential Studies Quarterly* (Spring, 1992): 323–35; "Excerpts From Interview with Nixon About Watergate Tapes and Other Issues." *The New York Times*. Sept. 4, 1977.
25. Frost, David, interviewer. "The Frost/Nixon Interviews."
26. Frost, David, interviewer. "The Frost/Nixon Interviews."
27. Subsequent release of a taped conversation reveals Nixon was indeed considering this option: The Associated Press. "Nixon Proposed Using A-Bomb in Vietnam War." *The New York Times*, March 1, 2002.
28. Interview with author, October 2022. On file.
29. "Daniel Ellsberg Explains Why He Leaked the Pentagon Papers." NPR, 2019.
30. Smith, David. "'I've Never Regretted Doing It': Daniel Ellsberg on 50 Years Since Leaking the Pentagon Papers," *The Guardian*, June 13, 2021.
31. Naughton, James. "Federal Warrant Is Issued for the Arrest of Ellsberg." *The New York Times*, June 26, 1971; Smith, "'I've Never Regretted Doing It.'"
32. "Walter Cronkite, Anchor for the CBS Evening News, Interviews Daniel Ellsberg." Famous-Trials. (Emphasis added.)
33. Interview with author, October 2022. On file.
34. Ibid.
35. Numbers are from one day when the jurors were publicly in court and numbers do not reflect three absent. The Associated Press. "Public Gets Look at Grand Jurors." *The New York Times*, July 28, 1973.
36. Shu, Spencer. "The Foreman of Watergate Grand Jury No. 1 Has Been Watching the Confrontations with Another President." *The Washington Post*, April 15, 2019.
37. Interview with author, October 2022. On file.
38. Rugaber, Walter. "Cord Reported to Link Mitchell to Bugging Plot." *The New York Times*, March 29, 1973.
39. Buchanan, Patrick. "A Special Presidential Consultant Comments on Questions of Justice." *The New York Times*, June 13, 1974.
40. "Transcript of a Recording of a Meeting among the President, John Dean, and H. R. Haldeman." *Nixon Presidential Library*. March 21, 1973.
41. Quote about Petersen is from White House tape, March 21, 1973, meeting of Nixon, Dean, and Haldeman. Transcript prepared by the White House Judiciary Committee staff.
42. The Secret White House Tapes. June 29, 1971.
43. Transcript of a recording of a meeting among the president, John Dean, and H. R. Haldeman in the Oval Office, on March 21, 1973, from 10:12 to 11:55 a.m.
44. "Subpoena Served on Thomas Jefferson to Testify at Aaron Burr's Trial for Treason, 13 June 1807." Library of Congress. For a discussion of presidents and former presidents who acted as witnesses, see also Rotunda, Ronald. "Presidents and ex-Presidents as Witnesses: A Brief Historical Footnote." *Law Forum*. 1 (1975).
45. "Public Gets Look at Grand Jurors."
46. Sirica, John J. *To Set the Record Straight.* (Norton, 1975.)

47. Sirica, *To Set the Record Straight*, 140.
48. "Public Gets Look at Grand Jurors."
49. Kohut, Andrew. "How the Watergate Crisis Eroded Public Support for Nixon," Pew Research Center, September 25, 2019.
50. Pregelj, Vladimir. "Letter to Richard Nixon," January 30, 1974. National Archives.
51. "Seven Members of the Watergate Grand Jury, Breaking Their . . ." United Press International, June 18, 1982.
52. Lardner Jr., George. "Starr Looks to Watergate's 'Road Map.'" *The Washington Post*, September 8, 1998.
53. "Grand Jury Report and Recommendation Concerning Transmission of Evidence to the House of Representatives." National Archives, 70105876.
54. From the indictment itself now released: https://lawandcrime.com/high-profile/watergate-roadmap-released-read-the-formerly-sealed-grand-jury-report-and-recommendation/.
55. "Department of Justice Memorandum," September 24, 1973.
56. *20/20, ABC News*. June 1982. Transcript on file with author.
57. *20/20, ABC News*. June 1982. Transcript on file with author.
58. Author's interview with Philip Lacovara, January 19, 2021.
59. Author's interview with Lacovara.
60. Herbers, John. "Tapes Released." *The New York Times*, August 6, 1974.
61. "Jurisdictional History of the Judiciary Committee." Government Publishing Office.
62. Rudalevige, Andrew. *The New Imperial Presidency: Renewing Presidential Power after Watergate*. (University of Michigan Press, 2006.)
63. See Elayne Edlund's appearance on ABC's *20/20*. For a reference to that interview, see, "Watergate Grand Jury Tried to Indict President Richard Nixon." UPI, June 17, 1982.
64. For a development of this argument see Brettschneider, Corey, and Jeffrey Tulis. "The Traditional Interpretation of the Pardon Power Is Wrong." *The Atlantic*, July 13, 2020.

CHAPTER 12: CODA: OUR CURRENT CRISIS

1. Steckelberg, Aaron. "Inside Trump's West Wing." *The Washington Post*, May 3, 2017.
2. Mueller, Robert. *Report on the Investigation into Russian Interference in the 2016 Presidential Election, Volume II*. U.S. Department of Justice, March 2019.
3. Volume II of the Mueller report.
4. Volume II of the Mueller report.
5. Morgan, Dan. "U.S. Reverses Position on Counsel Law." *The Washington Post*, March 2, 1999.
6. Starr, Kenneth W. "Referral from Independent Counsel Kenneth W. Starr in Conformity with the Requirements of Title 28, United States Code, Section 595(c)." United States Congress, 9 Sept. 1998.
7. Rudalevige, Andrews. *The New Imperial Presidency: Renewing Presidential Power after Watergate*. (University of Michigan Press, 2006.)
8. "From Governor to Grand Jury: An Interview with Freda Alexander." Digital Maryland. http://collections.digitalmaryland.org/cdm/ref/collection/saac/id/3495.
9. Glasser, Susan. "Forewoman Would Have Voted to Indict Clinton." *The Washington Post*, March 26, 1999.
10. Bork, Robert. "Against the Independent Counsel." Commentary. February 1993. https://www.commentary.org/articles/robert-bork/against-the-independent-counsel/. See also, Bork, Robert, "Prepared Remarks for Deputy Attorney General Eric Holder." *House Judiciary Subcommittee*. March 2, 1999. https://www.justice.gov/archive/dag/testimony/ictestimonydag.htm.

11. Bendavid, Naftali. "In Reversal, Reno Joins Opposition to Independent Counsel Statute." *Chicago Tribune*, March 3, 1999.

12. Mueller, Robert. *Report On The Investigation Into Russian Interference In The 2016 Presidential Election, Volume II.* U.S. Department of Justice, March 2019, p. 86.

13. Weissmann, Andrew. *Where Law Ends: Inside the Mueller Investigation.* (Random House, 2020), xiii.

14. Weissmann, Andrew. *Where Law Ends: Inside the Mueller Investigation.* (Random House, 2020.)

15. "Attorney General William P. Barr Delivers Remarks on the Release of the Report on the Investigation into Russian Interference in the 2016 Presidential Election." Department of Justice, April 18, 2019.

16. McPherson, Lindsey. "On Impeachment, Pelosi Prevailed over Judiciary Panel to Narrow Focus." Roll Call, December 11, 2019.

17. Bowden, John. "Collins: Trump Has Learned a 'Pretty Big Lesson' from Impeachment." The Hill, February 4, 2020. https://thehill.com/homenews/senate/481486-collins-trump-has-learned-a-pretty-big-lesson-from-impeachment/. The New York Times. "Officer's injuries, including concussions, show scope of violence at Capitol Riot.

18. NPR. "Read Trump's Jan. 6 Speech, A Key Part of Impeachment Trial." *NPR*, February 10, 2021. https://www.npr.org/2021/02/10/966396848/read-trumps-jan-6-speech-a-key-part-of-impeachment-trial.

19. Schmidt, Michael S., and Luke Broadwater. "Officer's Injuries, Including Concussions, Show Scope of Violence at Capitol Riot." *The New York Times.* February 11, 2021, updated July 12, 2021.

20. Helderman, Rosalind, et al. " 'Trump Said to Do So': Accounts of Rioters Who Say the President Spurred Them to Rush the Capitol Could Be Pivotal Testimony." *The Washington Post*, January 16, 2021.

21. Allen, Jonathan. " 'Call to Arms': Jan. 6 Panel Argues Trump Summoned the Violent Extremists." *NBC News*, July 22, 2022.

22. Dewan, Shaila. "Police Officer's Suicide after Jan. 6 Riot Is Ruled a Line-of-Duty Death." *The New York Times*, March 10, 2022.

23. Marcus, Josh, and Graig Graziosi. "Where Are You Nancy?': Audio of Rioters Stalking the Halls of the Capitol Revealed at Impeachment Trial." *The Independent*, February 10, 2021. https://www.the-independent.com/news/world/americas/us-politics/nancy-pelosi-staffers-capitol-riot-impeachment-b1800650.html.

24. Gangel, Jamie, Kevin Liptak, Michael Warren, and Marshall Cohen. "New Details about Trump-McCarthy shouting match show Trump Refused to Call Off the Rioters." *CNN*, February 12, 2021. https://www.cnn.com/2021/02/12/politics/trump-mccarthy-shouting-match-details/index.html.

25. Holder, Alex. *Unprecedented.* Discovery+, July 2022.

26. "One Year On, Republicans Still Don't Consider Biden the Rightful Winner." News Center, University of Rochester, December 22, 2021.

27. Trump's January 6 speech.

28. "Oath Keepers Leader Stewart Rhodes Calls on Militia Members to Prepare for Violence against 'Illegitimate' Biden Administration." Media Matters for America, January 20, 2021.

29. See Goldstein, Jared. "The Klan's Constitution." *Alabama Civil Rights & Civil Liberties Law Review* 9 (2018): 285.

30. *20/20.* ABC News. June 1982.

INDEX

Catron, John, 96, 97
censorship, 199–200
Chase, Samuel, 34–35, 38, 40, 41, 52–53, 57–60, 90
Cherokee People, 78
cinema, 196
ciphers, 45
citizenship, 103, 139, 143. *See also* equal citizenship; Fourteenth Amendment; personhood
civil disobedience, 240–41, 248–51, 256–57, 258–59, 262, 275. *See also* King, Martin Luther, Jr.
civil rights
  overview, 4–5
  1957 civil rights bill, 253
  1964 civil rights bill, 253–55
  American support for, 257
  anti-tyranny, 249, 250, 251, 252
  Bloody Sunday, 255
  businesses and, 174
  civil disobedience and, 240–41, 248–51, 256–57, 258–59, 262
  as constitutional, 174
  desegregation resistance, 241–42, 244
  Eisenhower and, 234, 236–37, 238–39, 241–47, 337n65
  gender equality and, 254
  KKK prosecuted, 161–62
  LBJ and, 253–54, 255–56, 257–58
  Niagara Movement, 178–79
  Parks and, 239
  political activism, 179
  President's Committee on Civil Rights, 220, 224–30, 232
  F. Roosevelt and, 217
  "To Secure These Rights," 229, 232
  study of, 219
  suing for, 161
  Supreme Court and, 174, 177–78
  Trotter vs. B.T. Washington, 176–77
  Truman and, 219–22, 227, 230–32
  B.T. Washington at White House, 176
  Wells vs. B.T. Washington, 177
  Wilson and, 173–74, 179–80

  See also equal citizenship; equal protection; King, Martin Luther, Jr.; Marshall, Thurgood; National Association for the Advancement of Colored People; personhood; segregation; Trotter, William Monroe; voting rights; Wells, Ida B.
Civil Rights Act (1866), 143
Civil Rights Act (1875), 165–69, 170
Civil Rights Act of 1957, 242–43
Civil Rights Act of 1964, 253–55, 261
Civil Rights Cases of 1883, 169, 255
Civil War
  Black soldiers in Union Army, 126–29
  Emancipation Proclamation and, 125
  ex Confederates and Johnson, 143
  Johnson and, 137–38
  Lincoln's philosophy, 118–19, 124, 130
Civilian Conservation Corp (CCC), 214
The Clansman (Dixon), 184, 197–98
The Clansman (play), 199
Clark, Mamie and Kenneth, 236, 333n55
Clark, Tom C., 219
class, 72
Clinton, Bill, 294–96, 299
Collins, LeRoy, 256
Colvin, Claudette, 239
Comey, James, 292–93
committee of executives, 9
common law, 24, 30
communism, 207–8, 253–54
Confederates. *See* Civil War
Congress
  Adams and, 25
  Black congressmen, 158, 159–60, 165–66
  Civil Rights Act (1866), 143
  Dred Scott and, 134
  habeas corpus, 77, 121–22
  impeachments, 299
  slavery and, 115, 120, 134
Connor, Bull, 250
conspiracy theories, 201
Constitution
  African Americans and, 11
  Article II, 115
  Article IV, Section 3, 95–96

newspapers
  of Democratic-Republicans, 32, 34, 37–38,
    51–52, 54 (see also *Aurora*)
  Douglass' Monthly, 113
  Douglass's print run, 305
  expansion of, 194–95
  Federal Republican, 66–68
  Guardian, 176
  Kentucky Gazette, 51
  Liberator, 85–86
  Lincoln and, 122
  Memphis Free Speech, 177
  New National Era, 162
  North Star, 89
  number of, 31
  as partisan, 31
  sabotage of, 67
  Sentinel of Freedom, 51
  Sunbury and Northumberland Gazette,
    37–38
  Wasp, 61
  See also *Aurora*; journalists; Sedition Act
Niagara Movement, 178–79
Nixon, Richard
  overview, 2, 7
  antisemitism, 268, 272
  Brookings Institution plot, 269–70
  Cox and, 282–83
  crisis overview, 265–66, 267
  Ellsberg Capital building attack, 271, 289
  Ellsberg's Vietnam evaluation, 274
  executive privilege, 280
  Fielding office break-in, 270–71, 289
  Frost interview, 272–73
  impeachment of, 286, 287–88
  indictment of, 284–86, 288–89
  King and, 243
  as lawyer, 3
  Lincoln's power and, 273
  New York Times Co. v. United States,
    268–69
  nuclear weapons, 274–75, 276
  Opponents List, 271–72
  pardoned, 288–91
  Pentagon Papers, 275–76 (see also *New York
    Times Co. v. United States*)
  power overview, 272–73

  recovering from, 267
  resignation of, 287–88
  Saturday Night Massacre, 282–83
  Watergate conspiracy, 277, 280, 287
  White House tapes, 280–82, 287, 288
  See also Grand Jury One
North Star (newspaper), 89
Northside Center for Child Development,
    333n55
nuclear weapons, 274–75, 276

Oath Keepers, 303–4
Otis, Gray, 82

Paine, Thomas, 31
pardons, 56, 288–91
*Parents Involved in Community Schools v.
    Seattle School District*, 262
Parks, Rosa, 239
parliamentary structures, 9, 21, 25
Paul, Alice, 204
Pence, Mike, 300, 301–2
Pentagon Papers, 268–69, 275. See also Water-
    gate conspiracy
Peoples, Ethel, 277–78
personhood, 92, 101, 132. See also abolitionism;
    citizenship; Douglass, Frederick; equal
    citizenship
Philadelphia, 28
Philadelphia Aurora (newspaper). See *Aurora*
Philadelphia Constitutional Convention
    (1787), 30
Pickering, Timothy, 27, 28, 36, 52
Pinckney, Charles Cotesworth, 101
Plessy, Homer, 174
Plessy v. Ferguson
  about, 169, 174–75
  Alexander and, 228–29
  Executive Order 9980 and, 231
  interpreting segregation, 193
  Marshall and, 223, 225–26
  Murray's bet, 235
  NAACP and, 222–23 (*see also* Marshall,
    Thurgood)
  Southern Manifesto and, 241
  struck down, 237
  See also *Brown v. Board of Education*

Roosevelt, Eleanor, 213, 217–18, 227–28
Roosevelt, Franklin Delano, Jr. (FDR), 212–13, 214–15, 217, 227–28
Roosevelt, Theodore, 176
Rosenstein, Rod, 292–93
Ross, Robert, 63
Rousseau, Jean-Jacques, 23
rule of law, 3, 4, 7. *See also* Grand Jury One; Nixon, Richard
Russia, 292–93

Saturday Night Massacre, 282–83, 297
Scalia, Antonin, 294, 296
Scott, Dred, 95–99. See also *Dred Scott*
Scott, Harriet, 95
secession, 118, 119, 133
"To Secure These Rights" (President's Committee on Civil Rights), 228–30, 232
Sedition Act (1798), 29–31, 33–43, 46–53, 56–58, 252
Sedition Act of 1918, 203
sedition laws, 25–26, 72–73, 75. *See also* free speech
segregation
    children and dolls study, 236
    Civil Rights Act and, 164–66
    Constitution and, 225–26, 251
    Douglass's legacy and, 169–70
    Eisenhower and, 236–37, 238–39, 241–47
    federal government, 190–91, 193, 226
    fighting desegregation, 241–42, 244
    Hayes and, 175–76
    Houston and, 222
    Marshall and, 222–23
    in military, 231, 233
    New Deal and, 215
    public accommodations, 226, 242
    in schools, 235, 244–46, 258, 262 (see also *Brown v. Board of Education*)
    "To Secure These Rights," 228–30
    Supreme Court and, 225
    as unequal, 194
    Wilson and, 180, 187, 190–94
    women's suffrage and, 205
    See also civil rights; *Plessy v. Ferguson*
self-government, 309n10
Senate, 37, 59, 158–59

Sentinel of Freedom (newspaper), 51
Separate Car Act, 174
Seymour, Horatio, 153
Shelby County v. Holder, 262
Shull, Lynwood, 216
Simmons, William Joseph, 200
Sirica, John, 279, 281–82, 286
Skowronek, Stephen, 8
slander, 25–26
slavery
    badges of slavery, 174
    Black Codes, 142
    Buchanan and, 93–94, 96–97, 98–99, 105–6
    Civil War and, 118–19
    Congress and, 115, 120, 134
    Constitution and, 16, 86–87, 88–89, 95–96, 98–105, 116, 131–32
    debates over, 96–97
    democratic crisis and, 6
    Democratic Party and, 94
    as divisive, 96–97
    Dred Scott, 95–100, 103–4, 114
    expanding, 86
    free Black people (*see* freedmen)
    free territories and, 95–96, 97–98, 101
    gag rule, 86, 317n5
    Jackson and, 76
    Jefferson and, 81
    Kansas-Nebraska Act, 105
    Lecompton Constitution, 105–6
    Lincoln and, 109, 113, 114–19, 123, 129–30, 132–33
    Madison and, 81
    Missouri Compromise, 95–96, 97, 98
    Northern agitators and, 107
    numbers enslaved, 86
    people as citizens, 102, 108
    people as property, 98, 101–2
    vs. preservation of Union, 96–97, 115, 124
    presidency and, 93
    protecting (see *Dred Scott*)
    re-enslaving people, 142
    relations with enslaved people, 61
    riots over, 68
    Supreme Court and, 96–98